Hwee Ling Lim

Constructing Learning Conversations

Hwee Ling Lim

Constructing Learning Conversations

Virtual Collaborative Learning Processes in Higher Education

VDM Verlag Dr. Müller

Imprint

Bibliographic information by the German National Library: The German National Library lists this publication at the German National Bibliography; detailed bibliographic information is available on the Internet at http://dnb.d-nb.de.

Any brand names and product names mentioned in this book are subject to trademark, brand or patent protection and are trademarks or registered trademarks of their respective holders. The use of brand names, product names, common names, trade names, product descriptions etc. even without a particular marking in this works is in no way to be construed to mean that such names may be regarded as unrestricted in respect of trademark and brand protection legislation and could thus be used by anyone.

Cover image: www.purestockx.com

Publisher:
VDM Verlag Dr. Müller Aktiengesellschaft & Co. KG, Dudweiler Landstr. 125 a, 66123 Saarbrücken, Germany,
Phone +49 681 9100-698, Fax +49 681 9100-988,
Email: info@vdm-verlag.de

Produced in USA and UK by:
Lightning Source Inc., La Vergne, Tennessee, USA
Lightning Source UK Ltd., Milton Keynes, UK
BookSurge LLC, 5341 Dorchester Road, Suite 16, North Charleston, SC 29418, USA

ISBN: 978-3-639-02558-3

TABLE OF CONTENTS

LIST OF FIGURES

LIST OF TABLES

CHAPTER 1

INTRODUCTION

This book presents a qualitative case study that aims to gain greater insight into the impact of online synchronous (chat) interaction on the learning process from a sociocultural constructivist perspective in the context of an online undergraduate unit. Given the sparse research on the effectiveness of chat interaction in supporting knowledge construction processes, this study developed a new methodological design that integrates discourse and social network analytical methods with survey perception analysis for examining the impact of chat interaction on facilitating participation, knowledge construction, and the quality of online learning experience of two different online tutorial groups. Findings from this study offer a rich account of the role of chat interaction in the construction of learning conversations for guiding the pedagogical design of collaborative-constructivist learning activities.

1.1 Background to the Research

In the context of education, interaction has been regarded as a crucial element in learning experiences (Dewey, 1938; Vygotsky, 1962/1986). In online learning contexts, interaction was identified as one of the major constructs in distance education research (McIsaac & Gunawardena, 1996). In this study, *online interaction* is defined as involving "a dialogue or discourse or event between two or more participants and objects which occurs synchronously and/or asynchronously mediated by response or feedback and interfaced by technology" (Muirhead & Juwah, 2004, p.13). According to Garrison and Anderson (2003), online interactions between and within student-teacher-content components in a virtual community of inquiry are significant for their possible impact on learning outcomes.

Studies have shown that online interaction has a vital role in the success of learning as it supports collaborative-constructivist learning strategies and fosters the building of learning communities (Garrison, Anderson, & Archer, 2000; Kanuka & Anderson, 1998). The availability of interaction opportunities has also been found to be significant for supporting student preferences for control of learning path, and contact with others that build relationships resulting in higher levels of student satisfaction and quality learning outcomes (Bonk, Daytner, Daytner, Dennen, & Malikowski, 2001; Bonk, Hansen, Grabner-Hagen, Lazar, & Mirabelli, 1998; Harasim, Hiltz, Teles, & Turoff, 1995; Sherron & Boettcher, 1997). With recent arguments that mere generation of computer-mediated dialogue may not necessarily lead to educationally productive collaboration and quality learning (Palloff & Pratt, 2003), research in online interaction at the level of higher education broadened from a focus on the quantity of dialogue to encompass the examination of the quality of online interaction (Hendriks, 2002; Lapadat, 2002; Rose, 2002).

The quality of *online asynchronous interaction*[1] in higher education has been extensively examined from a constructivist learning approach for indications of "sustained reflection and discourse" that are associated with knowledge building (Garrison, Anderson, & Archer, 2001, p.11; DeLaat & Lally, 2004). In contrast, the

---

[1] In technical terms, online asynchronous interaction refers to a dialogue, activity, or event that takes place in a delayed-time mode through a computer-mediated communication medium.

relatively less research carried out on the quality of *online synchronous* or *chat interaction*[2] has focused primarily on its effectiveness in enhancing social-emotional or community building aspects of collaborative learning and work group processes (Chou, 2002; Duemer, Fontenot, Gumfory, & Kallus, 2002; Mercer, 2003; Schwier & Balbar, 2002; Sudweeks, 2004; Sudweeks & Simoff, 2000) while its role in supporting knowledge construction remains unclear.

1.2 Statement of Problem

Studies on classroom conversational interactions in the constructivist learning framework have largely reported evidence of knowledge building processes and in some cases even indications of conceptual change among the learners.

For instance, Mason (2001) examined the effects of classroom collaborative oral discourse and reflective writing strategies on conceptual change in 12 young learners (9-10 years old) on the target science concept of decay, and learner perceptions of the value of such strategies. Data from individual in-depth interviews, observations of group discussion and product analysis were used to evaluate the participants' extent of prior knowledge and reflections on experiences. Results from the analyses showed evidence of knowledge revision particularly in discussions that displayed the use of "collaborative discourse-reasoning" or "argumentative dynamics" (Mason, 2001, pp. 324-325) in constructing shared knowledge.

Similarly, Meyer and Turner (2002) studied the impact of scaffolded instruction by teachers on the development of self-regulation processes of young learners (12 years old) in nine mathematics classes. Transcripts of whole-class discussions were examined for teacher responses that reflected scaffolding of understanding, learner autonomy and maintenance of positive learning environments. Responses from surveys on learners' own evaluation of their self-regulated learning strategies were used to confirm interpretations of the transcript data. The study presented results from the discourse analysis of classroom conversational interaction from one illuminative case which indicated the development and realization of self-regulated learning with high levels of scaffolding in teacher responses.

The advent of the synchronous computer-mediated communication (CMC) mode which replicates much of the feel of face-to-face communication in its similarity of conversation features (Kortti, 1999) presents two broad questions.

1. If face-to-face classroom conversational interactions have been found to support and indicate knowledge construction, can we also assume that online synchronous interactions in virtual classrooms support and indicate knowledge construction processes?

Based on the *sociocultural constructivist*[3] perspective that learning involves contextualized dialogic participation in the practices of the community, Crook and Light (2002) claimed that instant messaging[4] (IM) or similar synchronous CMC media

---

[2] In technical terms, online synchronous interaction refers to a dialogue, activity, or event that takes place in a real-time mode through a computer-mediated communication medium.
[3] This study uses the term *sociocultural* consistently from this point to refer to both variants of social and social-cultural constructivism. The research associated with constructivism is discussed in Chapter 2.
[4] *Instant Messaging* is service that alerts users when other defined users are online and allows real-time communication through private online chat areas (Microsoft Press, 2002).

support this process of enculturation by ensuring the continuity of established learning practices which are for most communities, largely rooted in face-to-face conversational exchanges. However, Edwards (2002) cautioned that the available technology presents only "a precondition for [knowledge construction] and does not simply constitute it" (section 5). Instead, Edwards (2002) suggested that an examination of the "directed analytical and creative conceptual communication practices" (section 5) is crucial for understanding the process of knowledge building.

While the synchronous CMC mode enables possibly the closest technological approximation to communication in face-to-face settings besides desktop conferencing[5], most studies have focused on its role in supporting social-emotional, community building or leadership aspects of collaborative learning rather than as a means for developing critical thinking (Haythornthwaite, Kazmer, Robins, & Shoemaker, 2000; Mercer, 2003; Schwier & Balbar, 2002; Sudweeks, 2003a; Sudweeks, 2004). Moreover, the examination of chat interaction in virtual classrooms is complicated by the absence of physical contact between participants with the attendant non-verbal turn-taking cues, and few appropriate analytical frameworks for chat discourse, hence prompting the second question.

2. If knowledge construction occurs during educational chat, will we know it when we see it? What/which analytical frameworks can be used to characterize and measure knowledge building processes in chat discourse?

The analytical frameworks for examining online educational exchanges have been mainly designed for asynchronous discussions; hence the classification schemes are typically more sensitive when applied to longer postings containing complete thoughts, extended reflection and reasoning than the shorter, condensed and more intense exchanges present in chat discourse. Nevertheless, there has been promising work carried out recently that examined the effectiveness of online synchronous interaction in supporting learning which were based on the established methodological tradition of discourse analysis.

Early work by Wegerif and Mercer (1997) resulted in an analytical framework, which when applied to the examination of peer talk in classroom discourse could better explain the nature and function of the discourse in collaborative learning processes. The framework consisted of three types of talk: *disputational, cumulative,* and *exploratory*; each of which could be further analyzed from dialogic role to the finer speech act and word levels. Wegerif and Mercer (1997) claimed a special status for exploratory talk as "a dialogical model of reasoning" (section 6, para. 1) since it is characterized by self-reflection and shifts of perspective by the speaker in the discourse. Later researchers, highlighted below, modified and extended this framework into the realm of *computer-mediated discourse[6]* (CMD) for investigating the impact of conversational roles and moves[7] on the coherence and depth of chat discourse.

---

[5] Desktop conferencing refers to the use of computers for simultaneous communication among geographically separated participants in a meeting with video, audio and/or compressed digital images transmitted over the Internet (Microsoft Press, 2002).
[6] Computer-mediated discourse refers to "the communication produced when human beings interact with one another by transmitting messages via networked computers" (Herring, 2003, p.1).
[7] Moves refer to the pragmatic intentions of utterances or turns at speech act level as interpreted from the context of the dialogue (Kneser, Pilkington, & Treasure-Jones, 2001).

Berzenyi (1999) formulated an interlocutor relationship theory as a tool for analyzing chat discourse and as a pedagogical model for developing awareness of audience issues among students in a university technical writing course. The framework consisted of four types of interlocutor relationships on "a continuum of conflict and cooperation: agonistic, hierarchical, dialectical, and emphatic" (Berzenyi, 1999, p.232) that could be applied to the characterization and analysis of online interlocutor relationships as represented by the discourse. The framework could also form an instructional strategy for the deliberate adoption of specific interactional roles and relationships by participants through role play activities during chat discussions. Berzenyi (1999) suggested that discourse of productive educational chat is mainly characterized by indicators of inclusive, dialectical relationships which, like *exploratory talk* (Wegerif & Mercer, 1997), reflect the presence of multiple perspectives in a relatively egalitarian environment with instances of constructive conflict or challenges.

More recently, the *Exchange Structure Analysis* (ESA) framework was developed for "capturing the grammar of turns between dialogue participants with the aim of gaining insights into their relative contributions and roles" (Kneser, Pilkington, & Treasure-Jones, 2001, p.67). The theoretical basis of ESA is informed by Sinclair and Coulthard's (1975) *transactional analysis* and modifications to it suggested in Stubbs (1981). With the unit of analysis set at the *turn*[8] in chat discourse, coding of chat transcripts using the exchange structure categories alone produces a straightforward quantitative count of the frequency and types of turns contributed during discussions. A more informative analysis of chat exchange patterns could be obtained by an examination of speech acts (Austin, 1962; Searle, 1969) or the pragmatic intention of turns using move categories, and further associating turns already coded at exchange structure and move levels, with anticipated argument and exchange structure roles.

Kneser et al. (2001) applied the ESA framework in the examination of the characteristics of chat discourse and evaluation of the effectiveness of online tutors in transferring discussion skills to postgraduate students in a distance learning course from a constructivist perspective. Transcripts from chat seminars were analyzed using ESA which was found to be sufficiently sensitive to identify differences between student and tutor roles, and the patterns in exchange roles adopted by tutors and students that indicate the degree of inclusiveness of participation by both parties in chat discussions. Based on the constructivist assumption that the tutor initially scaffolds interaction before transferring control to the students during the learning process, results from the quantitative discourse analysis indicated a pattern of tutor-domination rather than withdrawal of control in discussion which suggests a need for improvement to online tutor facilitation strategies. Kneser et al. (2001) highlighted the finding of large variations in chat discussion participation levels which were attributed to factors such as the English Language proficiency of participants (a mix of local UK and international non-native English speaking students), the highly directive facilitation style of the tutors, and the non-assessed status of the chat activity.

In addition, Cox, Carr, and Hall (2004) conducted a comparative study that examined the impact of course design, group dynamics, and facilitation styles on chat

---

[8] A turn is a contribution by a participant that is delimited by a carriage return in chat discourse (Kneser et al., 2001).

discussions in two university courses at undergraduate and postgraduate levels. Using a modified version of ESA, a quantitative analysis of transcripts from group chat sessions was carried out to identify participant roles adopted, inclusiveness of participation, and characteristics of chat discourse. Together with qualitative data from student surveys and interviews, the study concluded that the potential of chat was not fully realized in the two courses due to factors such as the highly directive facilitation style of the tutors, English Language proficiency of students, a lack of clear discussion objectives for students and tutors, and perceptions that the chat activity was weakly integrated into the course design.

Although both studies showed that the ESA framework could support the examination of educational chat discourse from the levels of dialogue roles to speech act, findings on the impact of chat interaction on the learning process were limited by the methodological designs adopted. For instance, in Kneser et al. (2001), chat transcripts from one class formed the sole data source and only quantitative measures of interaction were applied. Cox et al. (2004) examined groups from two courses which carried out different learning activities, namely general discussion and decision-making tasks during chat sessions. Both qualitative and quantitative measures of interaction were used on multiple data sources that included chat transcripts, survey and interview responses. However, both studies collected and analyzed a limited amount of transcript data which provided a partial account of the online learning process. The methodological designs of both studies are discussed further in Chapter 4.

Such a situation presents an opportunity to fill the gaps in current research and further current understanding on the impact of online synchronous interaction in facilitating the learning process from a sociocultural constructivist perspective with an in-depth case study in this work. The case study is an undergraduate unit identified as a particularly illuminative case exemplifying the instructional application of chat interaction. This single-embedded case study compares the learning experiences of two tutorial groups in the undergraduate unit and analyzes a complete dataset of chat transcripts collected over a whole semester (11 weeks), hence providing a fuller account of the quality of learning experience and online learning process over time which is supported by chat interaction. Additionally, the integration of discourse and social network analytical approaches in interpreting educational chat exchanges, when triangulated with self-reports of online learning experiences, form a new methodological design for examining the impact of online synchronous interaction on learning.

Since the real-time communication mode is both less convenient and more expensive to provide than the asynchronous mode (Anderson, 2003; Armitt, Slack, Green, & Beer, 2002), there are also fiscal as well as pedagogical imperatives to examine student perceptions of the impact of chat interaction on their learning experiences and the extent to which it satisfies their learning needs in order to justify current and future investments in such services. However, as noted by Parker (2004), it must be acknowledged that the adoption of such a "business model of higher education" (p.389) could be controversial at a time when the introduction of online learning had triggered a paradigm shift in the traditional perspective of education as the pursuit of knowledge for its own sake.

1.3 Statement of Purpose

The purpose of this study is to examine the impact of online synchronous interaction on the learning process from a sociocultural constructivist perspective in the context of an online undergraduate unit.

More specifically, this qualitative study aims to:
- examine the discourse of online synchronous interactions that are related to the content being learnt for indications of active participation and knowledge construction; and
- explore the perceptions of student participants on the value or impact of synchronous computer-mediated interactions in supporting collaborative learning and group work processes.

Ultimately, from the findings on the extent to which chat interaction supports the learning process and positive learning experiences, this study will determine if there are any implications for the theory and practice of online synchronous activity design from a collaborative-sociocultural constructivist perspective; specifically, the problems and opportunities associated with this kind of learning that could be drawn from the results.

1.4 Research Questions

The following questions are used to guide this study in the context of the *Organisational Informatics* (OI) undergraduate unit offered by Murdoch University, which was selected as a particularly illuminative case of the use of online synchronous interaction during *chat tutorials*[9]:

Research Question 1:
What do the overall patterns of task-oriented chat discourse reveal about engagement by participants with each other's contributions, interactional purposes, and the collaborative learning process in groups?

For Research Question 1 (RQ1), the method of *discourse analysis*[10] (DA) is used for the coding and analysis of the chat transcript dataset from two tutorial groups in terms of exchange structure and moves. Additionally, *social network analysis*[11] (SNA) is applied as both an analytical method and visualization tool for representing the coded turns/exchanges.

Research Question 2:
How do student participants perceive their experiences of chat tutorial interaction in terms of participation opportunities, adequacy of learning support, and quality of learning experience and collaborative work process?

For RQ2, data from student participant responses to an online survey administrated to the same two tutorial groups are analyzed with descriptive statistics and examined

---

[9] In technical terms, a chat tutorial refers to an instructional session supported by chat CMC medium and delivered over the Internet.
[10] As an analytical method, DA is a procedure of textual analysis used for studying "texts and talk in social practice" (Hepburn & Potter, 2004, p.180)
[11] SNA is "the disciplined inquiry into the patterning of relations among social actors, as well as the patterning of relationships among actors at different levels of analysis (such as persons and groups)" (Breiger, 2004, p.505).

from an interpretive perspective to reflect the participants' views on their online learning experiences. With this methodological approach, there could be further insight gained regarding the possible explanations underlying the patterns of task-oriented chat discourse found in RQ1. The analytical methods selected to investigate both research questions are discussed more fully in Chapter 4.

In addressing the research questions, three main assumptions are held.

Assumption 1:
In relation to the choice of CMC medium, it is assumed that the chat medium provides participants with relatively equal opportunities for contribution to discussions in an "egalitarian" learning environment (Kiesler, 1992, p.152).

In contrast to face-to-face communication, chat interaction is mainly text-based although some current chat applications such as Yahoo Messenger™ or Windows Messenger™ offer image and voice capability options to users. Based on the *reduced social cues* theory (Kiesler, Siegel, & McGuire, 1984), the largely text-based nature of the synchronous CMC medium is assumed to filter out static social context cues that affect human communication processes and behaviour which could also impact on the online learning process and educational experience.

With less "physical and psychological" indicators (Veerman, Andriessen, & Kanselaar, 2000, p. 6) such as physical appearance, gender, race, age and social status available for impression formation, the chat medium is held to offer the advantages of supporting discussions "aired in an egalitarian atmosphere" (Cutler, 1995, p.23) where participants are more likely to have (or perceive to have) equal opportunities (Herring, 2000) for contributing to the tutorial discussions and encouraging greater self-disclosure that builds ties that bind online communities (Haythornthwaite et al., 2000).

Assumption 2:
In relation to the pedagogical and methodological approaches based on sociocultural constructivism adopted, respectively, by the *Organisational Informatics* unit and this study, it is assumed that knowledge construction is supported by active participation in the dialogic learning process and greater control of the chat discussions by learners over time (Vygotsky, 1962/1986; 1978; Wertsch, 1985).

Being largely influenced by Vygotsky, sociocultural constructivist theorists regard learning as a process of "enculturation into a community of practice" (Cobb, 1994, p.13; Lave & Wenger, 1991) whereby guided participation in shared knowledge construction mediated by technical and/or psychological tools, provides learners with support that enables higher potentiality of cognitive growth, and leads to transformations in individual understandings with the appropriation of such shared knowledge.

This study views interaction as being crucial to the learning process and assumes that dialogic participation or engagement in instructional contexts such face-to-face lectures or chat tutorials, through bulletin boards or other CMC media, support individual and group knowledge construction processes. Within the *zone of proximal development* (ZPD) (Vygotsky, 1962/1986) established between the students, tutor, and the virtual learning environment, *scaffolding* as support from the tutor, peers, and the chat medium are held to influence participant experiences of the collaborative learning process. The *mediation means* of the synchronous CMC technology and the language of chat discourse enable, respectively, immediacy of interaction that reduces transactional distance (Moore & Kearsley, 1996) and the formation of learning conversations from which participants *appropriate* (Rogoff, 1990) for their own use the resulting shared understandings. This knowledge construction process is assumed to be empirically observable through an examination of the educational chat exchanges as well as student participants' self-reflections on their learning experiences.

Assumption 3:
In relation to the impact of online synchronous interaction on student satisfaction, it is assumed that chat tutorial interaction supports positive learning experiences given its close resemblance to face-to-face classroom interaction (Laurillard, 2002; Moore & Kearsley, 1996).

Interaction in chat tutorials offer possibly the closest technological approximation to face-to-face interaction in conventional classrooms given the unique combination of conversation features (Kortti, 1999) and immediacy of social presence (Short, Williams, & Christie, 1976) afforded by the synchronous CMC medium. The reduction of transactional distance between distant learners bridged by the immediacy of the online conversational interaction is held to result in higher levels of student satisfaction with the learning experience (Moore & Kearsley, 1996; Laurillard, 2002). Additionally, the close resemblance between the two learning environments is assumed to facilitate the transfer of formal learning behaviour since "students may find it easier to orient themselves when surrounded by familiar, albeit virtual, structures like classrooms, libraries, cafes" (Murphy & Collins, 1997, section 2, para. 8).

1.5 Key Assumptions of Study
This section outlines the key epistemological assumptions and the theoretical perspectives adopted in this study which is located within the qualitative research framework. Chapter 4 provides a fuller discussion of the philosophical and theoretical positions underlying the methodological approach of the study.

This study holds the *constructionist* epistemological position which assumes that "all knowledge, and therefore all meaningful reality as such, is contingent upon human practices, being constructed in and out of interaction between human beings and their world, and developed and transmitted within an essentially social context" (Crotty, 1998, p.42). Additionally, it is assumed that the knowledge attained is subject to change when shared or exposed to new perspectives during interaction (Duffy & Jonassen, 1991).

Constructionism forms the epistemological basis for a number of interpretive theoretical perspectives including the variants of radical and sociocultural constructivism. In this work, the term *constructionism* (Crotty, 1998) is used to refer to the *epistemological* position adopted in this study while *constructivism* refers to the range of *theoretical perspectives* available in the constructivist continuum ranging from radical to sociocultural constructivism.

This study adopts the *sociocultural constructivist* theoretical perspective (Vygotsky, 1962/1986) which foregrounds the social processes in knowledge building with the implicit assumption of the individual activity of cognitive re-organization. Hence, dialogic interactions between learners are regarded as crucial for supporting meaning negotiation leading to the construction of shared knowledge from which there could be individual appropriations of the shared understandings (Duffy & Cunningham, 1996; Rogoff, 1990). Based on these assumptions, this study focuses on educational chat interaction patterns/practices and applies methods drawn from discourse and social network analyses. Interpretation of the learning process is guided by sociocultural constructs of social interaction, ZPD, scaffolding, mediation means, and appropriation which have been re-interpreted from Vygotsky's original meanings by sociocultural theorists (Duffy & Cunningham, 1996; Rogoff, 1990; Wertsch, 1985).

The constructionist and sociocultural constructivist assumptions of this study locate it at the paradigmatic level within the *qualitative research framework* which studies phenomena in their natural settings and attempts to "make sense of, or to interpret, phenomena in terms of the meanings people bring to them" (Denzin & Lincoln, 2000, p.3). Given such an interpretive approach, this qualitative study aims to illuminate and gain deeper understanding of the knowledge construction process in context rather than prove beyond doubt the existence of events or relationships that correspond to some external reality.

1.6 Scope of Study
In keeping with the aims of this inquiry, the delimitations of this study are stated below, beyond which there are no attempts at generalization to a larger population although the findings may be extrapolated to similar cases.

The first delimitation concerns the sample. The *research site* is an online undergraduate unit which was selected based on the main criteria of accessibility, feasibility and relevance (Yin, 1993). It constitutes a single, particularly "information rich" (Patton, 2002, p.231) case from which one could potentially learn most (Stake, 1995) regarding the impact of chat interaction on the online learning process. The *participants* are a purposive sample comprising 24 students from two tutorial groups, two tutors, and the researcher. Participants from both tutorial groups (Groups 1 and 4) in this case study took part in the same learning activity involving weekly critical discussion on the same set of readings in WebCT™ chat tutorial rooms, supported by a tutor-facilitator and moderated by student presenter(s). However, different participants "have different renditions of the same event" (Yin, 1994, p.146). A between group comparison of educational chat interaction enables representation of the various perspectives leading to a more holistic understanding of the phenomenon and enhancing validity of the study through data triangulation. Chapter 3 provides a fuller description of the site and participants in this case study[12].

The second delimitation concerns the data. The primary data sources are archived chat tutorial logs and responses to a web survey from Groups 1 and 4 (G1 and G4). Interactions in the chat logs comprise contributions for establishing social, cognitive and teaching presences (Garrison et al., 2000) in an online learning community. In

---

[12] The case study is defined as a process of inquiry which examines "a phenomenon in its natural setting, employing multiple methods of data collection to gather information from one or a few entities (people, groups or organizations)" (Benbasat, Goldstein, & Mead, 1987, p.370).

order to examine chat discourse for indications of active participation and knowledge construction, only task-oriented turns that contain content directly related to the issues in the set-readings are selected for analysis. To explore perceptions of student participants on the impact of chat interaction in supporting collaborative learning and group work processes, self-reports of attitudes, behaviour and experiences specific to the chat tutorial context are obtained with open-ended and closed questions in a web survey. Chapter 4 provides a fuller discussion of the methodology adopted for data collection and analysis.

The third delimitation concerns the positionality of the researcher. In this study, the researcher is an *outsider* who is not directly involved in the design or teaching of the course. Besides ethical considerations, the covert observation of online interactions through *lurking* is not possible due to the WebCT™ chat feature which displays the identities of all participants logged into the chat room. The presence of a 'lurker' would be noticed and could cause disquiet among participants leading to alterations in normal interaction patterns.

The selection of two tutorial groups for comparison in this case study enables the adoption of a non-participant observer role for G1 and a participant observer role for G4. While the researcher's own participatory experiences inform the interpretation of G4 interactions from the transcript data, the *insider* perspective is mainly sought from a key informant (the unit coordinator) for clarifications on the content and context of G1 interactions. Even as insiders provide access to private online communities and 'native' insights on observed phenomena, this study acknowledges Delamont's (2004) caution on informants' use of "impression management" (p.224) whereby informants tell the researchers what s/he wants to hear, lie or hide information in order to protect themselves and their privacy. To corroborate the insights offered by the informant, multiple sources of data are utilized (Yin, 1994) such as archived chat tutorial logs, responses to a web survey, and unit document artifacts.

1.7 Significance of Research
In its areas of inquiry, this study is essentially cross-disciplinary as it involves the fields of education, linguistics, information and communication technology (ICT), and educational technology in its examination of the impact of online synchronous interaction in facilitating collaborative-constructivist learning and group work processes.

The significance of the research reported in this book covers the following aspects:
- refinement of the *Exchange Structure Analysis* coding scheme (Kneser et al., 2001) and development of a web survey instrument for gathering multiple perspectives on educational chat interaction;
- development of a new methodological design that integrates discourse and social network analytical methods with survey perception analysis for triangulation of different perspectives on chat interaction;
- in-depth understanding of the impact of chat interaction from the synthesis of findings from interpretive analysis of transcript data (gathered over an extended period of time) with participant perceptions of learning experiences; and
- provision of a holistic and rich account of the construction of learning conversations with a comparison of two different tutorial groups bounded by the highly personalized experiences of teaching and learning in a single case study.

In general, the findings from this study are likely to be significant to researchers who are concerned with the use of technology for online learning and the nature of educational chat discourse. This study may also be of interest to higher education professionals and faculty responsible for the provision and design of distance learning programmes. Funders and promoters of educational technology may benefit from a greater understanding of the role of synchronous CMC media in supporting the learning process. Finally, the findings may provide pedagogical guidance for online tutors in managing group participation and formulating strategies for the facilitation of learning conversations. The more specific contributions from this research are presented in Chapter 6.

1.8 Summary and Outline of Book

Interaction has a vital role in the success of online learning as it supports collaborative-constructivist learning strategies and fosters relational ties that bind virtual learning communities, leading to higher levels of student satisfaction and quality learning outcomes. Online synchronous interaction in virtual classrooms has been primarily examined for its role in supporting social-emotional aspects of learning while its role in developing critical thinking remains unclear.

This case study of an undergraduate unit, which exemplifies the instructional application of online synchronous interaction, aims to examine the impact of chat interaction on the learning process from a sociocultural constructivist perspective that could further understanding and contribute to the current sparse research in this area. With the application of a new methodological design that integrates discourse and social network analytical concepts in interpreting educational chat exchanges as well as survey perception analysis of online learning experiences, this study examines the learning processes of two online tutorial groups over time and the quality of learning experiences which are supported by chat interaction.

An overview of this book presented over the following chapters is provided below:

Chapter 2 reviews key concepts and assumptions of major learning theories on the form and function of interaction, characteristics and affordances of online learning environments and CMC modes in supporting educational interaction, the nature of computer-mediated discourse, and learner perceptions of online educational experiences. The literature review presents the background for examining three main concepts pertaining to the role of chat interaction in facilitating collaborative-constructivist learning and group work processes: *participation*, *knowledge construction*, and *quality of online learning experience*.

Chapter 3 presents the case study of the online undergraduate OI unit offered by Murdoch University. Background information is given on the pedagogical framework of the unit, its representation as a networked learning model and the profile of the students. A detailed description is provided of the aims and structure of the chat tutorial activity which is the focus of this study.

Chapter 4 states the constructionist and sociocultural constructivist theoretical assumptions of this study and locates it within the qualitative research framework. The research site and its associated actors are characterized as an instrumental single-embedded case study. The choice of the case study methodology is justified and the research stages are outlined. The inquiry procedures for investigating both research questions are described with specific mention of data sources and collection procedures, analytical instruments/methods, and validity of measures utilized.

Chapter 5 reports the quantitative and qualitative results from both research questions. RQ1 findings, which are based primarily on the analyst's interpretation of the educational interactions from the chat transcripts, are informed by survey results from RQ2 on student self-reports on online learning experiences. Insights gained from the synthesis of different perspectives enable a richer account of the impact of chat interaction on the learning process.

Chapter 6 discusses the substantive findings from Chapter 5 and their implications. This chapter concludes the book by summarizing the contributions and limitations of this study. Possible areas for further research are also recommended.

CHAPTER 2

LITERATURE REVIEW

2.1 Introduction

Learning through interaction is the main belief underlying most educational theories and classroom instructional practices. With the rapid adoption of online learning in higher education from the 1990s, educators had variously lauded (Harasim et al., 1995) or expressed reservations (Ramsden, 1992) over the viability of the new networked learning model in supporting interactions that result in quality learning experiences and outcomes. Such positions are likely to stem from the different conclusions drawn in the consideration of the following issues.

- How do people learn? How do we come to believe that learning occurs through interaction?
- Where does learning take place? In what environment(s) do learners interact?
- What supports learning? What is the nature of online educational interaction and discourse?
- What can be seen as evidence of learning? How do students perceive the quality of online learning experiences?

These issues frame the discussion in this chapter which reviews key concepts and assumptions of major learning theories on the form and function of interaction, the characteristics and affordances of CMC modes and online learning environments in supporting educational interaction, the nature of computer-mediated discourse, and learner perceptions of online educational experiences. The literature review presents the background for the study's examination of three main concepts pertaining to the impact of online synchronous interaction on the sociocultural constructivist learning process: *participation*, *knowledge construction*, and *quality of online learning experience*.

An overview of the chapter is provided below:

Section 2.2 discusses the concepts and philosophical assumptions of main learning theories that colour interpretations of the form and function of educational interaction, focusing on the sociocultural constructivist learning perspective adopted by this study.

Section 2.3 describes the types of interactions afforded by CMC technologies and contextualizes educational interaction within a virtual learning community model.

Section 2.4 reviews major approaches in the study of discourse and compares the nature of asynchronous and synchronous computer-mediated discourse.

Section 2.5 discusses the broad pedagogical Implications of student perceptions of online educational experiences, highlights quality assurance frameworks for evaluating distance education programs, and explains the use of data gathered on student self-reports of learning experiences within the context of the study.

Section 2.6 summarizes the main concepts and assumptions underlying the study that enable the research questions to be addressed.

2.2 Learning and Interaction

Although interaction is widely assumed to support learning, distance education literature offers various interpretations of the form and purpose of the activity. This section discusses the different philosophical and theoretical assumptions underlying objectivist and constructivist understandings of learning and their implications for the role of interaction in learning processes.

2.2.1 What is interaction?

The term *interaction* has been defined as "a transaction taking place between an individual and what, at the time, constitutes his environment" (Dewey, 1938, p.43), with educational interactions involving transactions between learners and the instructional environment. In online learning contexts, the concept of interaction encompasses learning activities carried out between human-human as well as human-computer or technology components (Sims, Dobbs, & Hand, 2002). The terms *interaction* and *interactivity* have been used interchangeably in distance and online learning literature to refer generally to "the form, function and impact of interactions in teaching and learning" (Muirhead & Juwah, 2004, p.13).

The term *interactivity* is largely held by the IT community to refer specifically to the characteristic of the technology medium which allows the user to carry out "conversational exchange of input and output, as when a user enters a question or command and the system immediately responds" (Microsoft Press, 2002, p.279). Interactivity has also been defined from the learning perspective as "the capability of participants to receive specific feedback of any length to their contributions from any other member of a CMC discussion" (Romiszowski & Mason, 1996, pp.445).

The focus of the study is on task-oriented, online synchronous (chat) interactions carried out in online tutorials that have specific pedagogical purposes. Hence, interactions of relevance to the study are those that occur in "formal educational contexts ... specifically designed to induce learning directed toward defined and shared learning objectives" (Anderson, 2002, para.6). Additionally, such dialogic transactions are held to be characterized by *interactivity* which is defined as

> the extent to which messages in a sequence relate to each other, and
> especially the extent to which later messages recount the relatedness
> of earlier messages ... Interactivity describes and prescribes the
> manner in which conversational interaction as an iterative process
> leads to jointly produced meaning ... it is a general enough concept to
> encompass both intimate, person-to-person, FTF communication and
> other forums and forms.
> (Rafaeli & Sudweeks, 1998, p.3).

The need to highlight the different understandings of these terms, support to some extent the observation that interaction is a multifaceted concept used to refer to a diversity of activities and contexts (Muirhead & Juwah, 2004). Anderson (2004) concurred that "it is surprisingly difficult to find a clear and precise definition of [interaction] in the educational literature" (p.43) even though the concept has long been regarded as crucial to learning. In an earlier paper, Anderson (2002) attributed such difficulties in arriving at a common understanding of interaction to "surface problems of definition and vested interests of professional educators" (para.1). The differences in perspectives on what constitutes the nature and purpose of interaction could also be traced to disagreements in other areas: the philosophical assumptions of the basic relationship between the individual and the environment; and the theoretical beliefs regarding what constitutes knowledge and learning.

Duffy and Cunningham (1996) explained that underlying philosophical orientations and epistemological beliefs invariably colour what is meant by knowledge and learning from different theoretical perspectives. Regarding the impact of such beliefs on instructional practice, Duffy and Jonassen (1991) noted that since educators normally utilize their past knowledge and/or personal experiences of learning in designing courses, the design would naturally implicitly or explicitly reflect their understandings of the learning process and hence constitute an expression of their theoretical beliefs on learning. In the following discussion, the broad philosophical assumptions underlying objectivist and constructivist learning perspectives are explained and contrasted for a better understanding of the role of interaction from these perspectives.

2.2.2 Philosophical assumptions of objectivism and constructivism
The objectivist view of the basic relationship between the individual and the environment is based on *realism* which is "the doctrine that there is an independently existing world of objective reality that has a determinate nature that can be discovered" (Schwandt, 2001, p.176). The ontological assumptions of objectivism also include the belief that this external structured world consists of stable properties and entities (Jonassen, 1991a). Objectivist epistemology claims that knowledge, although produced by individual thought processes, is ultimately "determined by the structure of the real world" and could be mapped on to learners (Jonassen, Davidson, Collins, Campbell, & Haag, 1995, p.10).

In contrast, constructivist philosophy is based on the doctrine of *subjectivism* which broadly holds that "all judgments [or interpretations] ... are *nothing but* reports of an individual speaker's feelings, attitudes, and beliefs" (Schwandt, 2001, p.241-emphasis in original). The ontological assumptions of constructivism include the belief in the existence of multiple realities based on individual experiences. In general, constructivist epistemology holds that knowledge is, by definition, a subjective interpretation imposed by the individual on the world. Furthermore, since multiple individual interpretations would lead to multiple realities, no one interpretation is necessarily less valid than another (Jonassen, 1991b) but this view is not taken to the extreme stance of either epistemological nihilism or solipsism (von Glasersfeld, 1995). Essentially, constructivism does not share the objectivist epistemological aim to achieve certainty in knowledge but regards constructed knowledge as dynamic and subject to change when exposed to new perspectives during interaction (Duffy & Jonassen, 1991).

2.2.3 Objectivism and implications for learning
Behaviourist and cognitivist learning theories share most of the ontological and epistemological beliefs of objectivism. From both perspectives, learning is regarded as a scientifically observable phenomenon manifested in human behaviour, when examined, would lead to an explanation of the "true nature of learning processes" and ultimately result in the "betterment of our world" (Cunningham, 1991, p.13). Learning is viewed as an attempt by the student to 'mirror' the structure of the

external world as interpreted by the instructor and gain this knowledge which would be common to all learners. Teaching involves mainly the transmission of information by the instructor that had been modelled on the structure of the real world (Jonassen, 1991b). The ultimate goal of learning is to achieve "complete and correct understanding" (Duffy & Jonassen, 1991, p.8) of reality since individual understandings are necessarily partial or biased.

Such objectivist assumptions are reflected in prescriptive instructional designs that focus on the pre-determination of content and learning objectives due to the belief in an unchanging reality, and the adoption of quantitative testing to evaluate the success of information transmission or internalization based on the premise that all learners could reach same level of understanding (Jonassen, 1991a). The design of distance education courses (particularly in computer-assisted instruction or CAI) based on objectivist principles emphasize linear sequencing of the learning process that starts by identifying instructional goals and ends with summative evaluation. Such 'drill and practice' courses, although acknowledged to be effective in teaching basic skills and knowledge, may not necessarily be appropriate when the complexity of content in certain subject domains require higher order conceptual understanding. Under such conditions, the advanced determination of acceptable performance indicators may not be possible or desirable (Winn, 1991).

Since behaviourist theorists strongly associate learning with behavioural modification, educational interaction involves the activities of information transmission by the instructor and/or environment to the learner, and the production of appropriate conditioned response(s) by the learner. Interactions are mainly designed for the instrumental *purposes* of enabling the transfer of information to the learner and providing opportunities for practicing stimulus-response sequences in order to maintain or reinforce associations (Ertmer & Newby, 1993).

Cognitivist theorists generally associate learning with the building of mental schemes to ultimately form a knowledge base that mirrors the external world. In contrast to the behaviourist transmission model, interaction involves the active acquisition of experiences by the learner from the instructor and/or environment, and the effective retrieval of processed information from the mind. Interactions are mainly designed for the following *purposes*: to enable learners "to impose order, stability, and meaning on experience" (Good & Brophy, 1990, p.56) so as to achieve a state of equilibrium with their environment from the Piagetian perspective; and to support the instructional approach of discovery learning which would activate the learners' intrinsic motivation and develop independent learning skills that could ultimately enhance information retention and retrieval (Bruner, 1966). A close reading of Bruner's (1961) account of the experimental studies on school children which examined their cognitive strategies in information gathering would reveal that the discovery learning approach is essentially teacher-centered and congruent with objectivist ideology. The question-answer activities carried out in the 'discovery' process reflect the underlying assumptions that the content information is already known to the instructor and that learners are in fact 'discovering' pre-determined information hidden in the tasks.

2.2.4 Constructivism and implications for learning
In what may seem to be a radical shift from the objectivist perspective of learning as the passive assimilation of de-contextualized concepts that mirror the structure of the

real world, the constructivist approach views learning as an active process involving individual interpretations of experiences, the sharing of multiple perspectives, and negotiation of meaning through interaction in authentic contexts. Teaching primarily involves the establishment of a facilitator or cognitive apprenticeship relationship with learners for the provision of guidance rather than strict control of instruction. Hence, the aim of learning is not to reach complete understanding of some ultimate reality, but to gain self-awareness or reflexivity which could enable learners to attain "real control over and responsibility for their beliefs" (Duffy & Cunningham, 1996, p.182).

Such subjectivist assumptions are reflected in instructional designs that emphasize flexibility in learning including the pre-determination of the main field of knowledge rather than its specific content. Given the belief that learners create multiple understandings, learning objectives are related to processes for knowledge development rather than the products (Ertmer & Newby, 1993). As noted in Jonassen (1991b), since "[c]riterion reference instruction and evaluation are proto-typical objectivistic constructs" (pp.29-31) incongruent with the constructivist approach, qualitative evaluation methods are used such as 'goals-free' approaches which adopt the standard of viability rather than 'correctness'.

In the context of distance learning, the design of constructivist distance education courses would reflect the "conversational paradigm" (Romiszowski & Mason, 1996, p.449). Hence, problem-based, situated learning approaches (Brown, Collins, & Duguid, 1989), and various strategies to reduce transactional distance (Moore & Kearsley, 1996) are adopted such as greater student control of the learning path, accessibility to 'tools' that increase communicative interaction, and goals-free evaluation through self-assessment or reflection on the learning experience (Jonassen, 1991a).

2.2.5 Interaction from constructivist learning perspectives

At this point, it would be necessary to describe the divergent perspectives on the learning process held by two schools of thought within the constructivist paradigm termed variously as *cognitive* or *radical* and *social* or *sociocultural* constructivism in the literature. Both approaches acknowledge that learning involves the elements of interaction and individual cognitive activity but they differ in the emphasis placed on the primacy of the contribution of each component.

To avoid confusion, this study uses the terms *radical* and *sociocultural* constructivism consistently in reference to the two approaches. The following discussion of their theoretical differences and similarities draws mainly from the detailed comparison in Cobb (1994) summarized in Table 2.1, and the works of Duffy & Cunningham (1996); Rogoff (1990); von Glasersfeld (1981; 1989; 1992; 1995; 1997a; 1997b); Vygotsky (1978) and Wertsch (1985).

Radical constructivism is termed as such since "it breaks with convention and develops a theory of knowledge in which knowledge does not reflect an 'objective' ontological reality, but exclusively an ordering and organization of a world constituted by our experience" (von Glasersfeld, 1981, section 1, para.14). The establishment of the epistemological basis for radical constructivism is largely attributed to the work of von Glasersfeld who was greatly influenced by Piagetian theories on the nature of knowledge and cognitive development. The constructs of *adaptation, equilibrium,* and *interaction* in Piaget's schema theory form the basis for radical constructivist view of learning which could be broadly stated as a "product of self-organization" (von Glasersfeld, 1989, section 6, para. 5) involving an iterative process whereby interaction in an experiential world produces a state of mental dissonance in the individual, to be resolved by adaptation or cognitive changes entailing the coordination of inner experiences with outer experiences, within the specific community, which would restore the individual to a state of equilibrium (von Glasersfeld, 1997a).

Table 2.1. Contrasts between constructivist perceptions of learning and interaction (adapted from Cobb, 1994)

| Issues | Constructivism | |
	Radical	Sociocultural

Proponents	- Piaget (1970; 1980); von Glasersfeld (1992).
	
	- von Glasersfeld developed the epistemological basis for Radical Constructivist (RC) perspective using
	  a) Piagetian concepts of assimilation and accommodation.
	  b) Cybernetics concept of viability rather than Truth.
	  c) Ethnomethodology (Mehan & Wood, 1975).
	  d) Symbolic interactionism (Blumer, 1969).
		- Vygotsky (1978); Rogoff (1990); Lave & Wenger (1991); Newman, Griffin & Cole (1989).
		
		- Sociocultural Constructivists (SC) were mainly influenced by Vygotsky's emphasis on the importance of social interaction with experts in the ZPD and the role of culturally developed sign systems as psychological tools for thinking.
		
		- SC adopted Vygotskian constructs of
		  a) ZPD/scaffolding
		  b) Interaction
		  c) Internalization/appropriation
		  d) Mediation tools

Learning	- A "product of self-organization" to eliminate mental perturbations (p. 14). - Involves coordination of inner experiences with outer experiences within community of practice.	- A process of "enculturation into a community of practice" (p.13) or "coparticipation in cultural practices" (p.14).
Primary process	- Individual processes (primary). - Sociocultural processes (secondary).	- Sociocultural processes (primary). - Individual processes (secondary).
Knowledge	- Refers to individual's "conceptual structures" that are considered viable "given the range of present experience within their tradition of thought and language" (von Glasersfeld, 1992, p.381 in Cobb, 1994, p.14).	- Refers to the "quality of individual interpretive activity" (p.15).
Interaction	- Refers to individual's "sensory-motor and conceptual activity" (p.14). - von Glasersfeld (1989) viewed interaction as a "source of perturbation" (p.136 in Cobb, 1994, p.14). - Communication is regarded as "a process of mutual adaptation" during which meaning is negotiated and modified by individual interpretations (p.14). - Foregrounded = learning as cognitive self-organization. - Backgrounded = implicit assumption of individual participation in cultural practices.	- Refers to "participation in culturally organized practices" (p.14). - Meaning negotiation as "a process of mutual appropriation" involving both tutor and learners using/co-opting each other's contributions (p.15). - Foregrounded = learning as acculturation through guided participation. - Backgrounded = implicit assumption of cognitively active constructing individual.
Tools	- Signs/symbols are tools for expression and communication of thought by the individual.	- Signs/symbols are representations of established meanings of disciplines or shared meanings established by a group or community of practice.

Since radical constructivism associates learning mainly with changes in personal cognitive structures, interaction involves individual "sensory-motor and conceptual activity" (Cobb, 1994, p.14) with the primary process being cognitive self-organization and the implicit assumption of individual participation in reciprocal sociocultural practices. Interactions between the "conscious intelligence and environment" (von Glasersfeld, 1981, section 1, para.15) are mainly designed for the *purposes* of providing "source[s] of perturbations" (von Glasersfeld, 1989, section 6, para. 5) and opportunities for mutual adaptation that lead to changes in individual interpretations of experiences from the world.

In response to criticism, particularly from sociocultural constructivists, that Piaget's theory of cognitive development ignores the role of social interaction, von Glasersfeld (1995) allowed that Piaget's works may not have provided details on the actual workings of social activities in the learning process, but maintained that a close reading would have shown Piaget's awareness of the role of interaction in supporting the process of learning as a source of perturbation. It would also have revealed the strong Piagetian belief in the capabilities of an active, exploratory learner as the reason behind the primacy of focus on individual rather than sociocultural processes (von Glasersfeld, 1997b). Hence, the distinct position taken by radical constructivists, in contrast to their sociocultural counterparts, that social interaction with other learners is considered on par with and thus not accorded any greater significance than those occurring with other environmental objects (von Glasersfeld, 1995).

In its philosophical orientation, *sociocultural constructivism* shares the belief of its radical counterpart that individual constructions of knowledge do not mirror reality. However, being largely guided by Vygotsky's work in the field of developmental psychology, sociocultural theorists emphasize the primacy of social rather than individual processes in knowledge building. The sociocultural constructivist view of learning could be broadly stated as a process of "enculturation into a community of practice" (Cobb, 1994, p.13) whereby guided social participation in shared knowledge construction, mediated by technical and/or psychological tools, provides learners with support enabling higher potentiality of cognitive growth, and leads to transformations in individual understandings with the appropriation of such shared knowledge. The social process of enculturation is considered primary with an implicit assumption of the individual cognitive dimension. Interactions between members of the community and the learning environment are mainly designed for the *purposes* of providing opportunities for discourse and appropriation that influence intellectual development.

The issue of whether the radical and sociocultural perspectives are reconcilable has generated debate. Duffy and Cunningham (1996) adopted the stand that there are irreconcilable philosophical differences between both approaches. Duffy and Cunningham (1996) claimed an essential incompatibility between the radical view of the learning which they interpreted as involving formal "constructions of reality" (p.176) and the sociocultural view that reality is always in flux within the social context. However, Jonassen (1991a) contended that the differences at the philosophical level could be seen in terms of relative positions on a continuum rather than from an exclusive either/or position. Von Glasersfeld (1992) offered a more conciliatory position that since both theoretical approaches view events through their own interpretive lens, an awareness of their grounding assumptions is necessary before judging the value of each approach.

From a pragmatic perspective, Cobb (1994) proposed that the two approaches could be seen as complementary, offering an account of the learning process that encompasses both individual cognitive activity and involvement in cultural practices of the community. The adoption of a pragmatic stand could lead to a more useful application of constructivism in educational practice since the sociocultural view does not adequately account for individual cognitive processes and the radical position does not fully explain the production and re-production of social practices of the community by individuals.

Essentially, radical and sociocultural constructivist interpretations of the concept of interaction differ in the following aspects. Radical theorists view interaction as mainly individual "sensory-motor and conceptual activity" (Cobb, 1994, p.14). Foregrounded is the individual activity of cognitive self-organization with the implicit assumption of individual participation in social processes. In contrast, sociocultural theorists regard interaction as mainly "participation in culturally organized practices" (Cobb, 1994, p.14). Foregrounded is the social activity of acculturation with an implicit assumption of the individual activity of cognitive re-organization.

In the context of this study, the sociocultural constructivist perspective is adopted which assumes that learning occurs primarily through conversational interaction that involves participation in online tutorial discussions guided by the tutor/peers, mediated by tools (print, web, CMC technologies and language), leading to construction of shared knowledge. The knowledge construction process and the transformations in individual understandings that occur when shared knowledge is "jointly produced and individually appropriated" (Rogoff, 1990, p.196) are assumed to be empirically observable through an examination of the chat discourse as well as from the student participants' self-reflection on their learning experiences.

2.2.6 Sociocultural constructs and relevance to study
Given the sociocultural constructivist position adopted by the study, the concepts of *social interaction*, the *zone of proximal development (ZPD)/scaffolding*, *mediation means*, and *appropriation* that form the theoretical basis of sociocultural constructivism are particularly relevant for guiding the examination of participation, knowledge construction, and quality of online learning experiences during the learning process. The following discussion explains these constructs which have largely been re-interpreted from Vygotsky's original meanings by sociocultural theorists (Duffy & Cunningham, 1996; Rogoff, 1990; Wertsch, 1985).

As explained in Wertsch (1985), Vygotsky's research on psychological development is based on the assumption that higher mental functions originate from social processes which could be empirically observed through the examination of the forms of psychological tools (mainly language) and social relation. Vygotsky theorized that learning occurs first on an external plane where participation in group interaction, during specific social contexts, influence the later internalization process of higher mental functions. Reflecting this theoretical perspective, this study views *social interaction* as having a crucial role in the learning process and assumes that dialogic engagement between members of the learning community in formal instructional contexts such face-to-face lectures and online synchronous tutorials, as well as other contexts that constitute the totality of the learning environment, could support individual and group knowledge construction.

The ZPD construct was developed by Vygotsky partly due to his concern over the narrow focus in educational psychology, at that time, on assessment methods that measured mostly the child's "intrapsychological accomplishment" or existing intellectual capability rather than provided insight on the impact of interaction or "interpsychological functioning" on the level of potential intellectual development (Wertsch, 1985, p.67). The ZPD is defined as "the distance between a child's 'actual developmental level as determined by independent problem solving' and the higher level of 'potential development as determined through problem solving under adult guidance or in collaboration with more capable peers" (Vygotsky, 1978, p.8 in Wertsch, 1985, pp.67-68). When interpreted by sociocultural theorists, the ZPD is taken to explain the learner's potential capacity for intellectual growth when given guidance or scaffolding in the form of tutor/peer support through interaction.

Duffy and Cunningham (1996) extended the Vygotskian concepts of ZPD and scaffolding in their contention that sources of scaffolding are not limited to the tutor and/or expert peers which would reflect an objectivist information-transmission instructional approach, but encompass the affordances of the whole learning environment which include "any artifacts in the environment ...as well as the cultural context and history" (p.183) contributed by learners. Hence, the ZPD could be construed as being established between the learner, tutor, and the learning environment which forms a "dynamic whole" (Duffy & Cunningham, 1996, p.185). The wider interpretations of the *ZPD* and *scaffolding* constructs are adopted for locating the constructs in the social, cultural, historical, and technological contexts of this study. Given that this study mainly focuses on educational interaction supported by the synchronous CMC medium, the additional technological dimension is crucial for representing the virtual learning environment that situate cognition and participation. Additionally, this study assumes that learner perceptions of the availability of peer/tutor scaffolding during collaborative discussions would influence their experiences of the learning process.

One of the premises in Vygotsky's theoretical framework is that mental processes could only be understood when there is understanding of the tools and signs that mediate them. Vygotsky distinguished between technical and psychological tools; technical tools refer to objects/instruments used chiefly for controlling the environment while psychological tools include "language; various systems for counting; mnemonic techniques ... all sorts of conventional signs" (Vygotsky, 1981, p.137 in Wertsch, 1985, p.79) for effecting changes in behaviour (others and oneself) rather than objects during social interaction. In contrast to the cognitivist view of the role of language as an instrument or "an internal technique for programming our discriminations, our behavior, our forms of awareness" (Bruner, 1966, pp.108-109), sociocultural theorists regard language as a means of mediation in knowledge development which is shaped by the demands of the communicative context and, in turn, changes the learning process.

In this study, both *technical* and *psychological tools* are held to play crucial roles in supporting the learning process. Technology is used to enable interaction at a distance and the synchronous CMC medium, with its characteristic of immediacy, is assumed to support the "reorganization and extension of our cognition" (Duffy & Cunningham, 1996, p.187) during online tutorials. The language used in chat discourse is a hybrid of both speech and writing that evolved from the limitations of the CMC medium or demands of communicative context.

Although the term *internalization* had been used in both Piagetian and Vygotskian accounts of cognitive development, Wertsch (1985) explained that the differences in both conceptualizations of internalization stemmed from their underlying assumptions of the origins of mental processes, nature of learning activity, and means of representation. The Vygotskian construct is defined as "a process involved in the transformation of social phenomena into psychological phenomena" (Wertsch, 1985, p.63) where cognition is primarily influenced by social processes. As sociocultural theorists applied the construct of internalization to account for the process by which shared understandings become part of individual constructions, they encountered the dilemma of trying to explain how "the external lesson is brought across a barrier into the mind of the [learner]" (Rogoff, 1990, p.195).

By avoiding the radical theorists' view of internalization as a separate process mediating between external and internal world, reflected also in Vygotsky's definition of internalization as "a process whereby certain aspects of patterns of activity that had been performed on an external plane come to be executed on an internal plane" (Wertsch, 1985. pp.61-62), Rogoff (1990) proposed that it would be possible to reconceptualize internalization as a process of *appropriation*. Rogoff (1990) explained that from the very start, as the learner participates in social interaction, s/he is contributing to the development of group practices and hence already has access to shared understandings in which the individual contributory component is indistinguishable from the totality of the shared construction. In this case, the notion of a separate process of internalization is superfluous since the individual is not "*taking* something from an external model" (Rogoff, 1990, p.195-emphasis in original). Instead, what is involved is the individual use or appropriation of that shared knowledge which s/he had a part in creating that would, in turn, transform individual understandings. Rogoff (1990) further described the process of appropriation as being analogous to the efforts made by cells to sustain themselves in a living organism. Just as cells undergo exchanges of nutrients and wastes through their porous membranes for survival in a living body, learners take part in social exchanges and appropriate for their own use the resulting shared understandings which are essential for enculturation into the community.

Rogoff's (1990) analogy of an organic environment where knowledge is "jointly produced and individually appropriated" (p.196) was refined by Duffy and Cunningham (1996) into a more sophisticated model of learning in an environment of distributed intelligence as suggested by the metaphor of Mind as Rhizome (MAR). This study adopts the concept of *appropriation* in a metaphorical MAR environment in which all minds are connected to other minds in various contexts forming communities. The connections are dialogic communicative events mediated by signs or tools from the context. Constructed knowledge is dynamic as a result of new connections (negotiated meanings) from interactions. As a result, "thinking is not an action that takes place within a mind within a body, but rather at the connections, in the interactions" (Duffy & Cunningham, 1996, p.177). Hence, this study focuses on the examination of technology-mediated dialogic interactions for a better understanding of the knowledge construction process.

2.2.7 Summary

Although interaction is widely assumed to support learning, the form and purpose of the activity have been variously interpreted in distance education literature. The apparent lack of common agreement on the concept was attributed to differences in implicit philosophical and theoretical assumptions of the learning process.

Within the constructivist paradigm, the sociocultural constructivist perspective of learning was adopted which regards social interaction between learners as crucial for supporting negotiation of meaning leading to the construction of shared knowledge from which there could be appropriation of the shared understandings. The knowledge construction process is assumed to be empirically observable through examining the discourse of educational chat interaction and from student self-reflections on learning experiences which were guided by the sociocultural constructs of social interaction, ZPD/scaffolding, mediation means, and appropriation.

In particular, the interpretation of ZPD as encompassing the learner, tutor and the learning environment was essential in this study for representing the totality of the virtual learning environment for situating participation in learning conversations. The next section describes the characteristics and affordances of online learning environments and CMC modes in supporting educational interaction in virtual learning communities.

2.3 Interaction in Virtual Learning Environments

Where does learning take place? In what environment(s) do learners interact? What types of interaction are supported in these environments? The move from constructing learning conversations in traditional classrooms to virtual learning environments presents benefits and challenges to educators. The range of educational interactions has been extended yet limited by technological decisions. At the same time, there is a need to reconceptualize learning communities as displaying both physical and virtual dimensions. This section describes the types of interactions afforded by CMC technologies and contextualizes educational interaction within a virtual learning community model.

2.3.1 Types of interaction

Due to concerns over a lack of consistency in the use of the term *interaction* in distance education literature, Moore (1989) introduced three types of interaction that are now widely described and accepted in the field of distance education: learner-content, learner-instructor, and learner-learner interactions. In Moore (1989), *learner-content* interactions are characterized by engagement between the learner and the "subject of study" that lead to "changes in the learner's understandings, the learner's perspective, or the cognitive structures of the learner's mind" (para. 3). *Learner-instructor* interactions are "interactions between the learner and the expert" (Moore, 1989, para. 5) that support the personalization of teaching-learning processes and provision of feedback. The pedagogical models of most distance education courses reflect these two types of interaction as students engage mainly in independent study supported by self-contained instructional materials and feedback from tutors. *Learner-learner* interactions refer to "inter-learner interaction, between one learner and other learners, alone or in group settings, with or without the real-time presence of an instructor" (Moore, 1989, para. 9). Moore (1989) regarded this type of interaction as representing a "new dimension of distance education" which normally eschews group/collaborative learning approaches due to the geographically separated learning parties. However, improved web/CMC technologies and the greater acceptance of constructivist learning approaches have paved the way for the application of peer learning strategies in online contexts.

Berge (2002) claimed that *learner-content* interaction is a "problematic formulation, as content cannot interact, hold a dialogue, or answer back" (p.185). Instead, Berge (2002) proposed that the concept be re-formulated from interaction *with* content to interaction *about* content that involves mental dialogue as learners "construct meaning, answer questions, or find the appropriate places to integrate incoming information into their existing schema" (p.185). It could be argued that such a re-formulation could result in significant differences in meaning and theoretical orientation. Semantically, the term 'interaction *with* content' implies an inclusive relationship between two parties whereas 'interaction *about* content' suggests a degree of remoteness between the learner and the subject/content being discussed. Theoretically, the concept of 'interaction *about* content' assumes the radical constructivist view of learning as primarily an individual cognitive activity involving the internalization of external knowledge into the internal mental schema while the term 'interaction *with* content' reflects the sociocultural view of the primacy of participation by all learning parties in the knowledge construction process. Moreover, Berge's (2002) claim does not take into account the capabilities of current and emergent technologies in supporting content that could be "programmed to take a more active part in student-content interactions" (Garrison & Anderson, 2003, p.44).

The advent of web and CMC technologies led to the development of various permutations from this basic set of three interactions. Hillman, Willis, and Gunawardena (1994) introduced a fourth type of interaction termed *learner-interface* interaction which Hirumi (2002) explained as involving the graphical user interface (GUI) as a "point or means of interaction between the learner and the content, instructor, fellow learners, or others" (p.142). More recently, six possible classes of interactions were proposed by Anderson and Garrison (1998), and Hirumi (2002) which are listed in Table 2.2.

Table 2.2. Six classes of interactions (Anderson & Garrison, 1998; Hirumi, 2002)

Anderson & Garrison (1998)	Hirumi (2002)
Learner-Teacher	Learner-Instructor
Learner-Content	Learner-Learner
Teacher-Content	Learner-Content
Learner-Learner	Learner-Others
Teacher-Teacher	Learner-Interface
Content-Content	Learner-Environment

2.3.2 Computer-mediated interactions
The availability of CMC technologies to facilitate engagement between learning parties in online contexts requires consideration of the capabilities and limitations of the media which could affect opportunities for interaction and learning processes. The following discussion covers the broad pedagogical issues associated with computer-mediated interactions while the technological characteristics of asynchronous and synchronous CMC modes are dealt with in section 2.4.

Computer-mediated interaction involves "communication between different parties separated in space and/or time, mediated by interconnected computers" (Romiszowski & Mason, 1996, p.439) and the use of CMC technologies such as "electronic mail, computer conferencing, and on-line databases" (Jonassen et al., 1995, p. 16). The use of CMC technologies to support learning in virtual environments prompted a re-examination of the theoretical assumptions of learning and the role of technology in the educational process.

Romiszowski and Mason (1996) explained that at the philosophical level, there were calls from the humanistic camp for greater social interaction against the mechanistic position which was held to promote user isolation. These developments occurred whilst there were debates within the field of psychology over constructivist philosophy and its subjectivist interpretation of learning. Learning theories naturally experienced the downstream effects of these ideological upheavals with a shift from behaviourist and cognitivist approaches to constructivism in which CMC technologies could play significant roles in supporting conversational and collaborative interactions that are held to result in knowledge creation.

Even as CMC technologies could facilitate engagement between learning parties, there were concerns over the design of online courses that had mostly resembled electronic versions of traditional correspondence courses, offering limited means and opportunities for communication between course participants and providing content that "are no more than print-based text dumped online" (Cashion & Palmieri, 2002, p. 55). Research has found the availability of interaction opportunities to be crucial in reducing transactional distance (Moore & Kearsley, 1996) and supporting student preferences for control of the learning process or contact with others that build relationships resulting in higher levels of student satisfaction and quality learning outcomes (Bonk et al., 2001; Bonk et al., 1998; Harasim et al., 1995; Sherron & Boettcher, 1997). Hence, the limited communication means available in most online courses had led to concerns over the quality of learning (Cashion & Palmieri, 2002; IHEP, 1999), student retention rates (Carr, 2000) and reinforced perceptions that online learning is an isolating experience and an inferior option compared to on-campus/face-to-face education (Hara & Kling, 1999; Kumar, Kumar, & Basu, 2002).

Studies that reported on the application of computer-mediated interaction in online learning reflect a concentration on the use of the asynchronous mode (Booth & Hulten, 2004; Buckingham, 2003; De Laat & Lally, 2004; Garrison, 2003; Kanuka & Anderson, 1998; Kanuka & Garrison, 2004; McLoughlin & Luca, 1999) rather than the synchronous mode to enable group, peer-to-peer and student-tutor interactions (Armitt et al., 2002; Duemer et al., 2002; Spencer & Hiltz, 2003; Sudweeks & Simoff, 2000). Greater experimentation by educators with a wider range of CMC tools resulted in comparative studies on the interaction patterns of both CMC modes (Bonk et al., 1998; Chou, 2002).

However, Bonk and Cunningham (1998) expressed concern that computer supported collaborative learning (CSCL) tools were being applied on an ad hoc basis by teachers who may not be informed by theoretical frameworks or conclusive studies on the capabilities of such tools in enhancing learning. To provide guidance to teachers in critically integrating CSCL tools into the educational setting, Bonk and Cunningham (1998) presented three theoretical perspectives on pedagogical use of collaborative technology: learner-centered, constructivist, and sociocultural. The authors viewed the sociocultural theory of learning as offering greatest promise in guiding instructional use of CSCL tools. An example of the critical integration of CSCL tools in an online course, theoretically grounded in sociocultural constructivism, was reported in Sudweeks (2003c). Sudweeks (2003c) described the use of an extensive range of text-based CMC tools including e-mail, Internet Relay Chat (IRC), I Seek You (ICQ), instant messaging (IM), Short Message Service (SMS), and WebCT™ supported bulletin board and chat rooms to enable communication among distant undergraduates involved in a collaborative group project.

2.3.3 Online interaction models
A number of taxonomies have been developed to classify online interactions which could be grouped into four types of interaction models: communication, purpose/task, activity based, and tool based models (Hirumi, 2002).

- *Purpose/task based models* categorize interactions in terms of their functionalities. Sims (1995) developed an Engagement-Control Model to guide the effective choice of multimedia interaction types based on the degrees of engagement (navigational, instructional) and control (learner, system) that are required of the learning context.

- *Activity based models* classify interactions in terms of their instructional purposes. Bonk and Reynolds (1997) proposed a framework of web-based instructional strategies when applied could promote "creative and critical thinking as well as cooperative learning" (p. 167).
- *Tool based models* group technology tools in terms of their capabilities in supporting educational interaction. Bonk and Kim (1998) presented a typology of cultural tools/artifacts and learning environments (formal, informal) that are associated with adult learning from a sociocultural constructivist perspective.

Of particular relevance to this study are *communication based models* that categorize interaction in terms of relationships or exchanges between actors or learning parties. Wedemeyer (1981) developed an early communication model that reflects instructional exchanges between and within teacher, learner, and content components (Figure 2.1). The model was considered significant for its explicit acknowledgement of the role of technology as a communicative mediation means in the context of distance education (Shale & Garrison, 1990).

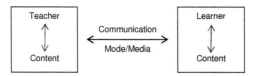

Figure 2.1. Distance education communication model (Wedemeyer, 1981, p.40)

Improved web and CMC technologies led to more complex interaction models that took into account varied types of interaction with other learning objects. Hirumi (2002) proposed a Three-Level Model of Planned ELearning Interactions that "delineates the relationship between fundamental communication-based interactions" (p.143) which could be used to guide the design of online interactions (Figure 2.2). Hirumi (2002) highlighted that the model is 'theory-free' in the sense that it does not "adhere to any particular learning theory or epistemology" (p.144) and could be flexible enough to accommodate any theoretical perspective.

In the model, Level I interactions represent activities that occur between the learner and self which include both cognitive and metacognitive processes. Level II interactions occur between the learner and other learners/objects while Level III interactions represent "a meta-level that transcend and serve to organize Level II interactions" (Hirumi, 2002, p.148).

Laurillard (2002) introduced a Conversational Framework based on the constructivist assumption that the articulation of individual reflections on experiences during dialogic interaction enables individual conceptual knowledge to be shared, critiqued and modified (Figure 2.3). The model represents activities that constitute "dialogic relationships" (Laurillard, 2002, p.86) within and between teacher and student participants. The activities are described as four processes that involve *discussion, adaptation, interaction,* and *reflection*. The model is claimed to be extendable to reflect the types of educational media that would be appropriate for supporting various learning interactions.

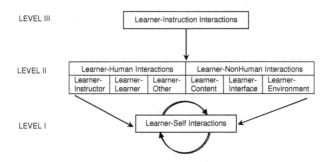

Figure 2.2. 3-Level Model of Planned ELearning Interactions (Hirumi, 2002, p.143)

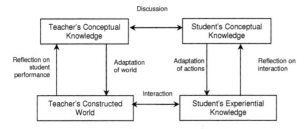

Figure 2.3. Conversational Framework (Laurillard, 2002)[13]

While communication based models reflect the transactional relationships between learning parties, they offer only a partial description of sociocultural constructivist learning process which involves participation in the practices of a *community*. Hence, this study adopts both communication and community based models (Anderson & Garrison, 1998; Garrison et al., 2000) described below for a fuller conceptualization of the learning process in a constructivist online learning environment.

2.3.4 Interaction frameworks of the study
Building on the basic interaction types introduced in Moore (1989), Anderson and Garrison (1998) presented a model in which online transactions between three macro-components of *student*, *teacher*, and *content* produce student-teacher, student-content, and teacher-content interaction types. In addition, transactions within each macro-component result in a sub-set of interactions: student-student, teacher-teacher, and content-content (Figure 2.4).

---

[13] Image source: http://www.learningandteaching.info/learning/pask.htm

The additional interaction types generated by this model include:
- *teacher-teacher* interaction that involves "teachers communicating with each other in order to enhance their teaching competencies" (Anderson & Garrison, 1998, p.104). Such forms of collegial contact during virtual conferences and/or the sharing of instructional resources through peer-to-peer technologies are considered vital to the establishment of communities of practice for educational professionals (Garrison & Anderson, 2003; Lave & Wenger, 1991).
- *content-content* interaction that relates to "learning resources that continuously improve themselves through their interaction, not only with learners, but also with other intelligent agents" (Anderson & Garrison, 1998, p.109). Examples of such forms of content available, at present, include Internet search engines, information alert and automated update services.
- *teacher-content* interaction that involves the professional functions of educators in creating course content and activities as well as monitoring or adapting the content to meet the needs of the instructional situation (Anderson, 2004).

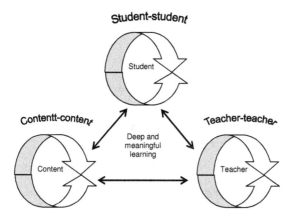

Figure 2.4. Types of Interaction (Garrison & Anderson, 2003, p.43; Anderson & Garrison, 1998)

In order to contextualize these interactions, Garrison et al. (2000) developed a *Community of Inquiry* (COI) model which was elaborated on and refined in subsequent publications (Anderson, 2004; Garrison, 2003; Garrison & Anderson, 2003; Kanuka & Garrison, 2004). The following discussion draws from these main sources in describing the model.

According to Garrison and Anderson (2003), the term 'community of inquiry' was originally used by Lipman (1991) to refer to a teacher-facilitated critical learning community where "students listen to one another with respect, build on one another's ideas, challenge one another to supply reasons for otherwise unsupported opinions, assist each other in drawing inferences from what has been said, and seek to identify one another's assumptions" (Lipman, 1991, p.15 in Garrison & Anderson, 2003, p.27). Based on this broad concept of a critical learning community comprising students and teachers and the constructivist assumption that knowledge building is a contextualized social process which occurs within such a community, the COI model is conceived as comprising three mutually interacting and reinforcing elements of cognitive, social, and teaching presences supported in online instructional environments by CMC technologies (Figure 2.5). The formation of such a community in online learning contexts represents an environment for "critical discourse and reflection" (Garrison & Anderson, 2003, p.27) where the dialogic education experience of sharing and negotiation of understandings could lead to "higher levels of learning" (Kanuka & Garrison, 2004, p.4).

Figure 2.5. Community of Inquiry Model (Garrison, Anderson, & Archer, 2000)

In the context of the COI model, *cognitive presence* is defined as "the extent to which participants in any particular configuration of a community of inquiry are able to construct meaning through sustained communication" (Garrison et al., 2000, p.4). The construct was also used to refer to "the intellectual environment that supports sustained critical discourse and higher-order knowledge acquisition and application" (Garrison & Anderson, 2003, p.55).

Social presence, a term first coined by Short, Williams, and Christie (1976), is used in this model to refer to "the ability of participants in the Community of Inquiry to project their personal characteristics into the community, thereby presenting themselves to the other participants as 'real people'" through the means of communication utilized (Garrison et al., 2000, p.4).

Teaching presence is defined in terms of three functions, namely, "the design, facilitation and direction of cognitive and social processes for the purpose of realizing personally meaningful and educationally worthwhile learning outcomes" (Anderson, Rourke, Garrison, & Archer, 2001, p.5). Although normally regarded as the main responsibility of the teacher, the constructivist orientation of the COI model holds that the teaching presence could also be established to some degree by a re-definition of student roles and through student-content interactions (Rourke, Anderson, Garrison, & Archer, 2001). As observed by Brabazon (2002), there are many roles situated between students and teacher that include paraprofessionals and administrators who hold teaching responsibilities.

The presence and interactions between these three elements in the COI model are considered "crucial prerequisites for a successful higher education experience" (Garrison et al., 2000, p.2). The cognitive presence reflects the "intellectual climate" (Garrison, 2003, section 2, para. 2) of the learning environment with the instructional objectives justifying its existence to the participants. The perception of an open or unthreatening social climate facilitates the knowledge sharing process necessary to sustain cognitive presence while the teaching presence structures and "mediates all these components" (Anderson et al., 2001, p.5). However, as educational communities are usually formed to attain "intended cognitive outcomes" (Garrison & Anderson, 2003, p.55), in this model, the social and teaching presences have mainly supportive or facilitative roles in the learning process.

The cognitive, social, and teaching presences in the COI model are operationalized by a template of categories and accompanying indicators (Table 2.3) for identifying and analyzing the presence of these elements in discursive online exchanges to improve "the practice of computer conferencing in higher education" (Garrison et al., 2001, p.2).

Table 2.3. Community of Inquiry categories and indicators (Garrison & Anderson, 2003, p.30).

Elements	Categories	Indicators (examples only)
Cognitive presence	Trigger event	Sense of puzzlement
	Exploration	Information exchange
	Integration	Connecting ideas
	Resolution	Apply new ideas
Social presence	Affective	Expressing emotions
	Open communication	Risk-free expression
	Group cohesion	Encouraging collaboration
Teaching presence	Design and organization	Setting curriculum and methods
	Facilitating discourse	Sharing personal meaning
	Direct instruction	Focusing discussion

A formal description of the template and preliminary findings of its application in the analysis of online asynchronous discussions were first reported in Garrison et al. (2000). Subsequent publications by the original co-authors and other researchers reported the application of the framework in identifying and evaluating the elements of *social presence* (Rourke et al., 2001; Stacey, 2000; Ubon & Kimble, 2004), *teaching presence* (Anderson et al., 2001; Stein & Wanstreet, 2004) and *cognitive presence* (Garrison, 2003; Garrison et al., 2001; Kanuka & Garrison, 2004; McKlin, Harmon, Evans, & Jones, 2002; Meyer, 2003; Meyer, 2004; Pawan, Paulus, Yalcin, & Chang, 2003) in asynchronous interactions in online higher education contexts.

A similar framework for conceptualizing the online learning environment was developed by Nolan and Weiss (2002). In the *Curriculum of Community* model, Nolan and Weiss (2002) proposed three locations for situating learning in virtual communities: Curriculum of Initiation and Governance, Curriculum of Access, and Curriculum of Membership. The model was claimed to function also as an analytical tool to examine curriculum components for additional insight on initiating and maintaining successful communities.

However, the *Curriculum of Community* model was not considered suitable in the context of this study for the following reasons:
- the model appears to be based on the structure of broader communities of interest rather than specific educational communities; and
- the model seems to present a set of practical guidelines for the design for online communities rather than offer a full articulation of the theoretical foundations for online learning communities.

This study adopts the conceptual frameworks based on the interaction and COI models developed by Anderson and Garrison (1998), and Garrison et al. (2000). The following discussion clarifies the extent to which the frameworks are applied.

Although most interaction types between *student*, *teacher*, and *content* macro-components are possible in the research site[14] which is an online undergraduate unit, this study focuses on *learner-teacher* and *learner-learner* interactions during online synchronous (chat) tutorials. This study adopts the COI model with its assumption that higher-order thinking in online learning contexts could be supported by the presence and interaction of the elements of cognitive, social and teaching presences.

In the context of the research site, the *teaching presence* is assumed to be reflected in the design of course materials/activities that structure the learning process, the specific instructional goals established for chat tutorials, and in the events of direct instruction and/or facilitation (carried out by the tutor and/or student-presenters) during the tutorial discussions.

This study acknowledges concerns regarding the use of a 'lean' text-based CMC medium (Daft & Lengel, 1986) to convey socio-emotional elements. However, it is assumed that compared to the asynchronous CMC mode, *social presence* could be more readily established by participants through the synchronous CMC mode which provides additional dimensions of immediacy and the natural conversational rhythm of face-to-face exchanges.

The *cognitive presence* is assumed to be supported by both elements of social and teaching presences with the knowledge construction process held to be reflected in the task-oriented chat exchanges as well as in participants' self-reflections on their learning processes.

However, this study does not utilize the template of categories and indicators developed by Garrison et al. (2000) for the analysis of the online synchronous discussions. Since the analytical framework had been designed mainly for the examination of asynchronous discussions (Garrison & Anderson, 2003), the classification scheme appears to be more sensitive when applied to longer postings. Given the shorter, condensed and more intense exchanges present in chat discourse, this study utilizes the *Exchange Structure Analysis* framework (Kneser et al., 2001) which will be discussed in Chapter 4[15].

The following discussion explains the conceptual distinctions between traditional and virtual communities, and describes the characteristics of online learning communities within which the educational interactions of relevance to this study are located.

2.3.5 Online environments and virtual learning communities
The culture and workings of communities have been examined by disciplines such as sociology and anthropology using various ethnographical methods such as case study and community study. Early anthropological studies focused on examining primitive societies as well as small towns and villages, with a seminal community study being the description of Middletown conducted by Robert and Helen Lynd

---

[14] The research site is described in Chapter 3.
[15] Refer to Chapter 4, section 4.4.1.

(Hammersley, 1998). With greater urbanization, modern anthropologists turned their attention to the study of cities and issues in contemporary societies.

According to Hammersley (1998), researchers from the *Chicago School of Sociology* employed a case study approach to investigate the city of Chicago for "the diversity and change characteristic of human behaviour (and particularly of modern social life)" (p.3). Other social studies looked at issues of class such as those carried out in the 1950s and 1960s by the *Institute for Community Study* on London's working-class areas. Later studies also examined the culture and workings of small groups and professional organizations such as medical and educational institutions. The basis for conventional conceptualization of communities in concrete, geographical terms could be attributed to the case/community study methodological approaches employed in such anthropological research which enable the direct observation and recording of physical places, social behaviour, and the various forms of contact that contribute to relationship-building and group formation.

Technological advances in CMC and the human desires for social-emotional contact as well as professional support, in increasingly dispersed urbanized societies, are among the motivational forces behind the rise of *virtual communities* (Thomsen, Straubhaar, & Bolyard, 1998). Attempts to define virtual communities in physical terms are fraught with difficulties since such communities are largely characterized by their ephemeral states. For instance, groups are formed in networked environments when individuals are drawn together by common interests or purposes; online personae are adopted which may bear no resemblance to the actual individuals; groups are usually self-regulated rather than being held accountable by external rules; and groups are disbanded easily when common goals have been reached or when areas of interests are not strong enough to continue to bind the individuals. Furthermore, the electronic evidence of interaction between members could be easily deleted, leaving no traces of the existence of such virtual groups (Rafaeli & Sudweeks, 1997; Thomsen, et al., 1998). Hence, the study of such virtual communities presents special methodological and ethical challenges to researchers which are discussed in Chapter 4.

According to Rafaeli and Sudweeks (1997), virtual communities could be considered "an enigma in traditional, rational and economic terms" (section 1, para. 4) as they differ so greatly from the conventional ideas held about the nature of communities. However, Jones (1998) contended that other than the territorial dimension, perceived differences between 'old' and 'new' communities are deceptive since virtual groups could just as easily be characterized by the "exclusivity, inflexibility, isolation, rigidity, homogeneity" of physical groups (p.9). Kolko and Reid (1998) added that the tendency for online groups to create their own forms of social stratification indicate that virtual communities could be "every bit as restrictive and oppressive as some real life ones" (p.217). Fernback (1997) clarified that even though conflict and division may be reflected in the *content* of discussion postings, CMC user groups are largely united in their collective ideological stand for "the principles of democracy and egalitarianism in [the] use of CMC" (p.46) in face of greater restrictions imposed on cyberspace freedom.

Virtual learning communities differ from the general "communities of interest" (Fernback, 1997, p.41) described above, yet share certain characteristics of face-to-face learning groups. Virtual learning communities are formed for pedagogical purposes with the justification of their existence based on their ability to facilitate the learning process and attain explicit educational outcomes. Such communities are also distinct from wider online groups in the following aspects: a lack of anonymity among group members, reduced mobility of individuals between groups, assessed/mandated participation in engineered instructional activities (Conrad, 2002), and the presence of "an institutional base" (Nolan & Weiss, 2002, p.306) for situating or supporting learning.

Learning communities are traditionally conceptualized as groups of students bound by the brick and mortar of educational institutions and the timing of class schedules. However, with the advent of online learning, pedagogical models have had to incorporate the concept of virtual environments for supporting critical discourse and collaborative group learning activities. Johnson and Johnson (1996) proposed a model of *technology-assisted cooperative learning* which is realized by the application of instructional technology to support cooperative learning groups to attain "higher achievement, more positive relationship, and greater psychological health" (p.1038). Garrison et al. (2000) developed the COI model for online learning which held the formation of a learning community as "an essential, core element of an educational experience when higher-order learning is the desired learning outcome" (Garrison & Anderson, 2003, p.22).

However, a *community of learners* theoretically conceptualized and labelled as such does not make it one. In other words, the provision of an online space for students to congregate in the form of an asynchronous forum or a chat tutorial room does not necessarily result in a community of learners. This study acknowledges the potential of networked learning envisioned as "effective learning environments [where] teachers and learners in different locations work together to build their understanding and skills related to a subject matter" (Harasim et al., 1995, p.3), but heeds the caution by Johnson and Johnson (1996) that "placing people in the same room and calling them a cooperative group does not make them one" (p.1025). Just as the degree of cooperation in groups is a matter of perception, the sense of 'community' in learning groups is also a matter of individual interpretation by the members. For students who have been herded together as 'captive' members into online groups, there must be something "that holds community together and forges an entity where there was none" (Conrad, 2002, section 6, para. 4).

In order to decipher the essence of a community, Baym (1998) presented a model of online community based on a three year ethnographic study of recreational asynchronous newsgroups in the early 1990s. The model comprises of pre-existing and emergent factors that could be used to explain the fundamental nature of a virtual community. Pre-existing or predicted factors include the external contexts, temporal structure, infrastructure of computer systems, purposes of usage, and characteristics of group and members that provide insight into the context of community development. By themselves, these predicted factors do not make a community. Instead, Baym (1998) hypothesized that online interaction among participants could result in "a dynamic set of systematic social meanings that enables participants to imagine themselves as a community" (p.38). Such emergent social meanings include forms of expressions, identity, relationship, and behavioural norms. The manifestation of such emergent social meanings in the group discourse and their appropriation for use by members contribute to the ties that bind and form the basis of group camaraderie.

In a recent study on student perceptions of an online learning community, Conrad (2002) concluded that there is a reciprocal relationship between *participation* and the development of a *sense of community*, and held that "participation in online learning activities exists before community, that it contributes to community, that it is the vehicle for maintaining community, and that it eventually becomes the measure of the health of community" (section 6, para. 3). Hence, Conrad (2002) suggested that the essence of an online learning community lies in both its "shared character and purpose" (section 6, para. 4), and further hypothesized that the emotional intensity of communal relationships between learners could be weaker in groups that display strong task orientation and pragmatic application of CMC tools in the learning process.

Although a detailed investigation into the essence of online learning communities is not within the scope of this study, this study holds that interaction as participation in the dialogic learning process is primary to the development of a sense of community in virtual learning groups. The development of communal relationships, in turn, contributes to the establishment of social presence that facilitates the knowledge building process necessary to sustain cognitive presence in the online communities of inquiry.

2.3.6 Summary
Advances in web/CMC technologies offer an ever-widening range of educational interactions involving human and non-human learning objects, but prompt concerns over the ad hoc application of CMC tools which are not guided by appropriate theoretical frameworks. In order to describe the educational transactions of relevance to this study and conceptualize the online learning process in a constructivist environment, an interactional framework (Anderson & Garrison, 1998) and *Community of Inquiry* (COI) model (Garrison et al., 2000) were adopted.

The virtual learning community conceptualized as the COI model was held to differ from, yet share the characteristics of both online communities of interest and face-to-face learning groups. Within the COI model, distant members of the online learning community congregate in virtual tutorial rooms to attain specific pedagogical aims, with the education experiences formed by the presence of social, cognitive, and teaching elements. The next section describes the dialogic interactions in virtual learning communities that support knowledge creation and compares the nature of computer-mediated discourse afforded by asynchronous and synchronous CMC modes.

2.4 Interaction and Online Discourse

What supports learning? What is the nature of online educational interaction and discourse in virtual learning communities? The sociocultural constructivist perspective assumes that participation in discursive practices of the community supports knowledge creation. In online contexts, the dialogic interactions between members of virtual learning communities form empirically observable manifestations of the knowledge construction process which are of specific relevance to this study. This section compares the nature of computer-mediated discourse afforded by asynchronous and synchronous CMC modes, and reviews major approaches in the study of discourse.

2.4.1 Asynchronous and synchronous CMC characteristics

When broadly described, computer-mediated communication (CMC) refers to

> both task-related and interpersonal communication conducted by computer. This includes communication to and through a personal or a mainframe computer, and is generally understood to include asynchronous communication via email or through use of an electronic bulletin board; synchronous communication such as "chatting" or through the use of group software; and information manipulation, retrieval and storage through computers and electronic databases.
> (Ferris, 1997, para.2)

In an educational context, CMC could additionally be regarded as "the use of networks of computers to facilitate interaction between spatially separated learners" (Jonassen et al., 1995, p.16). In contrast to face-to-face interaction which occurs under same-time/same-place conditions, CMC supports asynchronous (different-time/different-place) and synchronous (same-time/different-place) interactions. When conceptualized in terms of relative locations in space and time, these types of interactions could be represented in a matrix (Figure 2.6), with face-to-face interaction located in quadrant 1 and computer-mediated interactions located in quadrants 2 and 4 (Ngwenya, Annand, & Wang, 2004).

	Same place	Different place
Same Time	1	2
Different Time	3	4

Figure 2.6. Types of CMC interaction (Ngwenya, Annand, & Wang, 2004, p.323)

Asynchronous online communication, which could start and end at any time between users in different places, would be located in quadrant 4. It involves the occurrence of a dialogue, activity, or event in a delayed-time mode through the use of software applications such as e-mail, bulletin boards, or discussion forums. In online educational contexts, the design of collaborative group learning activities is largely centered around the use of bulletin boards or discussion forums where the asynchronous interactions are mainly manifested as textual contributions which could be composed, sent, saved, sorted by topic, chronology, or discussion threads, and accessed anytime/anywhere without proximity constraints. According to Lapadat (2002), these characteristics of "storage, dynamic additivity, and flexible sorting/searching" (section 2, para. 2) contribute to the interactivity of the asynchronous text-based medium.

Synchronous online communication, in contrast, requires communicating parties to be present at the same time for the event to take place and would hence be located in quadrant 2. It involves the occurrence of a dialogue, activity, or event in a real-time mode through the use of applications or services such as Voice over IP (VoIP), desktop video conferencing, and Internet Relay Chat (IRC). While video conferencing still faces constraints of bandwidth for audio/video synchronization, hardware/software costs and quality (Chan, Tan, & Tan, 2000), and VoIP is relatively new, IRC is currently easily accessible on the Internet with graphical user interfaces (GUI) offering greater convenience and usability compared to command-line interfaces available in the 1990s. Moreover, some chat applications such as Yahoo Messenger™ or Windows Messenger™ currently offer additional communication channels to users besides text such as image and voice capability options.

In technical terms, synchronous online communication or *chat* refers to "[r]eal-time conversation via computer. When a participant types a line of text and then presses the Enter key, that participant's words appear on the screens of the other participants, who can then respond in kind" (Microsoft Press, 2002, p.97). Such conversations are held in *chat rooms* which are "data communication channel[s]" that link computers, allowing participants to interact by sending text messages to one another in real time and such chat rooms are "often devoted to a particular subject or are conducted on a certain schedule" (Microsoft Press, 2002, p.97).

Online synchronous interaction in chat rooms are mainly manifested as textual messages, composed and sent by dyads or multiple parties who are logged in at the same time. Rather than being arranged in a topical order as in the case of asynchronous postings, chat messages appear chronologically on-screen "according to the sequence in which they are received" (Lapadat, 2002, section 2, para. 6) by the server and are prefixed by user login names which may or may not correspond to the actual names of the users. The transcripts of preceding exchanges "scroll up (and then off) each person's computer screen at a pace directly proportional to the tempo of the overall conversation" (Werry, 1996, p.51), offering a semi-permanent record of the proceedings which is generally not retrievable unless deliberately saved by the user or network administrator.

The focus of this study is on such online synchronous interaction in the context of chat tutorials that are supported by the WebCT™ learning management system (LMS)[16]. From the sociocultural constructivist learning perspective, both the CMC medium and LMS could be seen to play significant roles in supporting dialogic interactions by offering "an 'interpretive' zone that allows participants to share multiple perspectives or attitudes relative to a particular topic or issue" (Veerman et al., 2000, p.3). It could be argued that such a 'zone' could take the form of a chat

---

[16] The features of the learning environment supported by WebCT™ are described in Chapter 3.

tutorial room representing a virtual *same place* where distant students in *different time zones* congregate, hence locating online synchronous interaction in quadrant 3 (Figure 2.6) as well.

2.4.2 Studies in educational computer-mediated interaction

Studies that examined educational CMC interaction from a constructivist perspective have generally focused on the asynchronous mode which is assumed to support extended reflection (Harasim et al., 1995), and provide the time needed for learners to move beyond the phases of "sharing and comparing of information" (Pawan et al., 2003, p.120) to reach higher level 'integration' and 'resolution' phases of the critical thinking process where shared knowledge is synthesized and new knowledge created (Garrison et al., 2000). The prolonged period of discussion with accessibility to archived postings are held to both facilitate reflection by learners that could result in written responses that are "dense with meaning, coherent, and complete" (Lapadat, 2002, section 3, para. 3), as well as the development of a sense of community among virtual learners (Conrad, 2002).

Moreover, the asynchronous mode is believed to present learners with an ever-present "'window' for speaking" (Meyer, 2003, p.61) that is not subject to time constraints or competition for opportunities for participation which tend to be evident in face-to-face interactions. However, the asynchronous mode presents certain limitations that could be attributed to the features of particular CMC applications and human communication behaviour; for example, the availability of system generated information on the online status of other parties and whether one's postings have been viewed (Lapadat, 2002); as well as instances of participant procrastination leading to delays in replying or failures in responding to others' postings (Romiszowski & Mason, 1996).

Research on the asynchronous mode in higher education has mainly focused on the examination of the quality of online asynchronous discussions for the presence of cognitive and/or social-emotional dimensions considered necessary for developing critical thinking and collaborative skills among students. The methodological approach of content analysis, although rarely reported as being used on computer conferencing transcripts in the late 1980s (Mason, 1992), is currently widely adopted to examine electronic text generated from asynchronous discussions in a number of studies (Bonk et al., 2001; Booth & Hulten, 2004; De Laat & Lally, 2004; Garrison, 2003; Garrison et al., 2001; Hara, Bonk, & Angeli, 2000; Hendriks, 2002; Kanuka & Garrison, 2004; McKlin et al., 2002; McLoughlin & Luca, 1999; Meyer, 2003; 2004; Pawan et al., 2003; Rourke et al., 2001).

Even as Moore (1989) cautioned against relying on a single technological medium which could needlessly limit the range of interactions permitted in distance educational programs, there are relatively fewer studies on the use of instructional chat in higher education compared to the amount of research conducted on the asynchronous medium. Although research in the field of computer-supported collaborative work (CSCW) has been carried out on the impact of synchronous and/or asynchronous CMC on organizational communication and work group processes (McDaniel, Olson, & Magee, 1996; Siegel, Dubrovsky, Kiesler, & McGuire, 1986; Sproull & Kiesler, 1986; Sudweeks, 2004; Sudweeks & Allbritton, 1996;

Sudweeks & Simoff, 2005), researchers have observed that chat has only recently been applied for instructional purposes (Murphy & Collins, 1997; Werry, 1996).

The fewer studies on instructional chat could be attributed to factors such as the popularity of cognitive learning approaches that do not regard dialogue as crucial to the knowledge acquisition process (Polin, 2000); the predominance of perceptions that "promoting active asynchronous discussion is the best way to support interactivity in the online course" (Palloff & Pratt, 2003, pp.24-25); and the view that chat functions as an 'adjunct' to asynchronous interaction for enhancing social and communal relations (Lapadat, 2002; Mercer, 2003). Additionally, there are perceptions that chat is mainly for "recreational and social interaction" (Murphy & Collins, 1997, section 1, para. 4) which could be due to its traditional association, in the early 1990s, with fantasy and role-playing games in Multi-User Domains (MUD) or Multi-Object Oriented (MOO) virtual environments.

To some extent, the under-utilization of synchronous CMC in online course designs could also be attributed to the characteristics of the medium. The synchronous mode is held to lack the vital 'anytime' flexibility necessary to distance education models and the acquisition of good quality or stable synchronous applications could incur high costs (Chou, 2002). The medium tends to be vulnerable to technical problems involving reduction of communication bandwidth that may result in delays or disrupt the synchronization of responses (Herring, 1999). Such an unexpected loss of network connection could also lead to participants missing part of the discussion when they have reconnected as the textual record of preceding exchanges would have scrolled off their screens. In addition, the chronological linearity inherent in the real-time CMC mode means that messages may not appear on participants' screens according to the logical sequence of exchanges which could lead to discursive incoherence (Herring, 1999) in group discussions and undermine the dialogic process of knowledge construction.

Moreover, the synchronous mode may require tutors to have skills in the management of chat discussions which are complicated by factors such as the absence of face-to-face contact with group participants that could lead to uninhibited behaviour (Siegel et al., 1986) and the lack of conventional turn-taking cues which may result in the posting of multiple overlapping messages with the accompanying a loss of discussion focus (Pilkington & Walker, 2004). The mainly text-based synchronous medium may also entail additional skills from learners to fully participate in the discussions. In order to keep up with the rapid speed of chat discussions, participants may need to have prior experience in chat communication protocols (Pfister & Miihlpfordt, 2002), good typing skills, adopt linguistic conventions (Dykes & Schwier, 2003; Murphy & Collins, 1997) or 'Netspeak' and be proficient with the English language (Warschauer, 1996). Those who fail to keep up with the conversational flow may reduce participation in group discussions by retreating to the status of lurkers but may not necessarily be 'free-riders' (Albanese & van Fleet, 1984; Jones, 1984). Such peripheral participants could still be potentially productive members since no one could be expected to be "an active participant in all things, all the time" (Shumar & Renninger, 2002, p.6).

Some studies have presented results contrary to the assumption of the negative impact of the synchronous CMC medium on participation. In a study on task-oriented chat interaction, Hancock and Dunham (2001) found no significant relationship between typing speed on task error rate, turn coordination or task completion time. Similarly, McDaniel et al. (1996) found that the synchronous CMC medium did not have an impact on task completion nor was the nature of chat discourse perceived by the participants to be confusing or incoherent.

It has been contended that the synchronous CMC medium could support features in an online instructional environment that are familiar to learners and faculty, hence facilitating the transition from traditional face-to-face to online learning contexts. Murphy and Collins (1997) pointed out that recognizable metaphorical structures such as virtual tutorial rooms or cafés could virtually locate learners and interactions in familiar settings. Also, the close resemblance between chat and face-to-face exchanges, in terms of conversational rhythm, could facilitate the transfer of formal patterns of behaviour acquired in physical classrooms to virtual classrooms. Crook and Light (2002) added that since established learning practices for most communities are largely rooted in face-to-face conversational exchanges, the synchronous mode, with its close resemblance to the structure and rhythm of everyday 'talk', could be effectively interwoven into the "organized structure of formal communication" (p.167) evident in instructional settings such as tutorials or seminars.

While the asynchronous mode has the capability to 'expand' time which allows interactions to be "stretched out" (Shumar & Renninger, 2002, p.10), the synchronous mode has the capability to 'contract' time which makes it particularly appropriate for instructional activities that require interactivity, spontaneity, and fast decision-making (Murphy & Collins, 1997). The synchronous mode also provides a sense of immediacy and communicative presence that reduces transactional distance (Moore & Kearsley, 1996) between geographically separated parties engaging through a mainly text-based CMC medium. Such a sense of immediacy afforded by chat conversations could motivate involvement in interactions that provide "both intellectual and emotional content" to distant learning groups (Haythornthwaite et al., 2000, section 3.2, para. 16).

Sudweeks and Simoff (2000) presented a detailed study on the pedagogical impact of online synchronous activities on student motivation and participation in virtual tutorials or workshops. The chat interactions were analyzed through a variety of methods that include the quantitative analysis and visualization of participation patterns. The impact of chat tutorials on student motivation and participation were evaluated through a correlation of the quantitative analysis of interaction patterns with quantitative results from ratings in peer/tutor assessments of participation. Additionally, qualitative survey responses were also utilized to shed light on student perceptions of the effectiveness of online tutorials for learning. Findings from Sudweeks and Simoff (2000) indicated that online synchronous instructional activities with a sound pedagogical basis, such as "a cyclical process of interpretation, evaluation and reflection" (section 5), could support student motivation in the learning process.

Research on synchronous CMC interaction has mainly focused on examining the quality of online synchronous discussion for indicators of social-emotional presence in collaborative groups (Chou, 2002; Duemer et al., 2002; Haythornthwaite et al., 2000; Mercer, 2003; Spencer & Hiltz, 2003). Of particular relevance to this study are the more recent work that examined online synchronous interaction for indicators that chat discussions contribute to meeting formal pedagogical aims or enhance understanding of course content. In several studies, chat discussions were analyzed using content and discourse analytical methods for greater insight into participant engagement in argumentative dialogues for learning purposes (Veerman et al., 2000), and patterns of participation, chat exchange patterns, and participant roles during critical discussions (Cox et al., 2004; Kneser et al., 2001; Pilkington, Bennett, & Vaughan, 2000).

This study extends previous research in this area by examining task-oriented chat interaction for indications of active participation and knowledge construction during collaborative group learning processes. Analytical methods[17] of discourse and social network analyses are integrated with survey perception analysis for a fuller understanding of the learning process as evidenced by the chat discussion transcripts and student learning experiences. The following discussion compares two main approaches in the study of discourse and locates this study within the *discourse analysis* theoretical framework for the examination of dialogic interaction during electronic discussions.

2.4.3 Discourse Analysis and Conversation Analysis

Discourse analysis (DA) and conversation analysis (CA) are two similar, yet competing approaches to the study of discourse. The theoretical bases of the two approaches are described in this section while the specific methodological aspects relevant to the design of this study are discussed in Chapter 4.

Conversation analysis emerged within the discipline of sociology, in the late 1960s, at a time of paradigmatic upheavals which shaped its fundamental focus on the empirical study of social interaction and conduct (Clayman & Gill, 2004). The theoretical and methodological lineages of CA could be clearly traced to the contributions of Garfinkel (1967), Goffman (1955; 1983), and Sacks, Schegloff, and Jefferson (1974). At the paradigmatic level, CA is grounded in the tradition of *ethnomethodology* (a term coined by Garfinkel, 1967), which holds the phenomenological belief that since there is no external or objective reality, what could be known is based on subjective experiences which constitutes an individual's 'reality'. The focus of ethnomethodology is on the study of the ordinary methods used by ordinary members to get ordinary things done in the social world, with particular interest in *how* people get things done, their methods, shared norms, and understandings (Patton, 2002).

In congruence with its philosophical and methodological traditions, CA is considered essentially "the study of 'ethnic' (i.e. participants' own) methods of production and interpretation of social interaction" (Levinson, 1983, p.295). Goffman's (1983) work on interaction order laid the foundations for the assumption in CA that "social interaction is orderly in an individual, action-by-action, case-by-case, level" which is attributed to participants' access to knowledge of socially shared practices (Heritage, 2001, p.52). Therefore, as noted by Levinson (1983), CA focuses its areas of inquiry on *talk-in-interaction* and the identification of "recurring patterns" (p.287) in large corpora of naturally occurring conversations, in order to make explicit people's tacit

---

[17] The methods of discourse analysis, social network analysis and survey perception analysis adopted by the study are described in Chapter 4.

shared knowledge of how interaction is managed, and to ultimately enable "projectability" (p.297) or the anticipation of such interaction patterns in conversations. Sacks, Schegloff, and Jefferson synthesized the ideas presented by Garfinkel (1967) and Goffman (1983) in the development of CA methodology, which is characterized by its particular focus on the study of conversational organization that includes turn-taking, sequence organization, talk repair, and the overall structure of conversations (Sacks et al., 1974; Schegloff, Jefferson, & Sacks, 1977; ten Have, 2001).

Analysts adopting the CA method gather qualitative data, mainly through in-depth interviews and participant observation, in the form of naturally occurring talk rather than contrived examples of dialogue. Such empirical data are audio/video recorded and transcribed at various levels of detail (Levinson, 1983) from which patterns of interaction could be teased out and examined independently of the context or "the motivational, psychological or sociological characteristics of individuals" (Heritage, 2001 p.52). Heritage (2001) noted that two distinct branches of CA emerged from its central focus on conversational organization: CA as the study of ordinary conversation that analyzes "the institution *of* talk as an entity in its own right"; and CA as the study of institutional talk that examines "the management of social institutions *in* talk" (p.54-emphasis in original).

Discourse analysis, unlike conversation analysis, is a particularly "wide-ranging and slippery" concept (Taylor, 2001, p.8) which has been used to refer to a methodological approach, an analytical method, an area of research focus, as well as "a linguistic object that can be counted and described" (Potter, 2004, p.607). Although observed to be utilized mainly by researchers within the discipline of linguistics in the early 1980s (Brown & Yule, 1983), DA is currently regarded as "a contested disciplinary terrain where a range of different theoretical notions and analytical practices compete" (Potter, 2004, p.608). Hence, attempts to define DA have been fraught with difficulties given its origins and application in multiple disciplines including linguistics, sociology, psychology, communication, literary theory, and cultural studies (Potter, 2004).

In an attempt to bring some semblance of theoretical order to this highly fragmented concept, Potter (2004) extended the earlier work done in Potter and Wetherell (1987/2001) to develop an approach to DA, located in the discipline of social psychology, that aims to "make visible the ways in which discourse is central to action, the ways it is used to constitute events, settings and identities, and the various discursive resources that are drawn on to build plausible descriptions" (p.609). Broadly interpreted, Potter's (2004) approach to DA is based on three theoretical principles, namely, "discourse is *action-oriented, situated* and *constructed*" (p.609-emphasis in original).

The first principle that discourse is action-oriented borrows much from the CA methodological orientation of ethnomethodology and speech-act/turn-taking theory. In contrast to the traditional representational model of language as a "transparent, neutral and a 'do nothing' domain" (Wetherell, 2001a, p.189), this principle assumes that language performs "actions as parts of broader practices" and "*what discourse is doing*" could be observed in the data of talk and texts (Potter, 2004, p.609-my emphasis).

The second principle holds that discourse is situated in two ways: in the text, and in rhetorical purpose. In-text situation parallels CA's view that conversation is an orderly phenomenon, hence utterances or sentences are "responses to other actions, and they in turn set the environment for new actions" (Potter, 2004, p.609) which may or may not follow. Rhetorical situation refers to the view that the constructed discourse or accounts reflect their inherent "*offensive* and ... *defensive* rhetoric" (Potter, 2004, p.610-emphasis in original). This view signals a main area of divergence from CA and the possibility that DA could play "a key ethical and political role in showing how social phenomena are discursively constituted" (Hammersley, 2003, p.758).

The third principle holds that discourse is *constructed* from linguistic structure such as words or rhetorical devices, and *constructive* in its formation of versions of social realities. Potter (2004) clarified that this strand of "*discursive* constructionism" (p.610-emphasis in original) is distinct from conventional cognitive and social constructionism which appeal respectively to mental information-processing and internalization processes in order to explain the occurrence of the observed phenomena. Broadly interpreted, this principle holds that an examination of "people's practices" (Potter, 2004, p.610), which are believed to be reflected in the discourse, is sufficient by itself (independent of the context or participants) to explain the discursive process of shared reality construction. Hence, DA would not only shed light on the process but also ultimately reveal the *products* of discourse which are held to be "the institutions, modes of representation and cultural/materials discursive regimes which emerge as a result" (Wetherell, 2001b, p.393).

Reflecting CA methods, discourse analysts gather qualitative data through interviews, or the use of focus groups, in the form of naturally occurring talk including texts/documents that are part of everyday life and/or institutional life. Such empirical data are audio/video recorded, transcribed and coded to facilitate analysis rather than being intrinsic to the analysis as in the tradition of grounded theory (Potter, 2004). In terms of areas of inquiry that are specific to DA, Potter (2004) acknowledged that DA covers "an enormous variety of topics and asks a wide range of different questions ... that stretch the notion of discourse analysis well beyond breaking point" (p.611). Although claimed as an indication of the analytical adequacy of the DA approach, it could be argued such 'flexibility' leaves DA vulnerable to the criticism that it 'piggy-backs' on the methodological traditions established by CA and lacks its own distinctive paradigmatic features.

The lack of clarity in the literature on the status of DA as a paradigm or a method has added to the confusion and controversy surrounding this approach. Hammersley (2003) pointed out that if regarded as a *paradigm*, DA would be assumed to be grounded in its own set of ontological and epistemological beliefs, areas and methods of inquiry which are based on its disciplinary roots, to be used ideally at the exclusion of other paradigms in investigating the social world. If treated as a *method*, DA would be assumed to be informed by its philosophical and theoretical traditions in delineating the types of data (qualitative and/or quantitative) to be gathered that would illuminate the inquiry questions; the primacy of either the qualitative or quantitative method in the research design; the instruments to be used; and the criteria for judging the quality of the research findings. Furthermore, discourse analysis would be regarded as one out of other possible strategies to be adopted in the pursuit of specific research questions. In response, Potter (2003) stated that it is "confusing" (p.784) to regard DA as solely a paradigm or a method, since to do so, would firstly constrain DA in its engagement with other research methodologies and secondly, ignore the "web of theoretical and metatheoretical assumptions" (p.785) underlying DA.

In this study, both theoretical approaches of DA and CA discussed above could provide valuable insights regarding the educational discourse produced in computer-mediated learning contexts. However, at the philosophical level, when taken as they are, both approaches hold assumptions that present the following areas of problematic fit with the views held by the over-arching constructivist framework adopted in the study[18]:

- CA and DA hold that patterns of interaction could be interpreted solely from the discourse and independently of the context or participants, but constructivism seeks out and honours multiple perspectives.
- CA assumes that recurrent patterns of interaction identified in the discourse could ultimately be 'projected' (possibly as 'rules' of interaction) while constructivism aims to enhance understanding through inquiry.
- DA regards discourse as the main 'actor' in the construction of 'realities', but constructivism believes in the joint social construction of 'realities' through the negotiation of individual understandings.
- Potter's (2004) DA approach seems to have overtones of the critical, postmodern perspective while the 'milder' version of constructivism adopted by this study holds that even when issues of power are researched, it places no value judgments on different perspectives nor does it aim to redress power imbalances through interventions.

Hammersley (2003) observed that the viability of both approaches to the study of discourse could, in fact, lie in the extent to which they are modified in actual practice. Moreover, Potter (2004) noted an increasing blurring of the boundaries between the two approaches as DA has "picked up on some of the robust findings of conversation analysis, as well as its rigorous analytical approach" (p.621). Hence, this study turns to a DA approach grounded in the tradition of linguistics which is discussed below.

2.4.4 Discourse Analysis as theoretical framework
The term *discourse analysis* is defined, in the context of this research, as the study of "language in use" (Brown & Yule, 1983, p.1) which is based on two assumptions. The first assumption, which is basic to DA, holds that language is "a dynamic means of expressing intended meanings" rather than a static representational model (Brown & Yule, 1983, p.24). Hence, descriptions of language forms and patterns would take into account the environments in which they occur that includes the "relationship between the speaker and the utterance, on the particular occasion of use" (Brown & Yule, 1983, p.27) rather than solely the potential relationships between sentences. The second assumption, which diverges from Potter's DA approach, holds that the speaker/writer is at the centre of the communication process of meaning negotiation. Therefore, the examination of language use incorporates the perspectives of "people who communicate and people who interpret ... who have topics, presuppositions who assign information structure and who make reference" (Brown & Yule, 1983, p.ix).

---

[18] Refer to this chapter, section 2.2.

Based on these two assumptions, DA aims to describe how "forms of language are used in communication" (Brown & Yule, 1983, p.ix), which reflects one of the traditional concerns in linguistics, and to examine patterns of language used in communication; focusing on how "*humans* use language to communicate ... how addressers construct linguistic messages for addressees and how addressees work on linguistic messages in order to interpret them" (p.ix – my emphasis). In terms of its methodological position, Brown and Yule (1983) explained that DA is a cross-disciplinary approach that utilizes insights gained from other linguistic sub-disciplines such as sociolinguistics, psycholinguistics, computational linguistics, and pragmatics. Data analysis in DA involves not just the study of the textual data, but is balanced by a "consideration of the general principles of interpretation by which people normally make sense of what they hear and read" (Brown & Yule, 1983, p.x).

The areas of emphasis reflected in this DA theoretical framework parallel, to an extent, a typology of DA approaches suggested in Taylor (2001) for the study of different discourse aspects that are based on the assumptions that language is constitutive i.e. "it is the site where meanings are created and changed" (p.6) and situated in use. These four, possibly overlapping, approaches are labelled in this review as: *contextual, critical, linguistic,* and *interactional.*

The *contextual* approach is concerned with the use of special sets of language terms and their meanings that are associated with or constituted in particular topics, activities, or social-cultural settings. This approach reflects an area of interest in the study of language use which is situated not at the level of interaction but within specific social or cultural contexts. At the even higher level of 'society' or 'culture', the *critical* approach, which could overlap the contextual approach, involves the study of language patterns and related social institutional practices that empower and/or limit what people do and say.

The *linguistic* approach focuses on the study of language itself and patterns of variation in language systems that are related to its use by different individuals in various settings. In other words, the focus of inquiry is on "regularities within an imperfect and unstable system" (Taylor, 2001, p.8). The *interactional* approach regards the activity of language use as the main focus of discourse analysis. This approach assumes that conversational interaction patterns could be identified in terms of sequences whereby "any one person's contribution must follow on from that of the previous contribution and is inevitably shaped by what has gone before" (Taylor, 2001, p.8). Moreover, it assumes that meaning could be created within the interaction process and that the interactional context has a role in shaping the resultant patterns of language use. In this study, the context is taken to include not only the immediate in-text situation of utterances, but also factors such as the technology medium and learning environment.

The *linguistic* and *interactional* approaches would appear to most closely resemble and complement the early DA framework presented by Brown and Yule (1983). This study adopts a DA approach that integrates the views of both sets of authors which has the advantage of locating the framework in the established discipline of linguistics, hence providing a crucial theoretical basis for the examination of conversational turn-taking and interactional coherence in electronic discourse. The following discussion describes the characteristics of computer-mediated discourse with specific focus on chat discourse.

2.4.5 Computer-mediated discourse and chat discourse

Computer-mediated discourse (CMD) refers to "the communication produced when human beings interact with one another by transmitting messages via networked computers" (Herring, 2003, p.1). The study of computer-mediated discourse is held to be located within the field of CMC and "distinguished by its focus on *language and language use* in computer networked environments, and by its use of methods of discourse analysis to address that focus" (Herring, 2003, p.1-emphasis in original).

Interest in CMD stem from the emergence of a variety of *electronic language* (Collet & Belmore, 1996) which appears to defy traditional theoretical categories of text and speech that are based on the assumption that "physical contact is necessarily a part of human communication" (Reid, 1991, para. 1). As both asynchronous and synchronous computer-mediated discourse are largely text-based i.e., "messages are typed on a computer keyboard and read as text on a computer screen, typically by a person or persons at a different location from the message sender" (Herring, 2003, p.1), Yates (2001) pointed out that researchers have also been interested in the characterization of asynchronous and synchronous CMD as text or talk. Hence, as noted by Herring (2003), the broad areas of inquiry in CMD have included studies that examined the nature of CMD in comparison to written/spoken languages, the linguistic structure of asynchronous and synchronous discourse, online interaction management strategies, and issues of social practices and identity in online discourse.

The type of CMD of interest to this study is *chat discourse* which challenges "conventional understandings of the differences between spoken and written language" (Reid, 1991, para. 2). According to Ong (1982), research in language has concentrated so much on the study of written text that speech tended to be subsumed as a variant of writing. The consequence of such a perspective is the conventional assumption that speech is essentially the same as text, other than the lack of a textual form. However, the phenomenon of chat discourse would appear to blur such traditional characterization of speech and writing with its "text-based orality" (December, 1993, section 1, para. 2). While chat discourse displays the spontaneity of speech in its rhythm (given its element of synchronicity), it presents at the same time, the textual and structural forms of written language.

Studies that examined the features of chat discourse in comparison with speech (December, 1993; Kortti, 1999; Murphy & Collins, 1999; Werry, 1996) have largely identified *linguistic* features that are to similar face-to-face conversation such as the presence of turn taking, observer selection, opening sequences, self-repair, and intonation units. Features identified that are regarded as unique to chat discourse include the presence of explicit addressing, paralinguistic communication conventions (emoticons, emotags, acronyms), server messages, informality of language structure, and a lack of punctuation and capitalization.

Research on chat discourse includes studies that focus on the impact of the synchronous CMC medium on critical discussion and argumentation. For instance, Veerman et al. (2000) conducted an experimental study that examined the impact of peer coaching on the development of online argumentation skills among undergraduates in an educational technology course. Weger Jr. and Aakhus (2003) carried out an empirical study on the impact of the design features of the synchronous CMC medium on the quality of critical discussion and conversational coherence in public political Internet chat rooms using an argumentation analysis model. Stromer-Galley and Martinson (2004) conducted a comparative study that examined the impact of discussion topic (political versus recreational topics) on the coherence of chat discourse in public Internet chat rooms.

Of particular relevance to this study are the works by Kneser et al. (2001) and Cox et al. (2004) which examined *educational chat discourse* at transactional and exchange structure levels[19]. Kneser et al. (2001) examined the characteristics of chat discourse in order to evaluate the effectiveness of online tutors in transferring discussion skills to postgraduate students in a distance learning course. Transcripts from chat seminars were analyzed with an *Exchange Structure Analysis* (ESA) framework to identify exchange patterns of tutors and students that indicate the degree of inclusiveness of participation by both parties in an online learning environment. Cox et al. (2004) conducted a comparative study that examined the impact of course design, group dynamics, and facilitation styles in supporting effective online synchronous discussions in two university courses. Transcripts from chat discussions were analyzed with a modified version of the ESA framework to identify participant roles and inclusiveness of participation during learning conversations.

2.4.6 Chat as social conversation
The *Community of Inquiry* (COI)[20] adopted in this study holds that the presence and interactions between cognitive, social, and teaching presences are essential to a successful higher education experience (Garrison et al., 2000). In particular, positive perceptions of social presence are deemed to facilitate the knowledge construction process and support cognitive presence. Although not a primary area of focus in this study, the extent of social presence afforded by the synchronous CMC mode is nevertheless of some concern in the larger context of the online learning experience. Hence, it is necessary to briefly examine the issues concerning capabilities of text-based CMC in supporting social presence in online learning environments, with particular emphasis on the synchronous CMC mode.

Although distance education has largely embraced the capabilities afforded by CMC in increasing the interactivity of online courses, there are reservations over how CMC affects human communication processes and behaviour with their accompanying impact on knowledge construction and the online educational experience. The major theories developed to characterize the nature of CMC and account for its social impact in communication include: *social presence* (Short et al., 1976), *information richness* (Daft & Lengel, 1986), *reduced social cues* (Kiesler et al., 1984), *hierarchical flattening* (Sproull & Kiesler, 1986), and *social information processing* (Fulk, Schmitz, & Steinfield, 1990; Fulk, Steinfield, Schmitz, & Power, 1987).

According to Sherman (2001), these theories share the assumption that the largely text-based nature of CMC provides less information than face-to-face communication

---

[19] Findings from Kneser et al. (2001) and Cox et al. (2004) are described in Chapter 1, section 1.2. The Exchange Structure Analysis (ESA) framework for the analysis of chat exchanges is discussed in Chapter 4, section 4.4.1.
[20] Refer to this chapter, section 2.3.4.

for "forming impressions and making judgments of other people" (p.57), but differ in their positions on the resulting degree of impact on the social communication process. The term *cues-filtered out*, coined by Culnan and Markus (1987), is widely used to categorize the social presence, information richness, and reduced social cues models which, broadly interpreted, hold that since CMC technologies offer fewer means of conveying communicative information than the face-to-face mode, such loss of essential interactional cues that have been *filtered out* by text-based CMC modes could result in the phenomenon of *deindividuation* (Postmes, Spears, & Lea, 1998; 1999) which is characterized by the formation of negative, impersonal interpersonal perceptions, and/or the display of uninhibited or self-oriented communicative behaviour.

Given this study's focus on the impact of synchronous CMC on collaborative group learning processes, it is hence necessary to examine the possible implications of text-based chat on communication processes and participant behaviour in light of the theories discussed above. Although some chat applications such as Yahoo Messenger™ offer additional channels for conveying information through image and voice capability options (Figure 2.7), the WebCT™ chat facility in the research site is solely text-based (Figure 2.8). From the *cues-filtered out* theoretical perspective, solely text-based chat interactions are assumed to have low social presence, provide fewer interactional cues than face-to-face encounters and therefore more likely to result in negative interpersonal perceptions and uninhibited communicative behaviour.

However, the *social information processing* model claims that text-based CMC modes need not impact negatively on the social communication process since the need for affinity drives people to establish social relationships using whatever information available and through whichever means of communication that are at hand. As a result, in order to convey and/or obtain social information for perception formation, participants may actively "develop adaptive strategies" (Hancock & Dunham, 2001, p.107) or change their linguistic and/or interactional behaviour so as to facilitate information exchange and overcome the limitations presented by the communication means (Sherman, 2001).

Regarding the impact of text-based chat on *perception formation*, this study acknowledges that text-based chat may slow down the process of impression formation or establishment of social presence during online tutorials, but does not prevent it from occurring. In fact, the sense of immediacy of presence afforded by the synchronous CMC mode could facilitate or even heighten (Walther, 1996) the perceptions formed of other participants. Additionally, the *appearance screening* capability of the text-based CMC, which filters out static social context cues, could encourage greater self-disclosure that builds online bonds, reduce instances of online gender harassment (Herring, 2000), and lead to greater equality of participation (Siegel et al., 1986).

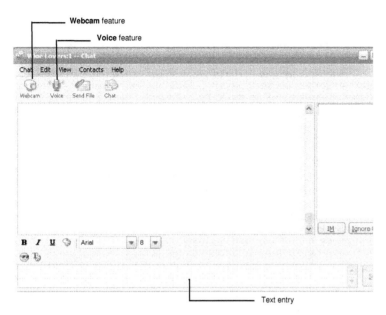

Figure 2.7. Yahoo™ chat application user interface

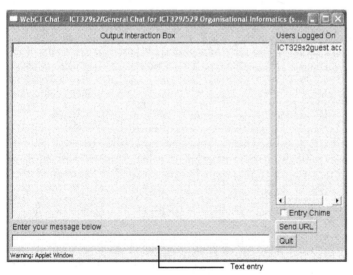

Figure 2.8. WebCT™ chat application user interface

It should be noted that other factors present in the research site[21], besides the CMC medium, could contribute to the establishment of social presence and sense of community such as the extended period of time (11 sessions) for participants to be acquainted with each other and acculturate to the social practices of their chat tutorial group; their prior knowledge of chat communication conventions; the scaffolding provided by unit resources such as the *Ecoms Guidelines* (Appendix A.5); and opportunities for face-to-face encounters during the weekly on-campus lectures.

The concept of *uninhibited behaviour*, as used by Sproull and Kiesler (1986) to describe CMC behaviour in an organizational context, refers to the "flouting of social conventions" (p.1508) and an increased willingness to communicate negative information or feedback. In the context of this study, the concept is taken to refer mainly to acts involving *flaming* or verbally abusive behaviour that could be disruptive to collaborative learning. As the sociocultural constructivist perspective holds that knowledge building involves the "active articulation" (Harasim, Calvert, & Groeneboer, 1997, p.150), sharing and negotiation of meanings from multiple perspectives, overly cooperative behaviour manifested as the withholding of opposing or negative points of view, although conducive to establishing an unthreatening social climate, are deemed undesirable for creating the mental 'perturbations' (von Glasersfeld, 1989) necessary for knowledge construction.

Some studies that found instances of uninhibited behaviour in CMC environments have associated the phenomenon to not only reduced social cues (Siegel et al., 1986) but also the factor of anonymity (Sproull & Kiesler, 1986). The extent to which *anonymity* is a factor in this study depends on how the concept is defined.

McLeod (1997) identified two kinds of anonymity in CMC contexts: technical and social anonymity. *Technical anonymity* refers to "the mechanical practices used to dissociate individuals from their inputs" (McLeod, 1997, p.225) that include the concealment of real names and spatial separation of individuals. *Social anonymity* refers to "individuals' subjective experience of anonymity—whether they believe they are anonymous and whether they believe others are anonymous to them" (McLeod, 1997, p.225) which could be affected by contextual variables such as group size, task, nature of relationship between participants, and length of acquaintance.

To some degree, the CMC environment in this study could display technical anonymity since the online tutorials are attended by distant students. However, if technical anonymity is taken to mean "not having participants' real names attached to their inputs" (McLeod, 1997, p.224), then the CMC environment is not anonymous since WebCT™ chat facility does not allow for the use of "pseudonymous" nicknames (Herring, 2003, p.7) and displays the names of all parties logged into the chat tutorial room.

It could be further argued that even when participants are spatially separated (without face-to-face contact) they may not be socially anonymous to one another. In the course of building online relationships and sense of community, Jacobson (1999) noted that "people may (and do) voluntarily disclose identifying information about themselves" (p.132). Herring (2000) also observed that not only do public IRC users

---

[21] The research site, which is an online undergraduate unit, is described in Chapter 3.

actively seek personal information on others' gender, they appear to not/not wish to conceal such information even when their gender place them at a disadvantage.

Leaving aside the issue of the truthfulness or falsity of such personal information revealed, it would appear that the CMC environment in this study does not exhibit 'true' anonymity in the sense of participants being totally unknown to each other by not having any knowledge or information about the other members in the tutorial group. As a result, instances of uninhibited behaviour during chat tutorials may not necessarily be associated with the factor of anonymity. Furthermore, uninhibited behaviour could be checked by other factors such as the moderated nature of the tutorial activity and tutor/peer assessments of participation in chat tutorial discussions.

At this point, it would be reasonable to conclude that even as the text-based synchronous CMC mode may slow down establishment of social presence during online interactions, various factors which are intrinsic and external to the chat medium offer other means for impression formation that could facilitate the learning process and enhance the overall online educational experience. The further concern regarding the claim of interactional incoherence in chat discourse and its possible impact on the dialogic knowledge construction process is discussed below.

2.4.7 Chat as learning conversation
In Werry's (1996) examination of the discursive properties of chat discourse, it was observed that in chat conversational sequences, "[e]ach utterance is simply displayed in the chronological order in which it is received by the IRC system ... [scrolling] up (and then off) each person's computer screen at a pace directly proportional to the tempo of the overall conversation" (p.51). Given this linear organization of conversational sequence, chat exchange structure[22] is considered distinctive from both traditional oral and written discourse for its juxtaposition of disparate conversational threads containing different speech acts and topics. Werry (1996) suggested that such organizational patterns in chat discourse could result in rapid topic shifts and a greater likelihood of "separate conversations intertwining" (p.51).

It is possible to take the stand that the above features of chat conversations are perceived by users as part and parcel of the appeal of the synchronous CMC mode, to be used or even exploited for creative language play (Herring, 1999; Jones et al., 2001) or "wit testing" in argumentative chat dialogue (Weger Jr. & Aakhus, 2003, p.35) and serve to differentiate experienced and 'newbie' members in chat communities. However, given the sociocultural constructivist perspective that knowledge is constituted in the learning conversations, the presence of such features could disrupt the dialogic learning process, impact on opportunities for participation in discussion or undermine the collaborative efforts by participants in meaning creation. The characterization of chat discourse as "brief, rapid messages" with multiple topics "interleaved in chronological rather than topical sequence" (Lapadat, 2002, section 2, paras. 6-7), leaves chat discourse vulnerable to claims of interactional incoherence (Herring, 1999) and the view that the synchronous CMC medium is incapable of supporting critical discussion that establishes cognitive presence in online learning contexts.

---

[22] The elements in the structure of pedagogical chat exchanges are discussed in Chapter 4, section 4.4.1.

In general, discourse incoherence could result from the lack of access to interactional management strategies such as knowledge of sentential structure, information from rhetorical and/or situational contexts, awareness of the principles of analogy, cooperation, turn-taking, and broader forms of sociocultural understandings (Brown & Yule, 1983). In the case of CMD, the following properties of the CMC media have additionally been cited as contributing to incoherence in online discourse:
- Synchronous CMC application designs that limit the quantity of text characters for each posting was found to prevent the "building of complete arguments" (Weger Jr. & Aakhus, 2003, p.31).
- The linear display of chat dialogue sequences on users' screens which juxtaposes disparate conversational threads was held to result in rapid changes in topic and a greater likelihood of overlapping utterances (Werry, 1996).
- The 'lean' CMC medium (Daft & Lengel, 1986) which reduces availability of non-verbal cues was held to disrupt the timing of turn-taking and organization of reference during discussions (Herring, 1999).

In particular, coherence in chat discourse could be problematic since the linear organization of conversational sequences on participants' screens may disrupt adjacency of turns and turn-taking sequences thereby violating the "no gap and no overlap" (Sacks et al., 1974, p.700) principles held necessary to the organization of orderly conversations.

The assumption that orderly talk is vital to coherence in conversations could be traced to theoretical developments on language use in the disciplines of linguistics and sociology. Broadly interpreted, *speech act theory* (Austin, 1962) assumes that any sentence or utterance could be used to perform three kinds of actions simultaneously: a locutionary, an illocutionary and a perlocutionary act (Brown & Yule, 1983). In other words, any sentence/utterance could be used by the speaker/addressor to achieve sentence meaning, intended meaning, and resultant effect on the receiver. Searle (1969) extended the concept of speech acts to include the constructs of direct and indirect speech acts; with indirect speech acts referring to the performance of illocutionary acts under the guise of other acts (Brown & Yule, 1983).

Levinson (1983) criticized the theory of speech acts for its failure to account for the issue of 'uptake' which involves the hearer/addressee understanding both the "force and content" of an utterance (p.237). In other words, speech act theory, as it is, does not explain how the hearer comes to interpret or recognize (rightly or wrongly) the intention of an utterance in a particular context. Furthermore, Brown and Yule (1983) pointed out that the theory does not account for instances when a single utterance may perform several illocutionary acts at the same time or when "a fairly extended utterance may be interpreted as a single act" (p.233). Nevertheless, speech act theory remains relevant in the field of discourse analysis for its significant foundational contribution to understanding discourse coherence and the role of adjacency pairs in the orderly sequencing of talk.

Later research pioneered by Goffman (1983) and Sacks et al. (1974) explored the issue of 'uptake' further in the respective disciplinary traditions of ethnomethodology and sociology. Goffman's (1983) work on interaction order suggested that participants' understanding of conversational organization could stem from access to some form of tacit, socially shared knowledge and practices (Brown & Yule, 1983; Heritage, 2001). Sacks et al. (1974) developed a model for the organization of conversational turn-taking to account for empirical observations of 'orderly talk' that became the basis of CA methodology. Based on the main assumption that there is an underlying system which manages turn-taking in conversations, Sacks et al. (1974) formulated a set of rules for "governing turn construction, providing for the allocation of a next turn to one part, and co-ordinating transfer so as to minimize gap and overlap" (p. 704). It is claimed that this model is free from constraints of context or topic and that examining conversational interaction at this level could indicate the extent of participants' understanding of the intentions of turns.

However, Sacks et al., (1974) highlighted several caveats in the use of this model: the proposed rules establish conditions for turn-taking sequences but do not guarantee their occurrences; and variations in the order of turns could be accounted for by other constructs such as adjacency pairs which "set constraints on what should be done in a next turn" (p.717).

Adjacency pairs, which resemble paired speech acts, are two-turn units such as question/answer or greeting/greeting and are defined by Levinson (1983) as sequences of two utterances that are

(i) adjacent
(ii) produced by different speakers
(iii) ordered as a *first part* and a *second part*
(iv) typed, so that a particular first part require a particular second (or range of second parts)
(Levinson, 1983, p.304-emphasis in original)

Additionally, turn-taking sequences could be extended with the presence of 'insertion' sequences (Brown & Yule, 1983) between each turn in an adjacency pair due to the use of indirect speech acts or 'repair mechanisms' to deal with turn-taking errors or violations (Sacks et al., 1974; Schegloff et al., 1977). The concept of adjacency pairs, as a technique for anticipating sequences of turns, is therefore "deeply inter-related with the turn-taking system" (Levinson, 1983, p.303) in contributing to a deeper theoretical understanding of discourse coherence[23] at the exchange level.

This study holds that the knowledge construction could be supported by the presence of coherence in chat discourse and the cooperative (Grice, 1967; 1978) rather than competitive efforts by participants in the dialogic process of meaning creation.

Discourse coherence is held to be indicated by the presence of topic relevance which is "*constructed* across turns by the collaboration of participants" (Levinson, 1983, p.315-emphasis in original). At the level of an exchange, the adjacency of turns sets the condition for subsequent turns and signals topic shifts. Hence, it could indicate elaboration in discussion, the expansion of a main topic to related sub-topics, or the presence of isolated topics that have been initiated but are not taken up in subsequent turns. Such patterns of coherence and topic relevance in the chat

---

[23] The concept of adjacency pairs in relation to the structure of pedagogical chat exchanges is discussed in Chapter 4, section 4.4.1.

discourse could thus indicate, to an analyst, the interactivity[24] of exchanges and depth of discussion generated by the participants.

Collaborative effort, as displayed in the discourse, is held to be indicated by the presence of symmetrical patterns of turn-taking/turn-passing. Based on the assumption that the turn-taking system regulates the distribution of opportunities of participation which could be "valued, sought, or avoided" by participants (Sacks et al., 1974, p.701), patterns of turn-allocation or turn-taking (orderly or overlapping) in the chat discourse could therefore indicate the extent to which participation opportunities were present in discussions. The degree of symmetry in turn-taking patterns could indicate whether participants compete to hold the floor (dominate the discussion) or collaborate in meaning negotiation such as by extending invitations to other participants to take up the next turn.

In congruence with DA methodological approach adopted, this study acknowledges that "*humans* use language to communicate" (Brown & Yule, 1983, p.ix-my emphasis). Therefore, the presence of coherence or incoherence in discourse is largely a matter of interpretation. This study recognizes that discourse analysis offers one interpretation (the analyst's) of what had happened during educational chat interactions. Therefore, it is necessary to also examine student perceptions of their experiences, discussed in the next section, for further insight into the collaborative group learning process.

2.4.8 Summary
Synchronous and asynchronous CMC modes offer different capabilities and constraints to facilitating interaction in online learning environments. The perception that a delayed-time CMC medium is more conducive for critical and reflective thinking led to a concentration in research and application of the asynchronous mode at the level of higher education. In contrast, the synchronous CMC mode is largely perceived to support social-emotional presence in collaborative groups with fewer studies researching the effectiveness of chat in supporting learning conversations. The under-utilization of synchronous CMC in online courses was attributed to the characteristics of the medium and the additional skills required from the tutor and learners in managing or coping with the online synchronous interaction and chat discourse.

Discourse analysis and conversation analysis present two similar, yet competing approaches to the study of discourse at the level of methodology and methods. While conversation analysis offers a well-established paradigmatic framework for studying talk-in-interaction, discourse analysis reflects a more fragmented theoretical background which overlaps to a great extent the CA methodological position and methods. This study adopted a DA theoretical framework located in the established discipline of linguistics for examining the discourse of educational chat.

While the concern that text-based chat discourse may affect the establishment of social presence was acknowledged, it was argued that social presence could be built through other means intrinsic to the chat medium and available from the research site. Regarding the further concern of interactional incoherence which could disrupt the dialogic learning process, it was held that discourse coherence could be taken as

---

[24] Refer to definition of interactivity by Rafaeli and Sudweeks (1998) in this chapter, section 2.2.1.

the presence of topic relevance with the adjacency of turns signalling interactivity in exchanges and depth of discussion. Additionally, knowledge construction could be facilitated by collaborative effort in meaning making as indicated by the presence of symmetrical patterns of turn-taking and availability of participation opportunities.

While the study of online discourse could offer one perspective on educational chat interaction, the next section discusses another perspective on the collaborative-constructivist group learning process provided by student perceptions of their experiences.

2.5 Student Perceptions of Online Learning Experiences

While educational chat discourse could provide valuable insight into the nature of online learning processes, student perceptions of their learning experiences offer another perspective on the phenomena. This section discusses the broad pedagogical implications of student perceptions of online educational experiences, highlights quality assurance frameworks for evaluating distance education programs, and explains the use of data gathered on student self-reports of learning experiences within the context of the study.

2.5.1 Student perceptions of online learning

Studies on student perceptions of online learning experiences have generally yielded mixed findings. Current online learning environments, supported by better technologies, are held to offer high quality interaction and a wide range of teaching approaches to enhance learning. The networked learning model for higher education proposed by Harasim et al. (1995) would move students from physical learning situations to globally connected learning communities, offer interactive instructional activities, support opportunities for communication between all parties in the learning process, and ultimately lead to "improvements in cognition and social interaction" (p.273).

A number of studies have reported online learner satisfaction over factors of convenience, flexibility of access and support from instructors/peers afforded by educational technologies (Bonk et al., 2001; Goh & Tobin, 1999; McLoughlin & Luca, 1999; Thomas, Jones, Packham, & Miller, 2004). Other studies found evidence of pedagogical benefits in terms of collaborative knowledge construction, critical thinking development (Armitt et al., 2002; Cooney, 1998; Hara et al., 2000; Kanuka & Anderson, 1998; Newman, Johnson, Cochrane, & Webb, 1997), and the achievement of comparable online learning outcomes (in terms of grades) to face-to-face courses (Hong, Lai, & Holton, 2003).

However, Hara and Kling (1999) observed that most studies on web-based instruction have focused on the benefits while glossing over the problems. Their study on student experiences with a web-based distance education course revealed student frustrations over the nature of online interactions (lack of timely feedback and visual cues), the management of communication (unclear task instructions), and technical problems that contributed to learner anxiety. Hara and Kling (1999) claimed that such difficulties encountered online could be major impediments to learning and have significant impact when "these frustrations so overwhelmed some students that they gave up on the formal content of the course" (p.23).

Other than problems related to the characteristics of CMC technology, later studies identified difficulties faced by participants who were not entirely comfortable with the collaborative learning process (Goh & Tobin, 1999; Hong et al., 2003), considered student-initiated online discussions of having less value than those contributed by traditional authority figures such as the teacher or subject expert (Teles, Gillies, & Ashton, 2001), and held certain expectations of online tutors that were based on previous educational experiences of face-to-face learning (Thomas et al., 2004).

While most studies have tended to examine students' retrospective perceptions of learning experiences, Kumar et al. (2002) examined *potential* students' "perceptions about virtual education and their willingness to enroll in a virtual education degree program" (p.134). The quantitative findings from a survey on participants from a rural mid-western US university indicate positive perceptions regarding the flexibility of online programs and its effectiveness for self-disciplined or motivated students. The study also found that, in comparison to on-campus education, there was skepticism over claims of the greater effectiveness of online learning and its ability to increase student-student or student-staff interactions.

In other words, in spite of the optimism expressed by Harasim et al. (1995) on the potential of networked learning, results from studies suggest that existing students have found that their online experiences do not exactly match their expectations and potential students are skeptical about the quality of online learning experiences. Such reported perceptions or experiences of online learning have both pedagogical and commercial implications.

2.5.2 Impact of student perceptions

McLoughlin (2003) noted that student perceptions of the quality of online learning where *quality* is defined as "student satisfaction with the online experience" (section 3, para. 4), could guide educators in the creation of learning experiences that meet student needs or expectations. The mid 1990s saw a shift in pedagogical direction towards the adoption of learner-centered and constructivist frameworks that currently ground most online instructional approaches. These instructional approaches emphasize greater student control of learning processes, more opportunities for CMC supported interaction, use of collaborative learning activities, and evaluation through self-assessment or reflection on learning experiences (Bonk & Cunningham, 1998; Jonassen et al., 1995). Gunawardena and Duphorne (2000) found evidence of "a significant, positive correlation" (p.111) between the use of such online learning approaches and student satisfaction with learning experiences which, the authors suggested, could translate to a greater likelihood of student re-enrolment for such experiences.

Student perceptions of learning experiences could have commercial implications for maintaining a competitive edge in the online education sector. The performance of educational institutions, in terms of graduate satisfaction ratings and institutional rankings, are readily available for comparison through organizations such as the *Australian Universities Quality Agency* and annual commercial college guides (*Good Universities Guide to Universities, U.S. News & World Report*). With increasing numbers of online courses available to consumers, the perceived 'quality' of a course could be a vital factor in educational product differentiation by affecting consumer confidence as reflected in "student application patterns" (Chun, 2002, p.20), enrolment, retention, and re-enrolment rates.

Carr (2000) observed that with the gradual maturation of the online education sector, university administrators and faculty were presented with discouraging figures suggesting that course retention and completion rates for online/distance education programs are generally lower than those for on-campus programs. Such results were initially attributed to the different measures of retention employed by various institutions and the statistical odds for attrition, given the mature profile of distant education students who tend to have more family or job commitments and responsibilities. However, the presence of "significant variation" (Carr, 2000, p.39) in online course completion rates among different educational institutions suggests that other factors such as the experience of online tutors, degree of contact/interaction between learning parties, or simply variations in the quality of online programs could contribute to determining attrition rates.

More recently, the premise that there are 'real' variations in online course quality was strengthened by findings from Rovai and Barnum (2003) which examined the learning experiences of 328 graduate students enrolled in 19 online graduate courses offered by a single university. Using self-report measures of learning, the authors gathered quantitative data through Likert-type questions in online surveys and from archived interaction data that reflected, respectively, active and passive student participation in terms of the number of messages posted and access to the discussion area without contribution. The study found "significant differences in perceived learning among the 19 on-line graduate courses taught by the same university" (Rovai & Barnum, 2003, p.68) which led the authors to call for the implementation of quality assurance in online programs.

2.5.3 Evaluation frameworks for online learning
According to Chun (2002), assessment of higher education quality could be carried out using four methodological approaches which involve the analyses of actuarial data, ratings of institutional quality, student survey information, and data from direct assessments of student learning.

Actuarial data include information on admission test scores, demographics of student population, staff-student ratio, breadth and depth of course offerings, and graduation rates. The data from *direct assessment* include information on course grades and scores from standardized tests or performance tasks that have been designed to "assess general academic skills or subject matter knowledge" (Chun, 2002, p.23). Data from *ratings of institutional quality* reveal faculty's or administrators' perceptions on the academic quality and/or reputation of other institutions while data from *student surveys* provide self-reported information on "collegiate experiences, satisfaction with their coursework and school, self-assessments of improvements in their academic abilities, and educational and employment plans" (Chun, 2002, p.21).

Since most existing guidelines on quality practices for higher education have been developed for application in traditional on-campus university settings (Chickering & Gamson, 1987; Ramsden, 1992), there have been efforts towards the development of quality assurance (QA) frameworks that take into account online learning contexts. Recently, several frameworks have been developed for the evaluation of online distance education programs and learner experiences in the higher education and vocational education/training (VET) sectors. The following studies have mainly used a combination of data from ratings of institutional quality (Cashion & Palmieri, 2002; IHEP, 2000; Yeung, 2001) and student surveys (Cashion & Palmieri, 2002; IHEP, 2000; Jurczyk, Kushner Benson, & Savery, 2004) to assess quality on the institutional and/or programmatic levels.

In order to assist stakeholders in making informed judgments on online distance education standards, the Institute for Higher Education Policy (IHEP) conducted a US-based study to determine whether existing quality benchmarks developed for all types of distance learning could be applied to Internet-based distance education. The study examined the importance of each benchmark to participant institutions and the degree to which the benchmarks are incorporated into their policies, procedures, and practices. A final set of 24 benchmarks considered "most essential to the success of an Internet-based distance education program at any institution" (IHEP, 2000, p.25) was compiled and further examined in later studies.

Yeung (2001) examined the relevance of the benchmarks from the perspective of the teaching faculty in the Hong Kong higher education context. Jurczyk et al. (2004) measured student perceptions of a web-based US graduate course before, during, and after its commencement, through the use of a questionnaire based on the IHEP quality benchmarks. Cashion and Palmieri (2002) carried out a large-scale research project in Australia to identify quality factors perceived as important by VET students, faculty, and organizations that "will provide a foundation for benchmarking online learning" (p.12). The study identified 11 positive and 8 negative factors, and survey findings indicate that a majority of VET respondents believed they were receiving a high quality online learning experience with *flexibility*, *responsive teachers* and *high quality materials* ranked as the three most important factors in a quality online learning experience.

It is necessary to clarify, at this point, that it is not within the scope of this study to evaluate institutional effectiveness or conduct a summative assessment of the quality of the research site. Instead, this study is concerned with student expectations and experiences of online synchronous tutorials within the context of the selected case which is an online undergraduate unit[25]. Rather than being a component of established institutional review procedures or practices, the self-reported information gathered through the web survey instrument in this study is used to offer another perspective, in addition to the analyst's interpretations from the transcripts of chat discussions, on what had happened during the online learning process. Such integration of multiple perspectives could offer a richer and more holistic account of the learning process which may then inform the theory and practice of online synchronous activity design from a sociocultural constructive perspective.

2.5.5 Summary
In spite of the optimism over the potential of networked learning, studies on student perceptions of online learning experiences have generally yielded mixed findings. Studies have reported learner satisfaction and frustration over technical and CMC factors as well as instructional approaches in online courses. These perceptions and experiences of online learning could have pedagogical and commercial implications, and suggest a need for the implementation of quality assurance in online programs. Various frameworks were recently developed for the evaluation of online distance education programs and learner experiences in the higher education/vocational training sectors which used a combination of data from ratings of institutional quality and student surveys.

In the context of this study, it was clarified that data from student self-reports of learning experiences were not intended for evaluating institutional effectiveness. Instead, student perceptions of chat tutorial experiences were used in conjunction with interpretations from the transcript data on chat interactions for a rich account of

---

[25] The research site is described in Chapter 3.

the online learning process. The next section summarizes the main concepts and assumptions discussed in this chapter.

2.6 Summary
This chapter reviewed the main literature related to learning and interaction, and covered key concepts of major learning theories, the characteristics and affordances of CMC modes and online learning environments, the nature of computer-mediated discourse, and learner perceptions of online educational experiences. The discussions in this literature review formed the background for the study's examination of three main concepts pertaining to the impact of online synchronous interaction on the sociocultural constructivist learning process: participation, knowledge construction, and quality of online learning experience.

In terms of philosophical orientation, this study is located within the constructivist paradigm reflecting the sociocultural constructivist theoretical perspective that interaction between learners is crucial for supporting the construction of shared knowledge from which there could be appropriation of the shared understandings. Hence, examination of the knowledge construction process was guided by the sociocultural constructs of social interaction, ZPD/scaffolding, mediation means, and appropriation.

In order to describe the educational interactions and conceptualize the online learning process in a constructivist environment, this study adopted an interactional framework (Anderson & Garrison, 1998) and *Community of Inquiry* (COI) model (Garrison et al., 2000) within which distant members of the online learning community were held to congregate in virtual tutorial rooms for attaining specific pedagogical aims, with their education experiences formed by the presence of social, cognitive, and teaching elements.

A discourse analysis (DA) theoretical framework located in the discipline of linguistics was adopted for examining the text-based chat discourse with the assumption that social presence could be built through various means which are intrinsic and external to the chat medium. Additionally, discourse coherence in the dialogic interactions was held to be supported by the presence of topic relevance as the adjacency of turns that signals interactivity in exchanges and depth of discussion. Furthermore, knowledge construction was held to be facilitated by collaborative effort in meaning making as indicated by the presence of symmetrical patterns of turn-taking and participation opportunities.

While the study of online discourse could offer one perspective on educational chat interaction, student perceptions of experiences provide another perspective on the collaborative-constructivist group learning process. In spite of the optimism over the potential of networked learning, studies on student perceptions of online learning experiences have reported both learner satisfaction and frustration over technical and CMC factors as well as instructional approaches in online courses. In the context of this case study, these perceptions and experiences of online learning could have pedagogical implications for the theory and practice of online synchronous activity design from a sociocultural constructive perspective.

The next chapter presents the case study of the online undergraduate unit offered by Murdoch University and describes in detail the aims and structure of the chat tutorial activity which is the focus of this study.

CHAPTER 3

THE CASE STUDY

3.1 Introduction

This chapter presents the research site which is an undergraduate unit of study. The following sections provide background information on the site, the participants, instructional events, and learning processes associated with the research context.

The research site is an undergraduate unit of study offered by the School of Information Technology at Murdoch University in Perth, Western Australia. The *Organisational Informatics* (OI) unit was identified as a particularly illuminative case of the application of online synchronous interaction in networked learning[26]. Furthermore, it met the following criteria enabling the examination of the research questions stated in Chapter 1:

- reliable accessibility for research purposes;
- pure or hybrid course delivery i.e., delivered entirely or partly through the Internet;
- main instructional activities held in a virtual environment;
- use of computer-mediated interaction modes; and
- use of online instructional activities involving critical discussion, with formal learning objectives, schedules, and assessment.

The evolution of the unit of study to its current manifestation was charted in the following publications: Sudweeks (2003a; 2003b; 2003c; 2004); Sudweeks and Simoff (2000; 2005). The following description of the unit drew from these main sources as well as personal communication with the first author (Dr. Fay Sudweeks) who is also the OI unit coordinator at Murdoch University.

The research site was originally a postgraduate course available from Sydney University in 1998. In 1999, it was modified and trialled as a third-year undergraduate unit at Murdoch University. With further modifications, the unit was offered to second-year undergraduates at Murdoch University in 2000 (Figure 3.1).

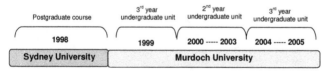

Figure 3.1. Developmental time-line of study unit from 1998-2005

After changes in name and course number, *Organisational Informatics* is available for third-year undergraduates at Murdoch University as

> a unit of study in the Information Systems Development and Information Systems Design streams within the Bachelor of Science degree [which examines] a range of contemporary information systems topics, concerning

---

[26] See Chapter 4 for description on screening and case selection procedures.

organizational, social and cultural aspects of the design and development of information systems.
(Sudweeks, 2004, p.89)

3.2 About *Organisational Informatics*
As stated in Sudweeks (2004), the OI unit aims to develop skills associated with "organizational aspects of the design and development of information systems" (p.90), including skills in critical assessment and management of issues related to knowledge building organizations by facilitating "reflective construction of knowledge" (p.90).

The OI unit is available in the second semester (13 weeks) of each academic year to students from Murdoch University who meet the pre-requisites of having studied certain first and second-year units. According to Dr. Sudweeks, student enrolment numbers reached a high of 151 in 2002, with 2005 reporting an enrolment of 52 students (personal communication, 13 June 2005). The profile of the participants is described in section 3.5.

The unit adopts a hybrid course delivery design that offers on-campus, face-to-face lectures and online tutorials. Its two main learning activities are a collaborative group project and online synchronous (chat) tutorial discussions which were reported in a number of publications by Dr. Sudweeks. The *group project* was examined in terms of student perceptions on the following aspects: student satisfaction with the collaborative work process (Sudweeks, 2003a), group communication, group dynamics, and perceptions of online learning in general and the project task in particular (Sudweeks, 2003c).

The studies generally found participant perceptions of "significant benefits from collaborating online" (Sudweeks, 2003c, p.182) that was supported by the quality of the work produced in terms of grades achieved. Participant comments on their experiences substantiated the findings:

> I think that the on-line group is a great idea for university courses. Why: It's so easy to see who is at meetings, record minutes, have tasks pinpointed. You have time to think before answering via email and the ability to get good written feedback ... So far it has been one of the best group experiences.
> (Sudweeks, 2003a, p.1444)

> ... no fights only good discussions, everyone has done their bit excellent it has been a pleasure to work in this group.
> (Sudweeks, 2003a, p.1445)

The *chat tutorial activity* was utilized as a case in several studies. For instance, Sudweeks (2004) examined changes in computer-mediated group processes over time, focusing on developmental and leadership characteristics of asynchronous and synchronous computer-mediated groups, of which the chat tutorials in the OI unit constituted the case for the synchronous computer-mediated group. Sudweeks and Simoff (2000) studied the chat tutorial activity for its effect on student motivation and participation, while Sudweeks and Simoff (2005) examined emergent leaders in collaborative virtual groups.

Main learning resources for the unit include a print *Resource Materials* reader (336 pages) and *Unit Outline* handout (Appendix A.1). Other electronic resources are available from the unit website which is described in section 3.3.

Since 1998, the OI unit assessment components underwent several changes. In 2002, the assessment changed from building a collaborative web portal to a group project that involved the collaborative planning and presentation of a proposal for a major event. From 2005, the reflective journals incorporated critiques on set-readings and reflections on tutorial discussions. The 2005 assessment components are provided in Table 3.1.

Table 3.1. 2005 *Organisational Informatics* assessment components (Sudweeks, 2005)

Assessment Components	Weightage
1. Research essay (individual)	(15%)
2. Group project: proposal for major event	(15%)
3. Reflective journals (individual)	(20%)
4. Tutorial presentation (individual)	(10%)
5. Discussion participation (individual)	(5%)
6. Examination (individual)	(35%)

Three areas of assessment of particular interest to this study are described below as they complement and support the chat tutorial learning activity: *reflective journals*, *tutorial presentation*, and *discussion participation*.

Reflective journals are student critiques of set-readings that are expected to include "reactions to the articles for each topic, and how they relate to the lectures, other topics and other material" (Sudweeks, 2005, p.4). The main pedagogical objective of this assessment/learning task is to enable students to experience "critically reviewing and recording … thoughts about the readings for the unit, as well as from a variety of other sources" (Sudweeks, 2005, p.4). Hence, in each journal (about 500 words in length), the student is expected to critically review the reading and pose at least one question related to the issue(s) in the reading for further discussion during the chat tutorial. Students are required to submit 11 journals (from Week 2 to Week 12 inclusive) to the tutorial group's bulletin board prior to the tutorial session to enable group members to read each other's critiques and the scheduled student presenter to collate questions and issues to raise during the discussion.

A compulsory one hour chat tutorial is held weekly (from Weeks 2-13) with the final session in Week 13 reserved for online presentations of the group projects. The tutorials are conducted in a seminar style, moderated by one or two student presenters in WebCT™ chat rooms and facilitated by the tutor. The pedagogical design and conduct of the chat tutorial are further described in section 3.5. *Tutorial presentations* by scheduled student presenters are assessed according to the following criteria: provision of "a clear [brief] summary, identification of key issues, knowledge of the topic, expressions of opinions on the topic(s), efforts to stimulate discussion, and management of the group discussion" (Sudweeks, 2005, p.5).

To ensure active involvement during tutorials, *discussion participation* is assessed by the tutor and peers based on the "level and quality of participation, effort, and sense of responsibility" (*Peer Assessment of Participation*, p.1 in Appendix A.2). Students are required to submit a *peer assessment* form to the tutor via e-mail at the end of the semester.

3.3 The Virtual Learning Environment

WebCT™ is a commercial learning management system (LMS) that is platform independent and accessible via the Internet through a web browser. The name *WebCT* stands for *Web Course Tools* which is "a suite of educational tools that allows the instructor/designer to create an interactive learning environment" (Rehberg, Ferguson, & McQuillian, 2001, p.63). WebCT™ is adopted by Murdoch University as its university-wide virtual learning environment (VLE) (Figure 3.2) that enables "the design, management and administration of computer-mediated learning, including delivery of course materials, support of course communications, student management, tracking and evaluation" (Sudweeks & Simoff, 2000, section 2).

teaching and learning centre

Welcome to WebCT @ Murdoch

Log in to WebCT

Log in to WebCT @ Murdoch by clicking the login button. If you are having difficulties with your password, see Logging into WebCT

Figure 3.2. The WebCT™ learning environment at Murdoch University

The OI unit home page (Figure 3.3) which is available via WebCT™ provides access to a range of learning resources.

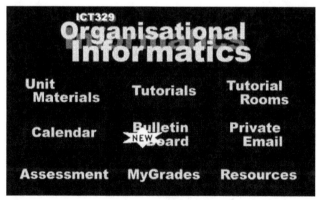

Figure 3.3. 2005 *Organisational Informatics* home page

Online learning resources for the unit were initially organized into three categories: materials for *Learning Tasks, Learning Resources*, and *Learning Supports* (Sudweeks, 2003a). According to Sudweeks (2003c), due to the need to "encourage more social cooperative learning" (p.175), a new collaborative online group project (proposal for a major event) was introduced in 2002 which prompted modifications to the VLE design to reflect the additional learner support necessary for facilitating online communication and group work. The structure of the VLE was therefore extended to four categories: resources for *Communication*, *Resources*, *Learner Support*, and *Assessment* (Figure 3.4).

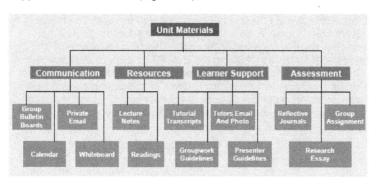

Figure 3.4. Extended *Organisational Informatics* VLE (Sudweeks, 2003c, p.176)

Since then, the unit coordinator had further refined the range of learning resources available from the unit website. A possible interpretation of the VLE structure in 2005 is presented in Figure 3.5. It should be noted that the VLE elements are not assigned to mutually exclusive categories and that in actual practice, some elements perform overlapping functions; for instance, the *calendar* could be a communication tool for conveying noteworthy events and an administration tool for organizing public and/or private diary entries. Similarly, the *tutor contact details/photo* could function as an administration element or a supporting resource element for establishing social presence of the online instructor.

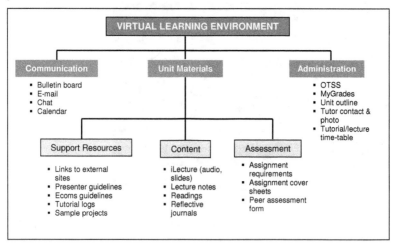

Figure 3.5. 2005 representation of *Organisational Informatics* VLE (adapted from Sudweeks, 2003c, p.176)

From this perspective, the VLE for the OI unit is organized into three main components: *communication*, *unit materials*, and *administration*. The *communication* component includes synchronous and asynchronous communication tools such as WebCT™ chat (Figure 3.6), bulletin boards, private e-mail, and a common calendar. The *administrative* component supports course organizational services such as self-enrolment in tutorial groups through the *Online Tutorial Signup System* (OTSS), the distribution of grades, access to lecture/tutorial schedules (Figure 3.7), and the *Unit Outline*.

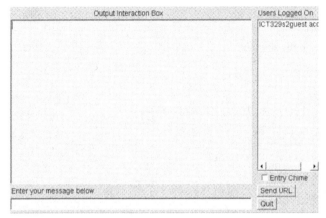

Figure 3.6. WebCT™ chat facility

Date	Week	Topic	
Jul 25	1	Introduction to the Unit and Organisational Informatics	PPS, RTF, PDF (2005)
Aug 1	2	Computer mediated communication in organisations	PPT, RTF, PDF (2005)
Aug 8	3	Group processes	PPT, RTF (2004)
Aug 15	4	Organisational culture	PPT, RTF (2004)
Aug 22	Non teaching break		
Aug 29	5	Virtual communities and organisations	PPT, RTF (2004)
Sep 5	6	Work and society in the Information Age	PPT, RTF (2004)
Sep 12	7	Globalisation	PPT, RTF (2004)
Sep 19	8	Computer-mediated collaborative work	PPT, RTF (2004)
Sep 19	8	Team Project due at 10:00am	

Figure 3.7. 2005 OI unit lecture schedule

The *unit materials* component is retained as "the hub of the site" (Sudweeks, 2003c, p.174) which had expanded significantly since its representation in Figure 3.4. The component consists of three sub-categories of learning materials: *content materials*, *support resources*, and *assessment resources*. *Content materials* and *support resources* provide access to main and secondary instructional materials such as iLecture notes (Figure 3.8) and links to external sites. The *assessment* sub-category provides access to assignments resources such as project requirements and peer assessment forms (Figure 3.9).

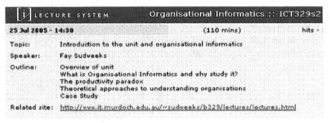

Figure 3.8. Content materials: iLecture resources

ICT329 Organisational Informatics (s2, 2005)

Homepage > **Assessment**

ICT329 Assessment Material	Reflective Journals	
• **Reflective Journals**	Due Date	8:00pm each Sunday, beginning 31 July.
• **Group Project**	Format	Individual work
○ **Groupwork Hints**	Length	500 words
○ **Cover Sheet (Word)**	Unit contribution	20% (11 journals)
○ **Diary (Excel file)**	Submission	Prepare in text format and post to your tu Sunday.
○ **Example Projects**	Aims	To enable you to identify and critically ass topic.
• **Research Essay**		To encourage you to have a deeper under
○ **Cover Sheet (Word)**		To provide a mechanism for encouraging r
○ **Guides to Referencing**		To provide a forum for you to think of broa
○ **Assignment Hints**	Your task:	A critique of the week's required read
• **Essay Writing Help**		Each week you are to submit a journal of
• **Peer Assessment**		- not a summary - of the readings. It shou including o o your opinion of the articles

Figure 3.9. Assessment resources

3.4 The OI Unit Pedagogical Framework

The pedagogical framework of the OI unit is based on the social constructivist view of learning (Vygotsky, 1962/1986) as "a cycle of interpretation, evaluation and reflection of content evolving into individual and shared knowledge" (Sudweeks & Simoff, 2000, section 3). In congruence with the unit's constructivist theoretical basis, instructional strategies emphasize "collaboration, personal autonomy, generativity, reflectivity, active engagement, personal relevance, and pluralism" (Sudweeks, 2004, p.83). Hence, main learning activities, namely, the group project and online tutorial discussions, are designed to develop "reflective construction of knowledge and active participation" (Sudweeks, 2004, p.85) and sustain "students' continuous engagement in discovering and applying knowledge and skills in the context of authentic problem solving" (p.92).

Reflecting the networked learning model (Harasim et al., 1995) that also underlies the OI instructional design, there is significant use of the VLE as "a digital educational environment" (Sudweeks, 2004, p.92) where students could access an extensive range of resources for their educational needs and the management of learning processes. The VLE also provides online spaces where learning could be situated in synchronous and asynchronous environments. Moreover, there is extensive use of CMC to not only support interaction during chat tutorials and the collaborative group work processes for the team project, but also to facilitate unit administration or assessment, such as electronic submission of coursework to the tutor via e-mail or posting of journals to the bulletin board. Essentially, the VLE plays a vital role in reducing transactional distance (Moore & Kearsley, 1996) usually perceived by students in distance courses.

3.5 The Online Synchronous Tutorial
Although the OI unit employs two main instructional activities described in section 3.2, the focus of this study is on the online synchronous tutorial. This section describes the participants, conduct and pedagogical design of the tutorial activity. While students in the OI unit used to be assigned to tutorial groups via a paper-based preferential system, from 2003, students could self-enroll in tutorial groups of their choice at the start of the semester through the OTSS. In 2005, there were four tutorial groups with 9 to 15 students in each group. Two of the four available tutorial groups (Groups 1 and 4) were selected for comparative study (Table 3.2).

Table 3.2. List of participants from Groups 1 and 4[27]

No.	Group 1	No.	Group 4
1.	Derek	1.	Evan
2.	Max	2.	Bill
3.	Alvin	3.	Mike
4.	Cliff	4.	Eric
5.	Colin	5.	Karl
6.	Ted[28]	6.	Jack
7.	Sam	7.	Ian
8.	Diane	8.	Pete
9.	James	9.	Robin
10	Alan	10	Lim (Researcher)
11.	Jason	11.	Fay (Tutor)
12.	Scott		
13.	Barry		
14.	Tony		
15.	Wendy		
16.	Rachel (Tutor)		

Even as all groups were involved in equivalent learning activities covering the same content areas, the greater differences displayed by Groups 1 and 4 in terms of student profile, group size, and tutors (Table 3.3) could provide valuable insight into the impact of chat interaction on their collaborative learning processes.

The compulsory one hour chat tutorials are held weekly (from Weeks 2-13) with the final session in Week 13 reserved for online presentations of the group projects. Hence, 22 tutorial sessions (11 sessions for each group) were examined in this study

---

[27] *Fay* and *Lim* are the only actual names retained in this study. The names of all other participants are pseudonyms.
[28] Ted withdrew from the unit on 15 October 2005.

i.e., from Weeks 2-12 (inclusive). The tutorials are conducted in a seminar style, facilitated by the tutor and moderated by one or two student presenters in WebCT™ chat rooms (Figure 3.10). The actors in the tutorials include the tutor (facilitator), the student presenter (moderator), and the students (participants) (Sudweeks & Simoff, 2000). The student presenter role is rotated among all the students in each tutorial group.

Table 3.3. Characteristics of tutorial groups 1 and 4

Characteristics	Group 1	Group 4
Tutorial time	- Morning session (10.30am)	- Evening session (7.30pm)
Group tutor	- Rachel[29] (Part-time staff)	- Fay (Full-time staff)
Group size	- 15 students, 1 tutor	- 9 students, 1 tutor, 1 researcher
Enrolment status	- 13 Internal, 2 External students[30]	- 4 Internal, 5 External students
Nationality	- Majority of international students, minority of Australian students	- Majority of Australian students, minority of international students
English Language proficiency	- Majority of ESL/EFL speakers, minority of native English speakers	- All native English speakers
Gender	- 3 female and 12 male students	- 1 female and 8 male students

ICT329 Organisational Informatics (s2, 2005)

Homepage **Tutorial Rooms**

ICT329
Organisational Informatics

Welcome to ICT329 Tutorials.
Click on the room that corresponds to your Tutorial Group number to enter it. For example, if you are in Group 1, you click on "Group 1", etc. All discussions in Tutorial Rooms are automatically logged and will be available to all ICT329 students shortly after each tutorial. Discussions in the General Chat rooms are not logged.

Group 1 Mon 10:30

Group 2 Mon 12:30

Group 3 Mon 16:30

Group 4 Mon 19:30

General Chat for ICT329 Organisational Informatics (s2, 2005)

General Chat for All Courses

Note: Conversations in the following rooms will be recorded:
Group 1 Mon 10:30, Group 2 Mon 12:30, Group 3 Mon 16:30, Group 4 Mon 19:30.

Figure 3.10. *Organisational Informatics* chat tutorial rooms

For tutorial sessions with *two presenters* (Figure 3.11), each presenter moderates a ½ hour discussion slot based on the critique of one reading and adopts the participant role when not presenting. Before the tutorial, each presenter prepares brief critiques on at least two of the week's readings before the tutorial. One critique is posted on the tutorial group's bulletin board and the other is presented during the tutorial. In addition, each presenter prepares questions for highlighting issues related to the reading and stimulating the discussion.

For tutorial sessions with *one presenter* (Figure 3.12), the sole presenter also prepares brief critiques on at least two of the week's readings before the tutorial and discusses both critiques during the tutorial. The sole presenter moderates the discussion for the entire session based on critiques of two readings.

---

[29] Other than the researcher (Lim) and Fay, participant names in this study are pseudonyms.
[30] Internal and external students, respectively, undergo the course on-campus and through distance learning mode.

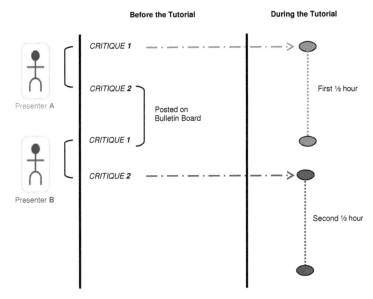

Figure 3.11. Tutorial session with two presenters

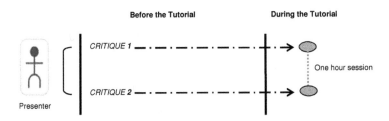

Figure 3.12. Tutorial session with one presenter

During the tutorial, the presenter starts the discussion by highlighting the main issues in the selected reading based on his/her critical evaluation of the article. The presenter is expected to moderate the discussion by "posing pertinent questions that bring out the main issues of the articles, stimulating discussions and encouraging participation by all members" (Sudweeks, 2003b, section 3). The tutor is present as a facilitator throughout the tutorial session and evaluates the performance of the presenter(s) as well as the extent of participation by other students in the discussion. The other students are expected to participate actively during discussions and evaluate the presenter(s) as part of *peer assessment of participation*.

Preparation for tutorial presentation is supported by online resources that include the following:
- *Reflective Journal* (Appendix A.3) which states the requirements for the critique;

- *Guidelines for Tutorial Presenters* (Appendix A.4) which states the responsibilities of the presenter; and
- *Ecoms Guidelines* (Appendix A.5) which highlights CMC conventions and netiquette[31]. Archived tutorial logs of sessions are available from the unit website to facilitate peer/self-evaluation and reflection on participation (Figure 3.13). The logs are also a convenient source for reference by students absent from tutorials for some reason.

Group No.	Tutorial Day/Time	Week
Group 1	Monday 10:30	2 3 4 5 6 7 8 9 10 11 12 13
Group 2	Monday 12:30	2 3 4 5 6 7 8 9 10 11 12 13
Group 3	Monday 16:30	2 3 4 5 6 7 8 9 10 11 12 13
Group 4	Monday 19:30	2 3 4 5 6 7 8 9 10 11 12 13

Figure 3.13. Tutorial logs

The chat tutorials are designed to introduce students, in an active and experiential way, to the theory and practice of computer-mediated work processes which are directly relevant to the course topics (Table 3.4).

Table 3.4. OI unit content topics (from *2005 Resources Material*)

Organisational Informatics Content Topics	
- Computer mediated communication	- Computer-mediated collaborative work
- Organisational design and group processes	- Organisational decision support systems
- Organisational culture	- Systems theory
- Virtual organisations and communities	- Managing information and information
- Work in the information age	technology
- Globalization	

Other than providing students with exposure to CMC processes, the tutorials also function as supportive virtual learning environments. As student presenters moderate by drawing less confident members into discussions, supporting views of others and keeping discussions relevant, they are essentially involved in establishing teaching presence in the online learning environment (Garrison et al., 2000).

Furthermore, student comments on tutorial experiences from earlier publications below suggest that in their roles as presenter or participant, they learnt to provide social-emotional and cognitive support to each other as they share individual knowledge and negotiate new understandings:

> …Although I never see any of our group, or might not get to know anyone personally, I feel that the bond here is better than my other tutorials. (Sudweeks & Simoff, 2000, section 4.4)

> … I am actually learning and gaining a lot of valuable knowledge and information. The discussion…provides my group members and me the chance of voicing out our ideas and opinions of the discussed topic after we had done our research and readings. (Sudweeks & Simoff, 2000, section 4.4)

---

[31] Netiquette is an abbreviation of network etiquette, referring to "[p]rinciples of courtesy observed in sending electronic messages" (Microsoft Press, 2002, p.361).

Essentially, the chat tutorial learning environment reflects the *Community of Inquiry* model (Garrison et al., 2000) described in Chapter 2. Moreover, the online tutorial pedagogical framework (Figure 3.14) that regards learning as "a cyclical process of interpretation, evaluation and reflection" (Sudweeks & Simoff, 2000, section 5), is reflected in the activities which involve critical review of readings, dialogic exchange of multiple perspectives, and student reflection on learning through the use of archived tutorial logs.

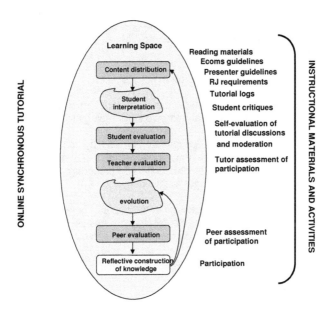

Figure 3.14. Online Tutorial Pedagogical Framework (adapted from Sudweeks, 2004, p. 93)

3.6 Summary

This chapter presented a detailed description of this study's research site, covering its initial form as a postgraduate course in 1998 at Sydney University to its current manifestation (in 2005) as an online undergraduate unit at Murdoch University. An updated representation of the VLE structure was provided that took into account changes to the unit yet to be reported in publications. The pedagogical framework of the OI unit and its main learning activities were described with particular focus on the chat tutorial activity and the participants which are of interest to this study. The next chapter locates and characterizes the OI unit and its actors as an instrumental case within the methodological framework of this study.

CHAPTER 4

RESEARCH METHODOLOGY

4.1 Introduction

As particular ontological, epistemological, and axiological beliefs held by researchers and their disciplines largely determine the kinds of knowledge sought, understood, and valued from the inquiry process, this chapter describes the methodological assumptions underlying this research, the procedures, and instruments for examining the impact of online synchronous (chat) interaction on the learning process from a sociocultural constructivist perspective in the context of the *Organizational Informatics* (OI) unit described in Chapter 3.

An overview of this chapter is provided below:

Section 4.2 identifies the philosophical assumptions and theoretical perspectives underlying the qualitative methodological framework adopted by this study.

Section 4.3 justifies the choice of the case research approach, characterizes this inquiry process as an instrumental case, establishes its units of analysis, sampling strategy and data sources, describes the data collection procedures, ethical considerations, and major research stages in this study.

Section 4.4 describes the methods and instruments adopted, namely, the *Exchange Structure Analysis* (ESA) coding scheme, *Social Network Analysis* (SNA) as analytical method and visual representation tool, and the web survey instrument.

Section 4.5 explains the procedures for processing the transcript and survey datasets.

Section 4.6 defines the constructs/measures utilized in data analysis and discusses validity issues associated with the instruments and data.

Section 4.7 summarizes the methodological design and procedures adopted by the study that enable the research questions to be addressed.

4.2 Methodological Considerations
4.2.1 Philosophical and theoretical perspectives
Historically, most research efforts in the natural and social sciences were based on objectivist epistemology; reflecting the view of *logical positivism* (a term popularized by Auguste Comte) which assumes that "only verifiable claims based directly on experience could be considered genuine knowledge" (Patton, 2002, p.92). The positivist belief in the privileged position of objective empirical findings as 'true' knowledge was ironically questioned within the scientific community by Kuhn (1961; 1970) who argued that scientific theories represent consensual understandings that are subject to change with the emergence of progressively more powerful explanations. The concept of multiple or subjective 'realities' that are socially constructed challenged the certainty of empirical knowledge, strengthened the constructionist movement and legitimized qualitative studies located epistemologically towards the subjectivist end of the objectivism-subjectivism continuum.

This study holds the *constructionist epistemological position* which is the view that "all knowledge, and therefore all meaningful reality as such, is contingent upon human practices, being constructed in and out of interaction between human beings and their world, and developed and transmitted within an essentially social context" (Crotty, 1998, p.42). Essentially, the kind of knowledge attainable is assumed to be constituted in the interaction with entities "against a backdrop of shared understandings, practices, language" (Schwandt, 2000, p.197) and subject to change when exposed to new perspectives during interaction (Duffy & Jonassen, 1991). The constructionist position could be regarded as being situated midway in the objectivism-subjectivism epistemological continuum as it does not assume that all knowledge exists independently of the mind to be discovered through objective methods, nor does it presuppose the possibility of subjectively imposing meaning that is "created out of nothing" (Crotty, 1998, p.9) onto objects of study.

Constructionism forms the epistemological basis for a number of interpretive theoretical perspectives including the variants of radical and sociocultural constructivism. In this work, the term *constructionism* (Crotty, 1998) is used to refer to the *epistemological* position adopted in this study while *constructivism* refers to the range of *theoretical perspectives* available in the constructivist continuum ranging from radical/cognitive to social/sociocultural constructivism. The terms *radical* and *sociocultural constructivism* are used consistently in this work with reference to the two theoretical positions.

The differences between radical and sociocultural constructivism as learning theories and their assumptions of the knowledge building process were discussed in Chapter 2. This section covers implications of the sociocultural constructivist conceptualization of meaning-making on this study's methodological decisions of research focus and design which are largely drawn from Cobb (1994) and summarized in Table 4.1.

In examining online tutorial episodes from a *sociocultural constructivist* framework, this study assumes that learning occurs during guided participation in culturally organized practices of schooling within a virtual learning community, and that participation supports learning by enabling appropriation of the shared knowledge constructed and transformations in individual understandings (Duffy & Cunningham, 1996; Rogoff, 1990). Given these assumptions, the design of this research focuses on interaction patterns, practices and learning experiences mainly at the tutorial group level. Whilst primacy is given to examining the impact of chat interaction on the collaborative learning process, there is also consideration of the affordances of the chat medium and virtual learning environment in supporting and situating interaction.

Table 4.1. Design implications for study from sociocultural constructivist perspective (adapted from Cobb, 1994)

		Sociocultural Constructivism
Theoretical constructs	**Interaction**	Online interaction seen as an example of culturally organized practices of schooling.
	Learning	Knowledge construction process explained by constructs of - *guided participation* or interaction in collaborative online learning process - *zone of proximal development* and *scaffolding* provided by online peers/tutor - *mediation means* of CMC technology and computer-mediated discourse - *appropriation* of shared knowledge constructed leading to transformations in individual understandings
Design issues	**Research focus**	Examination of knowledge construction process emphasizes - interpretations of group interaction patterns and practices - participant perspectives on learning experiences - consideration of the affordances of the chat medium and virtual learning environment in supporting and situating interaction - level of tutorial group as unit of analysis

Methods of discourse and social network analyses[32] are used to illuminate "shifts and slides of meaning" (Cobb, 1994, p.15) during the dialogic activities of meaning-making. Interpretive analyses of chat interaction patterns are balanced by the different perspectives captured in participant self-reports of learning experiences, enabling 'multivoiced' accounts that contribute to the credibility of findings (Denzin & Lincoln, 2000) by qualitative research standards which are discussed in the next section.

4.2.2 Qualitative framework of study
After establishing the theoretical assumptions of this study, the methodological framework most appropriate for addressing the research aims needs to be considered. In this work, the term *methodology* refers to the plan of action showing how answers to the research questions would be obtained while *methods* refer to instruments/techniques for data collection or analysis.

Although research methodologies are conventionally distinguished as *quantitative* or *qualitative*, there appears to be numerous characterizations of the two frameworks (Denzin & Lincoln, 2000; Goetz & LeCompte, 1984; Sudweeks & Simoff, 1998). This section highlights the distinctive aspects of quantitative and qualitative research identified by Sudweeks and Simoff (1998), and Denzin and Lincoln (2000) before describing the characteristics of this study that locates it within the qualitative research framework.

Denzin and Lincoln (2000) proposed five main areas of differences between qualitative and quantitative research (Table 4.2) which were held to stem from methodological preferences of disciplinary traditions in the physical and social sciences.

---

[32] The methods and instruments used in this study are described in section 4.4 of this chapter.

Table 4.2. Differences between quantitative and qualitative research frameworks (based on Denzin & Lincoln, 2000, pp.1-28)

Areas of Differences	Quantitative Research	Qualitative Research
Uses of positivism & postpositivism	- Reality can be fully captured - Knowledge is discovered - Use of deductive strategies - Use of complex statistical methods for generalization	- Reality can only be approximated - Knowledge is constructed - Use of inductive strategies - Use of simple statistical methods for "locating groups of subjects within larger populations" (p.9)
Acceptance of postmodern sensibilities	- Adopts positivist/postpositivist criteria of objectivity, reliability, internal and external validity	- Adopts constructionist, postmodern criteria of "verisimilitude, emotionality ... praxis, multivoiced texts ... dialogue with subjects" (p.10)
Capturing of individual point of view	- Use of objective inferential empirical methods and data	- Use of interpretive interview and observation methods
Examination of constraints of everyday life	- Use of controlled, experimental settings - Use of large, random cases - Adopts etic, nomothetic position	- Use of naturalistic, everyday settings - Use of particular cases - Adopts emic, idiographic case-based position
Provision of rich descriptions	- Use of impersonal, third-person prose - Detailed descriptions of social world irrelevant for generalization	- Use of first-person accounts - Rich descriptions valued for establishing credibility

Sudweeks and Simoff (1998) contrasted qualitative and quantitative methodologies along four research dimensions (Table 4.3). Although such a presentation possibly exaggerates their differences, it is claimed that the two methodologies display areas of commonality: their shared aim to "explain the implicit concepts" within the data (Sudweeks & Simoff, 1998, p. 32); and the fundamental character of theories developed as interpretations of the phenomenon studied.

Table 4.3 Dimensions of quantitative and qualitative research (based on Sudweeks & Simoff, 1998, pp.33-36)

Areas of Differences	Quantitative Research	Qualitative Research
Purpose of inquiry	- Explanation of observed phenomenon - Hypothesis testing and refinement	- Understanding of observed phenomenon - Emergent theory development
Role of investigator	- Objective observer - Active manipulator of experimental setting	- Active interpreter - Participant observer in naturalistic setting
Acquisition of knowledge	- Use of quantitative, numerical data - Construction of knowledge, explanations as models - Generalization, theory building from results	- Use of loosely structured textual data - Discovery of knowledge as interpretations - Extrapolation, theory building from results
Presentation of research	- Data reduction using graphical visualization methods	- 'Thick' interpretations of results using quotes from raw data

Drawing from these two sources, the main research dimensions of this study are presented in Table 4.4 and further explained below.

The constructionist and sociocultural constructivist theoretical assumptions of this study locate it at the paradigmatic level within the qualitative research framework. Hence, this inquiry process aims to gain deeper understanding of the impact of chat interaction on learning by observing learning processes in the natural setting of an existing online undergraduate unit and interpreting events "in terms of the meanings people bring to them" (Denzin & Lincoln, 2000, p.3).

Table 4.4 Dimensions of this study

Dimensions of Study	Description
Theoretical assumptions	- Reality can only be approximated - Knowledge is constructed
Area of inquiry	- Cross-disciplinary involving education, information technology, linguistics
Purpose of inquiry	- To seek greater understanding of the impact of chat interaction in supporting the collaborative-sociocultural constructivist learning process - To determine implications for the theory and practice of chat activity design from a sociocultural constructivist perspective
Object of inquiry	- Single case of online undergraduate unit in its naturalistic setting - Two tutorial groups examined within the single case (Groups 1 and 4): Group 1 participants (15 students, 1 tutor) Group 4 participants (9 students, 1 tutor and 1 researcher)
Acquisition of knowledge	- Discovery of knowledge as interpretations - Extrapolation of findings to similar cases
Positionality of researcher	- Non-participation observer role adopted for Group 1 and participant observer role adopted for Group 4 - Active interpreter of chat interactions in transcript data - Insider perspective from key informant
Choice of data types, sources & methods	- Data types/sources: Qualitative data from transcripts, responses to open-ended survey questions, course document artifacts Quantitative data from responses to closed survey questions - Instruments: ESA coding scheme Online survey Social network analysis software - Analytical techniques: Discourse analysis Social network analysis Descriptive statistics
Presentation of research	- 'Thick' interpretations of results from quotes from transcript data and responses to open-ended survey questions - Data reduction with descriptive statistics and graphical representation of interaction

With the use of a single case[33], knowledge discovered from the interpretive analysis of online interactions and self-reports of learning experiences are not claimed to be generalizable to wider populations. However, the findings may be *extrapolated* as "modest speculations on the likely applicability of findings to other situations under similar, but not identical, conditions. Extrapolations are logical, thoughtful, case derived, and problem-oriented rather than statistical and probabilistic" (Patton, 2002, p.584).

Since the qualitative researcher seeks to interpret the meaningfulness of the data from multiple perspectives, the human focus of inquiry therefore encompasses the participants and the practitioner. The positionality of the researcher is significant in the methodological design for determining the intensity of participants' voices in the form of 'thick' descriptions (Geetz, 1973). In this study, the researcher is an *outsider* who is not directly involved in the design or teaching of the course. The selection of two tutorial groups for comparison (described in Chapter 3) within this case enables the adoption of a non-participant observer role for one group (Group 1) and an active participant observer role for the other (Group 4).

While the researcher's experiences inform interpretations of Group 4 interactions, the *insider* perspective is sought from a key informant on Group 1 interactions. Even as insiders provide 'native' insights on observed phenomena, this study acknowledges

---

[33] The case research approach and sampling issues are discussed in this chapter, section 4.3.

Delamont's (2004) caution on informants' use of "impression management" (p.224) whereby informants tell the researchers what s/he wants to hear, lie or hide information in order to protect themselves and their privacy. Hence, the researcher's positionality in this study led to the choice of multiple data sources and methods[34] to corroborate insights offered by the informant (Yin, 1994).

At the methods level, discourse and social network analyses are applied to the transcript dataset. Qualitative responses in the survey dataset are subjected to interpretive content analysis while statistical analysis is applied to the quantitative survey data. Findings are presented as descriptive statistics, graphical representations, and network sociograms which are accompanied by appropriate quotes from the datasets to adequately represent participants' perspectives and the meanings they attach to the interactions.

---

[34] The data sources and methods are described in this chapter, sections 4.3 and 4.4 respectively.

4.3 Case Research Methodology

4.3.1 Justification of case research approach

For greater understanding of the online learning process in the context of the OI unit, this study has recourse to five major research approaches in social sciences: experiments, histories, archival analysis, surveys, and case studies (Yin, 1994). Experimental and historical approaches present difficulties of fit with this study's theoretical positions that entail examination of phenomena in natural settings and inquiry questions that focus on contemporary events. Although archival and survey research approaches are useful for respectively, unobtrusive observation of interaction and overcoming field constraints of establishing face-to-face contact with the geographically dispersed participants in this study, the exclusive adoption of the former approach offers only the analyst's perspective of interaction while the latter generally requires large sample sizes for statistically significant results.

While Sudweeks and Simoff (1998) regarded the case research approach as "research in which the researcher has direct contact with the participants and the participants are the primary source of the data. It follows, then, that the primary methods used in case research are interviews and direct observations" (p.35), Yin (1994) pointed out that "case studies are a form of inquiry that does *not* depend solely on ethnographic or participant-observer data" (p.11-emphasis in original) and "need not always include direct, detailed observations as a source of evidence" (p.14).

Yin (1994) considered the case research approach appropriate given the following conditions:

> when 'how' or 'why' questions are being posed,
> when the investigator has little control over events, and
> when the focus is on a contemporary phenomenon within some real-life context
> (Yin, 1994, p.1)

Additionally, Benbasat, Goldstein and Mead (1987) suggested that the case research approach could be useful when there is a lack of strong theoretical basis for the topic investigated or when little is known about the phenomenon.

This work defines the case research approach as a *process of inquiry* involving the examination of "a phenomenon in its natural setting, employing multiple methods of data collection to gather information from one or a few entities" (Benbasat et al., 1987, p.370). The choice of the case research approach is justified based on the following consideration of each of Yin's (1994) conditions:
  - *how' and 'what' questions* are posed by RQ1 and RQ2 stated in Chapter 1;
  - the researcher has no control over the design and teaching of the OI unit; and
  - the chat interactions for observation are relatively recent events within the context of an existing undergraduate unit.

Moreover, as most studies have focused on the socio-emotional rather than knowledge building aspects of synchronous CMC interaction (discussed in Chapter 2), the case research approach could also enable the generation of knowledge on a little known phenomenon.

4.3.2 The instrumental case study: Definition and design
This research effort into the impact of chat interaction on the learning process in the context of the OI unit is framed as a *case study* of "teaching and learning in one setting … It is highly personalized because teaching and learning are highly personalized … The system boundaries are not the skins of people, but are the boundaries around a particular experience" (Stake, 1988, p.257).

Stake (2000) identified three types of case studies: intrinsic, collective, and instrumental. While an intrinsic case study examines a case which itself is of interest and hence focuses on emic issues arising from the case, an *instrumental* case study aims to

> provide insight into an issue or to redraw a generalization. The case is of secondary interest, it plays a supporting role, and it facilitates our understanding of something else … the choice of case is made to advance understanding of that other interest.
> (Stake, 2000, p.437)

This inquiry process is characterized as an instrumental case study conducted to examine specific *etic* research issues involving the impact of chat interaction on the collaborative learning process of the OI unit. Hence, the research issues are given primary consideration and serve to conceptually structure the case design (Stake, 1995).

Drawing from Yin's (1994) model of case research design, the design of this instrumental case study reflects four main stages: *design definition, data collection, data analysis*, and *interpretation and implications* (Figure 4.1) whereby research purposes, questions, and theoretical assumptions are defined before the selection of case, methods/instruments, and data sources. In the next stage, instruments are piloted and refined followed by conduct of the main study and collection of data from multiple sources. During data analysis, there is systematic comparison of interpretations from transcript and survey datasets that form the primary data source in order to elaborate or expand on the findings from one method with another.

Data from primary and secondary sources are integrated in the interpretation of findings. Conclusions and implications are drawn based on the pre-defined conceptual framework and research questions. The units of analysis, sampling strategy, and data sources in this case study are elaborated below.

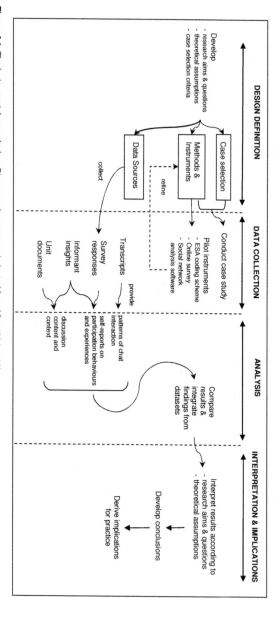

Figure 4.1. The instrumental case design: Stages and processes (adapted from Yin, 1994, p.49)

- *Units of analysis*
Decisions on units of analysis, in case research, are largely based on research purposes and questions (Yin, 1994). This study aims to examine the impact of chat interaction on the learning process in the OI unit context with particular focus on interaction and learning experiences at the tutorial group level. With the OI unit designated as the main case, the selection of two tutorial groups for comparison positions this inquiry as a Type 2 single-embedded case (Figure 4.2) whereby "within a single case, attention also is given to a subunit or subunits" (Yin, 1994, p.41).

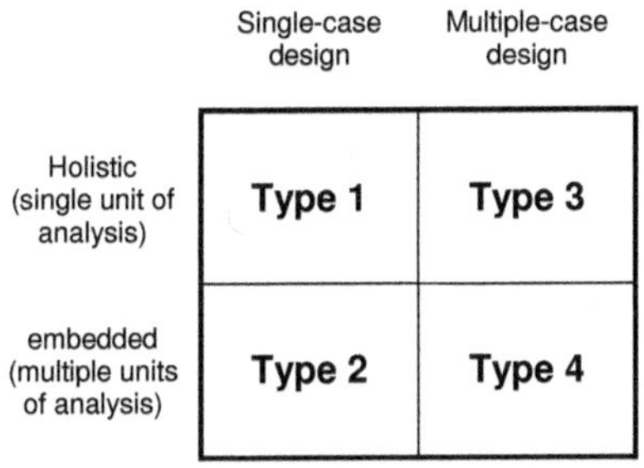

	Single-case design	Multiple-case design
Holistic (single unit of analysis)	**Type 1**	**Type 3**
embedded (multiple units of analysis)	**Type 2**	**Type 4**

Figure 4.2. Four variants of case study design (Yin, 1994, p.39)

- *Sampling strategy*
In congruence with the qualitative tradition of this inquiry, an *information-rich* case (Patton, 2002) was selected for study based on the criteria of potential for learning and in-depth understanding from the specifics of a particular case (Stake, 1995; 2000). This purposive sampling of a single illuminative case of the OI unit, which exemplifies the application of educational chat interaction, is based on the following practical rationale:
- accessibility for research purposes i.e., availability of site access and cooperation from unit coordinator, and
- limitations of resources i.e., within research time limit and budget.

Since "purposive samples require specific research justifications other than lack of money and availability" (Riffe, Lacy, & Fico, 1998, p.86) this sampling decision is also based on the following rationale:
- the satisfaction of case selection criteria (described further below) arising from conceptual framework of study and research questions;
- contribution to knowledge from the opportunity for greater understanding of the rare instructional application of synchronous computer-mediated activities in an online undergraduate unit when distance courses mainly apply online asynchronous learning activities which have been widely researched[35];
- contribution to improved pedagogical practices through insights from the research; and
- extrapolation of findings to similar situations.

Selection of a single illuminative case, although justifiable in terms of rarity of the phenomenon, could be vulnerable to the weakness of single-case designs when the

---

[35] See discussion in Chapter 2, section 2.4.

"case may later turn out not to be the case it was thought to be at the outset" (Yin, 1994, p.41). The site screening process based on the case selection criteria is briefly described below to explain the choice of the OI unit for study.

Given the initial broad area of research interest as the impact of online interaction on the collaborative learning process, a set of criteria below was developed to guide site selection.

1. Reliable accessibility for research purposes
2. Pure or hybrid course delivery viz, delivered entirely or partly through the Internet
3. Main instructional activities held in a virtual environment
4. Use of computer-mediated interaction modes
5. Use of online instructional activities involving critical discussion, with formal learning objectives, schedules, and assessment

In September 2004, six online courses were screened with four courses provided by Murdoch University and two courses offered by Open Learning Australia (Table 4.5). The courses are further described in Appendix A.6.

Table 4.5. Research sites identified for possible study

Educational Provider	Online Courses
Open Learning Australia & Curtin University of Technology	**REA11**: Applied Reasoning **NET24**: Virtual Communities
Murdoch Law School, Murdoch University	**LAW150**: Australian Legal System & LEG171: Legal Writing **LEG180**: Justices of the Peace and the Justice System
School of Veterinary Clinical Science, Murdoch University	**VET 620**: Diagnostic Imaging Unit for Masters of VET Studies Program
School of Information Technology, Murdoch University	**ICT329**: Organisational Informatics

The *Organisational Informatics* unit from Murdoch University was identified as most appropriate for this study since it met all the criteria (Table 4.6) and presented a rare opportunity to observe the extensive use of chat instructional activities in an online course established since 1998[36].

Table 4.6. Site selection by criteria

Site Selection Criteria	Online Courses					
	REA11	NET24	LAW150*	LEG180	VET620	ICT329
1. Reliable accessibility for research purposes	✗	✗	✓	✗	✗	✓
2. Pure or hybrid course delivery,	✓	✓	✓	✗	✓	✓
3. Main instructional activities held in a virtual environment	✓	✓	✓	✗	✓	✓
4. Use of computer-mediated interaction modes	✓	✓	✓	✗	✓	✓
5. Use of online instructional activities involving critical discussion, with formal learning objectives, schedules, and assessment.	✓	✓	✗	✗	✗	✓

*Includes LAW150: Australian Legal System and LEG171: Legal Writing

---

[36] See Chapter 3, section 3.1 on evolution of the OI unit.

- *Data sources and collection procedures*

The opportunity to use "many different sources of evidence" (Yin, 1994, p.91) offered by case research overcomes the limitations inherent in any single data source and provides different perspectives of the same phenomenon for triangulation. According to Stake (2000), triangulation has generally been assumed to be

> a process of using multiple perceptions to clarify meaning, verifying the *repeatability* of an observation or interpretation. But, acknowledging that no observation or interpretations are perfectly repeatable, triangulation also serves to *clarify meaning* by identifying different ways the phenomenon is being seen.
> (Stake, 2000, pp.443-444-my emphasis)

The use of multiple data sources, with their strengths balanced against their limitations (Table 4.7), enables the examination of educational chat interaction from different perspectives. While findings from transcripts reflect the analyst's interpretations of online interaction, the survey responses offer greater insight from the participants' perspective. Together with information from a key informant and unit document artifacts, triangulation of findings from these sources enables a more holistic understanding and representation of the phenomenon studied.

Both main and secondary data sources were used to address the research questions in this study (Table 4.8). The *tutorial logs* of Groups 1 and 4 (G1, G4) were collected over 11 weeks (August to October 2005) from the unit website after each weekly tutorial session. The complete chat transcript dataset comprised 22 sessions (11 from each group).

Student participant *survey responses* were gathered with an online survey administered from 24 October to 7 November 2005. The complete survey dataset comprised 13 returns from G1 and 8 returns from G4 with a respective response rate of 93% and 89% (Table 4.9).

Table 4.7. Data sources in this study: Strengths and limitations (adapted from Yin, 1994, p.80)

Data Sources	Strengths	Limitations
Archived tutorial logs (Primary data source) **Unit document artifacts** (Secondary data source)	- Stable and permanent for repeated review. - Retrievable with convenient electronic access and storage. - Unobtrusive observation of interaction. - Exact details provided of name, references and events. - Broad coverage of many events, in various settings, over varying time spans.	- Interpretive bias with secondary use of data which has to account for original intent of documents. - Partial rather than literal account of events since not every detail of online interaction could be captured by the WebCT™ chat facility e.g. timeline.
Responses from online survey (Primary data source) **Key informant** (Secondary data source)	- Targeted with direct relevance to areas of research interest. - Insightful with causal inferences of participants on interactions provided in self-reports of perceptions.	- Construct validity i.e., the extent to which the survey questions measure or elicit what they are intended to measure. - Response bias when respondents or informants reply with what they think the researcher wants to hear. - Inaccuracy with poor recall of learning experiences in self-reports.

Table 4.8. Main and secondary data sources for research questions

Research Questions	Data Sources	
	Main Data Sources	Secondary Data Sources
RQ1: What do the overall patterns of task-oriented chat discourse reveal about engagement by participants with each other's contributions, interactional purposes, and the collaborative learning process in groups?	Archived tutorial logs	Insights from staff participant on tutorial participation behaviours, experiences, discussion content and context.
RQ2: How do student participants perceive their experiences of chat tutorial interaction in terms of participation opportunities, adequacy of learning support, and quality of learning experience and collaborative work process?	Responses to online survey	Information from unit document artifacts on content and context of tutorial discussion.

Table 4.9. Online survey dataset and response rate

Group	No. of returns	%	Missing
1	13 out of 14*	93	1
4	8 out of 9*	89	1

* Derek (G1) and Karl (G4) did not submit survey returns.

Electronic *unit documents* such as reflective journals and presenter guidelines were downloaded from the unit website while the print *Resource Materials* reader was obtained from the unit coordinator. *Insights from staff participant* on tutorial participation behaviours, experiences, discussion content and context were gathered during informal meetings with unit coordinator.

4.3.3 Ethical considerations
Ethics in research refers to the obligation and accountability of the researcher to both the individual participant and society as a whole (Bromseth, 2002). Existing guidelines on ethical research conduct are largely based on the conventional dichotomy between public and private physical contexts, prove problematic when applied to the study of virtual communities since "what is 'public' and 'private' is not always clear, in conception, experience, label, or substance" (Waskul & Douglass, 1996, p.131).

King (1996) introduced two constructs of group accessibility and perceived privacy for determining the private/public nature of online communities under study. *Group accessibility* refers to "the degree with which the existence and access to a particular Internet forum or community is publicly available information" while *perceived privacy* is "the degree to which group members perceive their messages to be private to their group" (King, 1996, p.126). Essentially, private online communities are likely to be characterized by un-published URLs, membership conditions, and expectations of privacy. Hence, informed consent from participants may be required for the study of such groups.

However, the construct of perceived privacy does not account for individual differences in expectations of privacy since in online communities that are "recognized as 'public', participants can (and do) engage in 'private' forms of interaction" (Waskul & Douglass, 1996, p.132). Other factors for consideration in online research ethical frameworks could include the size and purpose of the online group, and extent of intrusiveness of study (Eysenbach & Till, 2001; Waskul & Douglass, 1996).

Based the literature, the two online tutorial groups selected for study display characteristics of *private* communities (Table 4.10) with restricted access to the password protected WebCT™ learning environment and likelihood of a high level of perceived privacy given a stable population where members know each other by their actual names over an extended period of 13 weeks. Even as archived logs of individual group discussions are available to a 'wider' community comprising all students enrolled in the OI unit, this wider community constitute authorized users of both WebCT™ and the unit website. Moreover, use of an online survey instrument that requires "active participation from informants" (Bromseth, 2002, p.41) could be regarded as a relatively intrusive research method. Hence, it is reasonable to conclude that informed consent from the online participants would be needed in this study.

Ultimately, ethical decisions in this study were governed by the institutional guidelines set by the *Murdoch University Human Research Ethics Committee* (HREC) that determined that a Human Research Ethics permit and informed consent from participants were required for this study which involved the secondary use of data created for another purpose, questionnaire administration, and evaluation of classroom learning for research purposes.

Table 4.10. Ethical factors: Online research design and group characteristics

Ethical Factors	Research Design and Online Group Characteristics
Group accessibility	- Access to WebCT™ chat tutorial rooms restricted to enrolled students in OI unit. - Condition placed on membership (enrolment in OI unit).
Perceived privacy	- Lack of anonymity among members (actual names known). - Stable group population over period of study (13 weeks).
Group size	- Group 1 (15 students, 1 tutor). - Group 4 (9 students, 1 tutor, 1 researcher).
Group purpose	- Collaborative learning through critical discussion of set-readings.
Degree of intrusiveness	- Participant observer researcher role adopted for Group 4. - Non-participant observer researcher role adopted for Group 1. - Administration of online survey to student participants. - Discourse analysis of chat tutorial transcripts. - Consultations with key informant who is both Group 4 tutor and OI unit coordinator.

Informed consent means that "research subjects have the right to know that they are being researched, the right to be informed about the nature of the research and the right to withdraw at anytime" (Ryen, 2004, p. 231). Although informed consent could be obtained prospectively or retrospectively (Eysenbach & Till, 2001), Murdoch University ethical guidelines required participant consent before conduct of the study which presented methodological risks of influencing future chat interaction patterns and losing potential participants when many opt out. Informed consent was obtained from the G1 tutor and Dr. Fay Sudweeks (unit coordinator/G4 tutor) in June 2005 (personal communication, 13 June 2005) before commencement of the main study.

The stages in obtaining informed consent from student participants are briefly described below.

- *Stage One: Notification and participant identification*

In Week 1 of semester 2 (2005), Dr. Sudweeks and researcher announced the research project and the specific tutorial group (G1) designated for study during the lecture. Details on the research purpose, action required of participants, relationship of the research project to their study in the OI unit, and participant confidentiality were provided. Voluntary participation was emphasized and should students not wish to participate, they had the option of joining other tutorial groups available for the unit without penalty. The same information was provided in an online *Information Letter and Consent Form* (Appendix A.7) available from the unit website in the event that not all students registered for the unit were present at the lecture. Students who agreed to be part of the project were asked to indicate formal consent via e-mail to the researcher.

In that week, all students in the OI unit self-enrolled in their preferred tutorial groups through the *Online Tutorial Signup System*. At that stage, it was decided that other than G1, an additional tutorial group (Group 4) would be included as a comparative case where the researcher would be an active participant in the tutorial discussions. Arrangements were made to incorporate Group 4 (G4) into the study design and informed consent procedures.

- *Stage Two: Formal consent*

During the first Group 4 tutorial session in Week 2, Dr. Sudweeks (G4 tutor) sought consent from the group members regarding participation in the study and active presence of the researcher during tutorials. With the consensual agreement of G4, the researcher attended the tutorials from Week 3. E-mail confirmations of formal consent were received from all participants by 25 August 2005.

This study acknowledges two possible areas of ethical risk to online participants: participant identification and conflict of interest presented by the roles of Dr. Sudweeks. The management of these risks involved the use of pseudonyms and restricted access to the survey data which are described below.

Although the "use of pseudonyms is widespread in chat room and virtual communities" (Jacobson, 1999, p.131), this feature is not supported by the WebCT™ chat facility. The actual names of participants in the tutorial logs were therefore replaced with pseudonyms by the researcher in all publications utilizing the data. Since Dr. Sudweeks waived privacy rights for the research site and self identification (personal communication, 13 June 2005), both were identified by actual names in this study.

Dr. Sudweeks is identified in the context of this study as a staff participant (unit coordinator, G4 tutor) and chief investigator/supervisor of this research project. A possible argument for conflict of interest could be presented by Dr. Sudweeks' duties in the management of the unit, assessment of the student participants' coursework/examination, and access (as chief investigator) to the survey data which included information on participants' experiences of tutorials managed and/or conducted by Dr. Sudweeks.

To avoid any potential conflict of interest, in Dr. Sudweeks' capacity as supervisor, she was not given access to the raw survey data or presented with any analyses of the survey data before the release of final unit grades to the student participants. As participant, Dr. Sudweeks received feedback on the research outcomes after the end of the semester and confidentiality was observed by referring to student participants by their pseudonyms.

4.3.4 Research stages in this study

With completion of site selection in 2004 and granting of ethical approval in April 2005, the main study was conducted between July 2005 and November 2005 when the OI unit was available to students in the second semester of the 2005 academic year. The major stages of this research are presented in Table 4.11.

Table 4.11. Major stages in research study

Major Research Stages	Time Frame
2004	
- Site selection process	Completed in Sept 2004
- Negotiation for site access	
2005	
- Ethics approval	Obtained on 29 Apr 2005
- Instrument development and refinement:	
Coding instrument development	Completed in Aug 2005
Online survey instrument development	Completed in Sept 2005
Evaluation of data visualization software	Completed in Sept 2005
- Data Collection:	
Participant identification & obtaining informed consent	Completed in Aug 2005
Transcript data collection (primary data source)	Completed in Oct 2005
Online survey administration (primary data source)	Closed on 7 Nov 2005
- Transcript data processing	Completed in Nov 2005
2006	
- Full transcript dataset coding	Completed in Jan 2006
- Survey data processing	Completed in Apr 2006
Full survey dataset coding	Completed in Apr 2006
- Data analysis	Completed in Jun 2006
- Feedback of research outcomes to participants	Completed in Aug 2006

The next section explains the methods of discourse analysis, social network analysis, and survey perception analysis, and describes the coding, visualization and survey instruments utilized to examine the impact of chat interaction on the collaborative-constructivist learning process.

4.4 Methods and Instruments

This section describes the methods and instruments utilized to examine task-oriented chat exchange patterns and student experiences of chat interaction during the collaborative learning processes of two tutorial groups in the OI unit.

An overview of this section is provided below:

Section 4.4.1 defines the discourse analysis method, explains the constructs of virtual classroom interaction and chat exchange structure, and describes the *Exchange Structure Analysis* (ESA) coding instrument developed for analyzing the transcript data.

Section 4.4.2 describes the background, significant concepts, and methods in *Social Network Analysis* (SNA), defines SNA as a qualitative method and explains areas of conceptual integration between SNA and ESA for analyzing chat exchanges. The processes of coding and analysis of the transcript data are summarized in a 5-stage model.

Section 4.4.3 justifies the choice of a web survey method, describes the survey development process and highlights features in questionnaire design for reducing survey error.

4.4.1 Discourse analysis: Method and coding instrument
Discourse analysis (DA) as a theoretical framework is defined as the study of "language in use" (Brown & Yule, 1983, p.1). As an analytical method, DA is a procedure of textual analysis for studying "texts and talk in social practice" (Hepburn & Potter, 2004, p.180) or "recorded talk" in specific communicative contexts (Schwandt, 2001, p.57). Although similar to *content analysis* in the sense that DA also uses procedures of sorting and categorizing textual data for quantitative and/or interpretive analyses, DA is distinctive for its focus on processes of communication, structures, interaction patterns of language in situated use (Taylor, 2001), and speech act functions realized by text or talk (van Dijk, 1997). Since this study examines synchronous computer-mediated discourse (CMD) which displays the spontaneity of speech and structural forms of written text, DA is adopted as the primary method for analyzing patterns of exchange (turn-taking) and moves (speech acts) in education chat interaction.

• *Representations of virtual classroom interaction and chat exchange structure*
Drawing from *transactional analysis* (Sinclair & Coulthard, 1992; Stubbs, 1983), *exchange structure theory* (Coulthard & Brazil, 1992), and further work by Pilkington (1999) and Kneser et al. (2001), this study's conceptualization of virtual classroom interaction, chat exchange system and structure are described below.
Sinclair and Coulthard (1992) conceptualized conventional classroom interaction as a hierarchy with the *lesson* as the highest unit, followed by *transaction, exchange*, and *move/act* (Figure 4.3a). A lesson is regarded as "the highest unit of classroom discourse, made up of a series of transactions" (Sinclair & Coulthard, 1992, p.33). Transaction boundaries are indicated by sets of preliminary and final exchanges which frame medial exchanges. Exchanges consist "minimally of contributions by two participants" (Coulthard & Brazil, 1992, p.64) which are moves with speech act functions. Pilkington (1999) proposed a similar representation of classroom

interaction as a hierarchical organization of *episode*, *exchange*, *turn*, *move*, and *predicate* (Figure 4.3b). The episode is the highest unit and comprises exchanges. An exchange is "the minimal unit of interactive discourse" (Stubbs, 1983, pp.28-29) consisting of at least an initiating and a responding turn, performed by a minimum of two participants. Turns consist of moves which indicate pragmatic intentions through their rhetorical predicate labels.

Figure 4.3a. Representation of classroom interaction (adapted from Sinclair & Coulthard, 1992, p.5)

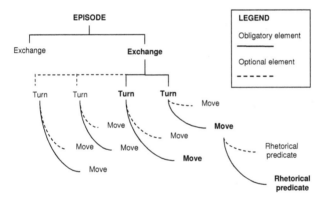

Figure 4.3b. Representation of classroom interaction (adapted from Pilkington, 1999, p.12)

Synthesizing the concepts presented in Sinclair and Coulthard (1992), and Pilkington (1999), this study developed a *virtual classroom interaction model* (Figure 4.4) for a broader representation of interaction, at levels higher than the exchange, which is specific to the online tutorial context. In this model, a *session*, like a lesson, is the highest unit of classroom discourse. It refers to the entire (1 hour) chat tutorial period and constitutes episodes and social spaces. *Social spaces* comprise utterances[37] on non-task related topics, marked by their location in the transitional area between episode boundaries and at the start/end of a session. *Episodes* comprise turns[38] on task related topics in discussion slots, within a session.

---

[37] While the terms *utterance* and *turn* are often used synonymously in DA literature, this could lead to confusion in this study which required a differentiation between contributions made within a session that are included and excluded from analysis. An *utterance* is defined in this study as "everything said by one speaker before another began to speak" (Sinclair & Coulthard, 1992, p.2). It is used in a broad sense to refer to all contributions made by participants within a session.
[38] The term *turn* is reserved for contributions that fall within episode boundaries.

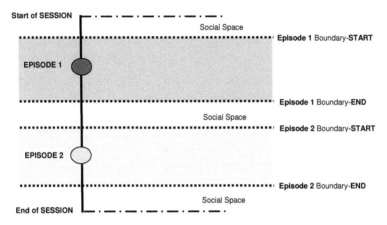

Figure 4.4. Virtual classroom interaction model: Session, episode and social spaces

The model frames interaction at the virtual classroom level as sessions, episodes, and social spaces, and forms the conceptual basis for transcript data segmentation into units of analysis during data processing[39]. Since the model reflects interaction at levels higher than the exchange, interactions at the levels of exchange, turn, and move are represented by an educational chat exchange system described below.

Interaction at exchange level is conceptualized as an *educational chat exchange system* which is a hierarchical organization of exchanges, turns and moves (Figure 4.5). Integrating the exchange structure concepts presented in Coulthard and Brazil (1992) which were further developed in studies by Pilkington (1999) and Kneser et al. (2001), a well-formed *chat exchange* consists of at least an initiating and responding turn, performed by a minimum of two participants. While in conventional spoken discourse, a *turn* is delimited by the start and end of a participant speaking, in chat discourse, "a carriage return effectively sends a message and automatically delimits a turn" (Kneser et al., 2001, p.67). A turn consists of at least one *move* which indicates its pragmatic intention at speech act level (Kneser et al., 2001).

Regarding the *sequence of turns* that forms an exchange, exchange structure theory holds that the organization of most non-pedagogical, 'everyday' conversational exchanges is sufficiently captured by the minimal unit [I-R], which consists "at least an initiation (I) from one speaker and a response (R) from another" (Stubbs, 1983, p.104). However, *pedagogical* exchanges are distinctive for their three-part structure of [I-R-<F>] or [I-R-<E>] (Mehan, 1985; Sinclair & Coulthard, 1992) where the optional third element, *Feedback* <F> or *Evaluation* <E>, constitutes an evaluative element in the sequence of turns.

---

[39] Data processing procedures are described in this chapter, section 4.5.

CHAPTER 4   93

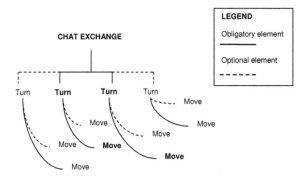

Figure 4.5. Educational chat exchange system: Exchange, turn and move

For instance, the following classroom exchange could be characterized as consisting of "an *initiation* by the teacher, followed by a *response* from the pupil, followed by [an optional] *feedback*, to the pupil's response from the teacher" (Sinclair & Coulthard, 1992, p.3-emphasis in original) that closes the exchange.

Example: Pedagogical exchange: [I-R-<F>] structure (adapted from Sinclair & Coulthard, 1992, p.33)

Teacher>>	Where does he live?	I		
Student>>	Rome.		R	
Teacher>>	Rome, yes.			F

A possible variation in turn sequence could take the form of [I-<RI>-R] where an optional element *Reinitiate* <RI> "functions as a response with respect to the preceding element and as an initiation with respect to the following one" (Coulthard & Brazil, 1992, p.71). As shown below, an initiation by the teacher is followed by a *Reinitiate* from the student that seeks clarification from the teacher on the previous turn before the exchange is completed.

Example: Variation of pedagogical exchange: [I-<RI>-R] structure

Teacher>>	Can anyone tell me what this chart means?	I		
Student>>	Where is the chart?		RI	
Teacher>>	Look at page two.			R

Kneser et al. (2001) proposed that the structure of *pedagogical chat exchange* comprised at least two elements: *Initiate* (I), and *Respond* (R), and up to four when inclusive of the elements *Reinitiate* (RI) and *Response-Complement* (RC) i.e., [I-R] or [I-<RI>-R-<RC>].

Example: Pedagogical chat exchange: [I-R] and [I-<RI>-R-<RC>] structures

Participant A>>	What are your thoughts on your own question?	I			
Participant B>>	haven't got a clue at the moment … give me a second to gather my thoughts and I'll let you know.		R		
Participant A>>	did you do ICT108? you should know why the internet was first developed	I			
Participant B>>	hmm wasn't the internet made for the army or something...		RI		
Participant C>>	arpa			R	
Participant A>>	military, yes				RC

As explained in Kneser et al. (2001), the term *Response-Complement* is used, instead of *Feedback* or *Evaluation* as practised by Sinclair and Coulthard (1992), to avoid the implication that evaluation is mandatory in a pedagogical chat exchange since the (RC) element may serve to communicate either acknowledgment or evaluative content.

Since (RC) is not exclusively an evaluative element and may convey acknowledgment, further variations of turn sequence in pedagogical chat exchanges are possible with a (RC) turn occupying the responding turn position after initiating turns (I) or (RI) i.e., [I-RC] and [I-<RI>-RC], which is originally reserved for a (R) according to Sinclair and Coulthard (1992). Additionally, a (RC) turn could be structurally located in the responding turn position after a (R) i.e., [I-R-<RC>]. Hence, this study holds that well-formed pedagogical chat exchanges may also display the structures of [I-RC], [I-<RI>-RC], and [I-R-<RC>] as shown below.

Example: (RC) positions in pedagogical chat exchanges: [I-RC], [I-<RI>-RC] and [I-R-<RC>]

Participant A>>	does everyone understand what i have said	I	
Participant B>>	yes, understood		RC
Participant A>>	internet drags you away from culture	I	
Participant B>>	how can the internet drag you away from culture, the internet is a culture	RI	
Participant C>>	ah		RC
Participant A>>	Antecedents are the contributing factors of Self-efficacy and are incorporated in the investigation of one?s degree of self-efficacy. What are some antecedents you can think of?	I	
Participant B>>	er... previous experience	R	
Participant C>>	yes - Remote working experience & training		RC

Based on the hierarchical educational chat exchange system described earlier, chat exchanges comprise turns and the pragmatic intentions of turns are identified by *moves*. *Speech act theory* (Austin, 1962; Searle, 1969) assumes that any sentence/turn could be used by the addressor/speaker to simultaneously perform a locutionary, an illocutionary and a perlocutionary act. The 'uptake' (Levinson, 1983) or interpretation (rightly or wrongly) of the turn's pragmatic intention, in a particular context, is held to be explained by a system of turn-taking rules or the concept of adjacency pairs which are two-turn units that "set constraints on what should be done in a next turn" (Sacks et al., 1974, p.717). Hence, a turn could be seen "as a realization of the speaker's intent to achieve a particular purpose" (Eggins & Slade, 1997, p.40).

Francis and Hunston (1992) noted that in the exchange analytical approach presented by Sinclair and Coulthard (1975), each turn indicates one move/speech act based on the analyst's interpretation of its *dominant* pragmatic function. However, this study allows that turns in educational chat discourse may perform more than one move because other than the immediate local context of the turn, the "extra-linguistic context" (Levinson, 1983, p.291) such as participant expectations about the purpose, and management routine of the online tutorial or speech event (Hymes, 1974) could contribute to a multitude of pragmatic intentions.

The constructs of virtual classroom interaction, chat exchange system and structure form the theoretical bases for the selection and refinement of the *Exchange Structure Analysis* coding scheme described below.

- *Background to Exchange Structure Analysis (ESA) coding scheme*

The *Exchange Structure Analysis* (ESA) coding scheme for dialogue analysis used in this study was originally developed by Kneser et al. (2001), and Cox et al., (2004) and could be traced to a larger DISCOUNT scheme presented in Pilkington (1997; 1999). Drawing from these sources, a brief account of the two schemes is provided below.

Based on *transactional analysis* (Sinclair & Coulthard, 1975; 1992; Stubbs, 1983) and *rhetorical structure theory* (Mann & Thompson, 1988), the DISCOUNT scheme was developed to "describe and evaluate educational discourse and, to mark representational levels of discourse which might be necessary for the generation of natural dialogues by machines" (Pilkington, 1999, p.2) such as Intelligent Tutoring Systems. DISCOUNT offers a hierarchical coding scheme with 4 turn categories, 26 moves and 97 rhetorical predicates for coding educational dialogue. Application of DISCOUNT to exchanges could reveal shifts in dialogue roles and participants who tend to hold the initiative, hence providing insight into learning processes. Although the examples of exchanges in Pilkington (1999) reflected mainly face-to-face interactional contexts, application of the scheme to computer-mediated discourse was not ruled out.

Kneser et al. (2001) noted that given its complexity of coding categories, DISCOUNT could prove cumbersome in actual practice and its application to large corpora could be highly time-consuming. Difficulties in inter-coder accuracy were reported in de Vicente, Bouwer, and Pain (1999) which found marked differences between two coders, after approximately 20 hours of training, mainly in the frequency of assigning rhetorical predicates labels to the same dataset. Given the large range of 97 labels at the predicate level of DISCOUNT, de Vincent et al. (1999) recommended a reconsideration of the categories in the scheme.

Since a thorough analysis of datasets with DISCOUNT could prove daunting in terms of time, complexity of coding categories, and accuracy of category assignment, Kneser et al. (2001) proposed a subset of DISCOUNT labelled *Exchange Structure Analysis* (ESA) that focuses the analysis at the levels of exchange and turn for "capturing the grammar of turns between dialogue participants with the aim of gaining insights into their relative contributions and roles" (p.67). The theoretical basis of ESA is informed by Sinclair and Coulthard's (1975) *transactional analysis* and modifications to it suggested in Stubbs (1981).

The ESA scheme, as presented in Kneser et al. (2001), comprised a set of *exchange structure categories* for coding turns initially at the exchange level which could then be associated with anticipated *exchange structure roles*. A further set of *move categories* enables the examination of pragmatic intentions of coded turns which could be associated with anticipated *argument roles* (Table 4.12). Essentially, when applied to educational chat discourse, coding of turns with the ESA scheme could

> determine who holds the initiative in a dialogue during particular phases of the dialogue or the dialogue as a whole. This, in turn, enables us to determine the degree of symmetry and inclusiveness of participation by looking for instances of particular categories of Exchange Structure analysis and the balance of these amongst participants (Kneser et. al., 2001, p.69)

Table 4.12. Kneser et al.'s (2001) categories in ESA scheme

Exchange Structure Category	Exchange Structure Role	Move Category	Argument Role
Initiate (I)	Initiator	Inform	Elaborator
	Initiator	Inquire	Inquirer
	Initiator	Reason	Explainer
Reinitiate (RI)	Reinitiator	Challenge or Disagree and Justify	Critic
	Reinitiator	Clarify	Clarifier
Respond (R)	Responder	Reason	Explainer
	Responder	Inform	Elaborator
Response-Complement (RC)	Finisher	Feedback	Evaluator
Stand Alone (SA)	Continuer	Inform and Reason	Narrator

Cox et al. (2004) further modified the ESA scheme by excluding the category of exchange structure roles, hence simplifying the association between *exchange structure* and *move* categories which could then be linked to respective *argument roles* (Table 4.13). Also, Cox et al. (2004) provided an explication of the ESA scheme with formal definitions of exchange structure and move categories to guide coding of educational chat exchanges (Table 4.14).

Findings from Kneser et al. (2001) and Cox et al. (2004) on the application of the ESA scheme to educational chat discourse were described in Chapters 1 and 2. This section focuses on the methodological designs (summarized in Table 4.15) and coding issues arising from the use of ESA in these studies with a brief mention of coding concerns raised in Carr, Cox, Eden, and Loopuyt (2002).

Table 4.13. Modified ESA scheme in Cox et al. (2004)

Exchange Structure Category	Move Category	Argument Role
Initiate (I)	Inform	Elaborator
	Inquire	Inquirer
	Reason	Explainer
Reinitiate (RI)	Challenge or Disagree and Justify	Critic
	Clarify	Clarifier
Respond (R)	Reason	Explainer
	Inform	Elaborator
Response-Complement (RC)	Feedback	Evaluator
Stand Alone (SA)	Inform and Reason	Narrator

Kneser et al. (2001) applied ESA to examining the characteristics of chat discourse and evaluating the effectiveness of online tutors in transferring discussion skills to postgraduate students in a distance learning course from a constructivist perspective. Transcripts from chat seminars were analyzed using ESA to identify the participants who tended to hold the initiative or dominate discussions. Inter-rater reliability score from the analysis of one chat session was a Kappa of 0.71 which falls within Krippendorf's 'tentative' range.

Table 4.14. Cox et al.'s (2004) definitions of coding categories (adapted from pp.185-186)

Exchange Structure Category	Definition
Initiate (I)	a contribution that anticipates a response and is not predicted from a previous turn
Reinitiating (RI)	a contribution that is a continuation of a current exchange and which anticipates a response, but which was not predicted from an earlier turn and which was not initial. Reinitiation can be negative feedback
Respond (R)	a contribution that is not initial, does not anticipate a turn and usually completes an exchange
Response-complement (RC)	a contribution that can be acknowledgement, feedback or evaluation. Response-complement signals intention to close the exchange, although it can be followed by a new exchange
Stand alone (SA)	contributions in which one participant continues to initiate, and where turns by the same speaker follow each other
Ill-informed turn (II)	a contribution that is an island, with no response to it

Move Category	Definition
Challenge	Statements requesting reasoning or fresh thinking
Justify	Reply with evidence or contraindication
Clarify	Questions of clarification
Feedback	Evaluative statements
Inform	Description/differentiation
Inquire	Questions requesting information
Reason	State causal proposition

Table 4.15. Methodological designs of Kneser et al. (2001) and Cox et al. (2004)

Research Focus	Participants	Methodology	Data Collection	Data Quantity
Kneser et al. (2001)				
Focus on symmetry of exchange roles indicating inclusiveness of participation.	- Postgraduates - 20 students (3-6/group) - 1 Tutor - 2 demonstrators (technical helpers)	Naturalistic setting. Quantitative discourse analysis of interaction patterns with ESA scheme.	Chat transcripts	Transcript data: - 1st 1-8 whole class chat sessions out of 11. - 1 private chat session between 2 students. - 1 private thread between demonstrators and tutor from one chat session.
Cox et al. (2004)				
Focus on factors affecting participation in chat discussions and impact of chat on learning.	Participants from 2 courses: - 8 from an undergraduate course; *Images of Africa* (IA) - 20 from a postgraduate course; *International Trade Bargaining* (ITB) in 2 groups (A=9; B=11)	Comparative case study. Quantitative and qualitative discourse analysis of interaction patterns with modified ESA scheme. Quantitative and qualitative analyses of interview and survey data.	- Chat transcripts - Observation in lab - Interview (ITB groups) - End-of-course student survey	Transcript data: - IA: all 3 chat sessions. - ITB: 8 chat sessions each from groups A and B out of over 20. Data presented from 4 sessions. Observation notes and survey data on both IA and ITB participants. Interview data from only ITB participants. Informal conversation with IA participants.

Kneser et al. (2001) attributed the score obtained mainly to "the possibility of a single category mismatch having knock-on effects for the selection of other categories after it" (p.71), particularly when there is strong inter-dependence between exchange structure categories. The concept of *prospective* or *continuous classification* (Sinclair & Coulthard, 1975; Stubbs, 1983) underlies the assumption in discourse analysis that each utterance is interpreted or classified in the light of structural predictions established by preceding utterance(s). In other words, as explained by Hepburn and Potter (2004), an utterance is "oriented to what comes before, and sets up an environment for what comes next" (p.190). Therefore, given the typical classroom exchange [I-R-RC], coding a turn as an *Initiate* places constraints on the interpretation of adjacent or following turns.

Other coding issues with ESA were highlighted in Carr et al. (2002) which compared participation patterns in two university courses using multiple data sources including transcripts from face-to-face and chat discussions, data from observation, interviews, and end-of-course student surveys. Application of ESA to the analysis of the transcript data revealed difficulties in interpreting structural relationships between chat turns posted in close proximity to each other. The study recommended the development of more categories and standardization of the practice of single or double-coding of turns at the move level.

Cox et al. (2004) conducted a similar comparative study that examined the impact of course design, group dynamics, and facilitation styles in supporting effective chat discussions in two courses at undergraduate and postgraduate levels. Quantitative analysis of transcripts of group chat sessions was conducted with a modified version of Kneser et al.'s (2001) ESA scheme to identify participant roles, inclusiveness of participation, and characteristics of educational chat discourse. Qualitative analyses of data from observation, student surveys, and interviews were also carried out. Inter-rater reliability for ESA was not reported in the study and details were not available on the approach for integrating results from ESA with data from other sources. However, Cox et al.'s (2004) study could be considered illuminative for its methodological design which triangulated findings from ESA with other data sources and its modification of the original ESA scheme.

- *Exchange Structure Analysis (ESA) coding scheme in current study*
The ESA scheme formulated for the examination of educational chat discourse in this case study is an extension of the method reported in Cox et al. (2004). The theoretical bases of the scheme stem from *discourse analysis* (Brown & Yule, 1983), *transactional analysis* (Sinclair & Coulthard, 1992; Stubbs, 1983), *exchange structure theory* (Coulthard & Brazil, 1992), and *speech act theory* (Austin, 1962; Sacks et al, 1974; Schegloff et al., 1977; Searle, 1969) which also underlie this study's conceptualization of virtual classroom interaction, chat exchange system and structure discussed earlier[40].

The ESA coding scheme developed by this study is described below and the general coding symbols used in the following discussion are explained in Table 4.16. The codebook for the ESA scheme (Appendix B.1) provides definitions of the coding categories, examples from chat exchanges, and explanations of the transcript data segmentation procedures.

Insights from the application of earlier versions of the scheme in studies (Carr et al., 2002; Cox et al., 2004; Kneser et al., 2001) led to the following refinements in the ESA coding scheme used in this study which enable the analysis of task-oriented

---

[40] Refer to page 107.

chat exchanges in online tutorial discussions for indications of active participation and knowledge construction:

- exclusion of the argument role category which was not particularly informative and could be confused with student-presenter and tutor-facilitator roles pre-determined by the chat tutorial activity;
- explicit association of each ES category to its own set of Move categories;
- addition of an *Other* category for coding Off-Topic and Repair turns that contain content not directly related to the issues in the set-readings i.e. non task-oriented turns;
- conceptualization of extended turn sequences to reflect control of discussion by participants; and
- standardization of the practices of single-coding turns at ES level and double-coding[41] at Move level.

Table 4.16. General coding symbols and description in current study

General coding symbol	Description
[ ]	Exchange boundaries
( )	EXCHANGE STRUCTURE (ES) and OTHER categories
{ }	MOVE category
< >	Optional item
$(_{fs}04.1.200)$	Turn label
/	Double/multiple assignment of categories
+	Extended turn sequence

The ESA scheme developed by this study analyzes chat exchanges at two main levels: Exchange Structure (ES) and Move levels (Table 4.17). Although the main focus of this study is on task-oriented turns, it is acknowledged that turns may serve to establish social or teaching presence (Garrison et al., 2000) in educational interactions. Hence, a separate *Other* category was created for such turns that are not coded at ES or Move level. These turns are classified as *Off-Topic* (OT) or *Repair* (RPR) with no further analysis.

Reflecting this study's conceptualization of the hierarchical educational chat exchange system, turns in episodes are first coded at the ES level according to four structural categories: *Initiate* (I), *Reinitiate* (RI), *Respond* (R), or *Response-Complement* (RC) to derive exchanges. As depicted in Figure 4.6, a top-down analysis starting at the ES level could reveal the structural organization of an exchange such as [I-RI-R-RC]. At the Move level, coded turns are further classified according to their associated moves (Table 4.18). For instance, a (RI) turn could be coded at the Move level as having the pragmatic intention to *Check* {CHK}, *Clarify* {CLA}, *Extend* {EXD}, or *Challenge* {CHA}.

---

[41] At the Move level, a turn may be double-coded when interpreted as simultaneously reflecting more than one pragmatic intention.

Table 4.17. Coding categories in current study: ES, Move and Other categories

Code	Description	Examples		
ES Level Category				
(I) Initiate	- initial in the exchange - not predicted from a previous turn - anticipates a following turn by another participant	Participant A>>Can anyone suggest the –'ve ways IFC can impact socially? Participant B>>decrease in physical exercise	I R	
(RI) Reinitiate	- not initial in the exchange - not predicted from earlier turn - anticipates a following turn by another participant (similar to an Initiate) - signals intention to continue the current exchange i.e. to start a sub-exchange that is related in content to the main exchange	Participant A>>Therefore, What is the impact of culture on the diffusion of interactive networks? Participant B>>organisational culture?	I RI	
(R) Respond	- not initial in the exchange - predicted from a previous turn - does not anticipate a following turn by another participant - usually closes an exchange but not always due to the possibility of a following (RC)	Participant A>> telephone is better communication than e-mail Participant B>> I would say they are different but to judge a technology without a context and say its better is a hard thing to do	I R	
(RC) Response-Complement	- not initial in the exchange - predicted from a previous initiating turn i.e. [I-RC] or [...RI-RC] - not predicted from an earlier turn; a turn that may follow a (R) i.e. [I-R-RC] - does not anticipate a following turn by another participant - signals intention to close the exchange - differentiated from (R) by conveying minimal information as acknowledgement or evaluation	Participant A>> But comp access is definitely cheaper than flying all the way to the other side of the world for business purpose rite Participant B>> yes	RI RC	
MOVE Level Category				
{INF} Inform	- describe or make observations of facts/events - state retrieved beliefs, definitions or rules - summarize/repeat information from memory or external sources	Participant>> like A says, a business can influence a culture to a certain extent Participant>> talking abt communication....	R I+	{INF} {INF}
{INQ} Inquire	- elicit or request for information - bid/solicit for favour that participants can permit or deny	Participant>> Do you agree that communication processes in VO are different from traditional organization?	I	{INQ}

{JUS} Justify	- defend a stated position (in previous or current turn) with information or evidence - challenge/dispute a stated position (in previous turn) with information or evidence	Participant>> assumption could be an imaginary fact	I+	{INF}
		Participant>> i.e. charlie chaplin(comedian) showed a joke of ascending stair, his theory proved to be funny or unreal in those days without any fact. But nowadays,like we see now, we have escalator	I	{JUS}
		Participant A>> so u are saying tt the company's reputation initiated the trust	RI	{CHK}
		Participant B>> i think it work both ways because trust can build ur company's reputation as well	R	{JUS}
{REA} Reason	- present problem-solution or cause-consequence - present support or contraindication for alternative hypotheses - state constructed (reasoned) beliefs or implications	Participant A>> This study was conducted on a group of employees of one of the largest computer organisations in the world. Therefore the study would not be representative of the entire nation of any of the countries, as these employees would be technologically focused for reason of the company that they are employed by.	I	{REA}
		Participant B>> agree	RC	{FBK-E}
		Participant A>> Is there a way to build trust in to a CMC technology?	I	{INQ}
		Participant B>> trust can also be gained from accountability ... if the only accountability is contact on CMC ... then its hard ... but external entities that are attached can help...	R	{REA}
{CLA} Clarify	- seek more information on previous turn(s) - make meaning clearer or understanding easier	Participant>> What do u mean?	RI	{CLA}
		Participant>> what kind of culture are you talking about	RI	{CLA}
{CHK} Check	- make certain the meaning of previous turn(s) - check readiness of participants, ascertain if there are any problems	Participant>> kinda like organisational groupthink?	RI	{CHK}
		Participant>> what about previous experience or exposure to it?	RI	{CHK}
{EXD} Extend	- describe or make observations of facts or events - state retrieved beliefs, definition or rules - summarize/repeat information from memory or external sources	Participant A>> trust may be developed from ppl comment on the vo or the image of the vo	I	{INF}
		Participant B>> also don't forget word of mouth and personal testimonies. they go far nowadays 2	RI	{EXD}
{CHA} Challenge	- propose/suggest another direction for discussion or thought - assert the need for another direction for discussion or thought	Participant>> So why bother with culture, and not stick to quantifiable methods like GDP, and uptake of IT?	RI	{CHA}
{FBK} Feedback	Feedback-Evaluation {FBK-E} - validate the truth/correctness of previous turn(s) - comment on the quality of the previous turn(s)	Participant A>> extrovers use the net to extend themselves while introvert use the net to remove themselves	I	{INF}
		Participant B>> agree	R	{FBK-E}
	Feedback-Acknowledgement {FBK-A} - report the state of the speaker - claim or acknowledge understanding/hearing of the previous turn(s)	Participant A>> how do u prove u worked whole weekend?	I	{INQ}
		Participant B>> the logging record..like this one...	R	{INF}
		Participant C>> time sheets	R	{INF}
		Participant A>> ok		RC {FBK-A}

OTHER Category			
(OT) Off-Topic			
	OT-Social (OT-S)	Participant>> Hes a married man!	**OT-S**
	- supports "development of group relationships" (Kneser et al., 2001, p.69) such as greetings, social banter and emoticons	Participant>> Thank you	**OT-S**
		Participant>> 3 mins	**OT-A**
		Participant>> Thanks, do you want to wrap it up?	**OT-A**
	OT-Administration (OT-A)		
	- deals with housekeeping issues for the OI unit and/or tutorial group such as time-calls and reminders	Participant>> i dowhy?	**OT-T**
		Participant>> [blank]	**OT-T**
	OT-Technical (OT-T)		
	- results from technical problems/issues such as mistyping and problems with network connections or equipment.		
(RPR) Repair	- to repair or correct a previous turn		
		Participant A>> and the results can be found in a long term...which most manager want it S.O.S	
	Repair-Self (RPR-S) whereby the 'speaker' of the trouble-source carries out the repair	Participant A>> I mean sonn as possible	**RPR-S**
		Participant A>> seeing more work brings on more stress thus ness gets done in the end	
	Repair-Other (RPR-O) whereby another participant (not the 'speaker' of the trouble-source) carries out the repair.	Participant B>> or less	**RPR-O**

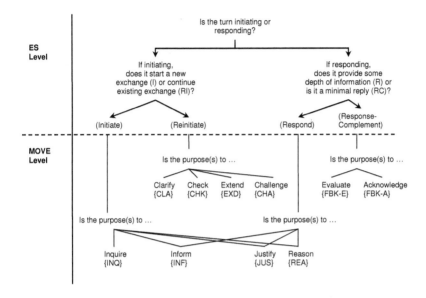

Figure 4.6. ESA scheme in current study: Coding at ES and Move levels

Table 4.18. ESA scheme in current study: Summary of associated ES and Move categories

Move	Exchange Structure			
	(Initiate)	(Reinitiate)	(Respond)	(Response-Complement)
{Inform}	1		1	
{Inquire}	1			
{Justify}	1		1	
{Reason}	1		1	
{Check}		1		
{Clarify}		1		
{Extend}		1		
{Challenge}		1		
{Feedback}				1

Note:
- (INITIATE) to {Inform}, {Inquire}, {Justify}, {Reason}
- (REINITIATE) to {Check}, {Clarify}, {Extend}, {Challenge}
- (RESPOND) to {Inform}, {Justify}, {Reason{}
- (RESPONSE-COMPLEMENT) to {Feedback}

As shown in the example below and Figure 4.7, while ES level analysis reveals the structural organization of the pedagogical chat exchange, Move level analysis indicates the communicative intentions underlying the turns constituting the exchange that could offer a more informative analysis of exchange. It should be noted that in this study, coding of structural positions and pragmatic functions of turns are largely guided by interpretations of their *relevance* to discussion context and content rather than consideration of the correctness or accuracy of content in the turns.

Example: ES and Move level analyses of a pedagogical chat exchange

		ES Level				Move Level
Participant A>>	What do you think of barber's paper-did you find it depressing? enlightening?	I				{INQ}
Participant B>>	which one? or both?		RI			{CHK}
Participant A>>	either			R		{INF}
Participant B>>	ah				RC	{FBK-A}

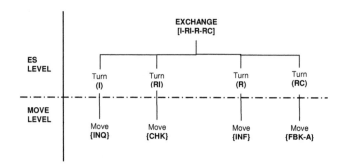

ES LEVEL

EXCHANGE
[I-RI-R-RC]

Turn (I) — Turn (RI) — Turn (R) — Turn (RC)

MOVE LEVEL

Move {INQ} — Move {CHK} — Move {INF} — Move {FBK-A}

Figure 4.7. ES and Move level analyses of a pedagogical chat exchange

The ESA scheme allows double-coding at the Move level when a turn is interpreted as simultaneously performing more than pragmatic function e.g., (RI) to both {*Clarify*} and {*Challenge*} as shown below. However, only the range of moves associated with the (RI) category could be assigned to the turn.

Example: A double-coded turn at Move level

		ES Level		Move Level
Participant A>>	do u think by using CMC small organization will be able to upgrade and increase productivity ?	I		{INQ}
Participant B>>	how small is small anyway, if it's just one office with 20 people or whatever then what's the point?		RI	{CLA/CHA}
Participant C>>	I agree		RC	{FBK-E}

In summary, given the focus of RQ1[42] on the analysis of task-oriented chat discourse for patterns of engagement by participants with each other's contributions and interaction during the collaborative learning process in groups, application of this refined ESA scheme to the transcript data could reveal the following:
- *extent of participation* as frequency/range of interaction turn and move types adopted by participants;
- *depth of information shared* as the presence of (R) that convey substantial information in contrast to (RC) that are minimal replies conveying acknowledgement or evaluation; and
- *knowledge construction* as sets of moves that indicate the presence of information sharing and topic development phases in exchanges that signal respectively, exchange of information as participants explore issues, and instances whereby the

---

[42] RQ1 was stated in Chapter 1. The operationalization of constructs in RQ1 as measures is explained in this chapter, section 4.6.

shared information is questioned, checked, clarified, or challenged which reflect meaning negotiation that builds new knowledge.

Moreover, greater understanding of the collaborative learning process in groups could be gained from examining *control of discussion* by participants as the presence of extended turn sequences shown below. An *extended turn sequence* is a sequence of two or more turns of the same ES type (by the same speaker) that may/may not immediately follow each other in the transcript due to system lag and/or use of multiple short postings by the participant in order to convey a message.

Example: Extended turn sequences in exchange: I-SEQ and R-SEQ

		ES Level	Move Level
Participant A>>	People who use e-mail regard it as less valuble than other modes of comm..	I+	{INF}
Participant A>>	We all use e-mail regularly do we agree/disagree why?	I	{INQ}
Participant B>>	Disagree. Depends on context	R+	{JUS}
Participant B>>	Email is great 4 work stuff	R	{JUS}

When these sequences are present as *Initiate*, *Reinitiate* and *Respond* types of extended turn sequences (I-SEQ, RI-SEQ, R-SEQ), they indicate efforts by participants to avoid being interrupted and ensure adequate 'speaking' time necessary to communicate the message. The presence of extended turn sequences in exchanges could therefore reflect control of discussion exerted by participants for various purposes during the learning process.

Although analysis of educational chat discourse through the ESA scheme could be illuminating, the results form a static representation of interaction during the learning process. The next section discusses the integration of social network analysis (SNA) with ESA for a more powerful analytical suite which could offer an interpretation of chat interaction that more closely represents the intuitive understanding of the dynamic to-and-fro pattern of turn-taking in exchanges of learning conversations.

4.4.2 Social network analysis
Social network analysis (SNA) is used in this study as "a set of methods for the analysis of social structures" (Scott, 2000, p.38) and as a visualization tool for representing actor and turn networks. This section provides an overview of the theoretical and empirical work in SNA, defines SNA as a qualitative method, its assumptions and significant concepts, and explains areas of conceptual integration between SNA and ESA in analyzing educational chat interaction.

The development of SNA, from the 1930s, to its current form was variously documented in Breiger (2004), Freeman (2000a; 2000b), Hanneman and Riddle (2005), Scott (2000), and Wasserman and Faust (1994). Drawing from these main sources, the following discussion highlights significant SNA methods and concepts from research in the disciplines of mathematics, psychology, sociology, and anthropology.

- *Representation of social networks: graphs and matrices*
The work of social psychologists, trained in the gestalt tradition, that explored group structure and dynamics contributed to the application of visual images as graphical representations of network features. In experimental human behaviour studies on the

association between psychological well-bring and social relations, psychiatrist Jacob Moreno (1932; 1934) created a *sociogram* (Figure 4.8) to represent the formal properties of social group structures. A sociogram is "one kind of graphic display [in two-dimensional space] that consists of points (or nodes) to represent actors and lines (or edges) to represent ties or relations" (Hanneman & Riddle, 2005, p.21).

Figure 4.8. A sociogram

The construction of a sociogram enables not only the visualization of existing actors and ties in a group, but also depicts the directional nature of interpersonal relations to illustrate sources of influence (Jennings, 1937) and path of information diffusion. Sociograms were utilized in Moreno, Jennings, and Stockton (1943) to display group and subgroup structures in classrooms based on friendship choices made by students. The fundamental concern of SNA in the nature of relational ties is succinctly captured by a *sociometric star* (Figure 4.9) representing "the recipient of numerous and frequent choices from others and who, therefore, held a position of great popularity and leadership" (Scott, 2000, p.10).

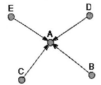

Figure 4.9. A sociometric star

According to Freeman (2000a), variations in sociograms introduced by Moreno included not only directed ties, but also *multiplex graphs* (Hanneman & Riddle, 2005) which depict more than one kind of relation for a set of actors as well as the use of different shapes, locations, and/or colours to highlight significant network structural features (Moreno & Jennings, 1944). In the field of *sociometry*, defined as "the measurement of interpersonal relations in small groups" (Wasserman & Faust, 1994, p.11), further sophistication in the interpretation and visual display of relational properties were introduced by the assignation of values to ties (Cartwright & Harary, 1956) in the form of signs for positive and negative relations such as *like* (+) or *dislike* (-), and/or numbers to indicate quantity/frequency in *valued graphs* (Figure 4.10).

While sociograms could adequately show immediate ties between actors, for larger datasets encompassing many actors, types and number of ties, mathematical representations as matrices offer clearer displays of network features. Wasserman and Faust (1994) attributed the early use of matrices for representing network data mainly to the pioneering work by Forsyth and Katz (1946), Harary and Norman (1953), and Harary, Norman, and Cartwright (1965).

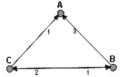

Figure 4.10. A directed and valued graph

Conventional sociological data consisting of actors and attributes are displayed in *case-by-variable matrices* where cases are represented by rows, and variables by columns (Figure 4.11). However, SNA does not usually handle attribute data but rather relational data which are not considered properties of independent actors. Hence, relational data consisting of actors and relations are typically organized in *case-by-case adjacency matrices* or sociomatrices (Wasserman & Faust, 1994) where cases are represented by both rows and columns, with relations represented by entries in matrix cells (Figure 4.12).

		Variables		
		Age	Gender	Grade
	Abe	20	Male	A+
Cases	**Ben**	22	Male	C+
	Cyn	18	Female	B+

Figure 4.11. Case-by-variable matrix

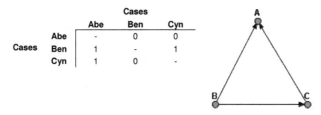

		Cases		
		Abe	Ben	Cyn
	Abe	-	0	0
Cases	**Ben**	1	-	1
	Cyn	1	0	-

Figure 4.12. Adjacency matrix and sociogram for friendship (*likes*) relation

In some instances, network studies have utilized data from different types of entities (Breiger, 1974; Galaskiewicz & Wasserman, 1989) to examine *affiliation networks* whereby "one set of actors is measured with respect to attendance at, or affiliation with, a set of events or activities" (Wasserman & Faust, 1994, p.40). Such data are captured by *case-by-affiliation matrices* (Scott, 2000) or *incidence matrices* (Wasserman & Faust, 1994) where cases are represented by rows, and affiliations of cases (in events, activities or organizations) are represented by columns (Figure 4.13).

		Affiliations		
		Event 1	Event 2	Event 3
	Abe	1	1	0
Cases	Ben	0	1	1
	Cyn	1	1	0
	Dan	1	1	1

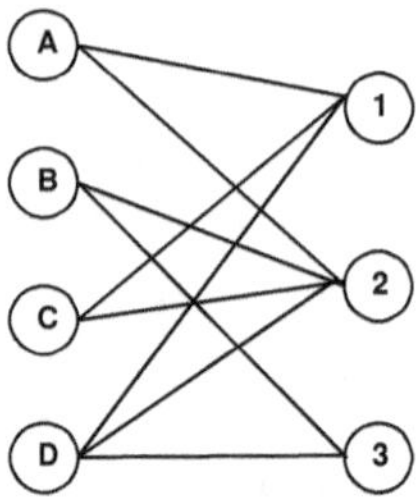

Figure 4.13. Case-by-affiliation matrix and sociogram (adapted from Wasserman & Faust, 1994, pp.299-301)

In this study, the concepts of valued, directed ties are fundamental to examining the extent of engagement in chat exchange patterns in terms of the direction and frequency of ties/turns sent and received by participants during the learning process. Relational data in the form of ties/turns are displayed as case-by-case adjacency matrices of actor and turn networks[43]. With the construction of matrices at exchange and episode levels, visualization of data as sociograms is supported by *NetMiner II* version 2.4.0 (Cyram, 2004). While other SNA programs such as UCINET 6.0 (Borgatti, Everett, & Freeman, 2002), STRUCTURE (Burt, 1991) and StOCNET 1.5 (Boer et al., 2004) are available for specialized network analysis and statistical procedures, NetMiner II is a commercial SNA program that supports both *network analysis* with SNA measures such as *degree*, *density*, *roles*, *centrality* and *graphical visualization* of data (Figure 4.14).

More details on NetMiner II features, system requirements, and limitations are available in Appendix B.2 and from http://www.netminer.com. Given rapid changes in the range and features of SNA programs (free and commercial), it is not possible to provide a definitive listing of available programs in this book. Recent comprehensive reviews of established and newer software could be found in Breiger (2004); Huisman and van Duijn (2004), Scott (2000), and from the *International Network for Social Network Analysis* (INSNA) at http://www.sfu.ca/~insna/ .

▪ *Theoretical developments in SNA: Concepts and empirical applications*

The distinct sociological orientation in SNA could be traced to theoretical and empirical work carried out in sociology and anthropology from 1930s to 1950s. Following the work of anthropologist A. R. Radcliffe-Brown in subgroup structures of social systems, Harvard researchers, W. Lloyd Warner and Elton Mayo conducted two classic studies which were on the Hawthorne electrical factory in Chicago (Roethlisberger & Dickson, 1939) and the New England community of 'Yankee City' (Warner & Lunt, 1941). Although these investigations produced significant empirical findings on the behaviour of work groups and cohesive structures in modern communities, of particular relevance to SNA was the use of sociograms in both studies to describe social structures found by the researchers.

[43] Processing of relational data for construction of adjacency matrices is described in this chapter, section 4.5.

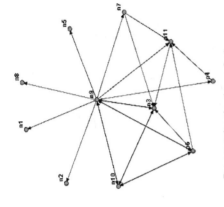

Representation of exchange: Adjacency matrix

cency Variable Name	EXG-3g4S11E1											☑ Dir
0	1	2	3	4	5	6	7	8	9	10	11	
	n1	n2	n3	n4	n5	n6	n7	n8	n9	n10	n11	
n1	0.0	0.0	0.0	0.0	0.0	0.0	0.0	0.0	0.0	0.0	0.0	
n2	0.0	0.0	0.0	0.0	0.0	0.0	0.0	0.0	0.0	0.0	0.0	
n3	0.0	0.0	0.0	0.0	0.0	0.0	0.0	0.0	0.0	0.0	1.0	
n4	0.0	0.0	0.0	0.0	0.0	0.0	0.0	0.0	1.0	0.0	1.0	
n5	0.0	0.0	0.0	0.0	0.0	0.0	0.0	0.0	0.0	1.0	0.0	
n6	0.0	0.0	1.0	0.0	0.0	0.0	0.0	0.0	1.0	0.0	1.0	
n7	0.0	0.0	1.0	0.0	0.0	0.0	0.0	0.0	0.0	1.0	1.0	
n8	0.0	0.0	0.0	0.0	0.0	0.0	0.0	0.0	0.0	0.0	0.0	
n9	0.0	0.0	1.0	1.0	1.0	1.0	1.0	1.0	0.0	1.0	1.0	
n10	0.0	1.0	1.0	1.0	0.0	2.0	1.0	0.0	1.0	0.0	0.0	
n11	0.0	0.0	3.0	0.0	0.0	0.0	1.0	0.0	1.0	1.0	0.0	

Representation of exchange: Sociogram

DISTRIBUTION OF DEGREE

MEASURES	VALUE	
	IN-DEGREE	OUT-DEGREE
SUM	26	26
MEAN	2.364	2.364
STD.DEV.	1.823	2.837
MIN.	1	0
MAX.	7	10
# OF ISOLATE	0	4
# OF PENDANT	6	1
INCLUSIVENESS(%)	100	63.636

Analysis of exchange: Degree

Figure 4.14. NetMiner II: Representations and analysis of a chat exchange

Sociograms were used in the Hawthorne and Yankee City studies to respectively, illustrate differences between observed and formal patterns of relationships in work groups, and to describe membership in formal/informal subgroups that constitute the social structure of a community. Although sociograms were mainly applied for *illustrative* rather than *explanatory* purposes, a study of 'Old City' (Davis, Gardner, & Gardner, 1941) on the internal structure of informal subgroups, formulated certain theoretical hypotheses on relationships between subgroups based on the interaction patterns present in the data.

According to Scott (2000), later work by Homans (1951) signalled a move towards the development of formal methods for the structural analysis of social groups based on particular theoretical orientations. From Homans' (1951) re-analysis of the data from the Old City study, emerged the current network technique of *blockmodeling* to partition matrices for discovering the presence of subgroups through their structural properties (Figure 4.15) as well as theoretical concepts of *frequency, duration, direction* and *transitivity* to explain interactional patterns. Homan's work was later extended to the field of *exchange theory* that emphasizes "social structure as the framework within which exchange processes take place and the structural change that result from these processes" (Molm & Cook, 1995, p.210).

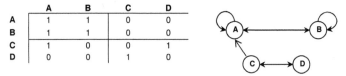

Figure 4.15. Blockmodeling: Blocked/partitioned matrix and sociogram for directed *marriage* relational ties of four families

The work of John Barnes, Elizabeth Bott, and Clyde Mitchell, on the effect of conflict/power in the formation and transformation of social structure, advanced the development of "formal techniques of network analysis with substantive sociological concepts" (Scott, 2000, p.27). The kinship studies conducted by Barnes (1954), and Bott (1955; 1956) marked the formal use of the social network concept as a framework and analytical method for the sociological interpretation of relations in social systems. Mitchell (1969) contributed a formal conception of a *network* as an interactional system involving "both a flow of information and a transfer of resources and services" (Scott, 2000, p.30). Other concepts from graph theory were also adapted by Mitchell to describe and measure the quality of relations that were precursors of current SNA concepts of *reciprocity, intensity, density*, and *reachability*.

Of particular relevance to this study is the extension of SNA to analyzing non-kinship based relationships by a group of Harvard researchers led by Harrison White in the 1960s. As Scott (2000) stated, they were mainly concerned with "the modelling of social structures of all kinds. There was no single theoretical focus to their work, the unifying idea being simply that of using algebraic ideas to model deep and surface structure relations" (pp.33-34).

The application of SNA primarily as a *method* to describe and model a wide range of relations could be seen in empirical studies that examined corporate interlocking (Levine, 1972; Scott 1991), diffusion of innovation (Rogers, 1979), information diffusion (Granovetter, 1974; Lee, 1969), world market structures (Burt, 1988), language change and variation (Labov, 1972; Milroy, 1987; 2000), terrorist networks (Krebs, 2002; Tsvetovat & Carley, 2005), and a more extensive list is available in Wasserman and Faust (1994)[44].

Freeman (2000b) reported that recent empirical work in social network analysis had extended to the field of computer-mediated communication (Garton, Haythornthwaite, & Wellman, 1997; Paolillo, 1999). In particular, more current studies had employed SNA methods in examining CMC-supported *learning networks*. In Lipponen, Rahikainen, Lallimo, and Hakkarainen (2001), and Aviv, Erlich, Ravid, and Geva (2003), asynchronous discussion postings were analyzed using a combination of SNA and content analysis methods to investigate participation patterns, learner network structures, and quality of knowledge construction process. In Haythornthwaite (2000; 2001), data from participant self-reports were analyzed using SNA to examine types of interaction and range of media used to support collaborative group work.

In contrast to these studies, the methodological design of this research incorporated *SNA and discourse analysis* in examining the impact of online *synchronous* interaction on the learning process of two tutorial groups over time as revealed by the chat transcript data. The patterns of participation, engagement in task-oriented exchanges, and knowledge construction revealed by both analytical methods are compared and integrated with findings from self-reports of learning experiences. The following section defines SNA as a method, justifies its location in the qualitative research framework, and explains areas of conceptual integration between ESA and SNA in analyzing chat exchanges.

• *SNA as qualitative method: Definition, assumptions and application in current study*
In this study, social network analysis is defined as a *method* enabling "the disciplined inquiry into the patterning of relations among social actors, as well as the patterning of relationships among actors at different levels of analysis (such as persons and groups)" (Breiger, 2004, p.505). The significance of the results is interpreted through the lens of the sociocultural constructivist theoretical perspective and the following assumptions specific to the method:

- Actors and their actions are viewed as interdependent rather than independent, autonomous units
- Relational ties (linkages) between actors are channels for transfer or 'flow' of resources (either material or nonmaterial)
- Network models focusing on individuals view the network structural environment as providing opportunities for or constraints on individual action
- Network models conceptualize structure (social, economic, political, and so forth) as lasting patterns of relations among actors
(Wasserman & Faust, 1994, p.4)

---

[44] Refer to Wasserman and Faust (1994, pp.5-6).

Essentially, the SNA method assumes the primacy of relational ties between social units and that "interactions between actors are the building blocks that sustain and define groups, whether learning groups, work groups, or other communities" (Haythornthwaite, 2001, p.213). Through examining structural patterns of ties, SNA aims to "understand properties of the social (economic or political) structural environment, and how these structural properties influence observed characteristics and associations among characteristics" (Wasserman & Faust, 1994, p.8).

Although SNA techniques include quantitative statistical analysis and/or the application of mathematical algorithms to analyzing or modelling relational data, this study views SNA as a *qualitative method* given the nature of network data that is analyzed which congrues with the qualitative research framework of the study. This study applies network analysis to textual data comprising turns/ties by actors engaged in dialogic interaction within an online collaborative learning context. Such relational ties are considered properties of "systems of agents" (Scott, 2000, p. 3) rather than individuals. The ties are regarded as means for the exchange of information, social and emotional support between participants of two chat tutorial groups, and subject to interactional opportunities and constraints present in the settings. Although these ties could be reduced to quantitative counts, they are necessarily social and/or cultural artifacts that require interpretation within their specific contexts (Breiger, 2004; Webster, Freeman, & Aufdemberg, 2001). Moreover, SNA is applied to transcript data which had been pre-coded according to the ESA scheme[45] and constructed as chat exchanges. It should be noted that while turns are categorized at both ES and Move levels in ESA, network analysis mainly utilizes information on turns coded at the ES level.

The overall validity of knowledge gained from SNA is evaluated through *methods triangulation* whereby interactional patterns of interest revealed through SNA are triangulated with the findings from discourse analysis with the ESA scheme and self-reports of learning experiences from the survey. The following section explains the areas of conceptual integration between SNA and ESA in analyzing educational chat exchanges.

▪ *Integration of SNA and ESA: Concepts of chat exchange, degree, actor type, reciprocity, inclusiveness*
As stated in section 4.4.1 of this chapter, a well-formed *chat exchange* is performed by a minimum of two participants and comprises at least two elements: *Initiate* (I), *Respond* (R), and up to four when inclusive of *Reinitiate* (RI) and *Response-Complement* (RC) i.e., [I-R] or [I-<RI>-R-<RC>].

From a SNA perspective, the concept of well-formed chat exchange remains fundamentally unchanged (Figure 4.16).
- A *node* represents a social unit which could be an individual (actor), an entity, group, organization, country, or an abstraction (point) i.e., nodes represent "discrete individual, corporate, or collective social units" (Wasserman & Faust, 1994, p.17).
- A *tie* represents a connection/link between two nodes which is regarded as "inherently a property of the pair and therefore is not thought of as pertaining simply to an individual actor" (Wasserman & Faust, 1994, p.18). A *connection* exists

---

[45] Refer to this chapter, section 4.4.1 for a description of the ESA coding scheme.

between a pair of nodes which has ties incident to and/or from each other e.g., i -> j, i <- j or i <-> j.
- A *relation* refers to the type of tie that exists between a pair of nodes and could be extended to refer to the "collection of ties of a given kind measured on pairs of actors from a specific actor set" (Wasserman & Faust, 1994, p.20).

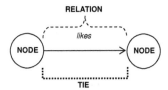

Figure 4.16. Node, tie and *likes* relation

Therefore, a chat exchange would basically comprise nodes, ties, and relations. Since nodes could be individuals or abstract entities, both actor and turn networks could be conceived from chat exchanges as shown below. In *actor networks*, the nodes are participants (n1, n2); ties are turns ($_{tu}$01.2.1, $_{tu}$01.2.2)[46] that link participants; and relations are the type of turns (I, R) present between the participants (Figure 4.17). In *turn networks*, nodes are turns ($_{tu}$01.2.1, $_{tu}$01.2.2); ties are the links between turns; and relations are the types of turns (I, R) exchanged in the interaction (Figure 4.18).

Example: Chat exchange: [I-R] structure

Turn No.	Participant	Turn	ES Level
($_{tu}$01.2.1)	n1>>	Do you think that Virtual Organisations should be based on High Reliability Organisations?	I
($_{tu}$01.2.2)	n2>>	not really, they are a special case	R

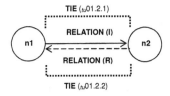

Figure 4.17. Nodes as actors in chat exchange

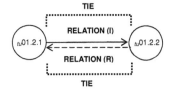

Figure 4.18. Nodes as turns in chat exchange

---

[46] Turn labels are explained further in section 4.5.

Building on chat exchanges constructed with the ESA scheme, this study applies the following SNA concepts of *degree*, *inclusiveness, actor type*, and *reciprocity* for greater understanding of the dynamic to-and-fro patterns of engagement in chat interaction.

The relations examined in the transcript dataset are "behavioral interaction" (Wasserman & Faust, 1994, p.18) involving 'talking' and initiating/responding in exchanges which are characterized by the transfer (one-way) or exchange (two-way) of nonmaterial resources (information). Given the nature of such relations, ties (as links or turns) are *directed* and *valued*. As shown by the following chat exchange and its representation as a sociogram, directed and valued ties indicate respectively, the communicative direction of the information exchange as *out-ties* (ties sent) or *in-ties* (ties received), and the frequency of the interaction as *degree* of connection between a node to other nodes adjacent to it.

The overall strength of connections among nodes in a network/group could be indicated by *network density* which is measured as the number of ties present in a network, expressed as a proportion of the maximum possible number of ties (Scott, 2000). However, application of this concept to actor-nodes in the transcript data presents several difficulties:
- besides limitations of time (1 hour tutorial) and group size (11 to 16 participants), there are no theoretical limits to the number of ties that could possibly be sent/received by each participant; and
- there are currently no benchmark network density values for comparison from research similar to the design of this study.

Example: A directed and valued chat exchange: Exchange and sociogram

No.	Participant	Turn	EXG-3-g4S11-E1							
45	n9	i was just wondering... if people are say..going to say a speech at a rally... do they need to read a copyright out first...so everyone knows								
53	n10	no robin - not by current copyright laws	R							
55	n6	hehehe, that's an interesting idea, robin	RC							
63	n3	if you're going to release something to the public you have to make an effort to copyright it before hand. you cant do it as an afterthought.	R							
68	n6	I just type © on all my docs =)		R						
75	n7	but if you make it public then its not copyrighted		R						
66	n10	but copyright is automatic on creation in form mike		R						
73	n3	its not automatic, you gotta go to the office and get your patent pending. My grandpa was denied a patent because his device was already being put to use.			R					
78	n11	patent is different to copyright				R+				
84	n11	you need to register a patent and pay a fee				R+				
86	n11	and you patent the product				R				
88	n7	ok					RC			
89	n4	oh ok					RC			
79	n6	isn't a patent where you can protect an idea?					RI			
87	n10	patents are for design mainly						R		
90	n6	so I pay to patent my design, but can copyright the content for free?							RI	
92	n10	well said jack - exactly!!								RC

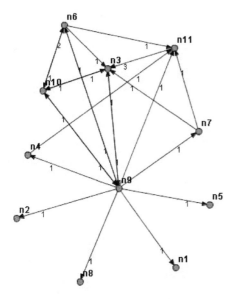

However, the level of connectivity of actor-nodes in a network to one another within an exchange could be examined in terms of *inclusiveness*. Inclusiveness is measured as the number of connected nodes, expressed as a proportion of the total number of nodes present in the network (Scott, 2000). Although inclusiveness is a parameter in measuring network density, the concept focuses on the presence or absence of ties between actor-nodes rather than the strength of ties among the nodes, as in the case of network density. Accordingly, application of inclusiveness necessitates the following theoretical assumption and data conditions:
  - ties/turns could be directed to all or specific actors in chat exchanges;
  - the presence of directed ties; and
  - the conversion of valued ties to binary ties.

Applying the concept of inclusiveness at the exchange level could therefore reveal instances when ties are present between certain actors, yet absent between other actors in the group. Such patterns in chat exchanges could indicate the extent to which actors are involved in tutorial discussions; and the exclusion and inclusion of certain participants from the dialogic process of knowledge construction. When ties are regarded as means for exchange of information, social and emotional support between participants, the presence or absence of such ties could also suggest the extent of learning support available to the participants in the group.

Actor-nodes are a finite set of participants belonging to two tutorial groups who function as distributors and/or recipients of information during tutorial discussions. Drawing from the concept of degree as the frequency of ties/turns sent (outdegree) or received (indegree) between actor-nodes, the extent of directional symmetry in the flow of information between actors during the collaborative learning process could be examined through the concept of *actor-node types*. Based on the overall tendencies

to send and/or receive ties, actors could be analyzed as four node types
(Wasserman & Faust, 1994) (Figure 4.19).
- *Isolate*: actor-node with no ties incident to or from it.
- *Transmitter*: actor-node with only ties originating from it.
- *Receiver*: actor-node with only ties terminating at it.
- *Carrier*: actor-node with ties incident to and from it.

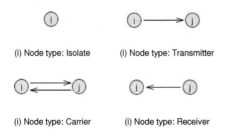

(i) Node type: Isolate   (i) Node type: Transmitter

(i) Node type: Carrier   (i) Node type: Receiver

Figure 4.19. Actor-node types: Isolate, Transmitter, Receiver, and Carrier

Hence, the proportion of actor-node types present at exchange or episode levels
could indicate the extent of symmetry and mutuality in information sharing during the
collaborative leaning process. Based on the concept of *reciprocity*, which refers to a
state whereby both actors in a dyad choose the other on a relation i.e. i <--> j
(Wasserman & Faust, 1994), reciprocation of choice at the group level could be
explored with a reciprocity index revealing the strength of tendency of the group
towards mutual exchange of information during the learning process.

Application of SNA to the *analysis* of chat exchanges coded with the ESA scheme
could further reveal the following aspects regarding engagement by participants with
each other's contributions and interaction during the collaborative group learning
process:
- *extent of engagement* by participants with each other's contributions as *degree*
  (outdegree, indegree) indicating directional flow of the information within the group.
  A finer analysis afforded by *actor-node types* and *group reciprocity* could show
  whether there was mutual sharing of information which is an essential aspect of the
  collaborative learning process.
- *opportunities for participation* as *inclusiveness* at exchange level indicating
  exclusion or inclusion of certain participants from the learning process, and extent
  of learning support available to the participants in the group.

Furthermore, application of SNA to the *visualization* of chat exchanges coded with
the ESA scheme could illustrate the following:
- *topic development* as turn networks with the presence of divergence in
  conversational threads suggesting greater depth of discussions, and
- *opportunities for participation* as actor networks with presence/absence of ties
  between actor-nodes in an exchange suggesting extent of involvement in the
  construction of learning conversations.

In addressing RQ1, *discourse analysis* was conducted using the ESA scheme for coding and analysis of the transcript dataset while *social network analysis* was applied to the coded turns/exchanges as an analytical method and visualization tool. The integrated application of the two approaches to the transcript dataset is summarized in a process model described below.

- *Process model for coding and analysis of transcript data*

Various models for coding and analysis of verbal or transcript data have been presented in the literature (Chi, 1997; Riffe et al., 1998; Sudweeks, 2004). Drawing from these sources, this study adopted a 5-stage model depicting an iterative process whereby research questions, assumptions, and constructs to be investigated inform the identification of the ESA scheme, development of coding categories, definitions and procedures (Figure 4.20).

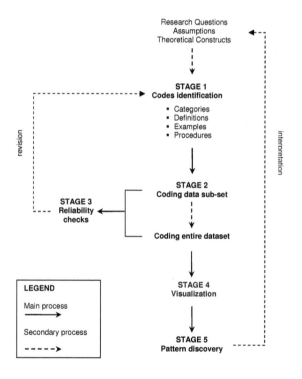

Figure 4.20. Process model for coding and analysis of transcript data

Preliminary application of the coding scheme to a data sub-set is followed by reliability checks on categories and procedures for ensuring that the coding instrument is able to measure the formulated constructs, leading to revisions of the scheme. The revised scheme is then re-applied to the entire transcript dataset after which an inter-rater reliability check is carried out. Coded data is transformed into matrices of actor or turn networks, displayed as figures or tables to facilitate interpretive analysis and pattern discovery using descriptive statistics and SNA measures. The results are then interpreted in light of the research questions and assumptions.

At this point, Stages 1, 2 and 4 had been described in sections 4.4.1 to 4.4.2 of this chapter. Findings from pattern discovery (Stage 5) and interpretations of the results from data analyses will be presented in Chapters 5 and 6 of this book. Issues on reliability and validity of the methods/instruments will be discussed in section 4.6.

Since transcript analysis would reflect primarily the analyst's interpretations of interactions, further insight could be gained from examining participant self-reports of learning experiences. The next section discusses the application of a web survey method for gathering student perceptions of learning experiences during chat tutorials.

4.4.3 Perception survey analysis
Conventional survey methods for examining social attitudes, behaviour, and group interactional processes include face-to-face interviews, telephone interviews, mail and fax surveys (Aaker, Kumar, & Day, 2004). The advent of web/CMC technologies led to new online survey methods such as e-mail and web surveys which are increasingly used to gather data in educational research (Cashion & Palmieri, 2002; Goh & Tobin, 1999; Mason & Weller, 2000; Rovai & Barnum, 2003).

This study uses a web survey method to address RQ2[47] which focuses on how student participants perceive their experiences of chat tutorial interaction in terms of participation opportunities, adequacy of learning support, and quality of learning experience and collaborative work process. This section justifies the choice of the web survey method, describes the survey development process, and highlights features in online questionnaire design for reducing survey error.

- *Web survey method: Definition, assumptions and justification*
The *web survey method* involves mainly the use of the Internet for the administration and return of surveys. A self-administered questionnaire is posted on a web site and respondents enter their answers directly into the online form. The completed questionnaire is submitted electronically to a host server usually with the performance of a single action such as when the respondents click on a SUBMIT button. Data from survey returns are subsequently downloaded to databases, data analysis packages, or spreadsheets (Gunn, 2002). In some cases, the survey results could even be viewed instantaneously by researchers as soon as each form is submitted, hence facilitating the monitoring of survey progress.

Adopting a survey approach for obtaining information on perceptions, attitudes, and behaviour entails the following assumptions:

- Respondents selected … are available and willing to cooperate.
- Respondents understand the questions.
- Respondents have the knowledge, opinions, attitudes, or facts required.
- Respondents are willing and able to respond.
(Aaker et al., 2004, p.227)

---

[47] RQ2 was stated in Chapter 1. The constructs and measures in RQ2 are discussed in section 4.6.

Furthermore, this study assumes that student respondents are capable of describing "their feelings (such as satisfaction), their behaviors ... their opinions" (Chun, 2002, p.21) or learning gains over time.

Besides surveys, it could be argued that methods such as tests yield scores/grades that most directly reflect the extent of student learning. However, Rovai and Barnum (2003) noted that such data may not be very informative for the following reasons:
- grades may not reflect what is learnt since marks awarded could be for other factors such as attendance; and
- evaluation in the constructivist framework is subjective hence "different teachers and even the same teacher over time are unlikely to assign grades consistently" (p.61).

Therefore, the *survey* method could be considered more appropriate than tests for eliciting data on experiences, attitudes, and behaviour during chat tutorials.

Self-report data on student experiences could be gathered from survey methods such as face-to-face interviews and focus group discussions (Wall, 2001), postal and online (e-mail/web) surveys. The choice of the *web survey* method is justified given the following main factors and constraints present in this study:
- *Respondent characteristics.* Since the participants comprised External students who undergo the OI unit on a distance learning mode[48], web surveys are appropriate when "the desired respondents are geographically diverse or hard to find" (Fricker Jr. & Rand, 2002, p.363). Moreover, as School of Information Technology undergraduates at Murdoch University, respondents have ready access to the Internet, computing facilities and are likely to be IT literate. Additionally, as third-year undergraduates, they would have participated in a number of university-wide, unit feedback web surveys conducted by the university's Teaching and Learning Centre (TLC) which are similar in format and style to the survey used in this study.

- *Timeliness.* Comparative studies on time needed to field online (e-mail/web) and postal surveys had mostly concluded that a faster turnaround time could be achieved with online surveys (Kiesler & Sproull, 1986; Schleyer & Forrest, 2000; Tse, 1998). Fricker Jr. and Rand (2002) argued that although CMC/web technologies enable rapid delivery and return of surveys, online survey methods offer overall timeliness only when additional time is not required at other stages of the survey process. However, Fricker Jr. and Rand (2002) acknowledged that overall timeliness may be possible when a closed IT literate population with ready Internet access is surveyed using "an all-electronic process" (p.357).

This study faces time constraints in terms of participant availability only within the semester period; the need to capture accounts of recent experiences as soon as possible to reduce the vulnerability of responses to events external to the study (Aaker et al., 2004); and the limited timeframe for the research project. Hence, face-to-face and postal methods that require more time in all survey stages were deemed unsuitable. Given that respondents are IT literate, with ready Internet access, timeliness was possible with a mainly electronic survey process involving the use of multiple channels of communication, at various stages of the survey, to facilitate contact with participants and survey administration (Table 4.19).

---

[48] Refer to Chapter 3 for a description of the participants in the case study.

Table 4.19. Means of communication in survey stages

Survey Stages	Communication means for survey information dissemination				
	Web	Bulletin Board	E-mail	Face-to-face lecture	Audio lecture
Solicitation of respondents	✓	✓		✓	✓
Obtaining informed consent			✓		
Announcement of survey	✓	✓	✓		
Survey administration and returns	✓				
Follow-up to survey nonresponses			✓		

- *Convenience.* Although both e-mail and web survey methods appear equally feasible given respondent characteristics and time constraints, e-mail surveys require more effort by respondents to download attachments or enter responses by re-editing original messages before returning the completed surveys via e-mail. These additional steps were found to impact on response rate when respondents did not know how to re-edit the original message (Schleyer & Forrest, 2000), or when the survey format was distorted in the e-mail edit mode (Tse, 1998). In contrast, the web survey method offers greater convenience and simplicity of steps with direct entry of responses into a web form.

- *Cost.* The cost of a survey is generally computed based on factors such as "professional time required to design the questionnaire, the questionnaire length, the geographical dispersion of the sample" (Aaker et al., 2004, p.236), and whether incentives are offered to respondents. Online survey methods usually involve expenditure related to the acquisition of software for electronic questionnaire design, administration, and analysis. Additionally, there may be other costs associated with obtaining programming, hosting, and technical help desk services. Schleyer and Forrest (2000) cautioned that cost comparisons between different survey methods tended to be complicated by the absence of cost reporting in studies and different definitions of survey cost.

In this study, the web survey process incurred monetary costs to the researcher mainly as service fees to the Teaching and Learning Centre (TLC) for use of *Remark Web Survey®* (Principia Products, 2005) software, technical assistance for survey administration and hosting, and participation incentives (Table 4.20). Moreover, it is acknowledged that respondents had to bear the online connection fees for accessing and returning the web questionnaire. Given a small sample size (below 25 participants) and the total fee incurred (A$604.44), the cost of the web survey may not necessarily be lower than conventional surveys. While cost is one factor, the final decision on the web survey method was based on an overall consideration of the factors and constraints in this study.

Table 4.20. Monetary cost factors in web survey

Monetary factors	Details	Amount
- Programming and administration fees to the Teaching and Learning Centre (TLC)	Survey services provided by TLC include access to staff, programming, testing, hosting, data storage and related technical support services.	A$300
- Participation incentive	3 shopping vouchers to randomly selected participants.	A$300
- Pre-testing with 6 participants	Printing and stationery.	A$4.44
	Total	A$604.44

With the choice of the web survey method, further decisions on question formulation, self-administered questionnaire format, and procedures for survey testing and administration are discussed below.

- *Web survey development process*
This study utilizes a 7-stage survey development process model (Figure 4.21) reflecting an iterative process whereby the research questions, assumptions and constructs to be investigated in the study determine the relevant information to be gathered from the respondents which then inform the construction of questions, the questionnaire layout, and choice of measurement scales. Pre-testing is conducted to identify areas of deficiencies leading to refinement of the original questions and re-organization of the questionnaire before actual survey administration. The quantitative and qualitative data obtained are coded, analyzed, and interpreted in light of the research question and assumptions. The significant issues in the development process are discussed below.

Stage 1. Question formulation
The specific information necessary to address RQ2 were defined as constructs and operationalized as survey questions which are provided in Appendix B.3. *Open-ended* and *closed* questions (Figure 4.22) were used to reduce methodological weaknesses inherent in the use of only one question type, capture self-reported information at varying depths and enable variations in "the amount of direction" (Payne, 1951/2004, p.142) in answering questions. Such varying opportunities for self-expression and qualification may serve to enhance both relevance of the survey and respondent interest.

Open-ended questions serve to obtain elaborations to responses in earlier questions and gather responses that could not be foreseen. Such verbatim responses constitute 'rich' descriptions that add to the credibility of the findings by qualitative research standards (Denzin & Lincoln, 2000). In closed questions, the *nominal* measurement scale with dichotomous categories (Figure 4.23) was used to obtain demographic information while *ordinal* scales with itemized categories (Figure 4.24a) and ranking order (Figure 4.24b) enable respondent expression of judgment on behaviours observed and self-report of own experiences/behaviours during chat tutorials.

Kahn and Cannell (1957/2004) held that establishing *common frames of reference* could reduce ambiguity in question interpretation and enhance perception of question relevance in the context of respondents' own experiences. This was achieved by explicitly incorporating references to the chat tutorial context in the question statements (Figure 4.25) so that "the respondent is instructed, as part of the question, with respect to the frame of reference which he is to employ" (Kahn & Cannell, 1957/2004, pp.66-67).

As verbal clarification by the researcher would not be possible for self-administered questionnaires, *clarity of language and expression* had to be ensured. Terms used such as *CMC, chat, ICQ, presenter, participant*, and *online tutorials* were not considered unfamiliar since these expressions were present in course readings and tutorial discussions. Since only the respondents could adequately judge the clarity of questions, pre-testing (Stage 3) was necessary.

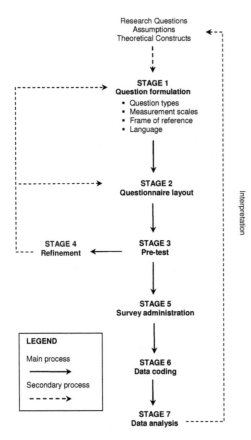

Figure 4.21. Process of web survey development

Open-ended question

7. Were there other factors that discouraged or inhibited you from contributing during tutoria
Please describe them below.

8. To what extent are the following factors important to you for online tutorials in this unit?

	Very important	Important
a. Opportunity to participate in discussions	○	○
b. Discussions are relevant to the unit readings	○	○

Closed question

Figure 4.22. Closed and open-ended web survey questions

12. Gender

○ Male
○ Female

Figure 4.23. Nominal measurement scale with dichotomous categories (Q.12)

3. How much help was available from your tutor and other students during online tutorials? Indicate your responses to the following statements from Strongly Agree to Strongly Disagree

	Strongly agree	Agree	Disagree	Strongly disagree
a. The tutor clarified issues on content that were raised during the discussion	○	○	○	○
b. The other students clarified issues on content that were raised during the discussion	○	○	○	○

Figure 4.24a. Ordinal scales with itemized categories (Q.3)

10. Rank the following factors on online tutorials in order of importance. For each factor, enter yo
from -

Most Important 5---4---3---2---1 Least Important.

(No ties allowed)

a. Opportunity to participate in discussions ☐

b. Discussions are relevant to the unit readings ☐

c. Communication skills in CMC environments are developed ☐

d. Understanding of course content is increased ☐

e. My online learning experience is enhanced with chat tutorials ☐

Figure 4.24b. Ordinal scales with ranking order (Q.10)

Frames of reference for concept of
participant and context of *online tutorials*

2. When you were not a presenter, as a participant during tutorial sessions for this unit, to what extent
following aspects of the online discussion easy for you? Indicate your responses to the following stater
Strongly Agree to Strongly Disagree

As a participant, I found it easy to

	Strongly agree	Agree	Disag
a. keep up with the speed of the discussion	O	O	O
b. contribute actively to the discussion	O	O	O

Figure 4.25. Frame of reference in web survey question

Stage 2. Questionnaire layout

A two-part self-administered, non-anonymous web questionnaire, with 17 questions
and a total of 55 discrete answers, was developed and presented as a single web
page. Part A of the questionnaire contains 11 focused questions that directly address
the issues in RQ2 while Part B contains 6 general questions that capture
demographic information with the final question dealing with participants' overall
experience with chat tutorials (Table 4.21).

Table 4.21. Organization of questions in web survey

Part A			Part B		
Question	Sub-questions		Question	Sub-questions	
1	a-f	6	12	-	1
2	a-d	4	13	-	1
3	a-b	2	14	-	1
4	a-d	4	15	-	1
5	a-i + probe	10	16	-	6*
6	-	1	17	-	1
7	-	1			
8	a-e	5			
9	a-e	5			
10	a-e	5			
11	-	1			
	Total	44		Total	11

*Note: Multiple selection of 6 options provided for this question.

Stages 3 & 4. Pre-test and refinement

The time needed for programming and hosting arrangements with TLC dictated that
pre-testing had to be conducted in two phases: *preliminary testing* via a draft print
version of the questionnaire (Appendix B.4) and *final testing* of the web survey
questionnaire. Preliminary testing was conducted from June 2005 to August 2005
with 4 students and 2 tutors from previous semesters who provided different
perspectives on experiences with the OI unit. Print versions of the questionnaire were
posted to trial respondents and five returns were obtained by August 2005. Final
testing of the web questionnaire was conducted in September 2005 mainly to assess
its usability before release.

Preliminary testing enabled evaluation of question clarity, layout of questionnaire, and overall *construct validity* of the questionnaire. Feedback from this phase led to the following refinements:
- rephrasing of questions for greater clarity and to avoid negative reporting of self-behaviour;
- re-ordering of questions to improve the logical flow of topics;
- removal of a question as the information could be obtained from the transcripts; and
- inclusion of several additional questions.

Stage 5. Survey administration
This stage comprised three main phases: survey announcement, administration, and follow-up on nonresponses. Information on survey commencement was disseminated via e-mail and bulletin board announcements in the OI unit website. Both e-mail and bulletin board messages provided similar details on the survey purpose, estimated time needed to complete it, URL of the web survey, participant confidentiality, and contact information of the researcher and supervisor. To encourage returns, there was mention of a token of appreciation (shopping vouchers) to randomly selected individuals for participating in the entire study (Appendix B.5).

The web survey was administered from 24 October 2005 to 7 November 2005 to both tutorial groups. While response rate was between 50% and 78% in the first week (Table 4.22), follow-up e-mail reminders resulted in a final response rate of 93% and 89% for Groups 1 and 4 respectively.

Table 4.22. Response rate of web survey

Event	Dates	Response rate			
		Group	No.		Missing
Survey release	24 October 2005	1	7 out of 14*	50%	7
		4	7 out of 9	78%	2
1st follow-up e-mail	28 October 2005	1	10 out of 14*	71%	4
		4	7 out of 9	78%	2
2nd follow-up e-mail	4 November 2005	1	13 out of 14*	93%	1
		4	8 out of 9	89%	1

*One G1 participant withdrew from the unit on 15 October 2005

Stages 6 & 7. Data coding and analysis
At the close of the survey, the returns were obtained from TLC in the form of an EXCEL file and checked for completeness and accuracy. *Completeness* pertains to whether a response is present for each question that should be answered. *Accuracy* refers to whether answers are "logically correct and acceptable" (Aaker et al., 2004, p.263) given the possibility that respondents may deliberately provide false information to mislead. The returns from both groups were found to be largely complete. While there were no patently nonsensical responses found, there were multiple returns by a respondent, in which case, only the last return was included in the dataset.

Given a nonprobabilistic sample, data from closed questions are subjected to descriptive statistical analysis while responses to open-ended questions are post-coded using categories that emerged from content analysis of the responses. The treatment of survey data is discussed further in section 4.5.

- *Design features in online questionnaire*
This section highlights the following main design features adopted in the web questionnaire and discusses the issues concerned with their utilization: choice of multiple-question web form layout, extent of input data validation, and implications of an *Unable to Judge* (UJ) option for closed questions.

Multiple-question and single-question sequential screen layouts for web surveys present both advantages and limitations. While the one-question-per-screen design reduces transmission time and the possibility of respondents getting 'lost', Schleyer and Forrest (2000) found the need to increase session time-out periods for survey completion. Couper, Traugott, and Lamias (2001) found that the multiple-question layout, where all questions are presented in a single web page, produced greater efficiency gains in terms of item completion time, download time, and time need for respondent orientation to questions. The choice of a *multiple-question layout* in this study is justified on the basis of simplicity of steps for survey completion, efficiency in respondent orientation to questions, and reduced online connection time as connection fees would be borne by participants who access the survey from home. With this layout, progress in survey completion would be indicated by the vertical scroll bar and question number which could minimize respondent confusion (Figure 4.26). In conjunction with the use of only one skip question at the end of the survey, the multiple-question layout could reduce respondent frustration and likelihood of survey abandonment.

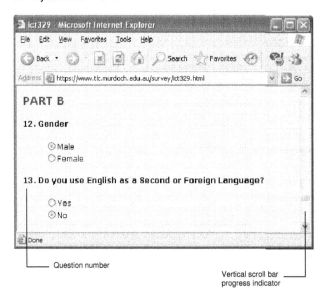

Figure 4.26. Progress indicators: vertical scroll bar and question numbers

Web surveys offer the advantage of automated *input data validation* for compelling respondents to answer every question (Fricker Jr. & Rand, 2002) that could enhance survey completion. However, this feature was found to be too restrictive when there are legitimate reasons for not answering and/or not knowing the answers to questions posed (Schleyer & Forrest, 2000). Dillman, Tortora, and Bowker (1998) cautioned that besides contributing to respondent frustration, this feature presents an ethical problem particularly when respondents have been assured of voluntary participation. In this study, input validation is limited to student name and ID data fields (Figure 4.27) for tracking return rates and associating self-reports of behaviour during tutorial discussions with observed participation patterns in the transcript data. To avoid measurement error manifested as answers reflecting social desirability bias, confidentiality of identity and information were explicitly stated at the start of the survey.

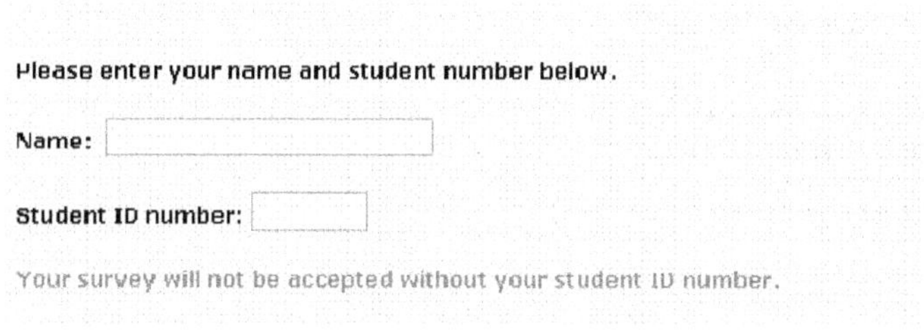

Please enter your name and student number below.

Name:

Student ID number:

Your survey will not be accepted without your student ID number.

Figure 4.27. Compulsory student name and ID fields in survey

Generally, noncommittal response options such as *Don't Know, No Answer,* and *Unable to Judge* (UJ) are included in survey questions to reduce respondent frustration and avoid "unrealistic assumptions about the expertness of a respondent or about the amount of information he possesses" (Kahn & Cannell, 1957/2004, p.71). However, the UJ option could contribute to *errors of central tendency* defined as "the tendency to avoid either extreme" (Ary, Jacobs, & Razavieh, 2002, p.232) manifested as the consistent selection of neutral/mid points in rating scales that were attributed to a number of causes: reduced motivation as a form of satisficing behaviour (Krosnick & Alwin, 1987); the establishment of a comfortable pattern of responding reinforced by unvarying response format (Herzog & Bachman, 1981) and confidentiality concerns (Aaker et al., 2004).

In this study, most closed questions in Part A provided a 4-point Likert-type attitudinal scale (*Strongly Agree-Strongly Disagree, Very Important-Not Important*) with an *Unable to Judge* (UJ) option offered only in Q.5 in a 5-point scale (Figure 4.28). This sparing use of the noncommittal option is based on the assumption that statements on interactional behaviour in the question accurately reflect the activities during chat tutorials. Feedback from the pre-test stage of the survey development process confirmed relevance of the statements to the actual experiences of respondents, and the expectation that the UJ option would be necessary for Q.5f and Q.5g which ask for answers pertaining to observed behaviour of *other* participants during discussions.

5. To what extent do the following statements accurately reflect your overall experience of online tutorials in this unit? Indicate your responses to the following statements from Strongly Agree to Strongly Disagree or Unable to Judge (UJ).

	Strongly agree	Agree	Disagree	Strongly disagree	Unable to judge
a. I had plenty of opportunities to participate in the discussion	○	○	○	○	○
b. I was able to make best use of the opportunities available for participation	○	○	○	○	○
c. I usually prefer to let the discussion develop before joining in	○	○	○	○	○
d. During discussions, I contributed my views even when I saw that others had already posted similar ideas	○	○	○	○	○
e. I usually contribute more to the discussion than the others	○	○	○	○	○
f. Everyone in the tutorial group contributed about the same amount to the discussion	○	○	○	○	○
g. The other students contributed different ideas to the discussion	○	○	○	○	○
h. I learned from other students' contributions during the discussion	○	○	○	○	○
i. I helped other students learn through my contributions during the discussion	○	○	○	○	○

Figure 4.28. *Unable to Judge* (UJ) option in Q.5

Later analysis of responses to Q.5 (reported in Chapter 5) revealed an interesting methodological aspect in the design of response formats. While selection patterns for Q.5f and Q.5g validated the design assumption that respondents may not have sufficient information/knowledge to provide an accurate answer pertaining to observed behaviour of other participants, the UJ option was used by some respondents in answering Q.5e to indicate an inability to provide an accurate report of *own* behaviour during tutorial discussions. Respondent explanations for selecting the UJ option indicated that factors associated with the synchronous CMC medium, namely, the lack of non-verbal cues in a text-based environment and rapid pace of discussion could have affected their ability to evaluate own behaviour during online interactions.

In summary, given that RQ2 broadly aims to explore the perceptions of student participants on the impact of chat interaction in supporting collaborative learning and group work processes, perception survey data gathered with the web survey method could reveal the following:
- *opportunities for participation* as self-reports on presence and exercise of perceived participation opportunities during chat tutorial discussions that could be further associated with factors identified by respondents to have both motivated and inhibited participation.
- *adequacy of learning support* as the extent of help perceived to be available from the tutor and peers on clarifying content issues during tutorial discussions.
- *quality of learning experience and collaborative work process* as the extent to which respondent expectations of online tutorial factors were satisfied by their experiences which could present certain implications for chat activity design.

Integration of survey findings from participant self-reports with the analyst's interpretations of interactions from the transcript dataset could enable the representation of various perspectives, leading to a more holistic understanding of the impact of chat interaction on the learning processing, and enhancing validity of the study through both method and data triangulation. The methodological treatment of the transcript and survey datasets for analysis is described in the next section.

4.5 Data Processing
This section explains the common pre-processing procedures for the transcript and survey datasets, and describes the treatment of survey data for descriptive statistical analysis and interpretive content analysis. The procedures in transcript data segmentation as units of analysis, construction of exchanges, and representations of actor/turn networks are described.

4.5.1 Data pre-processing for transcript and survey datasets
To maintain confidentiality of participant identity, which is part of the ethical considerations[49] in this study, actual names of participants from Groups 1 and 4 (G1, G4) were replaced with *pseudonyms* or *actor-node labels* (Table 4.23). However, the actual names of the researcher and Dr. Fay Sudweeks (G4 tutor /unit coordinator) were retained and the latter had waived privacy rights in the context of this project. Particular care was taken to ensure that actual names that appear in chat message headers, within messages, and responses to open-ended survey questions were replaced by respective pseudonyms.

Table 4.23. Groups 1 and 4 participants: Pseudonyms and actor-node labels

Group 1 Participants		Group 4 Participants	
n1.	Derek	n1.	Evan
n2.	Max	n2.	Bill
n3.	Alvin	n3.	Mike
n4.	Cliff	n4.	Eric
n5.	Colin	n5.	Karl
n6.	Ted[50]	n6.	Jack
n7.	Sam	n7.	Ian
n8.	Diane	n8.	Pete
n9.	James	n9.	Robin
n10	Alan	n10	Lim (Researcher)
n11.	Jason	n11.	Fay (Tutor)
n12.	Scott		
n13.	Barry		
n14.	Tony		
n15.	Wendy		
n16.	Rachel (Tutor)		

Further cleaning of the raw transcripts involved removing all system generated messages which provided time/date stamps of tutorial sessions and participant login/logout activities. *Private* chat[51] messages, when reflected in the transcript, were also removed. However, emoticons and other orthographic forms present in the messages were retained. Errors in spelling, grammar, and/or expression present in both datasets were retained. For a more accurate word[52] count with an EXCEL formula that distinguishes words using a space criterion, spaces were manually inserted or removed between words.

---

[49] Refer to discussion on ethical considerations in this chapter, section 4.3.
[50] Ted withdrew from the unit on 15 October 2005.
[51] The WebCT™ chat application supports *private chat* whereby a participant could send messages to designated receiver(s) in the chat room. These messages are hidden from the onscreen view of non-designated receivers and usually do not appear in the transcripts.
[52] In chat discourse, the definition of *word* includes emoticons and emotags.

4.5.2 Treatment of survey data

The web survey questionnaire was created with the *Remark Web Survey®* (Principia Products, 2005) software which also supports data retrieval and processing[53]. In this study, survey returns from both tutorial groups were downloaded into EXCEL (.xls) file format with worksheets showing all data in both numerical and text formats (Figure 4.29). In both formats, the data was displayed according to respondent and question number. Responses to closed questions were pre-coded by the survey software; hence minimal data processing was necessary for application of descriptive statistical analysis. Data from open-ended questions are post-coded using categories that emerged from interpretive content analysis of the responses. The *units of analysis* for the survey data are the tutorial group and individual participants. The complete survey dataset comprised 13 returns from G1 (93%) and 8 returns from G4 (89%).

4.5.3 Treatment of transcript data

The complete transcript dataset from G1 and G4 comprised 22 sessions or 44 episodes i.e., 11 sessions for each group with two episodes in each session (Table 4.24). Processing of the 'cleaned' transcript data involved three main phases: data segmentation, exchange and network construction which are described below.

Table 4.24. Transcript dataset by week, date, session and episode

Week	Date	Session	Episode	
1	25 July 2005	---	---	---
2	1 August 2005	1	1	2
3	8 August 2005	2	1	2
4	15 August 2005	3	1	2
5	29 August 2005	4	1	2
6	5 September 2005	5	1	2
7	12 September 2005	6	1	2
8	19 September 2005	7	1	2
9	26 September 2005	8	1	2
10	10 October 2005	9	1	2
11	17 October 2005	10	1	2
12	24 October 2005	11	1	2
13	31 October 2005	---	---	---

---

[53] More product details are available at http://www.principiaproducts.com.

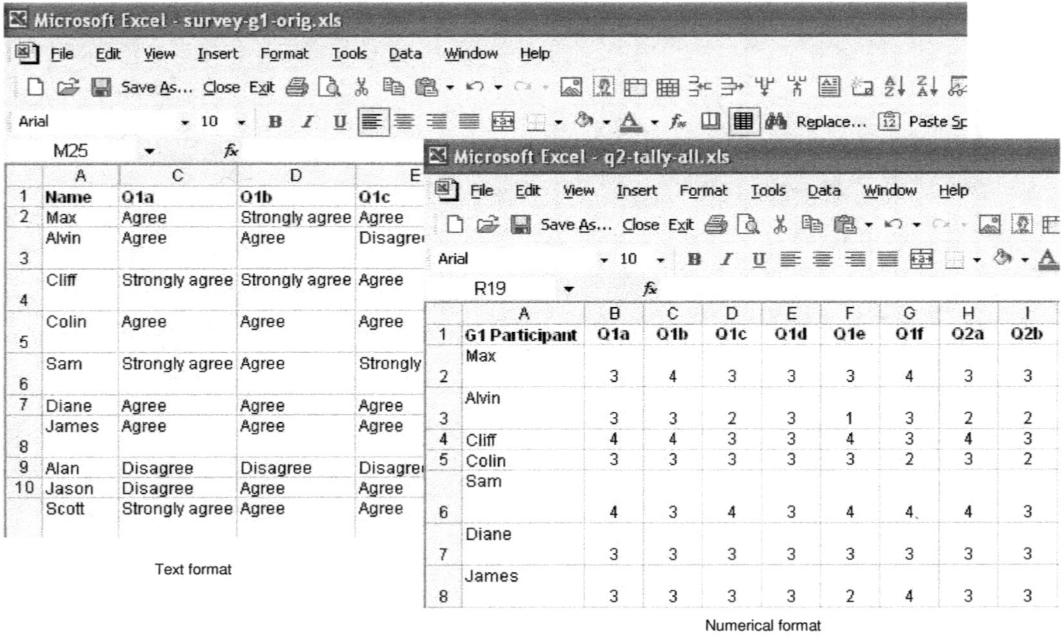

Microsoft Excel - survey-g1-orig.xls

File Edit View Insert Format Tools Data Window Help

Save As... Close Exit   B I U

Arial   ▾ 10 ▾   M25

	A	B	C	D	E
	Name	Q1a	Q1b	Q1c	
1	Max	Agree	Strongly agree	Agree	
2	Alvin	Agree	Agree	Disagree	
3	Cliff	Strongly agree	Strongly agree	Agree	
4	Colin	Agree	Agree	Agree	
5	Sam	Strongly agree	Agree	Strongly	
6	Diane	Agree	Agree	Agree	
7	James	Agree	Agree	Agree	
8	Alan	Disagree	Disagree	Disagree	
9	Jason	Disagree	Agree	Agree	
10	Scott	Strongly agree	Agree	Agree	

Text format

Microsoft Excel - q2-tally-all.xls

File Edit View Insert Format Tools Data Window Help

Save As... Close Exit   B I U   Replace.... Paste Sp

Arial   ▾ 10 ▾   R19

	A	B	C	D	E	F	G	H	I
	G1 Participant	Q1a	Q1b	Q1c	Q1d	Q1e	Q1f	Q2a	Q2b
1	Max	3	3	3	3	3	4	4	3
2	Alvin	3	4	3	3	3	3	3	3
3	Cliff	4	4	3	3	1	3	2	3
4	Colin	3	3	3	4	3	3	4	3
5	Sam	3	3	3	3	3	2	2	2
6		4	3	3	4	4	4	4	3
7	Diane	3	3	3	3	3	3	3	3
8	James	3	3	3	3	3	2	4	3

Numerical format

Figure 4.29. Survey returns from *Remark Web Survey*® Text and numerical formats

▪ *Transcript data segmentation: Units of analysis and reference normalization*
The virtual classroom interaction model[54] which frames interaction at the virtual classroom level as sessions, episodes and social spaces forms the conceptual basis for transcript data segmentation. The *units of analysis* for the transcript are conceptualized as a nested framework comprising sampling, context, and recording units (Shoemaker, 1996) (Figure 4.30). Interpretation of findings from the transcript dataset was carried out at group and individual levels[55].

- The *sampling unit* refers to the document that is selected for study i.e., the transcript of the *session* which formed the empirical basis for examining issues in RQ1.
- The *context unit* forms the portion of the text to be analyzed and delimits the scope of analysis within the data. Hence, it refers to the *episode* which is the context in which the recording unit is interpreted i.e., interpretations of meaning and pragmatic intention of turns/exchanges were made within the context of the episode where they were located.
- The *recording unit* forms what is actually measured within the context unit. Therefore, it refers to the elements coded or measured in an episode, which were the *turns* and *exchanges*.

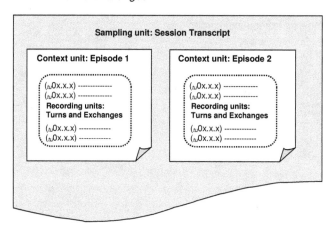

Figure 4.30. Transcript data: units of analysis (adapted from Shoemaker, 1996)

To maintain a *chain of evidence* (Yin, 1994), *standard referencing systems* were developed for turns and exchanges to indicate the origin(s) of the data. Reflecting the hierarchical structure of the units of analysis described earlier, the labelling system conveyed the following main information about the source of the recording units: group, session, episode, and item number of the turn or exchange (Figure 4.31). In network analysis, turns as nodes are identified by turn labels while actor nodes are identified by their assigned actor-node labels i.e., *n1*, *n2* (Table 4.23).

Figure 4.31a. Turn labels

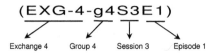

Figure 4.31b. Exchange labels

- *Chat exchange construction*

An overview of the data formatting process leading to exchange and network construction is provided in Figure 4.32. Turns derived from data segmentation (Figure 4.33) were exported to EXCEL spreadsheets that were organized by episode and each turn was numbered in sequential order.

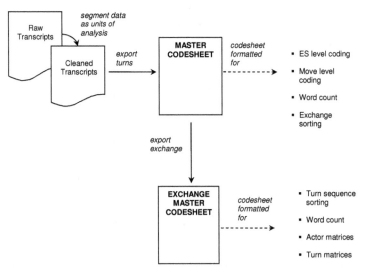

Figure 4.32. Transcript data formatting process

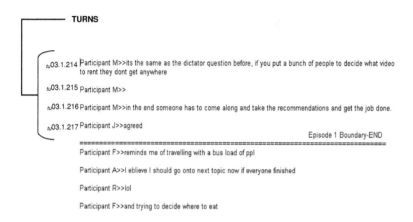

TURNS

$_{tu}$03.1.214 Participant M>>its the same as the dictator question before, if you put a bunch of people to decide what video to rent they dont get anywhere

$_{tu}$03.1.215 Participant M>>

$_{tu}$03.1.216 Participant M>>in the end someone has to come along and take the recommendations and get the job done.

$_{tu}$03.1.217 Participant J>>agreed

                                                                                    Episode 1 Boundary-END
==
Participant F>>reminds me of travelling with a bus load of ppl

Participant A>>I eblieve I should go onto next topic now if everyone finished

Participant R>>lol

Participant F>>and trying to decide where to eat

Figure 4.33. Turns in episode

Master codesheets for each episode (Figure 4.34) were therefore created as spreadsheets for coding turns in each episode according to the ESA scheme, sorting coded turns into exchanges and applying descriptive statistical analysis (Figure 4.35).

Since turns in the master codesheet were numbered sequentially and chat discourse is characterized by decoupled turns, coded turns were extracted from the master codesheet, further sorted into exchanges (Figure 4.36) and exported to EXCEL spreadsheets that were organized by episode. The constructed exchanges in each episode were labelled and their constituent turns retained their original item numbers. *Exchange master codesheets* for each episode (Figure 4.37) were therefore created from which adjacency matrices were constructed for network analysis and visualization as well as for the application of descriptive statistical analysis.

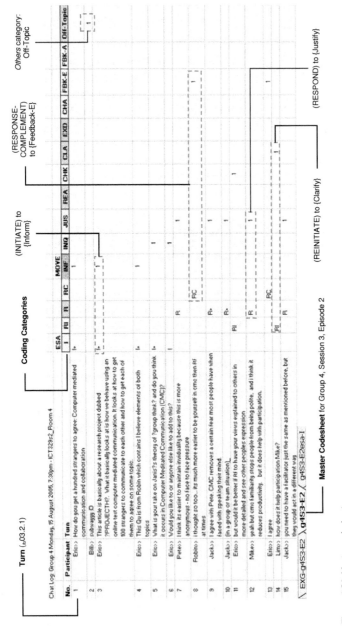

Figure 4.34. Master codesheet

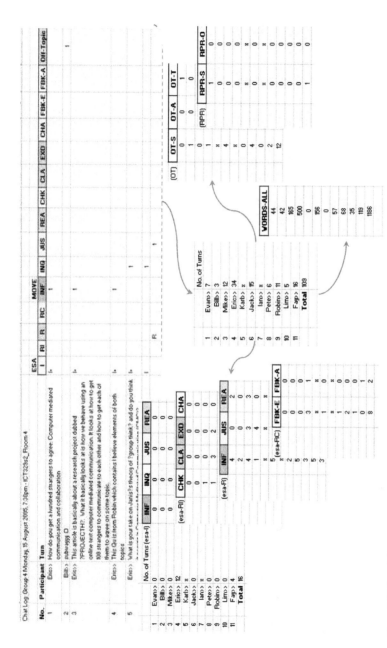

Figure 4.35. Descriptive statistics from Master codesheet

Master Codesheet

No.	Participant	Turn
1	Eric>>	How do you get a hundred strangers to agree: Computer mediated communication and collaboration
2	Bill>>	subwayyg :D
3	Eric>>	This article is basically about a research project dubbed ?PROJECTH?. What it basically looks at is how we behave using an online text computer mediated communication. It looks at how to get 100 strangers to communicate to each other and how to get each of them to agree on some topic.
4	Eric>>	This Qu is from Robin which contains I believe elements of both topics
5	Eric>>	What is your take on Janis?'s theory of ?group think? and do you think it occurs in Computer Mediated Communication (CMC)?
6	Eric>>	Would you like to or anyone else like to add to this?
7	Pete>>	I think its easier to maintain inviduality because this is more anonymous - no face to face pressure
8	Robin>>	i thought so too... its much more easier to be yourself in cmc then f/f at times
9	Jack>>	I agree with Pete. CMC removes a certain fear most people have when faced with speaking their mind.
10	Jack>>	(in a group or team situation)_
11	Eric>>	but would it be better if f/f to have your views explained to others in more detailed and see other peoples expression
12	Mike>>	yeah but cmc familiarity stops people from being polite, and i think it reduces productivity. but it does help with participation.
13	Eric>>	I agree
14	Lim>>	how does it help participation Mike?
15	Jack>>	you need to have a facilitator just the same as mentioned before, but they would act in a different way
16	Mike>>	if we were in a room right now sitting behind desks, we wouldnt be talking like we are now.

Exchange Master Codesheet

No.	Participant	Turn	Exchanges
1	Eric>>	How do you get a hundred strangers to agree: Computer mediated communication and collaboration	EXG-1-g4S3-E2
3	Eric>>	This article is basically about a research project dubbed ?PROJECTH?. What it basically looks at is how we behave using an online text computer mediated communication. It looks at how to get 100 strangers to communicate to each other and how to get each of them to agree on some topic.	
4	Eric>>	This Qu is from Robin which contains I believe elements of both topics	
5	Eric>>	What is your take on Janis?'s theory of ?group think? and do you think it occurs in Computer Mediated Communication (CMC)?	
6	Eric>>	Would you like to or anyone else like to add to this?	
7	Pete>>	I think its easier to maintain inviduality because this is more anonymous - no face to face pressure	
8	Robin>>	i thought so too... its much more easier to be yourself in cmc then f/f at times	
9	Jack>>	I agree with Pete. CMC removes a certain fear most people have when faced with speaking their mind.	
10	Jack>>	(in a group or team situation)_	
15	Jack>>	you need to have a facilitator just the same as mentioned before, but they would act in a different way	
12	Mike>>	yeah but cmc familiarity stops people from being polite, and i think it reduces productivity. but it does help with participation.	
13	Eric>>	I agree	
14	Lim>>	how does it help participation Mike?	
16	Mike>>	if we were in a room right now sitting behind desks, we wouldnt be talking like we are now.	

Figure 4.36. Sorting turns into an exchange

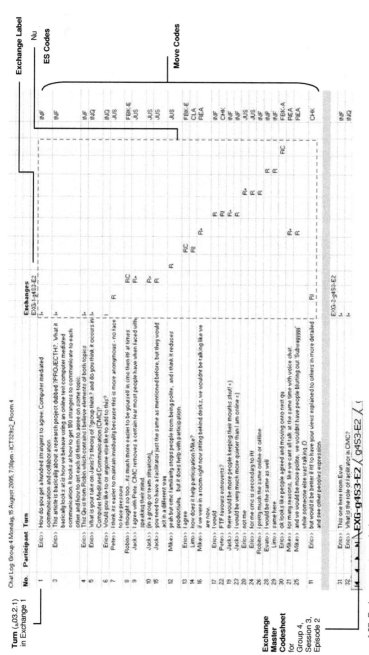

Figure 4.37. Exchange master codesheet

- *Network construction*

From chat exchanges, adjacency matrices of actor and turn networks were built. Turns in exchanges were transformed into directed and valued relational ties in adjacency matrices representing *actor networks*, with nodes as participants, (Figure 4.38) for analyses of degree, inclusiveness, actor-node types, and reciprocity[56] at levels of exchange and episode, and visualization as sociograms. In some instances, application of SNA measures required data reduction as the conversion of valued ties to dichotomous ties which were handled by NetMiner II.

From chat exchanges, turns were also transformed into directed relational ties in adjacency matrices representing *turn networks*, with nodes as turns, (Figure 4.39) mainly for the visualization of exchange conversational threads. Figure 4.40 shows the visualizations of actor and turn networks as sociograms.

Following the data treatment processes described in this section, analyses of transcript and survey datasets were conducted to address issues raised in the research questions of this study regarding the impact of chat interaction on the collaborative-constructivist learning process, and to specifically examine
- the discourse of task-oriented chat interactions for indications of active participation and knowledge construction; and
- the perceptions of student participants on the impact of chat interactions in supporting collaborative learning and group work processes.

The next section discusses the validity issues associated with the use of discourse and network analytical methods, and the web survey instrument. The constructs and measures specific to each research question which guided data analysis are also defined.

---

[56] Refer to this chapter, section 4.4.2 for a discussion on these SNA concepts.

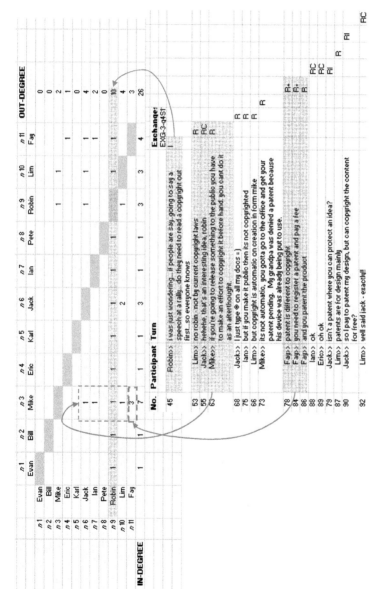

Figure 4.38. Chat exchange: Actor network adjacency matrix

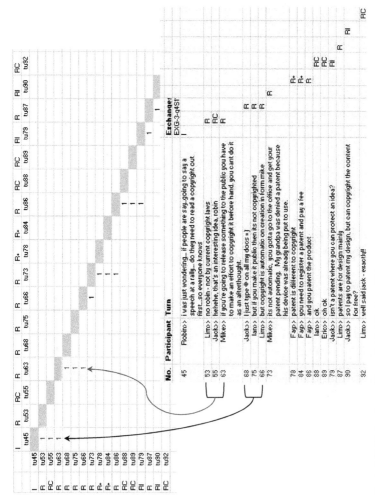

No.	Participant	Turn	Exchange: EXG-3-q4ST
45	Robin»	I was just wondering... if people are say..going to say a speech at a rally... do they need to read a copyright out first...so everyone knows	
53	Lim»	no robin - not by current copyright laws	R
55	Jack»	hehehe, that's an interesting idea, robin	RC
63	Mike»	if you're going to release something to the public you have to make an effort to copyright it before hand, you cant do it as an afterthought.	R
68	Jack»	just type © on all my docs =)	R
75	Ian»	but if you make it public then its not copyrighted	R
66	Lim»	but copyright is automatic on creation in form mike	R
73	Mike»	its not automatic, you gotta go to the office and get your patent pending. My grandpa was denied a patent because his device was already being put to use.	R
78	Fap»	patent is different to copyright	R+
84	Fap»	you need to register a patent and pay a fee	R+
86	Fap»	and you patent the product	R
88	Ian»	ok	
89	Eric»	oh ok	RC
79	Jack»	isn't a patent where you can protect an idea?	RC
87	Lim»	patents are for design mainly	RI
90	Jack»	so I pay to patent my design, but can copyright the content for free?	R
92	Lim»	well said jack - exactly!!!	RI

Figure 4.39. Chat exchange: Turn network adjacency matrix

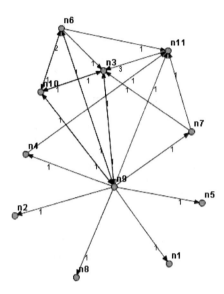

Figure 4.40a. Chat exchange: Actor network sociogram

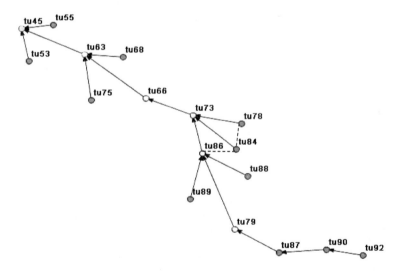

Figure 4.40b. Chat exchange: Turn network sociogram[57]

---

[57] In turn network sociograms, primary nodes that start an exchange or lead to divergent discussion threads could be highlighted with colours.

4.6 Validity Issues and Measures

This section identifies the main threats to reliability in the discourse analysis of the transcript data, the accompanying implications for social network analysis, and describes the practices undertaken to enhance the coding process. Validity in perception survey analysis is discussed with particular focus on content and construct validity of the survey instrument. Finally, this section defines the constructs and measures in RQ1 and RQ2 that guided data analysis in this study.

According to Yin (1994), reliability of a case study entails the demonstration that operations of the study (such as the data collection procedure) could be repeated with the *same results*. However, Sudweeks and Simoff (1998) argued that in online research, rapid changes in CMC/Internet technologies and application features imply that the "path of information communication" (p.31) is seldom stable. Also, given delays/time lags in synchronization and the creative use of language, participants on each side of the real-time link in this case study are likely to experience "a unique conversation" (Ruhleder, 2000, p.13).

This study acknowledges subjectivity with the use of a single case for in-depth understanding of the impact of chat interaction in facilitating the collaborative-constructivist learning process. Knowledge gained from this inquiry are based on interpretations in a specific time/context and not be claimed to be generalizable to wider populations. With the adoption of the standard of *authenticity* (Patton, 2000), the methodological design of this study emphasized the use of multiple data sources and methods for capturing 'rich' descriptions that add to credibility of the findings. Diverse perspectives were gathered for *triangulation* rather than the confirmation of a single interpretation of the online synchronous learning experience. This study holds that triangulation with methods of discourse analysis, social network analysis, and perception survey analysis in conjunction with data from transcripts, participant self-reports, unit document artifacts and a key informant added "rigor, breadth, complexity, richness, and depth" (Denzin & Lincoln, 2000, p.5) to this research effort. However, the issue of reliability is relevant to this study when regarded as the *consistent* application of coding categories to discourse data as discussed in the following section.

4.6.1 Reliability in discourse and social network analyses

The application of discourse analysis to the transcript data is an interpretive process involving "judgments about synonymy, paraphrase and other semantic intuitions" (Stubbs, 1983, p.75) which are exercised in tandem with an understanding of the conversational content and context. Riffe et al. (1998) recommended that in coding data containing latent content requiring interpretation of meaning by the analyst, reliability could be enhanced with the coding process "controlled by rules of procedure" (p.108) defined clearly and unambiguously in a codebook. Babbie (1990) suggested that coding reliability could be verified with other coder(s) with inter-coder reliability indicated by the degree of discrepancy between coders for a common transcript set.

Since social network analysis was conducted on transcript data which had been subjected to discourse analysis, enhancement of coding reliability would naturally impact on SNA interpretations of interactional patterns. In order to enhance reliability in the qualitative coding of the transcript data in this study, the following practices were carried out:

- *Codebook construction.* A codebook (Appendix B.1) was developed to guide the coding process using the ESA scheme. The codebook defined the major concepts and categories in the scheme with examples, explained the procedures for data segmentation and use of coding conventions.

- *Member check.* Member checking and verification of the qualitative coding were carried out with Dr. Fay Sudweeks in her roles as unit coordinator and G4 tutor on two occasions (22 November 2005, 23 February, 2006). The categories in the scheme were first explained and a copy of the codebook was provided to guide coding of an episode from the transcript dataset.

- *Intra-coder reliability check.* Since all transcript coding was carried out by the researcher, intra-coder reliability checks were carried out by pre-testing the coding scheme on a data sub-set consisting of 10 sessions (5 sessions from each group) (Table 4.25). Revisions to the coding scheme were made when certain categories and procedures were refined or discarded to ensure that the coding scheme was able to measure the formulated constructs. The reliability of category assignment to turns was enhanced when bottom-up coding from Move level led to occasional reconsideration of the ES category previously assigned. The researcher's role as participant observer also added to the reliability of interpreting the online interactions. The researcher participated in G4 tutorial discussions, read the set-readings for the OI unit, and attended all on-campus lectures to gain an understanding of the content and context of the chat interaction.

Table 4.25. Data sub-set used in reliability check

Week	Date	Session	Episode	
3	8 August 2005	2	1	2
5	29 August 2005	4	1	2
6	5 September 2005	5	1	2
7	12 September 2005	6	1	2
9	26 September 2005	8	1	2

4.6.2 Validity of perception survey analysis

The use of self-reported data is not without its problems but the validity of self-reports is generally held to be supported under certain conditions:
- the survey questions are unambiguous, refer to recent activities, and do not "intrude into private matters nor do they prompt socially desirable responses" (Kuh, 2001, section 3, para. 4);
- respondents have the knowledge, opinion, attitudes required (Aaker et al., 2004);
- respondents are willing and able to respond (Aaker et al., 2004); and
- respondents hold the view that "the questions merit a serious and thoughtful response" (Chun, 2002, p.23).

Although findings from Chesebro and McCroskey (2000) supported the validity of self-reports in the context of learning, this study acknowledges the following areas of vulnerability in the use of such data and describes the practices undertaken to enhance validity of self-reported data obtained.

While external validity, as generalizability of the survey findings, is moot in this single case study, *internal* validity is relevant in terms of content and construct validity of the survey instrument. Given the use of itemized categories (in closed questions) that are mainly sets of statements related to interactional behaviour during tutorials, there is a need to ensure *content validity* in the sense that the statements reflect accurately events occurring during the tutorials. At a higher level, there is a need to ensure *construct validity* of instrument as the appropriateness of the survey questions for eliciting the required information. Both issues of content and construct validity were addressed at the pre-test and refinement stages[58] of the survey development process, during which questions were added or discarded, rephrased and/or re-ordered that improved question clarity and layout of the instrument.

Additionally, measurement error as *error of central tendency* manifested in the consistent selection of neutral/mid points in rating scales (Ary et al., 2002) was reduced with the provision of an *Unable to Judge* (UJ) option only in one question (Q.5). The *Halo effect* (a term attributed to Thorndike, 1920 by Pike, 1999) whereby respondents "inflate reporting of their behavior, performance, or what they perceive they have gained from their college experience towards the more socially acceptable" (Chun, 2002, p.22) was minimized with the triangulation of evidence obtained from discourse and social network analyses of the transcript data.

4.6.3 Constructs and measures for research questions
A *theoretical construct* is an abstract, mental concept that represents an individual's idea of some aspect of the world such as 'engagement in participation' or 'collaborative learning process'. In order to establish a common representation of the construct necessary for building a shared understanding of its meaning, the construct has to be defined and the definition of its meaning should reflect the concept. The act of defining the construct involves making concrete the abstract concept through the process of *operationalization*. In the operationalization process, the construct is defined in measurable terms i.e., the theoretical construct is translated into a *measure* or concrete, empirically observable manifestation of the phenomenon such as 'Initiate turn' or 'inclusiveness'.

An overview of the operational definitions of the constructs and measures for the research questions in this study are provided in Table 4.26 and Table 4.27. The ESA and SNA measures used in RQ1 are matched to the respective constructs in each RQ1 sub-question. In RQ2, the survey questions constitute the operationalized measures for RQ2 constructs. Analyses of transcript and survey data obtained from G1 and G4 were guided by the measures and the results are presented in the next chapter.

---

[58] Stages in the web survey development process were discussed in this chapter, section 4.4.3.

Table 4.26. Research question 1 constructs and measures

RQ1.1: What do the overall patterns of task-oriented chat discourse reveal about engagement by participants with each other's contributions?

1.1.1 What is the extent of participation shown in exchange patterns?

	Measures	
ESA		**SNA**

(a) *Extent of participation* indicated by 3 categories: Present, Lurking, Absent.
Definition of PRESENT: a participant who is logged into the chat room and makes at least one contribution within session/episode boundaries.
Definition of LURKING: a participant who is logged into the chat room and makes no contributions within session/episode boundaries. A lurker participant is counted as present.
Definition of ABSENT: a participant who is not logged into the chat room.

Categories	Criteria	
	Logged in	Contribution made
Present	✓	✓
Lurking	✓	✗
Absent	✗	✗

(b) *Extent of participation* measured by
• Frequency of ALL turns by turn types.
Definition of TURN: a contribution that falls within Episode boundaries and identified by Session, Episode and Number
Definition of ALL turns: total number of TASK, Off-Topic and Repair turns.

(c) *Extent of participation* for tutors measured by
• Density of turn indicated by the association of total number of words to average turn length. The most active participants are associated with contribution of highest number of words and highest average turn length (Sudweeks & Simoff, 2005).
Definition of a WORD in chat discourse includes emoticons and emotags. An emoticon/emotag is counted as a word and may constitute a turn.

Definition of AVERAGE TURN LENGTH = $\dfrac{No.ofWords}{No.ofTurns}$

===== Application of ESA measures=====

1.1.2 Is there *engagement* in exchange patterns?		
ESA	**Measures**	**SNA**
====== Application of SNA measures======		*Extent of initiation* measured by (a) nodal degree (b) actor-node types (c) group reciprocity index
		Definition of DEGREE: the degree of connection between a node to other nodes adjacent to it. In directed graphs, nodal degree comprises of two elements - *outdegree* and *indegree*. Their numerical measures are the row and column sum (respectively) of am adjacency matrix.
		ACTOR-NODE TYPES (Wasserman & Faust, 1994) defined as - *Isolate* (0) is an actor-node with no ties incident to or from it i.e. if $D\_i(n)=0$, $D\_o(n)=0$ - *Transmitter* (1) is an actor-node with only ties originating from it i.e. if $D\_i(n)=0$, $D\_o(n)>0$ - *Receiver* (2) is an actor-node with only ties terminating at it i.e. if $D\_i(n)>0$, $D\_o(n)=0$ - *Carrier* (3) is an actor-node with ties incident to and from it i.e. if $D\_i(n)>0$, $D\_o(n)>0$
		RECIPROCITY INDEX formula = ratio of the maximum number of reciprocated ties to total number of ties (Cyram NetMiner v. 2.5 *User Manual*, 2004, p. 188).

RQ 1.2: What do the overall patterns of task-oriented chat discourse reveal about the interactional purposes of participants?

1.2.1 What types of ES turns are produced by the participants?	ESA	Measures	SNA
	ES turn types produced by participants measured by • frequency of (I) and (RI) contributed by participants • frequency of (R) and (RC) contributed by participants	======= Application of ESA measures=======	

1.2.2 What types of *Moves* are adopted by the participants?	ESA	Measures	SNA
	Types of Moves defined as • Moves associated with (I) include {INF, INQ, REA, JUS} • Moves associated with (RI) include {CHK, CLA, EXD, CHA} • Moves associated with (R) include {INF, REA, JUS} • Moves associated with (RC) include {FBK-E, FBK-A} *Range of Moves* intended by the participants measured by • maximum and minimum number of types of Moves adopted by participants	======= Application of ESA measures=======	

RQ 1.3: What do the overall patterns of task-oriented chat discourse reveal about the collaborative learning process in groups?

1.3.1 Is there *equality of participation*?

ESA	Measures	SNA
Equality of participation measured by • frequency of Initiate, Reinitiate and Respond extended turn sequences (I-SEQ, RI-SEQ, R-SEQ) An EXTENDED TURN SEQUENCE is defined as a sequence of 2 or more turns of the same ES type (by the same speaker) that may/may not immediately follow each other in the transcript.		*Equality of participation* measured by presence of • inclusiveness at exchange level = (total number of nodes - number of Isolates) / total number of nodes) *100 (NetMiner v.2.5, p.91) Definition of INCLUSIVENESS: the number of connected nodes expressed as a proportion of the total number of nodes present in the network (Scott, 2000, p.70). Definition of ACTOR-NODES: the participants in each exchange. Definition of CONNECTION: the existence of ties adjacent to and/or from a pair of actor-nodes Definition of ISOLATE: an actor-node with no ties incident to or from it.

1.3.2 Are there *information-sharing* and *topic development* phases in the exchanges?

ESA	Measures	SNA
Information-sharing is measured by • R-SEQ by participants • Move Sets 1 and 2 = frequency of {INF, EXD} Moves used for extended information giving and {JUS, REA} Moves that indicate defence/disputation of stated position with information and working through of implications or hypotheses. • Move Set 3 = frequency of {FBK-E, FBK-A} Moves that convey minimal information as evaluative content or acknowledgement. *Topic development* is measured by • Move Set 4 = frequency of {INQ, CHK, CLA, CHA } Moves that elicit more information to stimulate new discussion threads, make meaning clearer or understanding easier, and propose another direction for thought or discussion.		===== Application of ESA measures=====

Table 4.27. Research question 2 constructs and measures

Constructs and definitions	Measures as Survey Questions
RQ 2.1: How do student participants perceive their experiences of chat tutorials in terms of the opportunities for participation?	
Opportunities for participation during online tutorial discussions defined as ▪ perception of participation opportunities for self, and ▪ factors motivating and inhibiting participation.	*Perception of participation opportunities for self* measured by reports on ▪ presence/absence and use of participation opportunities (Q.5a; Q.5b). *Factors motivating and inhibiting participation* measured by reports on ▪ turn-taking behaviours (Q.5c; Q.5d). ▪ extent of difficulty/ease experienced in presenter and participant roles (Q.1; Q.2). ▪ impact of tutor and presenter facilitation styles on encouraging participation (Q.4a; Q4b). ▪ impact of tutor and peer assessment on encouraging participation (Q.4c; Q.4d). ▪ other factors (Q.6; Q.7).
RQ 2.2: How do student participants perceive their experiences of chat tutorials in terms of the adequacy of peer and tutor support?	
Learning support defined as extent of help available from tutor and other students in the group on clarifying content issues during tutorial discussions.	*Extent of learning support* measured by reports on ▪ availability of learning support from the tutor (Q.3a). ▪ availability of learning support from other students (Q.3b; Q.5e to Q.5i).
RQ 2.3: How do student participants perceive their experiences of chat tutorials in terms of the quality of learning experience and collaborative work process?	
Quality of learning experience and collaborative work process defined as ▪ the degree of fit between tutorial experiences to unit purpose of enhancing understanding of content. ▪ the relationship between the degree of satisfaction with 5 chat tutorial factors and their importance to the respondents, and overall perception of online learning experience for the unit. The 5 chat tutorial factors are defined as: (a) Opportunity to participate in discussions (b) Discussions are relevant to the unit readings (c) Communication skills in CMC environments are developed (d) Understanding of course content is increased (e) Online learning experience is enhanced with chat tutorials	*Degree of fit* between tutorial experiences and unit purpose measured by reports on factors affecting understanding of course content (Q.11). *Relationship between degree of satisfaction with and importance of chat tutorial factors* measured by ▪ the difference between percentage of respondents who reported levels of importance (Q.8) and satisfaction (Q.9) with 5 chat tutorial factors. *Overall perception of online learning experience for the unit* measured by reports on ▪ other factors/aspects of the online learning experience (Q.17).

4.7 Summary

Chapter 4 presented the methodological design of this qualitative case study and the underlying constructionist epistemological and sociocultural constructivist assumptions that guided decisions on data sources, data collection procedures, analytical methods, and instruments. The methods of discourse and social network analyses were described with particular focus on areas of conceptual integration between ESA and SNA in analyzing chat exchanges present in the transcripts. The development of the web survey instrument was described which gathered student perceptions of learning experiences for triangulation with evidence from the transcript data. This chapter also outlined the procedures for processing the transcript and survey datasets and discussed validity issues associated with the instruments and data. Finally, the constructs and measures for addressing the research questions in this study were defined. The next chapter presents the results from the analyses of the transcript and survey datasets which were guided by the constructs and measures in RQ1 and RQ2.

CHAPTER 5

RESULTS

5.1 Introduction

The previous chapter described the methodological design, analytical methods/instruments, constructs, and measures for examining educational chat interaction and learner experiences during online tutorial discussions in this case study. This chapter presents the results from transcript and survey data analyses which are discussed in order of research questions. This section reviews the aims of the study, research questions, data sources, and participants that form the background for understanding the results presented.

As stated in Chapter 1, the main purpose this study was to examine the impact of chat interaction on the learning process from a sociocultural constructivist perspective in the context of the OI unit. More specifically, the study aimed to:

- examine the discourse of task-oriented chat interactions for indications of active participation and knowledge construction; and
- explore student perceptions on the impact of chat interactions in supporting collaborative learning and group work processes.

In order to address these aims, two main research questions were formulated to guide the inquiry process.

RQ1. What do the overall patterns of task-oriented chat discourse reveal about engagement by participants with each other's contributions, interactional purposes, and the collaborative learning process in groups?

RQ2. How do student participants perceive their experiences of chat tutorial interaction in terms of participation opportunities, adequacy of learning support, and quality of learning experience and collaborative work process?

For RQ1, transcripts of chat tutorials were subjected to discourse and network analyses of turns/exchanges which were visualized as actor and turn networks. For RQ2, quantitative and qualitative survey data were subjected, respectively, to descriptive statistical analysis and interpretive content analysis.

The complete transcript dataset from two tutorial groups in this case study (G1, G4) comprised 22 sessions or 44 episodes i.e., 11 sessions for each group with two episodes in each session (Table 5.1). The transcripts reflected dialogic participation in equivalent learning activities involving critical discussions on set-readings which were facilitated by the tutor and moderated by one or two student presenters in WebCT™ chat tutorial rooms[59].

The complete survey dataset comprised 13 returns from G1 (93%) and 8 returns from G4 (89%). The survey dataset included student participant responses to closed and open-ended questions on learning experiences during chat tutorials (Table 5.2).

---

[59] See Chapter 3 for a description of the chat tutorial activity.

Table 5.1. Transcript dataset by date, session and episode

Date	Session	Episode
1 August 2005	S1	S1-E1, S1-E2
8 August 2005	S2	S2-E1, S2-E2
15 August 2005	S3	S3-E1, S3-E2
29 August 2005	S4	S4-E1, S4-E2
5 September 2005	S5	S5-E1, S5-E2
12 September 2005	S6	S6-E1, S6-E2
19 September 2005	S7	S7-E1, S7-E2
26 September 2005	S8	S8-E1, S8-E2
10 October 2005	S9	S9-E1, S9-E2
17 October 2005	S10	S10-E1, S10-E2
24 October 2005	S11	S11-E1, S11-E2

Table 5.2. Survey dataset and final response rate

Group	Response rate	Missing
1	13 out of 14* (93%)	1
4	8 out of 9* (89%)	1

* Derek (G1) and Karl (G4) did not submit survey returns.

The two tutorial groups selected for comparative study comprised 27 participants including two tutors i.e., the staff participants, and the researcher (Table 5.3). The researcher was a participant observer in G4 from session 2 (S2). There were no changes to G4 participant numbers at the close of transcript and survey data collection. In G1, one participant (Ted) attended sessions 1-9 (S1 to S9) but discontinued the unit on 15 October 2005. The transcript data from Ted was included in the analyses and he was considered *absent* for S10 and S11. Accordingly, survey return rate from G1 was based on 14 student participants.

Table 5.3. Groups 1 and 4 participants: Pseudonyms and actor-node labels

No.	Group 1	Node Label	No.	Group 4	Node Label
1.	Derek	n1	1.	Evan	n1
2.	Max	n2	2.	Bill	n2
3.	Alvin	n3	3.	Mike	n3
4.	Cliff	n4	4.	Eric	n4
5.	Colin	n5	5.	Karl	n5
6.	Ted*	n6	6.	Jack	n6
7.	Sam	n7	7.	Ian	n7
8.	Diane	n8	8.	Pete	n8
9.	James	n9	9.	Robin	n9
10.	Alan	n10	10.	Lim (Researcher)	n10
11.	Jason	n11	11.	Fay (Tutor)	n11
12.	Scott	n12			
13.	Barry	n13			
14.	Tony	n14			
15.	Wendy	n15			
16.	Rachel (Tutor)	n16			

* Derek (G1) and Karl (G4) did not submit survey returns.

Since characteristics of the two groups were described in Chapter 3, the main differences and similarities in student participant profile are highlighted in Table 5.4.

Table 5.4. Profile of participants

Characteristics	Group 1 Participants	Group 4 Participants
Gender	- 3 female and 12 male students	- 1 female and 8 male students
English Language proficiency	- Majority of ESL/EFL speakers, minority of native English language speakers	- All native English language speakers
Nationality	- Majority of international students, minority of Australian students	- Majority of Australian students, minority of international students
Age range	- From early to mid-20s	- From early to mid-20s
Location	- Residence in Western Australia	- Residence in Western Australia

Given the small number of participants involved in this study, statistical results from group comparison were not checked for significance. Instead, validity of results was established through methods and data triangulation[60]. The difference in group size (G1=16, G4=11) did not preclude quantitative comparisons based on the transcript data since the average attendance rate was found to be similar between groups (G1=79%, G4=81%) (Table 5.5). The following sections in this chapter present the results from the data analyses in order of research question and implications of the results will be discussed in Chapter 6.

Table 5.5. Groups 1 and 4: Attendance for all Episodes

Episode	G1 No.	%	G4 No.	%
S1-E1	13	81	8	73
S1-E2	13	81	8	73
S2-E1	15	94	8	73
S2-E2	15	94	8	73
S3-E1	13	81	9	82
S3-E2	14	88	9	82
S4-E1	13	81	10	91
S4-E2	14	88	10	91
S5-E1	15	94	9	82
S5-E2	15	94	9	82
S6-E1	13	81	8	73
S6-E2	13	81	9	82
S7-E1	11	69	9	82
S7-E2	12	75	9	82
S8-E1	10	63	8	73
S8-E2	10	63	8	73
S9-E1	13	81	9	82
S9-E2	13	81	9	82
S10-E1	13	81	8	73
S10-E2	13	81	9	82
S11-E1	8	50	11	100
S11-E2	8	50	11	100
% Total		1731.3		1781.8
% AV		**78.7**		**81.0**

Note: Total number of participants in G1=16; G4=11.
The number of participants here refer to those who are not absent for the episode

---

[60] Refer to discussion on validity issues in Chapter 4, section 4.6.

5.2 Results for Research Question 1: Engagement in Chat Exchanges

In RQ1, the constructs of *engagement* in chat exchanges, *interactional purposes*, and the *collaborative learning process in groups* were formulated to guide the analysis of task-oriented chat discourse for indications of active participation and knowledge construction. These constructs were operationalized as ESA and/or SNA measures which were defined in Chapter 4[61].

This section presents the results from the application of ESA and SNA measures to examining *engagement* by participants with each other's contributions defined as the *extent of participation*, and *extent of initiation and receiving of responses* present in the patterns of task-oriented chat discourse.

5.2.1 Extent of participation

The *extent of participation* was operationalized as the following measures:
(a) Participation category
(b) Frequency of ALL turns by turn types

(a) Participation category

In measuring extent of participation, it was necessary to first establish that participants were in a position to contribute to the discussion. Besides conventional measures of presence as dichotomous states of *present* or *absent*, the nature of synchronous CMC enables participants to inhabit a grey state of *lurking*, where participants are logged into the chat tutorial room, yet they make no contributions to the discussion.

In discourse analysis, 'talk and text' usually form the main empirical basis for study and analysis. Participants are 'visible' to the analyst mainly through their contributions to the conversation as turns sent to other participants. Lurker participants, therefore pose empirical and methodological challenges to the analyst: If they say nothing, are they there? Should they be included or excluded from consideration in quantitative discourse analysis? In social network analysis, the above quandary is less apparent since the receipt of a turn constitutes the establishment of a tie that links an actor to another in the network. Hence, lurker participants who are logged in, receive ties sent by others, yet do not send any ties, are included in the count of actors that make up the network. In this study, for both discourse and social network analyses of chat exchanges, lurker participants were regarded as present and included in the count of participants that make up the network or group in each episode.

The measure of Participation Category was used to classify participants by the number of episodes that they were *Present*, *Lurking* or *Absent*. The criteria of each category are shown below and the results from both groups are summarized in Table 5.6.

Participation Category	Criteria	
	Logged in	Contribution made
Present	✓	✓
Lurking	✓	✗
Absent	✗	✗

---

[61] Refer to Chapter 4, section 4.6.

Table 5.6. Groups 1 and 4: *Present, Lurking* or *Absent* participants for all episodes

G1		Participation Categories		Episodes	G4		Participation Categories		Episodes
No.		Present	Lurking	Absent	Total	No.	Present	Lurking	Absent	Total
1.	Derek	9	3	10	22	1. Evan	14	0	8	22
2.	Max	18	2	2	22	2. Bill	13	2	7	22
3.	Alvin	22	0	0	22	3. Mike	18	0	4	22
4.	Cliff	20	0	2	22	4. Eric	22	0	0	22
5.	Colin	16	0	6	22	5. Karl	10	0	12	22
6.	Ted	15	1	6	22	6. Jack	21	1	0	22
7.	Sam	22	0	0	22	7. Ian	20	0	2	22
8.	Diane	16	1	5	22	8. Pete	14	0	8	22
9.	James	13	0	9	22	9. Robin	19	0	3	22
10.	Alan	17	5	0	22	10. Lim	19	1	2	22
11.	Jason	11	0	11	22	11. Fay	22	0	0	22
12.	Scott	12	2	8	22	Total	192	4	46	242
13.	Barry	10	2	10	22	%	**79.3**	**1.7**	**19.0**	100.0
14.	Tony	18	0	4	22					
15.	Wendy	20	0	2	22					
16.	Rachel	17	5	0	22					
	Total	256	21	75	352					
	%	**72.7**	**6.0**	**21.3**	**100.0**					

A between group comparison showed that out of 22 episodes,
- G1 participants were *present* for a lower percentage of episodes i.e., logged in the tutorial chat room and made at least one contribution to the discussion, compared to G4 participants.
- G1 participants were *lurking* for a higher percentage of episodes i.e., logged in the tutorial chat room but made no contribution to the discussion, compared to G4 participants.
- G1 participants were *absent* for a higher percentage of episodes i.e., not logged in the tutorial chat room and made no contribution to the discussion, compared to G4 participants.

The results suggest that G1 participants, as a whole, by being *present* in fewer episodes, *absent* and *lurking* in more episodes than G4 participants, display a lower extent of participation in tutorial discussions. Although the tutors were expectedly not *absent* from any episode, Fay (G4 tutor) was *present* in all 22 episodes while Rachel (G1 tutor) was *present* in 17 which suggest a different extent of tutor participation in facilitating the tutorials.

(b) Frequency of ALL turns by turn types
The *ALL turns* measure was used to indicate extent of participation by the number of turns produced according to *Repair* (RPR), *Off Topic* (OT) and *TASK* turn types that constitute ALL turns[62]. The application of this measure raises a methodological question: Would the number of turns produced by presenters be considerably different from other students in the group as to preclude quantitative comparisons of turns produced for all episodes? This study adopted the assumption, held in

---

[62] ALL turns comprise the total number of turns within an episode that have been coded as TASK, OT and RPR.
TASK turns contain content directly related to the issues in the set-readings discussed in the episodes.
Off-Topic (OT) turns contain content that are *not* directly related to the issues in the set-readings but deal with social, administration and technical issues.
Repair (RPR) turns serve to correct perceived errors in earlier turns.
The coding categories were defined in the codebook (Appendix B.1) and Chapter 4 (section 4.4.1).

Sudweeks and Simoff (2005), namely, given that the presenter would be expected to contribute more turns than the others, but each student would also be appointed as presenter, it was assumed that "contributions to the discussions from each participant were potentially equalised" (p.7) across all sessions/episodes examined.

The results show that on average, compared to G1, G4 participants contributed more turns of every turn type for all episodes (Table 5.7).

Table 5.7. Groups 1 and 4: Frequency of ALL turns by turn types

G1		No. of Turns			G4			No. of Turns		
No.		TASK	OT	RPR	ALL TURNS	No.		TASK	OT	RPR	ALL TURNS
1.	Derek	103	7	1	111	1.	Evan	217	53	7	276
2.	Max	129	21	2	152	2.	Bill	111	57	1	169
3.	Alvin	291	26	3	320	3.	Mike	179	40	1	220
4.	Cliff	175	20	1	196	4.	Eric	424	165	7	596
5.	Colin	81	11	0	92	5.	Karl	146	28	1	175
6.	Ted	144	12	0	156	6.	Jack	395	173	7	575
7.	Sam	121	3	0	124	7.	Ian	393	143	9	545
8.	Diane	244	48	3	295	8.	Pete	245	23	2	270
9.	James	79	8	0	87	9.	Robin	239	172	6	417
10.	Alan	57	0	1	58	10.	Lim	213	39	0	252
11.	Jason	100	11	1	112	11.	Fay	552	184	8	744
12.	Scott	69	16	0	85		Total	3114	1077	49	4239
13.	Barry	120	36	1	157		%	73.5	25.4	1.2	100.0
14.	Tony	200	38	2	240		AV	283	98	5	385
15.	Wendy	215	25	2	242						
16.	Rachel	36	40	0	76						
	Total	2164	322	17	2503						
	%	86.5	12.9	0.7	100.0						
	AV	135	20	1	156						

A further comparison of TASK and OT turns revealed that, compared to G4, G1 participants produced a higher percentage of TASK turns in tandem with a lower percentage of OT turns. Since OT turns contain content that are *not* directly related to the issues in the set-reading(s), the results suggest that although G4 participants displayed a greater extent of participation by contributing more turns of every turn type, G4 tutorial discussions were less relevant in content to the discussion topic(s). This possibility will be further explored in the examination of interaction purposes of TASK turns in section 5.3.

The results also reveal an interesting aspect in the extent of participation by the tutors. Both tutors contributed approximately twice the average number of OT turns within their respective groups mainly for supporting group relations (OT-S) and group management (OT-A), which was expected given their role as tutor-facilitator (Table 5.7, Table 5.8). However, within their respective groups, Fay contributed the highest number of TASK turns while Rachel was the lowest contributor of TASK turns that contain content directly related to the set-reading(s). Essentially, although both tutors participated actively in establishing *social* and *teaching presence* (Garrison et al., 2000) through OT-S/OT-A turns, the higher frequency of TASK turns by Fay suggest a greater degree of involvement in formation of *cognitive presence* in G4 through the sharing of information directly related to the course content during discussions.

Table 5.8. Tutors: Distribution of OT turn types

Tutor	OT-S	OT-A	OT-T	Total
	Distribution of OT Turns			
Rachel	27 (67.5%)	13 (32.5%)	0 (0.0%)	40 (100%)
Fay	120 (65.2%)	50 (27.2%)	14 (7.6%)	184 (100%)

Further examination of tutors' extent of participation was conducted by measuring *turn density* (Sudweeks, 2004; Sudweeks & Simoff, 2005) which is based on two criteria.

(i) Total number of words for all episodes
(ii) Average turn length in words

The density of turn is indicated by the association of total number of words to average turn length i.e., the most prolific participant is associated with the contribution of the highest total number of words for all episodes *and* highest average turn length in words. The density of TASK turns was examined with this measure for indicating tutor activity level specific to contributions that are directly relevant to the course content.

Table 5.9 ranks G1 and G4 participants in order of total number of TASK words for all episodes and average TASK turn length in words. The results show that within their respective groups, Rachel displayed the lowest density of turn with both lowest total number of TASK words and average turn length. However, Fay produced the second highest total number of TASK words in G4 accompanied by a relatively low average turn length.

When results from both measures of TASK turn density and frequency of TASK turns are considered, the findings suggest a pattern of tutor participation whereby Rachel maintained a weak tutor presence with infrequent, terse and short contributions whereas Fay established a more visible presence through frequent, dense and short contributions to tutorial discussions.

Table 5.9. Groups 1 and 4: TASK turn density

G1	TASK Words		AV TASK turn length	G4	TASK Words		AV TASK turn length
	TASK Turn Density				*TASK Turn Density*		
Alvin	2936	Derek	19.0	Jack	5296	Mike	14.9
Cliff	2707	Colin	18.4	**Fay**	**5090**	Bill	14.9
Wendy	2211	Scott	17.4	Eric	3881	Jack	13.4
Derek	1959	Cliff	15.5	Pete	3220	Evan	13.2
Tony	1889	Jason	14.4	Ian	3154	Pete	13.1
Colin	1493	Wendy	10.3	Evan	2862	Robin	12.0
Ted	1440	Alvin	10.1	Robin	2862	Lim	10.8
Jason	1435	Ted	10.0	Mike	2671	**Fay**	**9.2**
Diane	1338	Max	9.6	Lim	2300	Eric	9.2
Max	1235	Tony	9.4	Bill	1649	Karl	8.9
Scott	1198	James	8.6	Karl	1293	Ian	8.0
Sam	956	Barry	8.0				
Barry	954	Sam	7.9				
James	680	Alan	6.0				
Alan	340	Diane	5.5				
Rachel	**128**	**Rachel**	**3.6**				

In the following section, the construct of *engagement* is further examined with SNA measures which afforded an interpretation of the concept that more closely represents the intuitive understanding of the dynamic to-and-fro pattern of turn-taking in conversational exchanges.

5.2.2 Extent of initiation and receiving of responses

The *extent of initiation and receiving of responses* was operationalized as SNA measures[63].
(a) Nodal degree of actors
(b) Actor-node types and group reciprocity

The measure of *degree* was used to indicate the communicative direction of information exchange as *out-ties* (ties sent) or *in-ties* (ties received) and the frequency of the interaction as *degree of connection* between an actor and other adjacent actors. Drawing from the concept of degree, directional symmetry in the flow of information during the collaborative learning process was examined with the related measures of *actor-node types* (Receiver and Carrier) and *group reciprocity* indicating symmetry/mutuality in information sharing at actor and group levels respectively.

(a) Nodal degree of actors

The activity of actor-nodes was measured by *nodal degree* which comprised two elements: *outdegree* (D_o) and *indegree* (D_i) which indicate, respectively, frequency of ties sent and received by adjacent actors. Application of this measure assumes the condition that turns in chat exchanges could be directed to all or specific actors in the group. The numerical measures of outdegree and indegree are the row and column sum (respectively) of an adjacency matrix (Table 5.10) and the full degree dataset is provided in Appendix C.1.

Table 5.10. Outdegree and indegree for episode G4S3-E1: Row and column sum in adjacency matrix

		n1	n2	n3	n4	n6	n8	n9	n10	n11	OUT-DEGREE
		Evan	Bill	Mike	Eric	Jack	Pete	Robin	Lim	Fay	
n1	Evan		1	4	9	2	1	1	2	4	24
n2	Bill	1		1	1	0	1	1	2	0	7
n3	Mike	3	1		5	2	1	1	1	2	16
n4	Eric	35	31	31		33	33	31	31	33	258
n6	Jack	6	3	8	8		7	4	4	7	47
n8	Pete	0	0	1	7	1		1	3	7	20
n9	Robin	2	1	2	2	1	1		0	2	11
n10	Lim	1	0	2	3	1	1	0		0	8
n11	Fay	9	6	7	7	10	16	6	6		67
IN-DEGREE		57	43	56	42	50	61	45	49	55	**458**

Table 5.11 shows the sum of out/in-ties in G1 and G4 by episode, summarizes the out/indegree of each group by the mean according to episodes, and presents the standard deviation of outdegree (SD (D_o)) and indegree (SD (D_i)) from the mean of each group by episode. The standard deviations reported for (D_o) and (D_i) show the quantified variability of actor-nodes in the respective activities of sending and receiving ties within the group.

---

[63] SNA concepts of degree, actor-node types and reciprocity were explained in Chapter 4, section 4.4.2.

A within group comparison of the standard deviations of (D_o) and (D_i) for all episodes showed consistently higher SD for (D_o) compared to (D_i)[64]. The presence of a higher SD (D_o) suggests that actors in the group tended to differ more greatly in the number of ties that they send. A lower SD (D_i) suggests that actors in the group tended to receive similar numbers of ties. Hence, results from a within group comparison of SD (D_o) and SD (D_i) indicate wider variability in the tendency of actors to send ties than receive ties within the group[65] which suggests a hierarchical, 'teacher-oriented' engagement pattern within both groups that could be attributed to the tutorial activity structure.

Table 5.11. Groups 1 and 4: Sum of ties, mean degree and standard deviation of degree by episode

Episode	Sum of Ties		Mean Degree		SD Outdegree		SD Indegree	
	G1	G4	G1	G4	G1	G4	G1	G4
S1-E1	380	281	29.2	35.1	63.2	42.0	3.1	10.9
S1-E2	308	257	23.7	32.1	73.5	31.4	0.9	5.8
S2-E1	979	170	65.3	21.3	203.1	26.0	2.9	8.8
S2-E2	865	663	57.7	82.9	163.6	74.9	4.9	8.8
S3-E1	426	458	32.8	50.9	88.6	75.6	5.3	6.3
S3-E2	326	249	23.3	27.7	54.9	41.1	4.5	5.7
S4-E1	282	392	21.7	39.2	57.9	52.1	4.1	7.9
S4-E2	625	471	44.6	47.1	59.7	56.1	7.4	14.9
S5-E1	693	327	46.2	36.3	163.8	34.7	3.8	5.4
S5-E2	451	432	30.1	48.0	70.2	44.2	12.0	8.3
S6-E1	411	566	31.6	70.8	79.2	74.6	9.5	9.9
S6-E2	648	256	49.8	28.4	146.6	26.4	3.9	7.1
S7-E1	523	626	47.5	69.6	127.0	60.0	3.2	4.3
S7-E2	235	64	19.6	7.1	48.6	8.5	3.5	2.4
S8-E1	306	322	30.6	40.3	68.9	40.3	9.0	10.4
S8-E2	255	279	25.5	34.9	40.4	45.3	3.6	6.7
S9-E1	730	320	56.2	35.6	179.8	32.5	4.4	9.4
S9-E2	578	260	44.5	28.9	143.5	39.2	11.2	6.2
S10-E1	242	115	18.6	14.4	42.8	36.9	2.7	4.3
S10-E2	464	217	35.7	24.1	117.9	20.5	4.7	11.2
S11-E1	248	410	31.0	37.3	62.0	26.0	3.5	13.3
S11-E2	236	455	29.5	41.4	58.5	29.1	4.2	8.8

Note:
- One *sum of ties* score was reported since the sum of out-ties is equal to the sum of in-ties in an adjacency matrix.
- The *mean degree* indicates the average degree of the nodes in the network. One mean is reported for each episode since the same set of ties is considered although from different directions. In other words, a tie sent is also a tie received, hence the mean of both out/indegree are equal.
- The *population* SD formula was applied since the participants in each group constituted the whole population in this case study and there is no generalization from sample to a wider population.
- The values for *standard deviation* obtained for this dataset does not indicate the proportion of data within a given range of standard deviations from the mean since the assumption of a normal distribution is not held here. Instead, the SD values indicate whether there were more or fewer ties above or below the mean.

Efforts by the student presenter to direct and/or stimulate discussion could mean that ties were mainly sent by the presenter for the episode and directed to all rather than specific students in the group hence accounting for findings of higher SD (D_o) and lower SD (D_i). This interpretation was supported when the frequency of out-ties by

---

[64] Given a dataset that is skewed positively for outdegree and skewed negative for indegree, the values for standard deviation obtained for this dataset does not indicate the proportion of data within a given range of standard deviations from the mean since the assumption of a normal distribution is not held here. Instead the SD values indicate whether there were more or fewer ties above or below the mean.
[65] This variation in SD (D_o) and SD (D_i) found was not unexpected in the analysis of directed and valued ties since it was assumed that turns in chat exchanges could be directed to all or specific actors in the group. Hence (D_o) and (D_i) would not necessarily be the same for an episode.

presenters were compared to the mean degree for each episode (Table 5.12). In both groups, the frequency of presenter out-ties was consistently above the mean degree for the episode. Interestingly, Fay was found to send more ties than the assigned G4 presenters in four episodes (S2-E2, S4-E1, S5-E2, S9E-2) while Rachel's frequency of out-ties was consistently lower than the G1 presenters. While the tutor-facilitator role entails joint responsibility with the presenter in moderating and stimulating discussions, the results reveal another aspect of difference in tutor involvement in the learning process.

Table 5.12. Groups 1 and 4: Frequency of presenter/tutor out-ties and mean degree by episode

G1 Episode	Mean Degree	No. of Presenter Out-ties	No. of Tutor Out-ties	G4 Episode	Mean Degree	No. of Presenter Out-ties	No. of Tutor Out-ties
S1-E1	29.2	243	0	S1-E1	35.1	144	34
S1-E2	23.7	278	1	S1-E2	32.1	101	62
S2-E1	65.3	824	2	S2-E1	21.3	87	32
S2-E2	57.7	667	4	S2-E2	82.9	191	**224**
S3-E1	32.8	339	1	S3-E1	50.9	258	67
S3-E2	23.3	219	3	S3-E2	27.7	137	48
S4-E1	21.7	217	0	S4-E1	39.2	111	**168**
S4-E2	44.6	213	2	S4-E2	47.1	166	145
S5-E1	46.2	659	0	S5-E1	36.3	124	59
S5-E2	30.1	279	5	S5-E2	48.0	62	**166**
S6-E1	31.6	305	0	S6-E1	70.8	266	45
S6-E2	49.8	557	0	S6-E2	28.4	71	70
S7-E1	47.5	448	0	S7-E1	69.6	210	118
S7-E2	19.6	180	1	S7-E2	7.1	28	14
S8-E1	30.6	237	6	S9-E1	35.6	115	51
S8-E2	25.5	137	1	S9-E2	28.9	75	**123**
S9-E1	56.2	679	2	S10-E1	14.4	112	1
S9-E2	44.5	541	28	S10-E2	24.1	73	43
S10-E1	18.6	163	37				
S10-E2	35.7	444	0				
S11-E1	31.0	194	0				
S11-E2	29.5	183	0				

Note: There were no presenters assigned for S8 and S11 in G4.

A between group comparison of SD (D_o) and (D_i) for all episodes (Table 5.11) showed
- higher SD (D_o) for G1, compared to G4, for most episodes except 1 episode (S8-E2).
- lower SD (D_i) for G1, compared to G4, for most episodes except 3 episodes (S5-E2, S7-E2, S9-E2).

The SD (D_o) results show a pattern of greater divergence in G1 outdegree and more convergence in G4 outdegree. This suggests that in G4, out-ties were more likely to originate from more actors other than the presenter while most out-ties sent in G1 could be attributed to the presenter. The SD (D_i) results show a pattern of greater convergence in G1 indegree while there is greater divergence in G4 indegree. This suggests that in-ties received by G4 actors were more likely to be specifically directed to them while most in-ties received by G1 actors were likely to be addressed to the entire group.

When interpreted within the collaborative learning context, the results suggest that more G4 actors were involved in the distribution of information/ties which were likely to be received by specific actors in the group. Even as G4 presenters and/or the tutor moderated the discussion, more G4 participants tended to initiate turns and attend to what was said in previous turn(s) by responding directly to the participant(s) who contributed the turn(s). In contrast, fewer G1 participants tended to be involved in the sending of ties which were mainly received by all actors in the group. In other words, G1 presenters were more likely than other participants in the group to initiate turns with information distributed generally to all in the group.

(b) Actor-node types and group reciprocity
While the measure of nodal degree showed different overall tendencies by actors in both groups as distributors of information and the recipients of such information, a finer analysis with the measures of actor-node types and group reciprocity could indicate whether there was mutual sharing of information, which is an essential aspect of the collaborative learning process.

In the analysis of *actor-nodes types*, participants in each episode were categorized as Isolates (0), Transmitters (1), Receivers (2) and Carriers (3)[66]. Where $D_i(n)$ and $D_o(n)$ denote nodal indegree and nodal outdegree of directed ties respectively, each actor-node type is defined below.

- *Isolate* (0) has no ties incident to or from it i.e. if $D_i(n)=0$, $D_o(n)=0$.
- *Transmitter* (1) has only ties originating from it i.e. if $D_i(n)=0$, $D_o(n)>0$.
- *Receiver* (2) has only ties terminating at it i.e. if $D_i(n)>0$, $D_o(n)=0$.
- *Carrier* (3) has ties incident to and from it i.e. if $D_i(n)>0$, $D_o(n)>0$.

This part of the analysis focuses on *Receiver* and *Carrier* node types at episode level for the following reasons:
- There would be no Isolates given the assumption that turns could be directed to all or specific actors in chat exchanges, and the nature of the tutorial activity during which presenters post *metastatements*[67] (brief summaries of set-reading(s) and/or introductory comments) at the start of each episode that are interpreted as being addressed to all participants in the group[68]. Hence, at episode level, the default node type would be *Receiver* since all actor-nodes would have at least one tie incident to it.
- There would be no Transmitters since any default Receiver node that sends a tie would be categorized as a *Carrier* which has ties incident to and from it.

Table 5.13 summarizes the predominant node type(s) adopted by G1 and G4 actors for all episodes.

A between group comparison showed that:
- G1 actors were *Receivers* in 15.5% of all episodes compared to 4.1% in G4.
- G1 actors were *Carriers* in 84.5% of all episodes compared to 95.1% in G4.

---

[66] Sources: Wasserman and Faust (1994, p.128); Cyram NetMiner v. 2.5 User Manual (2004, p. 92). See also Chapter 4, section 4.4.2.
[67] See codebook (Appendix B.1) for Metastatement definition and example.
[68] In actor networks, this study does not assume that actors send ties to themselves, hence the diagonal in the adjacency matrix is ignored.

Table 5.13. Groups 1 and 4: Actor-node types

G1		No. of Episodes			G4		No. of Episodes		
		Receiver	Carrier	Total			Receiver	Carrier	Total
n1.	Derek	1	11	12	n1.	Evan	0	14	14
n2.	Max	2	18	20	n2.	Bill	3	12	15
n3.	Alvin	0	22	22	n3.	Mike	0	18	18
n4.	Cliff	2	18	20	n4.	Eric	1	21	22
n5.	Colin	6	10	16	n5.	Karl	0	10	10
n6.	Ted	2	14	16	n6.	Jack	2	20	22
n7.	Sam	3	19	22	n7.	Ian	0	20	20
n8.	Diane	2	15	17	n8.	Pete	0	14	14
n9.	James	0	13	13	n9.	Robin	1	18	19
n10.	Alan	7	15	22	n10.	Lim	1	19	20
n11.	Jason	1	10	11	n11.	Fay	**0**	**22**	22
n12.	Scott	4	10	14		Total	8	188	196
n13.	Barry	3	9	12		%	**4.1**	**95.9**	100.0
n14.	Tony	0	18	18					
n15.	Wendy	1	19	20					
n16.	Rachel	**9**	**13**	22					
	Total	43	234	277					
	%	**15.5**	**84.5**	100.0					

Note: The total number of episodes refers to episodes in which participants were not absent.

These results suggest that G1 actors were more likely to only receive ties, hence displaying an asymmetrical directional flow of information than G4 actors. In contrast, G4 actors were more likely to both send and receive ties, thus displaying greater mutuality in sharing information than G1 actors. Additionally, a comparison of the predominant node type of *tutors* indicated that Rachel was a Carrier for 13 (59.1%) episodes while Fay was a Carrier for 22 (100%) episodes.

A further analysis of *group reciprocity* was conducted with a reciprocity index that indicates the strength of tendency of the group towards mutuality/reciprocation of choice at the episode level. In directed relationships, reciprocity is present when both actors in a dyad choose the other on a relation such as exchange of information i.e., i <--> j (Wasserman & Faust, 1994). The level of reciprocity for each episode was obtained with a *reciprocity index* based on the formula: *ratio of the maximum number of reciprocated ties to total number of ties* (Cyram NetMiner v. 2.5 User Manual, 2004, p.188).

Application of the reciprocity index assumes the following data conditions:
- presence of directed ties, and
- conversion of valued ties to dichotomous ties[69].

The value obtained with the reciprocity index could range from 0 to 1; indicating the likelihood of a sent tie to receive a tie in return[70], within an episode. If the value = 0, then there is no tendency to reciprocate; if the value = 1, the tendency is maximal i.e., all ties are reciprocated in the episode.

---

[69] Although there may be some loss of information with this procedure, data reduction is necessary for a cleaner description of ties at the group level. See also Chapter 4, section 4.5.3 on transcript data processing.
[70] Source: Wasserman and Faust (1994, p.514).

Results from the application of the reciprocity index (Table 5.14) show
 - G1 reciprocity values ranged from 0.93 (S5-E1) to 0.40 (S9-E2).
 - G4 reciprocity values ranged from 1.00 (S7-E1) to 0.60 (S10-E1).

Table 5.14. Groups 1 and 4: Reciprocity values by episode

Episode	Reciprocity Values	
	G1	G4
S1-E1	0.63	0.85
S1-E2	0.72	0.84
S2-E1	0.60	0.81
S2-E2	0.64	0.98
S3-E1	0.61	0.91
S3-E2	0.59	0.71
S4-E1	0.46	0.69
S4-E2	0.69	0.79
S5-E1	**0.93**	0.92
S5-E2	0.59	0.94
S6-E1	0.69	0.98
S6-E2	0.57	0.87
S7-E1	0.55	**1.00**
S7-E2	0.65	0.72
S8-E1	0.89	0.89
S8-E2	0.62	0.82
S9-E1	0.87	0.95
S9-E2	**0.40**	0.86
S10-E1	0.55	**0.60**
S10-E2	0.74	0.85
S11-E1	0.59	0.90
S11-E2	0.70	0.88

Note:
- Reciprocity values could range from 0 to 1. If the value =0, then there is no tendency to reciprocate; if the value =1, the tendency is maximal i.e. all ties are reciprocated in the episode (Wasserman & Faust, 1994).
- Given the narrow range of values, results are displayed with two decimal places.

A between group comparison of reciprocity values revealed that G4 reciprocity levels were generally higher than G1 for most episodes (besides S5-E1 and S8-E1) indicating a greater tendency towards reciprocation of ties. When considered together with findings from actor-node type analysis, group reciprocity analysis confirmed the impression that compared to G1, mutuality in information exchange was more evident in G4 and G4 may be a more balanced group in terms of information exchange during the collaborative learning process.

5.2.3 Summary
Regarding *engagement* by participants with each other's contributions as the *extent of participation*, and *extent of initiation and receiving of responses* present in chat interaction, comparative group analyses showed greater engagement in the collaborative learning process by G4, compared to G1, in terms of contributions of turns, overall tendencies to send or receive ties, mutuality in information exchange and reciprocation of choice.

More specifically, application of ESA and SNA measures showed that:
 - compared to G1, G4 participants displayed a greater extent of participation by being *present* in more episodes, *lurking* in and *absent* from fewer episodes, and contributing more turns of every turn type.

- G4 displayed a less hierarchical interactional pattern than G1 with more G4 actors, besides the presenters and/or the tutor, who tended to send ties, and a greater tendency to respond directly to actors rather than send ties generally to all in the group as in G1.
- G4 actors were predominantly *Carriers*, hence displaying greater mutuality in sharing of information than G1 actors who were largely *Receivers*.
- G4 was a more balanced group with greater reciprocity in information exchange than G1.

Between tutor comparisons showed different levels of engagement in facilitating tutorials with Fay displaying a greater involvement in the learning process compared to Rachel by
- being *present* in more episodes;
- contributing more TASK turns that share information related to the course content;
- maintaining a more visible presence through frequent, dense and short contributions that exceeded the frequency of out-ties by presenters in some episodes; and
- adopting the *Carrier* actor-node type in more episodes.

The next section presents the analyses of TASK turns at the finer levels of structural organization and pragmatic intentions for a more informative interpretation of the engagement patterns observed.

5.3 Results for Research Question 1: Interactional Purposes

Earlier findings suggested that compared to G4, G1 tutorial discussions were more relevant to the issues in the set-reading(s), but there was less likelihood of reciprocity or sent ties receiving a tie in return in G1 exchanges. This section presents the results from a finer analysis of *interactional purposes* of exchanges defined as the *turn* and *Move types* adopted by participants.

This part of the analysis was conducted with ESA measures which are the ES and Move coding categories. Results from ES level analysis are first presented showing interactional purposes of turns contributed based on structural categories. Results from Move level analysis are then shown revealing pragmatic intentions of turns contributed that provide a more informative interpretation of interactional purposes in exchanges.

5.3.1 Turn types in chat exchanges

The concept of *turn types* was operationalized as the ES categories: *Initiate* (I), *Reinitiate* (RI), *Respond* (R), and *Response-Complement* (RC) that reflect the structural organization of chat exchanges[71]. Analysis of these structural elements as frequencies of ES turn types produced could reveal depth of information exchange and extent of collaboration during chat interaction.

In the ESA scheme, TASK turns are classified at ES level as (I), (RI), (R), or (RC) with the following characteristics:

- An *Initiate* anticipates a subsequent turn by another participant which leads to the start of a new exchange.
- A *Respond* replies to a previous turn and usually signals the close of the current exchange.
- A *Response-Complement* replies minimally to a previous turn, conveying acknowledgement or evaluation, and signals the close of the current exchange.
- A *Reinitiate* turn, as intermediary question or statement, responds to a previous turn, anticipates a subsequent turn by another participant which continues the current exchange.

A between group comparison showed that all four ES turn types were produced by both groups, but in varying proportion of the group's total number of ES turns (Table 5.15)[72].

- G1 produced higher percentages of (I) and (RC) compared to G4.
- G4 produced higher percentages of (RI) and (R) compared to G1.

The results suggest different tendencies between groups towards giving/sharing of substantial information in exchanges. While (R) and (RC) share certain structural characteristics[73], a (R) is distinguished from (RC) by its provision of new/additional information through elaboration and/or explanation while a (RC) is a minimal reply conveying evaluation or acknowledgement as shown below. Hence, the higher percentage of (R) taken together with lower percentage (RC) produced by G4

---

[71] Refer to the codebook (Appendix B.1) and Chapter 4, section 4.4.1 for definitions and examples of ES categories.
[72] The full ES turn type dataset is provided in Appendix C.2.
[73] Both (R) and (RC) turns are not initial in exchanges and usually signal the intention to close the exchange.

participants suggest that they were more likely to receive replies that convey substantial information i.e., [I-R]. In contrast, the higher percentage of (RC) coupled with a lower percentage of (R) produced by G1 participants imply that they tended to receive responses that share less depth of information i.e., [I-RC].

Table 5.15. Groups 1 and 4: Distribution of ES turns

G1		No. of ES Turns				G4		No. of ES Turns			
No.		I	RI	R	RC	Total	No.	I	RI	R	RC	Total
1. Derek	16	24	54	9	103	1. Evan	53	25	128	11	217
2. Max	48	9	49	23	129	2. Bill	38	10	45	18	111
3. Alvin	56	18	156	61	291	3. Mike	47	10	118	4	179
4. Cliff	67	11	72	25	175	4. Eric	47	35	261	81	424
5. Colin	46	2	21	12	81	5. Karl	19	12	80	35	146
6. Ted	47	9	55	33	144	6. Jack	57	69	228	41	395
7. Sam	22	2	60	37	121	7. Ian	46	31	247	69	393
8. Diane	100	10	68	66	244	8. Pete	47	33	146	19	245
9. James	24	7	33	15	79	9. Robin	23	14	146	56	239
10. Alan	13	2	27	15	57	10. Lim	24	37	133	19	213
11. Jason	35	7	52	6	100	11. Fay	184	64	252	52	552
12. Scott	32	0	22	15	69	Total	585	340	1784	405	3114
13. Barry	39	11	32	38	120	%	18.8	10.9	57.3	13.0	100.0
14. Tony	109	10	61	20	200						
15. Wendy	48	19	100	48	215						
16. Rachel	5	4	4	23	36						
Total	707	145	866	446	2164						
%	32.7	6.7	40.0	20.6	100.0						

No.	Participant	Turn	EXG-4-g1S3-E1					
46	Wendy>>	Well, students are assigned into groups/teams to complete a project so that students will be prepared for participation in the business world.	I+					INF
47	Wendy>>	objective is to promote techniques and procedures requisite to being effective team members and leaders.	I+					INF
48	Wendy>>	When you are in a group, it is important to discuss with each other about improving interpersonal relationships among team members, group communication skills, and group cohesiveness.	I+					INF
49	Wendy>>	Besides, clarity and specificity of team goals, procedures, and roles should be organized fairly.	I+					INF
50	Wendy>>	agree?	I					INQ
51	Alvin>>	yeah			RC			FBK-E
52	Sam>>	yep			RC			FBK-E
53	James>>	100%			RC			FBK-E
54	Alan>>	ye one person shoulnd't do all the work			R			JUS
55	Tony>>	yes			RC			FBK-E

No.	Participant	Turn	EXG-4-g4S3-E1				
56	Eric>>	What are your impressions of being able to work within a team?	I+				INQ
57	Eric>>	My Personal Thought	I+				INF
58	Eric>>	Well to put it simply I believe that being able to work within a team enables you to voice your opinions and ideas on what should happen on the task. As well as adding to a more satisfied work environment which gives high moral with the workers being included in the decision making process.	I+				INF
59	Eric>>	Does anyone have any comments?	I+				INQ
60	Eric>>	Does anyone agree or disagree with this?	I				INQ
61	Jack>>	I believe working in a team facilitates this, but doesn't ensure it will happen		R			JUS
62	Evan>>	workplace seem to be moving more towards goal oriented jobs		R			INF
63	Eric>>	so each team is assigned a goal and must perform to the specific goal			R		INF
64	Pete>>	Being able to voice an opinion is important - so is role definition and defining what it is you exactly have to produce.		R			INF
66	Bill>>	and communication and honestly with one another is a big factor			R		INF
70	Jack>>	it's like saying a team is only the sum of its parts...a teams success is interlinked with the success and desires of its individual members			R		REA
65	Robin>>	I found sometimes working in teams....occasionally there tends to be one dominate person, and tends to lead to the team and that can cause disagreements		R			INF
67	Mike>>	if you have too many leaders it doesnt work.		R			REA
71	Eric>>	But if it is a small group it is possible			R		JUS
68	Lim>>	sometimes being in a team/group doesn't mean you can voice any opinion - you are just another warm body		R			JUS

Additionally, the results suggest different extent of collaboration in the learning process of the two groups. A (RI) being an intermediary question/statement, responds to a previous turn, anticipates subsequent turn(s) by other participants which form sub-exchanges or conversational threads that branch from the main exchange. In G1, the lower percentage of (RI) coupled with a higher prevalence of (I) imply a greater tendency to start competing new exchanges rather than follow up on previous turns. The reverse pattern observed in G4 suggests greater collaborative efforts to actively attend to the meaning/implications of others' contributions and further develop the topic of discussion through reinitiating turns as opposed to only focusing on own contributions. These results substantiated earlier findings that compared to G4, G1 discussions reflected lower reciprocity levels at the episode level for the exchange of information.

A between tutor comparison showed distinct differences in proportion of ES turn types produced (Table 5.16).
- Rachel produced mainly (RC) at 63.9% followed by (I) at 13.9% for all episodes.
- Fay produced mainly (R) at 45.7% followed by (I) at 33.3% for all episodes.

Table 5.16. Tutors: Distribution of ES turns

	Distribution of ES Turns				
Tutor	I	RI	R	RC	Total
Rachel	5 (13.9%)	4 (11.1%)	4 (11.1%)	23 (63.9%)	36 (100%)
Fay	184 (33.3%)	64 (11.6%)	252 (45.7%)	52 (9.4%)	552 (100%)

Note: Frequencies of ES turns extracted from Table 5.15.

The prevalence of (I) was expected given the tutors' roles as facilitators with the responsibility of directing/stimulating discussions. Since the tutors are expected to offer social support and evaluation that constitute *social* and *teaching presences* in a *Community of Inquiry* (Garrison et al., 2000), the high percentage of (RC) produced by Rachel was also expected. However, the marked difference in percentages of (R) by Fay (45.7%) and Rachel (11.1%) suggests that Fay contributed substantially more information to discussions than Rachel. The results substantiated earlier findings that Fay was more involved in G4 discussions, compared to Rachel, by contributing more TASK turns that share information related to the course content.

While ES level analysis revealed interactional purposes of turns contributed based on structural categories, results from Move level analysis that identified the communicative intentions underlying the turns are presented below.

5.3.2 Moves in chat exchanges

In Move level analysis, TASK turns previously coded as (I), (RI), (R), or (RC) were further categorized according to interpretations of their pragmatic functions. For instance, a turn coded as (I) at the ES level could be interpreted to have a communicative intention to *Inquire* {INQ} at the Move level[74]. Analyses of Moves as *frequencies*[75] and *range* of Move types adopted could reveal the underlying interactional purposes of turns sent by participants which form the basis for a later examination of information-sharing and topic development phases during the collaborative group learning process. In this section, results from comparative group and tutor analyses of Moves associated with each ES turn type are first described followed by discussion of the results.

The concept of *Move types* was operationalized as the following Move categories associated with each ES turn type:
- (I) associated Moves {INF, INQ, JUS, REA}
- (RI) associated Moves {CLA, CHK, EXD, CHA}
- (R) associated Moves {INF, REA, JUS}
- (RC) associated Moves {FBK-E, FBK-A}

Table 5.17[76] shows the frequency and percentage of Moves associated with ES turn types adopted by G1 and G4 participants for all episodes.

Table 5.17. Groups 1 and 4: Distribution of Moves for all episodes

	(I) associated Moves					(R) associated Moves			
	I-{INF}	I-{INQ}	I-{JUS}	I-{REA}	Total	R-{INF}	R-{JUS}	R-{REA}	Total
G1	550	146	6	14	716	448	321	98	867
	76.8%	20.4%	0.8%	2.0%	100.0%	51.7%	37.0%	11.3%	100.0%
G4	326	251	2	10	589	1131	479	180	1790
	55.3%	42.6%	0.3%	1.7%	100.0%	63.2%	26.8%	10.1%	100.0%

	(RI) associated Moves					(RC) associated Moves		
	RI-{CHK}	RI-{CLA}	RI-{EXD}	RI-{CHA}	Total	RC-{FBK-E}	RC-{FBK-A}	Total
G1	79	43	8	17	147	395	51	446
	53.7%	29.3%	5.4%	11.6%	100.0%	88.6%	11.4%	100.0%
G4	189	117	27	9	342	356	49	405
	55.3%	34.2%	7.9%	2.6%	100.0%	87.9%	12.1%	100.0%

A between group comparison of *(I) associated Moves* (Figure 5.1)[77] found
- little difference in the percentages of I-{JUS} and I-{REA} which was expected since it is not common to *Justify* or *Reason* at the start of a new exchange.

---

[74] Refer to the codebook (Appendix B.1) and Chapter 4, section 4.4.1 for definitions and examples of Move categories.
[75] The sum of all Moves may not tally with sum of ES turns due to double-coding at Move level.
[76] The full Move dataset is provided in Appendix C.3.
[77] Data for Figures 5.1 to 5.4 were based on Table 5.17.

- both groups mainly initiated exchanges to provide information, but G1 tended to adopt I-{INF} more than G4.
- G4 was more likely to initiate exchanges with questions than G1 i.e., I-{INQ}.

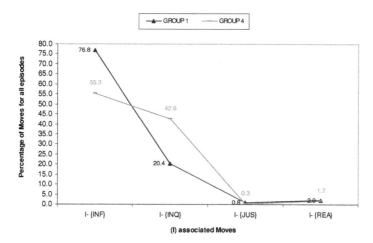

Figure 5.1. Groups 1 and 4: Comparison of (I) associated Moves

A between group comparison of *(RI) associated Moves* (Figure 5.2) found
- little difference in the percentages of RI-{CHK}, RI{CLA} and RI-{EXD}.
- a larger 9% difference in the percentage of RI-{CHA} with G1 more likely to Reinitiate to *Challenge* than G4.

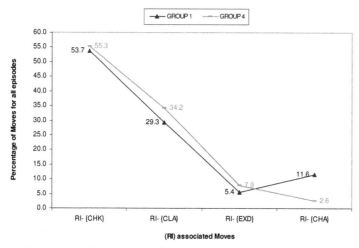

Figure 5.2. Groups 1 and 4: Comparison of (RI) associated Moves

A between group comparison of *(R) associated Moves* (Figure 5.3) found
  - little difference in the percentage of R-{REA}.
  - both groups mainly responded to give information, but G1 was more likely to R-{INF} than G4.
  - G1 was more likely respond for defending/disputing what was said in current or previous turns than G4 i.e., R-{JUS}.

A between group comparison of *(RC) associated Moves* (Figure 5.4) found little difference in the percentages of RC-{FBK-E} and RC-{FBK-A} adopted by both groups.

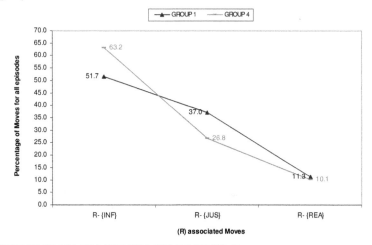

Figure 5.3. Groups 1 and 4: Comparison of (R) associated Moves

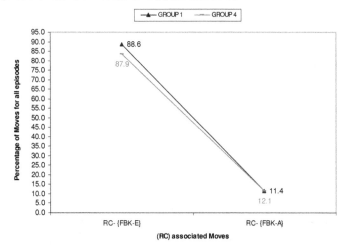

Figure 5.4. Groups 1 and 4: Comparison of (RC) associated Moves

- *Discussion of (I) associated Moves*

Findings at ES level showed that G1 produced a higher percentage of (I) compared to G4 (Table 5.18).

Table 5.18. Groups 1 and 4: Summary distribution of ES turns

	Distribution of ES Turns				
	I	RI	R	RC	Total
G1	707 (32.7%)	145 (6.7%)	866 (40.0%)	446 (20.6%)	2164 (100%)
G4	585 (18.8%)	340 (10.9%)	1784 (57.3%)	405 (13.0%)	3114 (100%)

Note: Data extracted from Table 5.15.

Move level analysis revealed that while both groups mainly adopted I-{INF} for providing information or making observations (see examples), G4 displayed a more balanced distribution of I-{INF} and I-{INQ}. The results suggest that besides information giving, G4 tended to use questions for starting discussions and stimulating debate whereas G1 tended to concentrate on giving information than eliciting information from others at the start of exchanges.

No.	Participant	Turn	EXG-7-g1S11-E2			
80	Sam>>	i am from south africa and they just accepted the use of CCTV recently a few years ago	I			INF
81	Cliff>>	have they been effective?		RI		CHK
83	Sam>>	yep, southafrica is one of the crime centers of the world...anyway i belive that CCTV is ggod and will expand in the near future			R	INF

No.	Participant	Turn	EXG-11-g4S11-E2			
136	Robin>>	they use CCTV at my mum's work where they thought it was a bomb... etc... its become a handy tool there	I			INF
139	Fay>>	they thought it was for a bomb?		RI		CHK
148	Robin>>	no.. they used it because a package was left.. and because they could see it on CCTV they were able to asses if it was a bomb or not			R	INF

- *Discussion of (RI) associated Moves*

ES level analysis found that G4 produced a higher percentage of (RI) compared to G1. Move level analysis showed that both groups used (RI) mainly to {CHK} and {CLA}. As shown below, RI-{CHK} is used to make certain the meaning of previous turns, usually through statements or closed questions that specify the information to be confirmed as options provided by the speaker. RI-{CLA} is used to seek more information on previous turns for making meaning clearer usually through open-ended questions.

In terms of the learning processes in both groups, the presence of RI-{CHK} suggests a degree of familiarity with the content/issues under discussion in order to be able to offer alternative perspectives. The presence of RI-{CLA} suggests an awareness of a knowledge gap or the incongruity of ideas/views presented in previous turns. The significance of the pattern of RI-{CHK} and RI-{CLA} found will be further examined (in section 5.4 of this chapter) in terms of topic development in the collaborative learning process.

No.	Participant	Turn	EXG-10-g4S3-E1							
166	Eric>>	This one is from Bill	I+							INF
168	Eric>>	How often should ?GroupThink? activities, suggestions and discussions take	I+							INQ
170	Eric>>	place for a heathly workplace and how often should procedures in a workplace be	I+							INQ
171	Eric>>	updated and changed?	I+							INQ
172	Eric>>	Would you like to or anyone else like to add to this?	I							INQ
173	Jack>>	as often as needed...which is kind of a paradox, given that it'd be up to the group to decide when it was required		R						REA
175	Eric>>	or to management organising the groups			R					INF
174	Fay>>	and they may not recognise it			R					INF
178	Robin>>	so if they (the group) don't recognise it then should management decide?? or just leave it to the group				RI				CHK
184	Bill>>	i think pete said or somthing said it earlier.. the works know from first hand experience (shop floor) what works well and what doesn't						R		INF
187	Pete>>	i think you have a have a feel for when the group is stagnating vs when its comfortable...simplest way is to ask, I suppose.						R		REA
188	Eric>>	i agree							RC	FBK-E

No.	Participant	Turn	EXG-5-g1S3-E1						
60	Wendy>>	If teamwork is implemented and supervised effectively, it can work in wondrous ways in successfully meeting the objectives.	I+						INF
61	Wendy>>	However, there is an issue raised by Hollander, a business ethicist, that because team leaders are in a position of authority, they may perform poorly and nonetheless be rewarded for their behavior.	I+						INF
62	Wendy>>	How should one resolve on the issue on how to equally reward (or punish) both the team leaders and their team members once they achieve their goals?	I+						INQ
63	Wendy>>	Besides, whose benefits have priority? Opinions?	I						INQ
64	Ted>>	if their still achieving their goals, why punish them?		RI					CLA
65	Alvin>>	if they haven't reach, then maybe need punish			R+				REA
69	Alvin>>	one of the team work option is they need 2 monitor each other in case have any mistake			R				REA

A particularly interesting result is the higher percentage of RI-{CHA} adopted by G1 compared to G4. RI-{CHA} is used to propose or assert the need for another direction for discussion/thought (see examples). While the presence of RI-{CHA} may mean more *disputational talk* (Wegerif & Mercer, 1997) in G1, which is characterized by conflict and disagreement, this study regards RI-{CHA} as a necessary element in the social constructivist learning process. RI-{CHA} Moves are sources of 'perturbation' (von Glasersfeld, 1989) that prompt debate and reconsideration of ideas presented which signal efforts at meaning negotiation. When coupled with a prevalence of I-{INF} and R-{INF}, as in both groups, it could be argued that the interactional patterns of both groups reflect more closely the characteristics of *exploratory talk* (Wegerif & Mercer, 1997) as participants cooperate to share information yet contribute critical responses that prompt efforts from others to justify or explain their views.

No.	Participant	Turn	EXG-4-g1S5-E1						
80	Colin>>	Question: Would a Virtual Organisation be successful if the particiapants are not willing to participate? How could you increase the likely hood for participants to want to participate?	I						INQ
91	Cliff>>	if there is no incentive to participate, then why bother?		RI					CHA
94	Colin>>	well thats right, i guess to begin with people would be there for a similar reason, they have the choise to participate within the virtual community			R				JUS

No.	Participant	Turn	EXG-16-g4S6-E1					
236	Ian>>	Do you think people who spend more of there time on the net chatting in msn, ICQ,	I+					INQ
237	Ian>>	yahoo etc... lack social communication skills when in Face to face situations	I					INQ
244	Fay>>	i think we have the notion of causality here - which i talked about in the lecture today	R+					INF
250	Fay>>	perhaps these ppl who use chat a lot may never have had good social skills	R					INF
251	Ian>>	they use it as a substitute		R				INF
255	Lim>>	but following the flow of discussion here is a skill		R				JUS
256	Fay>>	good point hwee - we are developing different skills			R+			JUS
258	Fay>>	skills in multitasking and multithread conversations			R			JUS
259	Eric>>	ok					RC	FBK-A
260	Ian>>	we are able to skim read better					R	INF
262	Jack>>	is it really a new skill which must be learnt? I would argue if you already have adequate literacy skills you will simply be given the opportunity to use those.					RI	CHA

- *Discussion of (R) associated Moves*

ES level analysis found that G4 produced a higher percentage of (R) compared to G1. Results from Move level analysis indicate that both groups used (R) mainly to {INF}. Compared to G4, the higher percentage of R-{JUS} observed in G1 is likely to be related to the prevalence of G1 RI-{CHA} found earlier suggesting efforts by G1 participants to defend/dispute challenges with information or evidence (see example). The low prevalence of R-{REA} in both groups which is used to present constructed beliefs or extended reasoning (see example) is noteworthy and the implications will be discussed in Chapter 6.

No.	Participant	Turn	EXG-8-g1S6-E1					
79	Tony>>	How about people hook into internet and no spending time with family	I					INQ
96	Derek>>	Honestly I believe the issue is not the internet, but the personality of the users. There are those who will be heavy users and still be socially active and vice versa. The internet just magnifies the behaviour. The internet cant be blamed for people who abuse it.	RI					CHA
98	Wendy>>	true			R+			JUS
102	Wendy>>	I also strongly believe that it depends on their own personality n behaviors			R+			JUS
103	Wendy>>	also what do they do using the internet			R			JUS

No.	Participant	Turn	EXG-12-g4S11-E1					
192	Fay>>	i wonder if he knew what impact "i have a dream" would become?	I					INQ
195	Lim>>	if it had been copyrighted, it probably wouldn't have reached so many people		R				REA
196	Ian>>	i think he had no idea of the scope it would have the speech and thats why they tried to get as much coverage and neglected the copyright		R				REA

- *Discussion of (RC) associated Moves*

ES level analysis found that G1 produced a higher percentage of (RC) compared to G4. Move level analysis revealed little difference in the proportion of RC-{FBK-E} and RC-{FBK-A} adopted by both groups. The results suggest that both groups primarily used RC-{FBK-E} to provide evaluative responses, comment minimally on the quality of previous turns by indicating agreement, disagreement, or neutrality which was expected in the context of topic-based discussions (see examples). RC-{FBK-A} was also adopted, but to a lesser degree for phatic functions i.e., establish social contact or acknowledge the hearing of previous turns by reporting the state of the speaker.

No.	Participant	Turn	EXG-8-g1S3-E1								
80	James>>	a group has a common goal which is important than there personal goals	I								INF
81	Wendy>>	true					RC				FBK-E
82	Max>>	true					RC				FBK-E

No.	Participant	Turn	EXG-15-g4S4-E2								
195	Jack>>	One quick question I wanted to ask: If Hofstede isn't entirely accurate, does that make Maitland's article less reliable?	I								INQ
202	Fay>>	not necessarily					R+				JUS
203	Fay>>	what if she found her propositions didn't hold					R+				JUS
205	Fay>>	that might indicate the assumptions were invalid					R+				JUS
207	Fay>>	she actually went on to do further study with those propositions					R+				INF
212	Fay>>	but i like the article, as i said, because it showed innovative thinking and has a good overview					R				JUS
209	Ian>>	ok						RC			FBK-A
210	Eric>>	hmm intersting						RC			FBK-E

Table 5.19 shows the frequency and percentage of Moves associated with ES turn types adopted by the tutors for all episodes.

Table 5.19. Tutors: Distribution of Moves for all episodes

Tutor	(I) associated Moves					(R) associated Moves			
	I-{INF}	I-{INQ}	I-{JUS}	I-{REA}	Total	R-{INF}	R-{JUS}	R-{REA}	Total
Rachel	0	5	0	0	5	4	0	0	4
	0.0%	100.0%	0.0%	0.0%	100.0%	100.0%	0.0%	0.0%	100.0%
Fay	105	77	1	1	184	164	70	19	253
	57.1%	41.8%	0.5%	0.5%	100.0%	64.8%	27.7%	7.5%	100.0%

Tutor	(RI) associated Moves					(RC) associated Moves		
	RI-{CHK}	RI-{CLA}	RI-{EXD}	RI-{CHA}	Total	RC-{FBK-E}	RC-{FBK-A}	Total
Rachel	1	3	0	0	4	21	2	23
	25.0%	75.0%	0.0%	0.0%	100.0%	91.3%	8.7%	100.0%
Fay	35	25	4	0	64	39	13	52
	54.7%	39.1%	6.3%	0.0%	100.0%	75.0%	25.0%	100.0%

When findings from ES and Move level analyses were considered, a between tutor comparison showed the following patterns of interactional purposes adopted:

- Fay's use of *(I) associated Moves* was spread among I-{INF, INQ, JUS, REA} while Rachel adopted only I-{INQ} for all episodes. The results suggest that compared to Rachel, Fay produced a higher percentage of (I) turns that were relatively balanced between initiating to give information and using questions to elicit more information during discussions.

- A similar pattern was observed in Fay's distribution of *(R) associated Moves* to include R-{INF, JUS, REA}, whereas Rachel used only R-{INF}. This suggests that Rachel produced a lower percentage of (R) turns which were mainly replies that state information from external sources rather than responses that defend/dispute stated positions or present constructed beliefs/reasoning.

- Although there was little difference in the percentage of (RI) produced by both tutors, Move level analysis revealed very different uses of (RI). While the greater proportion of *(RI) associated Moves* comprised RI-{CHK} and RI-{CLA} for both tutors, Rachel reinitiated primarily to {CLA} i.e., seek more information on previous turns to make meaning clearer through open-ended questions. In contrast, Fay had a more balanced distribution of {CLA} and {CHK} reflecting additional attempts to ascertain the meaning of previous turns through statements or closed questions that specify the information to be confirmed. None of the tutors adopted RI-{CHA} which was expected since it could be regarded as a relatively aggressive Move for facilitators.

- Given the marked difference in the percentage of (RC) produced by both tutors (Rachel=63.9%, Fay=9.4%), it was interesting to find similar patterns in their use of *(RC) associated Moves.* Both tutors adopted RC-{FBK-E, FBK-A} with a greater proportion of RC-{FBK-E} for contributing evaluative comments on previous turns.

5.3.3 Move range

Based on the ESA scheme, Moves represent pragmatic purposes of turns and reflect the rhetorical tactics used by participants to achieve certain interactional purposes. In the context of collaborative learning, use of a wide range of Moves indicates more effort by participants to provide information, convey meaning, prompt, probe, or shape the direction of discussions. The presence of such efforts could reflect the extent of learning support available from peers and the tutor in collaborative group learning processes. Results from the analysis of *Move range*, operationalized as the maximum and minimum number of Move types used by participants for all episodes, are shown in Table 5.20.

Table 5.20. Groups 1 and 4: Move Range

	Range of (I) associated Move Types				Range of (R) associated Move Types		
	Max 4	3	2	1	Max 3	2	1
Frequency of G1 participants	1 (6.3%)	5 (31.3%)	9 (56.3%)	1 (6.3%)	11 (68.8%)	4 (25.0%)	1 (6.3%)
Frequency of G4 participants	2 (18.1%)	3 (27.3%)	6 (54.6%)	0 (0.0%)	10 (91.0%)	1 (9.0%)	0 (0.0%)
	Range of (RI) associated Move Types				Range of (RC) associated Move Types		
	Max 4	3	2	1	Max 2		1
Frequency of G1 participants	3 (18.8%)	7 (43.8%)	3 (18.8%)	3 (18.8%)	15 (93.8%)		(6.3%)
Frequency of G4 participants	4 (36.4%)	3 (27.3 %)	4 (36.4%)	0 (0.0%)	11 (100.0%)		0 (0.0%)

Note: There are 4 Move types associated with both (I) and (RI); 3 Move types associated with (R), and 2 Move types associated with (RC).

A between group comparison of Move range showed that:
- out of the 4 Moves associated with (I) and (RI), a greater percentage of G4 participants used at least 3 (I) and (RI) associated Moves compared to G1.
- out of the 3 Moves associated with (R), a greater percentage of G4 participants used the full range of Moves compared to G1.
- out of the 2 Moves associated with (RC), 100% of G4 participants used the full range of Moves compared to G1.

Table 5.21 compares the range of Moves adopted by both tutors for all episodes. The results show that both tutors used the full range of Moves associated with (RC). However, compared to Rachel, Fay used a much wider range of Moves associated with (I), (RI) and R).

Overall, G4 was found to use a broader range of Moves associated with each ES turn type for all episodes compared to G1. The results suggest a greater tendency by G4 to provide information, convey meaning, prompt, probe, or shape the direction of discussions. The display of such interactional purposes reflects greater involvement by G4 participants in supporting the group learning process. Additionally, the wider Move range used by Fay, compared to Rachel, suggests greater efforts in tutor scaffolding, hence substantiating earlier findings that Fay maintained a more visible tutor presence and was more involved in G4 learning processes. Implications of the findings on Move range will be discussed in Chapter 6 in terms of availability of tutor and peer learning support.

Table 5.21. Tutors: Summary of Move Range

	Rachel	Fay
Range of (I) associated Move Types	1	4
Range of (RI) associated Move Types	2	3
Range of (R) associated Move Types	1	3
Range of (RC) associated Move Types	2	2

Note: Data summarized from Table 5.19.

5.3.4 Summary

ES and Move level analyses revealed additional facets in earlier findings on engagement by participants in each other's contributions with results that indicated the underlying interactional purposes of chat exchanges. Earlier findings suggested that compared to G4, G1 discussions were more relevant to the issues in the set-reading(s) but displayed lower levels of reciprocity. ES and Move level analyses substantiated these findings with results showing less collaborative effort in G1 exchanges as participants tended to concentrate on starting rivaling exchanges rather than follow up the meanings of previous turns or elicit information from others. Although G1 discussions were more relevant, responses by participants were likely to take the form of (RC) turns that convey less depth of information.

Comparative group analyses at Move level showed a greater focus by G1, compared to G4, on initiating to provide information than eliciting information from others at the start of exchanges, and responding to justify as a consequence of the use of more challenges. A broader Move range found in G4 suggested greater efforts by participants to support the group learning process by using Moves that serve to provide information, convey meaning, prompt, probe, and shape the direction of discussions

Results from tutor comparison substantiated earlier findings on different levels of tutor engagement in facilitating tutorials. Compared to Rachel, there was stronger effort by Fay to scaffold interactions in G4 by contributing greater depth of information with (R), initiating to both give information and elicit information, and adopting a wider range of Moves.

The next section extends the findings on interactional purposes of exchanges by further examining the ES and Move turn types identified in broader terms of participation equality and knowledge construction during the collaborative group learning process.

5.4 Results for Research Question 1: Collaborative Learning Process in Groups
Building on earlier findings on engagement by participants with each other's contributions and interactional purposes of turns in exchanges, this section presents the results from a broader analysis of the *collaborative learning process in groups* defined as the presence of *equality of participation,* and *information-sharing and topic development* in chat exchanges.

5.4.1 Equality of participation
The construct *equality of participation* was operationalized as the following SNA and ESA measures:
(a) Inclusiveness of learning network
(b) Frequency of *Initiate, Reinitiate* and *Respond* extended turn sequences

(a) Inclusiveness of learning network
The SNA measure of *inclusiveness*[78] is defined as the number of connected nodes expressed as a proportion of the total number of nodes present in the network (Scott, 2000). This measure was used to determine the *level of connectivity* of actor-nodes in a network to one another within an exchange. In this part of the analysis, *actor-nodes* are defined as the participants in each exchange. A *connection* exists between a pair of actor-nodes which has ties incident to and/or from each other i.e., i -> j, i <- j or i <-> j. An *Isolate* is an actor-node with no ties incident to or from it.

The value of inclusiveness was computed with the following formula; where N=nodes; I=Isolates.

$$\frac{\sum N - \sum I}{\sum N} \times 100$$

The inclusiveness value obtained could range from 0 to 1; indicating the level of connectivity of actor-nodes in a network/group to one another within an exchange. If the value = 0, then there are no connections/ties between all the actor-nodes (Isolates); if the value = 1, all the actor-nodes are connected to one another at the exchange level. Therefore, a 4 actor-node network that contains 1 Isolate would have an inclusiveness of 0.75 or <1 (Scott, 2000, pp. 70-71) (Figure 5.5). The inclusiveness value obtained at the exchange level could therefore reveal instances when ties are present between certain actors, yet absent between other actors in the group. Such patterns in chat exchanges could indicate the extent to which actors are involved in tutorial discussions; and the exclusion and inclusion of certain actors from the dialogic process of knowledge construction. When ties are regarded as means for exchange of information, social and emotional support between actors, the presence or absence of such ties could also suggest the extent of learning support available to the actors in the group.

Application of the inclusiveness measure necessitates the following data conditions and theoretical assumption that are explained below:
- the presence of directed ties;
- the conversion of valued ties to dichotomous ties; and
- ties/turns could be directed to all or specific actors in chat exchanges.

---

[78] The SNA concept of inclusiveness was discussed in Chapter 4, section 4.4.2.

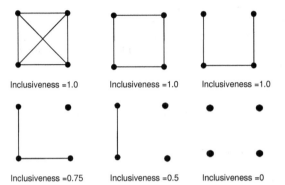

Inclusiveness =1.0   Inclusiveness =1.0   Inclusiveness =1.0

Inclusiveness =0.75   Inclusiveness =0.5   Inclusiveness =0

Figure 5.5. Comparisons of inclusiveness in a 4 actor-node network (adapted from Scott, 2000, p. 71)

Although inclusiveness is a parameter in the measure of network density, this analysis focuses on the presence or absence of connections between actor-nodes rather than the strength of ties among nodes as in the case of network density. Accordingly, while *direction* of ties is meaningful for establishing existence of connections, the *value* of ties that indicates frequency/intensity of connections is not necessary for determining presence or absence of connections between actors.

Although *actor-nodes type* analysis conducted previously[79] shares the assumption that ties/turns could be directed to all or specific actors in a network, Isolates were not expected at the episode level since metastatements by presenters at the start of each episode, that are interpreted as being sent to all, would have established a connection between all actors in the network. In this section, inclusiveness analysis was carried out at the *exchange* level where *Isolates* could be expected in exchanges when discussions involve a subset of actor-nodes with ties incident to and/or from one another that exclude other actors in the same network.

The inclusiveness values for all exchanges are shown in Table 5.22 and Table 5.23. The frequency and percentage of exchanges with inclusiveness of <1 and =1 are summarized in Table 5.24.

A between group comparison showed
- G1 exchanges with inclusiveness of <1 comprised 1.6% (3) of all exchanges (189).
- G4 exchanges with inclusiveness of <1 comprised 4.3% (11) of all exchanges (257).

The results suggest that when equality of participation was measured in terms of connectivity of actors to one another other at the exchange level as indicated by the presence or absence of ties, there was a small difference (2.7%) between both groups in the percentage of exchanges where actors within the same network were not involved in the discussions i.e. Isolates in exchanges.

---

[79] Refer to this chapter, section 5.2.

Table 5.22. Group 1: Inclusiveness values of exchanges for all episodes

G1	Inclusiveness Value of Exchange															
Episode	EXG-1	EXG-2	EXG-3	EXG-4	EXG-5	EXG-6	EXG-7	EXG-8	EXG-9	EXG-10	EXG-11	EXG-12	EXG-13	EXG-14	EXG-15	EXG-16
S1-E1	1.00	1.00	**0.15**	1.00	1.00	1.00	1.00	1.00								
S1-E2	1.00	1.00	1.00	1.00	1.00											
S2-E1	1.00	1.00	1.00	1.00	1.00	1.00	1.00	1.00	1.00	1.00	1.00	1.00	1.00	1.00	1.00	
S2-E2	1.00	1.00	1.00	1.00	1.00	1.00	1.00	1.00	1.00	1.00	1.00	1.00				
S3-E1	1.00	1.00	1.00	1.00	1.00	1.00	1.00	1.00	1.00	1.00						
S3-E2	1.00	1.00	1.00	1.00	1.00	1.00	1.00	1.00	**0.14**	1.00						
S4-E1	1.00	1.00														
S4-E2	1.00	1.00	1.00	1.00	1.00	1.00	1.00	1.00	1.00	1.00	1.00	1.00	1.00	1.00	1.00	
S5-E1	1.00	1.00	1.00	1.00	1.00											
S5-E2	1.00	1.00	1.00	1.00	1.00	1.00	1.00	1.00	1.00	1.00	**0.27**					
S6-E1	1.00	1.00	1.00	1.00	1.00	1.00	1.00	1.00	1.00	1.00	1.00					
S6-E2	1.00	1.00	1.00	1.00	1.00	1.00	1.00	1.00	1.00							
S7-E1	1.00	1.00	1.00	1.00	1.00	1.00	1.00	1.00	1.00	1.00	1.00	1.00	1.00	1.00	1.00	1.00
S7-E2	1.00	1.00	1.00	1.00	1.00	1.00	1.00	1.00								
S8-E1	1.00	1.00	1.00	1.00	1.00	1.00	1.00	1.00	1.00	1.00						
S8-E2	1.00	1.00	1.00	1.00	1.00	1.00	1.00									
S9-E1	1.00	1.00	1.00	1.00	1.00	1.00	1.00	1.00								
S9-E2	1.00	1.00														
S10-E1	1.00	1.00	1.00	1.00	1.00	1.00										
S10-E2	1.00	1.00	1.00	1.00	1.00											
S11-E1	1.00	1.00	1.00	1.00	1.00	1.00										
S11-E2	1.00	1.00	1.00	1.00	1.00	1.00	1.00									

Note:
- Inclusiveness values could range from 0 to 1. If the value =0, then there are no connections between all the actor-nodes (Isolates); if the value =1, all the actor-nodes are connected to one another at the exchange level.
- Given the narrow range of values, results are displayed with two decimal places.

Table 5.23. Group 4: Inclusiveness values of exchanges for all episodes

G4 Episode	Inclusiveness Value of Exchange																				
	EXG-1	EXG-2	EXG-3	EXG-4	EXG-5	EXG-6	EXG-7	EXG-8	EXG-9	EXG-10	EXG-11	EXG-12	EXG-13	EXG-14	EXG-15	EXG-16	EXG-17	EXG-18	EXG-19	EXG-20	EXG-21
S1-E1	1.00	**0.50**	1.00	1.00	**0.25**	1.00	1.00	**0.38**	1.00												
S1-E2	1.00	1.00	1.00	1.00	1.00	1.00	1.00	1.00	1.00												
S2-E1	1.00	1.00	1.00	1.00																	
S2-E2	1.00	1.00	1.00	1.00	1.00	1.00	1.00	1.00	1.00	1.00	1.00	1.00	1.00	1.00	1.00	1.00	1.00	1.00	1.00	1.00	1.00
S3-E1	1.00	1.00	1.00	1.00	1.00	1.00	1.00	**0.56**	1.00	1.00	1.00	1.00									
S3-E2	1.00	1.00	1.00	1.00																	
S4-E1	1.00	1.00	1.00	1.00	1.00	1.00	1.00	1.00	1.00	1.00	1.00										
S4-E2	1.00	1.00	1.00	1.00	1.00	1.00	1.00	1.00	1.00	1.00	1.00	1.00	1.00	1.00	1.00						
S5-E1	1.00	1.00	1.00	1.00	1.00	1.00	1.00	1.00	1.00	1.00	1.00	1.00									
S5-E2	1.00	1.00	1.00	1.00	1.00	1.00	1.00	1.00	1.00	1.00	1.00	1.00	1.00	1.00							
S6-E1	1.00	1.00	1.00	1.00	1.00	1.00	1.00	1.00	1.00	1.00	1.00	1.00	1.00	1.00	1.00	1.00	1.00	1.00			
S6-E2	1.00	1.00	1.00	1.00	1.00	1.00	1.00	1.00	1.00	**0.67**	1.00										
S7-E1	1.00	1.00	1.00	1.00	1.00	1.00	1.00	1.00	1.00	1.00	1.00	1.00	1.00	1.00	1.00	1.00					
S7-E2	1.00	1.00	1.00																		
S8-E1	1.00	1.00	1.00	1.00	1.00	1.00	**0.25**	1.00	1.00	1.00	1.00	1.00	1.00	1.00	1.00	1.00	**0.75**	1.00			
S8-E2	1.00	1.00	1.00	1.00	1.00	1.00	1.00	1.00	1.00	1.00	1.00										
S9-E1	1.00	1.00	1.00	1.00	1.00	1.00	1.00	1.00	1.00	1.00	1.00										
S9-E2	1.00	1.00	1.00	1.00	1.00	1.00	1.00	1.00													
S10-E1	1.00																				
S10-E2	1.00	1.00	**0.22**	**0.78**	1.00	1.00	1.00	1.00	1.00	1.00	1.00										
S11-E1	1.00	1.00	1.00	1.00	1.00	1.00	1.00	1.00	1.00	1.00	1.00	1.00	1.00	1.00	1.00	1.00					
S11-E2	1.00	**0.18**	1.00	1.00	1.00	1.00	1.00	1.00	1.00	1.00	1.00	1.00	1.00	**0.82**	1.00	1.00	1.00	1.00	1.00	1.00	1.00

Note:
- Inclusiveness values could range from 0 to 1. If the value =0, then there are no connections between all the actor-nodes (Isolates); if the value =1, all the actor-nodes are connected to one another at the exchange level.
- Given the narrow range of values, results are displayed with two decimal places.

Table 5.24. Groups 1 and 4: Distribution of exchanges with inclusiveness of =1 and <1 for all episodes

| | Frequency of Exchange | | | |
| | Inclusiveness =1 | | Inclusiveness <1 | |
Episode	G1	G4	G1	G4
S1-E1	7	6	1	3
S1-E2	5	9	0	0
S2-E1	15	4	0	0
S2-E2	13	21	0	0
S3-E1	10	11	0	1
S3-E2	9	4	1	0
S4-E1	2	11	0	0
S4-E2	15	15	0	0
S5-E1	5	12	0	0
S5-E2	10	15	1	0
S6-E1	11	18	0	0
S6-E2	9	10	0	1
S7-E1	16	17	0	0
S7-E2	8	3	0	0
S8-E1	10	16	0	2
S8-E2	7	11	0	0
S9-E1	8	11	0	0
S9-E2	2	8	0	0
S10-E1	6	1	0	0
S10-E2	5	9	0	2
S11-E1	6	15	0	0
S11-E2	7	19	0	2
Total	186	246	3	11
%	98.4	95.7	1.6	4.3

A further examination of *tutors as Isolates* in exchanges with inclusiveness of <1 showed that
- out of 3 G1 exchanges with inclusiveness of <1, Rachel was an Isolate in 66.7% (2) of the exchanges (Figure 5.6).
- out of 11 G4 exchanges with inclusiveness of <1, Fay was an Isolate in 18.2 % (2) of the exchanges (Figure 5.7).

The results indicate that compared to Rachel, Fay was involved in the discussions for a substantially larger percentage of exchanges which substantiated earlier findings that Fay was a Carrier in all episodes; displaying greater mutuality in the sharing of information than Rachel during the learning process.

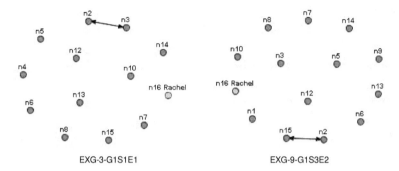

Figure 5.6. Rachel as Isolate in exchanges: EXG-3-G1S1E1, EXG-9-G1S3E2

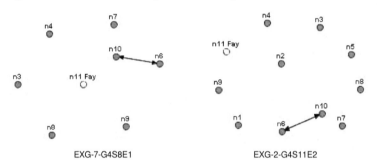

Figure 5.7. Fay as Isolate in exchanges: EXG-7-G4S8E1, EXG-2-G4S11E2

(b) Frequency of extended turn sequences
Findings from inclusiveness analysis showed the presence or absence of connections between actor-nodes implying the inclusion or exclusion of actors from discussions at the exchange level. In this part of the analysis, the construct *equality of participation* was operationalized as the ESA measure of frequency of *extended turn sequences* which could indicate extent of control exercised by certain participants in exchanges through which others may be excluded from discussions.

An *extended turn sequence*[80] is a sequence of two or more turns of the same ES type (by the same speaker) that may/may not immediately follow each other in the transcript due to system lag and/or use of multiple short postings by the participant in order to convey a message. Through the posting of multiple turns, the sender avoids being interrupted and maintains a hold on the floor i.e., the 'speaking' time necessary to communicate the message. At the same time, assuming that participants have a degree of understanding regarding their roles in the dialogue, the pragmatic intentions of turns, and the system of turn-taking that minimizes 'gap and overlap' in conversations (Sacks et al., 1974), other participants in the group are likely to refrain from posting their own messages until the perceived completion of the turn sequence.

---

[80] Extended turn sequences were defined with examples in the codebook (Appendix B.1) and discussed in Chapter 4, section 4.4.1.

In terms of equality of participation, the use of extended turn sequences could therefore reduce opportunities for contributing to the discussion while certain participants such as the presenters or tutors signal their continued intention to hold the floor. When these sequences are present as *Initiate*, *Reinitiate* and *Respond*[81] types of extended turn sequences i.e., I-SEQ, RI-SEQ, R-SEQ (see examples), they signal efforts by participants to avoid being interrupted, thereby exerting control of discussion for various purposes during the learning process.

No.	Participant	Turn	EXG-1-g1S2-E2					
1	Diane>>	this brings me to the next article	I+					INF
2	Diane>>	the 3rd one which looks at video conferncing	I+					INF
3	Diane>>	Video conferencing, as mentioned in the lecture	I+					INF
4	Diane>>	is a form of asynchronous communication	I+					INF
5	Diane>>	real-time communication	I+					INF
6	Diane>>	time for a question	I+					INF
7	Diane>>	Do you think that mediums like video conferencing fill the void of in interpersonal warmth and social interaction that something like email lacks? Or is it overrated? (also consider technical issues/ jerks and lags in video streaming)	I+					INQ
8	Diane>>	answers/opinions anyone?	I					INQ

No.	Participant	Turn	EXG-7-g1S2-E2					
124	Alvin>>	but how about someone using ur id??????????	RI+					CHA
127	Alvin>>	i means maybe in the lab, the person next 2 u c ur username and password, and use ur id 2 login	RI					CHA

No.	Participant	Turn	EXG-1-g4S3-E2					
9	Jack>>	I agree with Pete. CMC removes a certain fear most people have when faced with speaking their mind.	R+					JUS
10	Jack>>	(in a group or team situation)	R+					JUS
15	Jack>>	you need to have a facilitator just the same as mentioned before, but they would act in a different way	R					JUS

The social constructive learning framework adopted in this study assumes that knowledge construction is supported by initial scaffolding by the tutors and gradual withdrawal of learning support as students gain greater control of the chat discussions over time (Vygotsky, 1962/1986; Wertsch, 1985). Patterns in the use of extended turn sequences by the tutors over time (22 episodes) could therefore indicate whether reduced control of discussion was present in the collaborative learning process. Additionally, findings from the measure could also suggest the extent to which the tutors were involved in providing learning support.

Within each group, R-SEQ was found to constitute the largest percentage of all extended sequences (Table 5.25) but there were noteworthy differences in the proportion of I-SEQ, RI-SEQ and R-SEQ between the groups.

A between group comparison showed
- a higher percentage of I-SEQ produced by G1 compared to G4.
- higher percentages of R-SEQ and RI-SEQ produced by G4 compared to G1.

The results on *I-SEQ* suggest a greater tendency by G1 participants to hold the initiative in discussions by using multiple (I) turns at the start of new exchanges. When considered together with earlier findings that I-{INF} was the predominant (I) associated Move type adopted by G1, it presents the possibility that G1 pattern of I-SEQ usage was due to the tutorial activity structure whereby presenters were

---

[81] (RC) extended turn sequences were found to be rare. By definition, (RC) turns convey minimal information and function to close the current exchange. Hence, (RC) extended turn sequences were excluded from analysis.

expected to outline the scope of discussions at the start of episodes, stimulate and moderate discussions.

Table 5.25. Groups 1 and 4: Distribution of extended turn sequences for all episodes

G1 No.		Extended Turn Sequence				G4 No.		Extended Turn Sequence			
		I-SEQ	RI-SEQ	R-SEQ	Total			I-SEQ	RI-SEQ	R-SEQ	Total
1.	Derek	1	3	3	7	1.	Evan	12	4	30	46
2.	Max	9	1	7	17	2.	Bill	10	2	8	20
3.	Alvin	10	5	38	53	3.	Mike	9	0	19	28
4.	Cliff	16	1	4	21	4.	Eric	10	4	50	64
5.	Colin	4	0	5	9	5.	Karl	4	2	9	15
6.	Ted	6	0	7	13	6.	Jack	12	8	28	48
7.	Sam	4	0	9	13	7.	Ian	11	4	43	58
8.	Diane	19	1	17	37	8.	Pete	13	4	24	41
9.	James	5	0	3	8	9.	Robin	5	2	18	25
10.	Alan	4	0	2	6	10.	Lim	2	4	12	18
11.	Jason	7	1	13	21	11.	Fay	49	6	74	129
12.	Scott	4	0	5	9		Total	137	40	315	492
13.	Barry	12	2	9	23		%	27.8	8.1	64.0	100.0
14.	Tony	12	1	6	19						
15.	Wendy	11	1	31	43						
16.	Rachel	1	0	0	1						
	Total	125	16	159	300						
	%	41.7	5.3	53.0	100.0						

Further analysis on patterns of I-SEQ (Table 5.26) found that:
- in 100% (22) of G1 episodes, the highest frequency of I-SEQ produced in each episode was attributable to the assigned presenter.
- in 77.8% (14) G4 episodes, the highest frequency of I-SEQ produced in each episode was attributable to the assigned presenter[82]. Fay contributed more I-SEQ than the presenters and the highest frequency of I-SEQ for four episodes (G4S4-E1, G4S4-E2, G4S5-E2, G4S9-E2).

The results substantiated earlier findings[83] on nodal degree that compared to G4, G1 displayed a more hierarchical engagement pattern with presenters more likely than other participants to initiate turns with information distributed generally to all. Regarding equality of participation, the results suggest that G1 presenters tended to exercise greater control over the initiation of new exchanges while both G4 presenters and Fay were observed to participate in this activity.

The higher percentages of *R-SEQ* and *RI-SEQ* in G4, when considered with the main use of R-{INF} and RI-{CHK}[84], suggest the tendency to extend 'speaking' time for the purpose of sharing information at some depth with multiple (R) turns. Additionally, G4 participants were likely use RI-SEQ to control the discussion for the purpose of developing the main exchange or re-directing discussions to make certain the meaning of previous turns. Although control of discussion suggested through extended turn sequences implies the exclusion of certain participants from the learning conversation, the effect may not necessarily be detrimental to learning. The significance of these results will be further discussed in Chapter 6.

---

[82] In G4, there were no presenters assigned for S8 and S11
[83] Refer to this chapter, section 5.2.2.
[84] Refer to this chapter, section 5.3.2.

Table 5.26. Groups 1 and 4: I-SEQ by presenters and tutors

G1	No. of (I)-SEQ			G4	No. of (I)-SEQ		
Episode	Presenter I-SEQ	Tutor I-SEQ	Highest frequency of I-SEQ for episode	Episode	Presenter I-SEQ	Tutor I-SEQ	Highest frequency of I-SEQ for episode
S1-E1	3	0	3	S1-E1	4	1	4
S1-E2	5	0	5	S1-E2	3	1	3
S2-E1	11	0	11	S2-E1	3	0	3
S2-E2	8	0	8	S2-E2	7	6	7
S3-E1	5	0	5	S3-E1	6	3	6
S3-E2	5	0	5	S3-E2	3	1	3
S4-E1	2	0	2	S4-E1	2	5	5
S4-E2	2	0	2	S4-E2	2	4	4
S5-E1	4	0	4	S5-E1	3	2	3
S5-E2	1	0	1	S5-E2	2	4	4
S6-E1	5	0	5	S6-E1	5	1	5
S6-E2	6	0	6	S6-E2	3	2	3
S7-E1	11	0	11	S7-E1	3	3	3
S7-E2	4	0	4	S7-E2	1	0	1
S8-E1	8	0	8	S9-E1	5	0	5
S8-E2	4	0	4	S9-E2	2	4	4
S9-E1	8	0	8	S10-E1	1	0	1
S9-E2	2	1	2	S10-E2	2	0	2
S10-E1	4	0	4				
S10-E2	5	0	5				
S11-E1	5	0	5				
S11-E2	4	0	4				

Note: There were no presenters assigned for S8 and S11 in G4.

The tutors' use of extended turn sequences over 22 episodes were next examined for indications of declining prevalence of I-SEQ, RI-SEQ and R-SEQ. Table 5.27 shows the frequency of extended turn sequences produced by both tutors over 22 episodes. Table 5.28 partitions the data into two sets comprising the sum of extended turn sequences for the first and last 11 episodes (S1-E1 to S6-E1, S6-E2 to S11-E2 respectively).

Since Rachel was found to use only one extended turn sequence in total (I-SEQ), it was not possible to observe meaningful changes over time in her case. However, the results for Fay show a declining prevalence of I-SEQ and R-SEQ over time while the frequency of RI-SEQ remained unchanged for the first and last 11 episodes.

Regarding equality of participation, the results suggest that Rachel exerted minimal control over discussions which reflects a more passive facilitation style. Although Fay's prolific use of extended sequences reflects a more directive facilitation style, with corresponding implications of reduced opportunities for other G4 participants to contribute to discussions, the observed shift towards the use of fewer I-SEQ and R-SEQ in the last 11 episodes points to a gradual withdraw of control indicative of a collaborative learning process.

The patterns found in the tutors' use of extended turn sequences over time present certain implications for availability of learning support as *teaching* and *cognitive presences* within the *Community of Inquiry* (COI) model (Garrison et al., 2000) that will be discussed in Chapter 6. The next section presents the results from the analysis of Moves for indications of information-sharing and topic development during the collaboration group learning process.

Table 5.27. Tutors: Extended turn sequences by episode

Rachel	No. of Extended Turn Sequences			Fay	No. of Extended Turn Sequences		
Episode	I-SEQ	RI-SEQ	R-SEQ	Episode	I-SEQ	RI-SEQ	R-SEQ
S1-E1	0	0	0	S1-E1	1	0	3
S1-E2	0	0	0	S1-E2	1	0	4
S2-E1	0	0	0	S2-E1	0	0	4
S2-E2	0	0	0	S2-E2	6	1	6
S3-E1	0	0	0	S3-E1	3	0	1
S3-E2	0	0	0	S3-E2	1	0	1
S4-E1	0	0	0	S4-E1	5	0	4
S4-E2	0	0	0	S4-E2	4	1	5
S5-E1	0	0	0	S5-E1	2	0	2
S5-E2	0	0	0	S5-E2	4	1	5
S6-E1	0	0	0	S6-E1	1	0	6
S6-E2	0	0	0	S6-E2	2	0	1
S7-E1	0	0	0	S7-E1	3	0	5
S7-E2	0	0	0	S7-E2	0	0	2
S8-E1	0	0	0	S8-E1	4	0	4
S8-E2	0	0	0	S8-E2	7	1	2
S9-E1	0	0	0	S9-E1	0	1	7
S9-E2	1	0	0	S9-E2	4	0	0
S10-E1	0	0	0	S10-E1	0	0	0
S10-E2	0	0	0	S10-E2	0	0	3
S11-E1	0	0	0	S11-E1	0	1	7
S11-E2	0	0	0	S11-E2	1	0	2
Total	**1**	**0**	**0**	**Total**	**49**	**6**	**74**

Table 5.28. Tutors: Frequency of extended turn sequences for 1st and last 11 episodes

	Rachel			Fay		
	I-SEQ	RI-SEQ	R-SEQ	I-SEQ	RI-SEQ	R-SEQ
1st 11 episodes	0	0	0	28	3	41
Last 11 episodes	1	0	0	21	3	33

Note:
- Data summarized from Table 5.27.
- 1st 11 episodes comprised S1-E1 to S6-E1; last 11 episodes comprised S6-E2 to S11-E2.

5.4.2 Information-sharing and topic development

Building on earlier findings on Moves and extended turn sequences, this section presents the results from the application of ESA measures to examining the *collaborative learning process in groups* defined as the presence of *information-sharing and topic development* phases in chat exchanges. Sociograms are presented using SNA visualization techniques to illustrate turn networks.

The presence of *information-sharing* in the chat exchanges was operationalized as
(a) Frequency of R-SEQ.
(b) Frequency of {INF, EXD} Move used for extended information giving, and {JUS, REA} Moves that indicate working through of implications or hypotheses.

The presence of *topic development* in the chat exchanges was operationalized as (c) Frequency of {INQ, CHK, CLA, CHA} Moves that elicit more information to make meaning clearer/understanding easier and propose another direction for thought or discussion.

(a) R-SEQ frequency for information-sharing
A *R-SEQ* is a sequence of two or more (R) turns by the same speaker that may/may not immediately follow each other in the transcript. While the significance of R-SEQ was previously examined as control of discussion exercised by participants, this part of the analysis focuses on the implications of R-SEQ for information-sharing.

The presence of R-SEQ may indicate efforts by participants to explain, elaborate, or expand on own (current) or previous turns by others through the provision of more information than could usually be conveyed through a single turn. Hence, R-SEQs could reflect phases in exchanges where participants were involved in information-sharing at some depth.

Earlier findings[85] from a comparative group analysis showed that:
- R-SEQ formed the largest percentage of all extended turn sequences produced within both groups.
- G4 produced a higher percentage of R-SEQ (64%) compared to G1 (53%).
- Fay contributed the highest frequency of R-SEQ within G4 while Rachel did not produce any R-SEQ.

In terms of information-sharing, the results suggest while information-sharing was present in both groups, G4 participants tended to explain and/or elaborate at greater length in responses, hence providing more depth of information with the use of multiple (R) turns than G1 participants. Additionally, compared to Rachel, the prolific use of R-SEQ by Fay indicates a deeper involvement in both the provision and exchange of information for scaffolding the learning process.

(b) Move frequency for information-sharing: {INF, EXD, JUS, REA}
While findings on R-SEQ showed depth of information shared, Move level analysis afforded a finer interpretation of the information-sharing phase in exchanges. In this part of the analysis, *information-sharing* was operationalized as the presence of the following Move sets. The main pragmatic purposes of the Moves are explained in Table 5.29.

- *Set 1*: I-{INF}, R-{INF}, RI-{EXD}
- *Set 2*: I-{JUS}, I-{REA}, R-{JUS}, R-{REA}
- *Set 3*: RC-{FBK-E, FBK-A}

---

[85] R-SEQ was analyzed in this chapter, section 5.4.1. See results in Table 5.25.

Table 5.29. Descriptors for Move Sets 1-3

Move Set	Description
Set 1	
{INF}	- serves to provide information that are observations of facts, events or beliefs.
{EXD}	- used in responses that provide additional information or qualify what was said in previous turns.
Set 2	
{JUS}	- functions to defend or dispute a stated position with information/evidence.
{REA}	- functions to present implications, hypotheses or meanings generated from critical reflection or integrated with what was said in earlier turns.
Set 3	
{FBK-E}	- used in responses that comment briefly (can be single word) on the quality or correctness of previous turns.
{FBK-A}	- used in responses that report briefly (can be single word) the state of the speaker or claim understanding/hearing of previous turns.

In *Set 1*, the combined presence of I-{INF}, R-{INF}, and RI-{EXD} indicates exchange of information or experiences as participants explore issues under discussion (see examples).

No.	Participant	Turn	EXG-11-g4S11-E2				
136	Robin>>	they use CCTV at my mum's work where they thought it was a bomb... etc... its become a handy tool there	I				INF
139	Fay>>	they thought it was for a bomb?	RI				CHK
148	Robin>>	no.. they used it because a package was left.. and because they could see it on CCTV they were able to asses if it was a bomb or not		R			INF

No.	Participant	Turn	EXG-3-g1S3-E2				
12	Wendy>>	In fact, text-based CMC is commonly being compared to face-to-face communication because we can't even see each other?s facial expressions which would lead to confusions or misunderstandings.	I+				INF
14	Diane>>	and misinterpretations	RI				EXD
16	Derek>>	hence the evolution of emoticons	RI				EXD
15	Wendy>>	However, text-based CMC can significantly encourage everyone to contribute into teamwork progresses and elimate emotional boundaries which can lead to negative effects. Just like our online tutorial sessions right? :P	I				INQ
17	Alan>>	ye		RC			FBK-E

In *Set 2*, the combined presence of I-{JUS}, R-{JUS}, I-{REA}, and R-{REA} indicates a more advanced phase of information-sharing involving not only the provision of information retrieved from external sources, but also reasoning and critical reflection by participants (see examples).

No.	Participant	Turn	EXG-5-g4S8-E1				
58	Jack>>	it was harder to agree upon an event	I+				INF
62	Jack>>	but that's probably because it was left to our own imagination	I				JUS
61	Robin>>	yes it was		RC			FBK-E
72	Eric>>	We came together on an idea very early into the project		R			INF

No.	Participant	Turn	EXG-10-g1S4-E2				
119	Cliff>>	if the company follows third world culture, they should just overthrow the dictator and make the whole country one big company. until they get overthrown by a bigger company	I				REA
120	Derek>>	wouldnt be the first time oil companies have done exactly that...		R			INF
122	Jason>>	Organisational colonisation huh		R			INF

No.	Participant	Turn	EXG-2-g4S3-E1					
39	Fay>>	so what is the correct term for your group project?	I+					INQ
40	Fay>>	team or group?	I					INQ
41	Pete>>	But even a group with belonging, inclusion, exclusion and consensus would still fit the definition of a soccer riot.	R+					REA
45	Pete>>	I think the definition must also include a notion of purpose within an ethical framework for a group to be a team	R					REA
47	Fay>>	how about interdependency pete?			RI			CHK
48	Pete>>	That would work...a level of individualism maintained as well				R		JUS
50	Fay>>	ok sounds like we just about have consensus on the diff between team and group					RC	FBK-A

A between group comparison showed similar percentages of both *Set 1* and *Set 2* indicating that participants from both groups took part in the provision of additional information and reasoning activities respectively (Table 5.30). From a sociocultural constructivist perspective, the results suggest that participants are involved in the exchange and comparison of individual interpretations of concepts hence forming a *Zone of Proximal Development* (Vygotsky, 1978) for supporting intellectual growth during chat interaction.

Table 5.30. Groups 1 and 4: Move Sets 1 and 2 indicating information-sharing

G1		Move Set 1				Move Set 2			
No.		I- {INF}	R- {INF}	RI- {EXD}	Total	I- {JUS}	R- {JUS}	I- {REA}	R- {REA}	Total
1.	Derek	10	20	3	33	0	21	1	13	35
2.	Max	40	28	0	68	0	20	1	1	22
3.	Alvin	43	53	1	97	0	83	0	20	103
4.	Cliff	49	35	1	85	2	28	0	10	40
5.	Colin	39	9	0	48	0	6	1	6	13
6.	Ted	40	23	0	63	0	26	0	6	32
7.	Sam	16	30	0	46	0	26	0	4	30
8.	Diane	76	58	1	135	4	10	10	0	24
9.	James	17	22	1	40	0	4	0	7	11
10.	Alan	7	21	0	28	0	6	0	0	6
11.	Jason	30	26	0	56	0	17	0	9	26
12.	Scott	28	12	0	40	0	8	0	2	10
13.	Barry	29	9	1	39	0	23	0	0	23
14.	Tony	92	55	0	147	0	6	1	0	7
15.	Wendy	34	43	0	77	0	37	0	20	57
16.	Rachel	0	4	0	4	0	0	0	0	0
	Total	550	448	8	1006	6	321	14	98	439
	%				46.2					20.2

G4		Move Set 1				Move Set 2			
No.		I- {INF}	R- {INF}	RI- {EXD}	Total	I- {JUS}	R- {JUS}	I- {REA}	R- {REA}	Total
1.	Evan	34	83	7	124	0	33	0	12	45
2.	Bill	21	35	0	56	0	10	0	0	10
3.	Mike	34	54	0	88	0	25	3	39	67
4.	Eric	21	166	5	192	0	81	0	15	96
5.	Karl	12	57	0	69	0	19	0	4	23
6.	Jack	25	136	3	164	1	57	1	36	95
7.	Ian	31	158	1	190	0	72	1	17	90
8.	Pete	18	90	6	114	0	35	4	23	62
9.	Robin	12	101	0	113	0	41	0	5	46
10.	Lim	13	87	1	101	0	36	0	10	46
11.	Fay	105	164	4	273	1	70	1	19	91
	Total	326	1131	27	1484	2	479	10	180	671
	%				47.5					21.5

A further analysis of *Move Set 3* was conducted which examined the combined presence of RC-{FBK-E, FBK-A} that function to convey *minimal* information as acknowledgement or evaluation without depth of explanation or elaboration (see example). The results in Table 5.31 show that G1 produced a higher percentage (20.5%) of *Set 3* Moves that indicate exchange of minimal information compared to G4 (13%) which substantiated earlier findings that G1 was less likely than G4 to provide information at some depth.

No.	Participant	Turn	EXG-1-g1S7-E2					
1	Cliff>>	The second article I will present is a sequel of sorts to the first one. Also written by Benjamin Barber, it is called Ballots Versus Bullets, and was written in October 2001, just one month after the terrible events of the 11th September.	I+					INF
2	Cliff>>	To win the War on Terrorism, Barber argues, the US, Britain and it allies (of which, of course, Australia is one) must target the despair and hopelessness that terrorism exploits. Do you agree?	I					INQ
3	Derek>>	Personally, to win that war, the issues that caused terrorism to arrise need to be addressed		R				INF
4	Cliff>>	ok good					RC	FBK-A
6	Tony>>	i agree with derek					RC	FBK-E

Table 5.31. Groups 1 and 4: Move Set 3

G1		Move Set 3			G4		Move Set 3		
No.		RC-{FBK-E}	RC-{FBK-A}	Total	No.		RC-{FBK-E}	RC-{FBK-A}	Total
1.	Derek	7	2	9	1.	Evan	10	1	11
2.	Max	20	3	23	2.	Bill	13	5	18
3.	Alvin	52	9	61	3.	Mike	2	2	4
4.	Cliff	22	3	25	4.	Eric	71	10	81
5.	Colin	10	2	12	5.	Karl	34	1	35
6.	Ted	32	1	33	6.	Jack	38	3	41
7.	Sam	35	2	37	7.	Ian	62	7	69
8.	Diane	61	5	66	8.	Pete	18	1	19
9.	James	15	0	15	9.	Robin	52	4	56
10.	Alan	12	3	15	10.	Lim	17	2	19
11.	Jason	5	1	6	11.	Fay	39	13	52
12.	Scott	12	3	15		Total	356	49	405
13.	Barry	30	8	38		%			13.0
14.	Tony	17	3	20					
15.	Wendy	44	4	48					
16.	Rachel	21	2	23					
	Total	395	51	446					
	%			20.5					

Overall, even as there was little difference between the two groups in the percentage of *Set 1* and *Set 2* Moves indicative of information-sharing, results from the analyses of Move Set 3 and R-SEQ imply that less information was shared between G1 participants compared to G4 during discussions

(c) Move frequency for topic development: {INQ, CHK, CLA, CHA}
While the collaborative group learning process was held to be supported by information-sharing between participants in the previous measure, another crucial facet in learning conversations is the presence of *topic development* whereby the shared information is questioned, checked, clarified, or challenged. Essentially, the presence of topic development in chat exchanges could signal phases of meaning negotiation that build new knowledge.

In this part of the analysis, *topic development* was operationalized as the presence of Move Set 4. The main pragmatic purposes of the Moves are explained in Table 5.32.
- *Set 4*: I-{INQ}, RI-{CHK}, RI-{CLA}, RI-{CHA}

Table 5.32. Descriptors for Move Set 4

Move Set	Description
Set 4	
{INQ}	- functions to elicit more information with a question that may stimulate discussion on a new topic hence initiating a new exchange.
{CHK}	- used in responses to make certain the meaning of previous turns in exchanges with questions/statements that may start sub-exchanges.
{CLA}	- used for seeking additional information on what was said in previous turns with questions or statements that may start sub-exchanges.
{CHA}	- serves to propose/assert the need for another direction for discussion or consideration that may start sub-exchanges.

In *Set 4*, the combined presence of I-{INQ}, RI-{CHK}, RI-{CLA}, and RI-{CHA} indicates participant involvement in meaning negotiation, as the shared information is questioned, checked, clarified, and challenged (see examples).

No.	Participant	Turn							EXG-2-g1S11-E2
11	Sam>>	There seems to be mixed opinions from the public on having cctv, I would like to hear some of the opinions from you guy. Do you think CCTV is good or bad??	I+						INQ
12	Sam>>	does it cause more harm that good??	I						INQ
13	Cliff>>	i think they're good, the only bad thing imo is that they are only of any use AFTER a crime has been committed		R					JUS
17	Wendy>>	good		R+					JUS
18	Wendy>>	for security reasons		R					JUS
20	Sam>>	yep definatly					RC		FBK-E

No.	Participant	Turn							EXG-1-g4S3-E1
14	Eric>>	Is there a fundamental difference between a group of people and a team	I+						INQ
15	Eric>>	of people? Why is an individual able to hide their individuality in a	I+						INQ
16	Eric>>	group, but apparently not in a team?	I+						INQ
19	Eric>>	Would you like to or anyone else like to add to this?	I						INQ
24	Pete>>	Is it because team members have roles which are accountable to the entire team, but a group is just a collective?		RI					CHK
25	Jack>>	Yeah, is there a big difference between the two situations?			RI				CLA
30	Robin>>	i think because is a good, like pete says your held accountable.....certain things are expected of you, and if you don't do them can lead to consequences.....where as in a group situation like a leacture.....you can just sorta blend in the background					R		REA
31	Eric>>	I concur						RC	FBK-E

No.	Participant	Turn							EXG-3-g1S2-E1
62	Max>>	I prefer this kind of case to be f2f	I						INF
64	Diane>>	Does everyone think so?		RI+					CHK
67	Diane>>	Should bad news be delieverd f2f?		RI					CHK
82	Wendy>>	but if u deliver bad news thru CMC is more convenient			R				REA
84	Diane>>	Convenience vs occurence of miscommunication?				RI			CHK
87	Wendy>>	wat's the point of introducing CMC if its not for convinient n for improvements in decision making					RI		CHA
88	Diane>>	i think there has to always be a combination of f2f and cmc						R+	INF
89	Diane>>	in most situations						R	INF
91	Wendy>>	tru :)						R+	JUS
94	Wendy>>	can never rely on one thing only ;)						R	JUS

The implications of *Set 4* Moves in terms of topic development in chat exchanges are explained below.

- The presence of I-{INQ} signals the formation of a new conversational thread in an episode that opens discussion on another aspect of the issue(s) in the set-readings(s).
- The presences of RI-{CHK} and RI-{CLA} indicate attempts to progress further in understanding the topic by questioning rather than merely accepting the shared information.
- The presence of RI-{CHA} suggests efforts at critical appraisal of what was said in previous turns, resulting in the proposal of alternatives for further discussion.

Topic development in chat exchanges could be visualized as sociograms depicting *turn networks*. In turn networks, *nodes* are turns, *ties* are the directional links between turns and *relations* are the types of turns exchanged. The following sociograms of exchanges illustrate the development of discussion strands that branch from the main conversational thread as indicated by the presence of I-{INQ}, RI-{CHK}, RI-{CLA} and RI-{CHA} Moves (Figure 5.8).

No.	Participant	Turn	EXG-8-g1S1-E1				
103	Barry>>	sorry for asking this but wat does human-centered mean	I				INQ
105	Diane>>	like human-focused		R+			INF
108	Diane>>	or based on human needs		R			INF
106	Barry>>	oooh ok			RC		FBK-A
107	Alvin>>	is it like A.I.????			RI		CHK

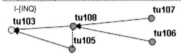

EXG-8-G1S1E1

No.	Participant	Turn	EXG-6-g1S1-E1				
82	Wendy>>	an issue will be why people still making n upgrading newer applications if win3.1 is so good?	I				INQ
84	Cliff>>	it's becasue win 3.1 is not good		R			JUS
93	Sam>>	and the graphics are not to hot			R		JUS
94	Barry>>	yea				RC	FBK-E
85	Alvin>>	technically speaking, play game		R			INF
91	Barry>>	ppl r probably upgrading and making new technology because its never enough		R			JUS
92	Alan>>	they want more features, power etc.		R			INF
96	Diane>>	the perpetual hunt for more			R		INF
101	Sam>>	development cant be stopped			R		INF

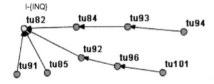

EXG-6-G1S1E1

Figure 5.8a. Topic development with I-{INQ} in two abridged exchanges within an episode

No.	Participant	Turn	EXG-4-g4S3-E1						
69	Fay>>	what is the best way to resolve conflicts in a team?	I+						INQ
72	Fay>>	as an example, if you had conflict in your team project, how would you deal with it?	I						INQ
73	Robin>>	i think open communication....and perhaps also having time during the project just to discuss if any problems come with other team members	R						INF
74	Jack>>	if it was over the internet there would be a lot of flaming! =)	R						INF
81	Jack>>	In an ideal world you would want to discuss the problem among all members of the team and come to a unanimous consensus	R						INF
82	Lim>>	in not so ideal world Jack?		RI					CLA
87	Jack>>	there would be a last-minute decision made by someone in a dictatorship-like role			R				INF
92	Evan>>	but a good dictator might be able to get things done faster				R			JUS
93	Jack>>	it's good to be the king, but only if you're seen to be a "good" king (which obviously differs depending on who you ask)					R		JUS
85	Pete>>	Democracy if there are an odd number of people in the team? The will of the majority?			R				INF
86	Robin>>	what if there isn't a majority??				RI			CLA
88	Eric>>	what if the will has made a bad choice				RI			CLA
90	Evan>>	democracy allows for check and balances against bad decisions,					R		INF
91	Pete>>	Democracy is the freedom to make choices...even if they're bad. Its the price for social cohesion					R		JUS

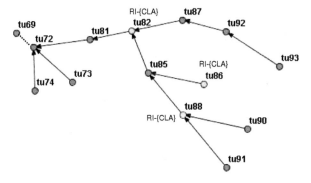

Figure 5.8b. Topic development with RI-{CLA} in abridged exchange

No.	Participant	Turn	EXG-7-g4S1-E1											Code
151	Evan>>	Sorry guys but to get back on topic - Pete asked the question - What sub cultures or ?communities of practice? would you expect to find within an organization? anyone like to discuss there experiences	I+											INQ
157	Evan>>	pete this was your question anything you would like to add	I											INQ
175	Ian>>	i found that there may be less communication	R											INF
159	Pete>>	Engineers tend to follow their profession - Reliability Engineers are the most reliable, Control Engineers like to have the situation under control , and Electrical Engineers just look for the coloured wire.! :-).	R+											INF
163	Pete>>	I think there are different communities of practice - definite groups who use information systems in distincty patterns.	R											INF
162	Robin>>	i find network adminstrators.......can well kinda be a bit no it alls at times		R										INF
164	Jack>>	I find that from techies...esp. at Rocko campus!			R									INF
169	Evan>>	i agree - they tend to hoard knowledge - you find alot of them are afraid if you know to much you might take their job			R									JUS
171	Eric>>	Likewise but it is there job to know what is wrong so that they may fix the problem asap even if some of them are impatient				R+								JUS
172	Eric>>	and less understanding				R+								JUS
174	Eric>>	when it comes down to the end users problem only at times though				R								JUS
178	Jack>>	Wouldn't it be in their best interests to educate others about how to fix certain "smaller" problems so they can concentrate on larger issues?				RI+								CHK
180	Jack>>	I'm referring more to end users				RI+								CHK
182	Fay>>	good point jack					RC							FBK-E
183	Ian>>	its benificial as a whole to do that				R								INF
189	Jack>>	Maybe I'm thinking more from a managers' point of view?				RI								CHK
190	Pete>>	The other problem is that immediate problems may not be seen as a priority by management.				R								INF
191	Robin>>	but as a priority to the user with the problem						R						INF
192	Jack>>	I think "my" business would be more effecient and productive if end users were capable of fixing problems (and perhaps not making them in the first place)...						R						REA
198	Eric>>	What if the end user has no technical expertise to fix the problem							RI					CHA
201	Jack>>	that's where the IT Pro should spend a little extra time educating the person, rather than just fixing the problem								R				REA
203	Eric>>	but it takes time to learn new things which the organisation may not want to waste									R+			JUS
204	Eric>>	if it is not beneficial								R				JUS
206	Jack>>	they may not learn a lot, but if they learn enough to save 10 minutes while they would wait for someone else to fix the problem, that's a net gain in my book										R		REA
207	Eric>>	agreed											RC	FBK-E
212	Ian>>	i think training a organisation can be of immense value										R		INF
213	Eric>>	at a cost if it does not increase production											R+	JUS
216	Eric>>	like training them to use a chat system may or may not increase productivity it depends if the organisation will profit from it											R	JUS

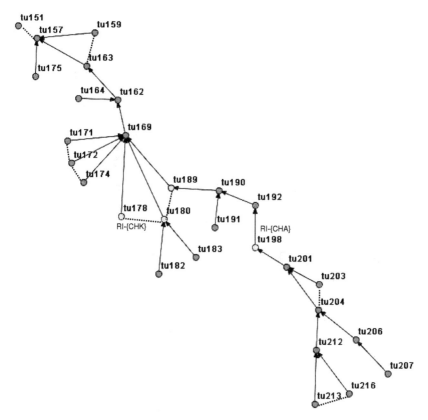

Figure 5.8c. Topic development with RI-{CHK} and RI-{CHA} in abridged exchange

A between group comparison of *Move Set 4* (Table 5.33) showed
- a 5% difference in the percentage of *Set 4* Moves produced by G1 and G4 that
  indicate topic development, hence suggesting a slightly greater tendency by G4
  participants towards extending discussions in both direction and depth.

Table 5.33. Groups 1 and 4: Move Set 4 indicating topic development

G1		Move Set 4				G4		Move Set 4			
No.	I-{INQ}	RI-{CHK}	RI-{CLA}	RI-{CHA}	Total	No.	I-{INQ}	RI-{CHK}	RI-{CLA}	RI-{CHA}	Total
1. Derek	8	19	1	2	30	1. Evan	19	10	7	1	37
2. Max	7	3	4	2	16	2. Bill	18	8	2	0	28
3. Alvin	14	12	3	2	31	3. Mike	11	7	3	0	21
4. Cliff	17	5	2	4	28	4. Eric	26	6	20	4	56
5. Colin	6	0	2	0	8	5. Karl	7	9	3	0	19
6. Ted	7	3	5	1	16	6. Jack	31	44	21	3	99
7. Sam	6	2	0	0	8	7. Ian	15	24	5	1	45
8. Diane	10	7	2	0	19	8. Pete	25	19	8	0	52
9. James	10	2	4	0	16	9. Robin	11	9	5	0	25
10. Alan	6	1	1	0	8	10. Lim	11	18	18	0	47
11. Jason	5	5	2	0	12	11. Fay	77	35	25	0	137
12. Scott	5	0	0	0	5	Total	251	189	117	9	566
13. Barry	10	2	8	0	20	%					18.1
14. Tony	16	6	3	1	26						
15. Wendy	14	11	3	5	33						
16. Rachel	5	1	3	0	9						
Total	146	79	43	17	285						
%					13.1						

An overall between group comparison of the percentage distribution of Move Sets 1 to 4 (Figure 5.9) revealed that:
- in G1, information-sharing (*Set 1*, *Set 2* and *Set 3*) comprised a slightly larger proportion (86.9%) of all Moves compared to G4 (81.9%).
- in G4, topic development (*Set 4*) comprised a slightly larger proportion (18.1%) of all Moves compared to in G1 (13.1%).

Group 1: Distribution of Move Sets 1 to 4   Group 4: Distribution of Move Sets 1 to 4

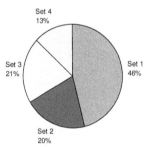
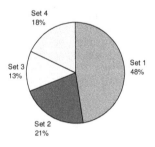

Figure 5.9. Groups 1 and 4: Distribution of Move Sets 1 to 4

On the whole, results indicated the presence of topic development phases in the chat exchanges of both groups reflecting participant involvement in the activity of meaning negotiation during the collaborative learning process. However, compared to G1, G4 participants were more likely to develop main conversational threads further in terms of direction and depth. A broader comparison of the distribution of all Move Sets suggested a stronger focus in G1 on the provision and exchange of information than development of discussion threads.

Although the analyses in this chapter had focused mainly on TASK turns that contain content directly related to the set-readings, this study acknowledges that educational exchanges may serve other purposes such as the establishment of *social presence* (Garrison et al., 2000; Short, Williams, & Christie, 1976) and *teaching presence* (Garrison et al., 2000). The ESA scheme categorized group communication within episode boundaries as TASK, Off-Topic (OT) and Repair (RPR) turns. *Cognitive presence* could be represented by contributions coded as TASK turns while the elements of *teaching* and *social presence* could be represented by contributions sub-categorized as OT-Administration (OT-A) [86] and OT-Social (OT-S) respectively. OT-Technical (OT-T) turns could be held to reflect the technology-based virtual environment where the educational interactions are situated.

A between group comparison showed that both groups produced OT turns of each sub-category in approximately the same percentages, with OT-S constituting the greatest proportion within G1 and G4 (Figure 5.10).

Group 1: Distribution of Off-Topic turns   Group 4: Distribution of Off-Topic turns

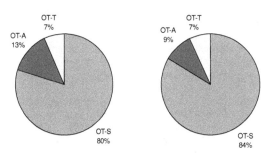

Figure 5.10. Groups 1 and 4: Distribution of Off-Topic turns

A between tutor comparison (Figure 5.11) revealed that both tutors produced mainly OT-S and OT-A for the respective purposes of development of social relations within each group, and class management or administration.

---

[86] OT-Social (OT-S) - supports "development of group relationships" (Kneser et al., 2001, p.69) such as greetings, social banter and emoticons.
OT-Administration (OT-A) - deals with housekeeping issues for the OI unit and/or tutorial group such as time-calls and reminders.
OT-Technical (OT-T) - results from technical problems/issues such as mistyping and problems with network connections or equipment.
See definitions and examples in codebook (Appendix B.1) and in Chapter 4, section 4.4.1.

Rachel: Distribution of Off-Topic turns   Fay: Distribution of Off-Topic turns

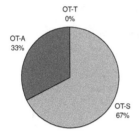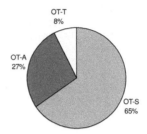

Figure 5.11. Tutors: Distribution of Off-Topic turns

5.4.3 Summary

The analysis of the *collaborative learning process in groups* in terms of *equality of participation* showed that both groups displayed relatively equal levels of inclusiveness at the exchange level with connections present between actors that facilitate the exchange of information within the network. The connections were utilized mainly by G1 presenters for maintaining greater control over the initiation of new exchanges (with I-SEQ) while in G4, the tutor and presenters were both involved in the activity. Compared to G1, G4 tended to exercise control over responding turns to ensure 'speaking' time for sharing information at some depth and re-directing the main conversational thread to elicit more information.

Both *information-sharing and topic development* phases in chat exchanges were found indicating participant involvement in the comparison of individual understandings of concepts and meaning negotiation of shared information which are characteristic of the collaborative-constructivist learning process. Additionally, compared to G4, there was slightly greater concentration by G1 on the activity of information-sharing than the development of discussion threads.

Although Fay established an overall stronger tutor presence than Rachel, and provided more learning support at the initial stages of the learning process, there was a gradual withdrawal of tutor control and scaffolding over time with the use of fewer I-SEQ and R-SEQ in the last 11 episodes. In contrast, Rachel exercised minimal control over discussions through extended turn sequences and provided less learning support as an Isolate in a larger percentage of exchanges than Fay.

Since the totality of an online educational experience encompasses the communication of task-oriented and non task-oriented information, an analysis of OT turns showed that both groups produced OT-S, OT-A and OT-T turns for conveying social meanings, dealing with administrative and technical matters respectively. Both Rachel and Fay were found to produce mainly OT-S and OT-A turns which was consistent with their role as tutors. When interpreted within the *Community of Inquiry* model (Garrison et al., 2000), the findings suggested that all three elements of cognitive, social and teaching presences that constitute an effective online educational experience were present in the interactions captured by the transcripts. The next section summarizes the findings presented for RQ1.

5.5 Summary of Results for Research Question 1

In this chapter, sections 5.2 to 5.4 presented the results for RQ1 that examined task-oriented chat interaction for a deeper understanding of engagement by participants with each other's contributions, interactional purposes and the collaborative learning process in groups. Transcript data was subjected to discourse and network analyses of turns/exchanges, and descriptive statistical analysis. The results were presented as tables, figures, sociograms of actor and turn networks, and illustrated with qualitative examples of chat exchanges where relevant.

Results from comparative group analysis showed that G4 displayed a higher extent of *engagement* than G1 in terms of contributions of turns, overall tendencies to send or receive ties, mutuality in information exchange, reciprocation of choice, and by simply being *present* in more episodes. In particular, compared to G1, G4 displayed a less hierarchical turn-taking pattern with more participants besides the presenters and/or the tutor, sending ties to others. G4 also tended to respond directly to specific participants than direct ties generally to all in the group.

Further analysis on *interactional purposes* underlying turns in exchanges both substantiated and revealed different facets in earlier findings. Compared to G4, G1 tended to start competing exchanges rather than follow up meanings of previous turns and G1 responses tended to convey less depth of information. The results substantiated findings of a lower reciprocity level and a more asymmetrical information exchange pattern in G1. G1 also tended to provide information than elicit information from others at the start of exchanges and respond to defend/dispute turns as a consequence of the use of more challenges. G1 displayed a narrower Move range suggesting less effort to provide information, convey meaning, prompt, probe, and shape the direction of discussions than G4.

During the *collaborative group learning process*, although there were relatively equal levels of inclusiveness between groups, the connections were utilized mainly by G1 presenters for maintaining control over the initiation of exchanges while in G4, the tutor and presenters were both involved in the activity. Compared to G1, G4 tended to exercise control over responding turns for sharing information at some depth and eliciting information. Both groups were involved in the comparison of individual understandings of concepts and meaning negotiation of shared information which are characteristic of the collaborative-constructivist learning process. However, compared to G4, G1 tended to focus on the activity of information-sharing than the development of discussion threads. The finding that task-oriented and non task-oriented information were exchanged during chat interaction suggested that the elements of cognitive, social and teaching presences (Garrison et al., 2000) that constitute an effective online educational experience were present in the interactions captured by the transcripts.

Results from tutor comparison showed greater engagement by Fay in terms of contributions of turns, and by being a Carrier and *present* in more episodes than Rachel. There was stronger effort by Fay to scaffold interactions in G4 by contributing greater depth of information, initiating to both give information and elicit information, and adopting a wider range of Moves. Although Fay established an overall stronger tutor presence than Rachel and provided more learning support at the initial stages of the learning process, there was gradual withdrawal of tutor control and scaffolding over time. In contrast, Rachel exercised minimal control over discussions and provided less learning support as an Isolate in a larger percentage of exchanges than Fay. However, both tutors were found to provide social and administrative support as OT turns which was consistent with their facilitator role.

The results from RQ1 presented were based primarily on the analyst's interpretation of the educational interactions from the transcript dataset. The next section presents the results for RQ2 on student experiences of chat interactions during online tutorials. Comparisons of findings from the transcript analysis with self-reported data could enable better understanding of the construction of learning conversations.

5.6 Results for Research Question 2: Opportunities for Participation

This section forms the start of the second part of Chapter 5 that presents the results for RQ2 which focuses on student experiences of chat tutorial interaction in terms of participation opportunities, adequacy of learning support, and quality of learning experience and collaborative work process. The main data source and participants are briefly reviewed before the results are presented.

5.6.1 Survey dataset and participants

Data on experiences of chat tutorial interaction were obtained by a web survey administered to G1 and G4 student participants[87]. While there were no changes to G4 student participant numbers at the close of the survey (G4=9), one G1 participant (Ted) attended sessions 1-9 (S1 to S9) but discontinued the unit on 15 October 2005. Accordingly, survey return rate from G1 was based on 14 student participants.

The survey dataset comprised 13 returns from G1 (93%) and 8 returns from G4 (89%)[88]. The data included responses to closed and open-ended questions on learning experiences during chat tutorials. Given the small number of participants involved, validity of results was established through triangulation of methods and data. Hence, survey results presented for RQ2 were also discussed in relation to earlier findings from the transcript dataset.

Demographic data from the survey show that the participants comprised both genders, from various cultural backgrounds, with different EL proficiency levels and previous experience with chat media prior to attending the online tutorials (Table 5.34). The participants were also between early to mid 20s and residing in Western Australia at that time[89].

Table 5.34. Demographic data from survey

Characteristics	Group 1 Participants	Group 4 Participants
Gender	- 3 female and 12 male students	- 1 female and 8 male students
ESL/EFL speakers	- 5 ESL/EFL speakers - 8 native English language speakers	- 8 native English language speakers
Cultural background	- a mix of african, asian and caucasian students	- a mix of asian and caucasian students
Prior chat experience	- 10 students used chat media at least *monthly* - 3 student *hardly ever/never* used the chat media	- 8 students used chat media at least *monthly*

5.6.2 Opportunities for participation

In RQ2, the constructs of *participation opportunities*, *adequacy of learning support*, and *quality of learning experience and collaborative work process* were formulated to guide the analysis of student perceptions on the impact of chat interaction in supporting the collaborative learning process. The constructs were operationalized as survey questions which were stated in Chapter 4[90].

---

[87] The web survey was administered only to student participants in both tutorial groups. The web survey form is provided in Appendix B.3.
[88] Refer to Table 5.2 in this chapter for final survey return rate.
[89] This information was gathered from OI unit administration documents and the unit coordinator.
[90] Refer to Chapter 4, section 4.6.

This section presents the results from examining *participation opportunities* defined as the *perception of participation opportunities*, and *factors motivating and inhibiting participation* during chat tutorials.

(a) Perception of participation opportunities
Participation opportunities perceived to be available during chat tutorials were measured by the following questions where respondents indicated their extent of agreement on a 5-point scale from *Strongly Agree* (SA) to *Strongly Disagree* (SD) and *Unable to Judge* (UJ):
- Q.5a: *I had plenty of opportunities to participate in the discussion.*
- Q.5b: *I was able to make best use of the opportunities available for participation.*

Results from a between group comparison show (Table 5.35)
- more intense agreement (*SA*) in G4 that participation opportunities were available.
- more intense agreement in G1 that perceived participation opportunities were exercised.
- overall greater agreement (*SA&A*) in G4 on the presence and use of participation opportunities during tutorial discussions.

Table 5.35. Groups 1 and 4: Presence and use of participation opportunities (Q.5a, Q.5b)

		SA	A	D	SD	UJ
5a. I had plenty of opportunities to participate in the discussion	G1	3 (23.1%)	8 (61.5%)	2 (15.4%)	0 (0.0%)	0 (0.0%)
	G4	3 (37.5%)	5 (62.5%)	0 (0.0%)	0 (0.0%)	0 (0.0%)
5b. I was able to make best use of the opportunities available for participation	G1	4 (30.8%)	7 (53.8%)	1 (7.7%)	0 (0.0%)	1 (7.7%)
	G4	0 (0.0%)	7 (87.5%)	1 (12.5%)	0 (0.0%)	0 (0.0%)

Although the results suggest that participation opportunities were largely perceived to be available and exercised in both groups, several G1 respondents disagreed on the availability of participation opportunities and there were respondents from both groups who indicated an inability to fully utilize opportunities perceived to be available. To account for the results, responses to five sets of questions posed in the survey which explore possible factors affecting participation during online tutorials are presented below.

(b) Factors Motivating and Inhibiting Participation
The factors motivating and inhibiting participation were measured by the following five sets of questions (listed in Table 5.36). Identification of these possible factors affecting participation was guided by the literature and previous research. The results were interpreted mainly in relation to the earlier finding of overall greater agreement in G4 compared to G1 on the presence and use of participation opportunities during tutorial discussions.

- *Set 1*: Q.5c and Q.5d for turn-taking behaviours
- *Set 2*: Q.1and Q.2 for presenter and participant roles
- *Set 3*: Q.4a and Q4b for tutor and presenter facilitation styles
- *Set 4*: Q.4c and 4d for tutor and peer assessment of participation
- *Set 5*: Q.6 and Q.7 for other factors

Table 5.36. Question sets 1-5: Factors motivating and inhibiting participation

Set 1	To what extent do the following statements accurately reflect your overall experience of online tutorials in this unit?
Q.5c	I usually prefer to let the discussion develop before joining in
Q.5d	During discussions, I contributed my views even when I saw that others had already posted similar ideas
Set 2	As a *presenter*, I found it easy to
Q.1a	keep up with the speed of the discussion
Q.1b	manage the discussion to keep it relevant to the topic
Q.1c	answer questions from others during the presentation
Q.1d	initiate the discussion on the reading(s)
Q.1e	explain and justify my views during the presentation
Q.1f	communicate my views without face-to-face contact with other students during the discussion
	As a *participant*, I found it easy to
Q.2a	keep up with the speed of the discussion
Q.2b	contribute actively to the discussion
Q.2c	explain and justify my views during the discussion
Q.2d	communicate my views without face-to-face contact with other students during the discussion
Set 3	I was encouraged to participate in the discussion by
Q.4a	the facilitation style of the *tutor*
Q.4b	the facilitation styles of *student presenters*
Set 4	I was encouraged to participate in the discussion by
Q.4c	the assessment of my participation by the *tutor*
Q.4d	the assessment of my participation by *other students*
Set 5	
Q.6	Were there other factors that *encouraged* or *motivated* you to contribute to tutorial discussions in this unit?
Q.7	Were there other factors that *discouraged* or *inhibited* you from contributing to tutorial discussions in this unit?

In *Set 1*, when turn-taking patterns are expected to affect perception and exercise of participation opportunities (Sack et al., 1974; Schegloff et al., 1977), it is likely that compared to G1, G4 respondents would report greater tendencies towards
- making early contributions to discussions (Q.5c) in the form of higher frequencies of SD/D than SA/A, and
- responding with additional views/information during discussions (Q.5d) as higher frequencies of SA/A than SD/D.

A between group comparison (Table 5.37) found that:
- a higher percentage of G1 respondents reported the tendency to let the discussion develop before joining in.
- a higher percentage of G4 respondents reported the tendency to contribute views even when others had posted similar ideas.

Table 5.37. Groups 1 and 4: Turn-taking behaviour (Q.5c, Q.5d)

		SA	A	D	SD	UJ
5c. I usually prefer to let the discussion develop before joining in	G1	3 (23.1%)	8 (61.5%)	2 (15.4%)	0 (0.0%)	0 (0.0%)
	G4	3 (37.5%)	0 (0.0%)	4 (50.0%)	1 (12.5%)	0 (0.0%)
5d. During discussions, I contributed my views even when I saw that others had already posted similar ideas	G1	2 (15.4%)	7 (53.8%)	4 (30.8%)	0 (0.0%)	0 (0.0%)
	G4	5 (62.5%)	1 (12.5%)	2 (25.0%)	0 (0.0%)	0 (0.0%)

The results suggest that compared to G1, G4 respondents were less likely to refrain from making early and additional contributions to discussions. Therefore, turn-taking behaviour could be one of the factors accounting for the greater agreement in G4 on the presence and use of participation opportunities.

In *Set 2*, when difficulties experienced by respondents in their roles as presenter and participant are expected to affect the perception and use of participation opportunities (Chou, 2002; Pilkington & Walker, 2004), it is likely that compared to G1,
- G4 respondents in both roles would report less difficulty (as higher frequencies of SA/A than SD/D) with all aspects of tutorial discussions.

A between group comparison of respondent experiences as *presenter* (Table 5.38) found:
- G1 presenters reported difficulties with all aspects of online communication and management of discussion.
- G4 presenters indicated difficulties in two aspects i.e., explanation/justification of views (Q.1e) and communication via a text-based medium (Q.1f).
- a higher percentage of G1 presenters (23.1%) reported difficulties with explaining/justifying views and communicating via a text-based medium than G4 (12.5%).

Table 5.38. Groups 1 and 4: Respondent experiences as Presenter (Q.1)

As a **presenter**, I found it easy to		SA	A	D	SD
1a. keep up with the speed of the discussion	G1	4 (30.8%)	6 (46.2%)	3 (23.1%)	0 (0.0%)
	G4	5 (62.5%)	3 (37.5%)	0 (0.0%)	0 (0.0%)
1b. manage the discussion to keep it relevant to the topic	G1	3 (23.1%)	9 (69.2%)	1 (7.7%)	0 (0.0%)
	G4	3 (37.5%)	5 (62.5%)	0 (0.0%)	0 (0.0%)
1c. answer questions from others during the presentation	G1	2 (15.4%)	9 (69.2%)	2 (15.4%)	0 (0.0%)
	G4	3 (42.9%)	4 (57.1%)	0 (0.0%)	0 (0.0%)
1d. initiate the discussion on the reading(s)	G1	2 (15.4%)	9 (69.2%)	2 (15.4%)	0 (0.0%)
	G4	4 (50.0%)	4 (50.0%)	0 (0.0%)	0 (0.0%)
1e. explain and justify my views during the presentation	G1	5 (38.5%)	5 (38.5%)	2 (15.4%)	1 (7.7%)
	G4	2 (25.0%)	5 (62.5%)	1 (12.5%)	0 (0.0%)
1f. communicate my views without face-to-face contact with other students during the discussion	G1	6 (46.2%)	4 (30.8%)	3 (23.1%)	0 (0.0%)
	G4	4 (50.0%)	3 (37.5%)	1 (12.5%)	0 (0.0%)

Note: Bill (G4) submitted a blank response to Q.1c.

A between group comparison of respondent experiences as *participant* (Table 5.39) found:
- participants from both group reported difficulties with all aspects of online communication during tutorial discussions.
- a higher percentage of G4 participants reported difficulties with keeping pace with the discussion (Q.2a), explanation/justification of views (Q.2c), and communication via a text-based medium (Q.2d).
- a higher percentage of G1 participants reported difficulties with contributing actively to the discussion (Q.2b).

The results suggest that:
- as *presenters*, G1 respondents found more difficulty with all aspects of online communication and management of discussion than G4.
- as *participants*, G4 respondents found more difficulty in three aspects of online communication during discussions than G1.

Table 5.39. Groups 1 and 4: Respondent experiences as Participant (Q.2)

As a **participant**, I found it easy to		SA	A	D	SD
2a. keep up with the speed of the discussion	G1	4 (30.8%)	6 (46.2%)	3 (23.1%)	0 (0.0%)
	G4	1 (12.5%)	4 (50.0%)	3 (37.5%)	0 (0.0%)
2b. contribute actively to the discussion	G1	0 (0.0%)	9 (69.2%)	4 (30.8%)	0 (0.0%)
	G4	2 (25.0%)	4 (50.0%)	2 (25.0%)	0 (0.0%)
2c. explain and justify my views during the discussion	G1	1 (7.7%)	9 (69.2%)	3 (23.1%)	0 (0.0%)
	G4	1 (12.5%)	5 (62.5%)	2 (25.0%)	0 (0.0%)
2d. communicate my views without face-to-face contact with other students during the discussion	G1	5 (38.5%)	6 (46.2%)	2 (15.4%)	0 (0.0%)
	G4	3 (37.5%)	3 (37.5%)	2 (25.0%)	0 (0.0%)

The factor of roles seems to partially account for the greater agreement in G4 on the presence and use of participation opportunities compared to G1. Although G4 respondents as *presenters* reported less difficulty with all aspects of tutorial discussions compared to G1, G4 respondents as *participants* reported more difficulty than G1 with three aspects of online communication during discussions. Since there was no clear finding from this part of the analysis indicating an inverse correspondence between extent of agreement over presence/use of participation opportunities, and level of difficulty experienced in both roles, other possible factors affecting participation are examined below.

In *Set 3*, when facilitation styles of the tutor and/or presenter are expected to affect perception and exercise of participation opportunities (Cox et al., 2004; Kneser et al., 2001), it is likely that
- G4 respondents would indicate greater agreement (as higher frequencies of SA/A than SD/D) regarding the positive impact of tutor and/or presenter facilitation styles on encouraging participation.

A between group comparison (Table 5.40) found:
- unanimous agreement in G4 that participation was encouraged by the *tutor's* facilitation style compared to 76.9% in G1.
- a higher percentage of G1 respondents reported that participation was encouraged by the *presenter's* facilitation style.

Table 5.40. Groups 1 and 4: Facilitation styles of tutor and presenters (Q.4a-4b)

I was encouraged to participate in the discussion by		SA	A	D	SD
4a. the facilitation style of the *tutor*	G1	2 (15.4%)	8 (61.5%)	3 (23.1%)	0 (0.0%)
	G4	2 (25.0%)	6 (75.0%)	0 (0.0%)	0 (0.0%)
4b. the facilitation styles of *student presenters*	G1	1 (7.7%)	11 (84.6%)	1 (7.7%)	0 (0.0%)
	G4	1 (12.5%)	6 (75.0%)	1 (12.5%)	0 (0.0%)

The results suggest that while the tutor facilitation style primarily motivated participation in G4, participation in G1 was largely encouraged by the presenter's facilitation style. These results also substantiated findings from RQ1 that Fay was more involved in G4 discussions and maintained a more visible tutor presence than Rachel. While facilitation style could be one of the factors accounting for greater agreement in G4 on the presence and use of participation opportunities, the results raise certain implications regarding tutor control of discussion which will be discussed in Chapter 6.

In *Set 4*, when tutor and/or peer assessment of participation are expected to affect mainly *exercise* of participation opportunities (Sudweeks & Simoff, 2000), it is likely that compared to G1,
- G4 respondents would indicate greater agreement (as higher frequencies of SA/A than SD/D) regarding the positive impact of tutor and/or peer assessment on encouraging participation.

A between group comparison (Table 5.41) found that:
- a higher percentage of G4 respondents reported that participation was encouraged by *tutor* assessment.
- a higher percentage of G1 respondents reported that participation was encouraged by *peer* assessment.

Table 5.41. Groups 1 and 4: Tutor and peer assessment of participation (Q.4c-4d)

I was encouraged to participate in the discussion by		SA	A	D	SD
4c. the assessment of my participation by the *tutor*	G1	4 (30.8%)	6 (46.2%)	3 (23.1%)	0 (0.0%)
	G4	2 (25.0%)	5 (62.5%)	1 (12.5%)	0 (0.0%)
4d. the assessment of my participation by *other students*	G1	2 (15.4%)	8 (61.5%)	3 (23.1%)	0 (0.0%)
	G4	1 (12.5%)	3 (37.5%)	3 (37.5%)	1 (12.5%)

The results suggest that assessment by the tutor rather peers may be one of the factors accounting for the greater agreement by G4 respondents over the exercise of participation opportunities.

While *Sets 1* to *4* comprised closed questions which examine factors located from the literature and previous studies as possibly affecting participation in learning interactions, *Set 5* consisted of two open-ended questions (Q.6 and Q.7) for capturing other factors regarded by respondents as affecting participation during tutorial discussions. The response rate for both questions is shown in Table 5.42.

Table 5.42. Groups 1 and 4: Response rate for Q.6 and Q.7

Group	Survey Returns	Q.6 and Q.7	
		Completed	Blank
G1	13	10 (76.9%)	3 (23.1%)
G4	8	6 (75%)	2 (25%)

Note: Both response rate for Q.6 and Q.7 were identical.
Completed returns refer to instances where answers were given.
Blank returns refer to instances where no answers were given.

In *Set 5*, analysis of the responses to the open-ended questions revealed three main common factors that both motivated and inhibited participation in both groups:
- the synchronous CMC medium,
- the presenter, and
- the quality of online interaction.

Other motivating factors provided by respondents included the issues in the set-readings and English language proficiency of other participants. Other inhibiting factors included gender (minority of female participants in both groups) and participant's own lack of preparation for tutorial discussions.

The *synchronous mode* of the online tutorials was singled out by some respondents as motivating participation for the following reasons:

> The main factor i think that because it was not face-to-face i felt abit more at ease at putting forward my opinions. I am quite a shy person and at times i think that my ideas are wrong or not correct, so at times abit hesitant to put them forward. The tutorial being online really did help. Gave me more confidence. [Scott]

> I guess this system and method will be used widely in the working environment it is good to get the practical experience now in university then later i twill be useful... [Tony]

Other respondents noted that the novelty of a chat tutorial experience inspired greater collaborative efforts during the learning process but the excitement over the CMC medium diminished over time.

> It was the novelty of a new type of tutorial - and the desire to make it "work"... [Pete]

> At the beginning of the semester, perhaps the first 6 weeks or so, it was quite fun participating in the tutorials; they were almost like a novelty. However as the semester wore on it became less of a novelty and, although it was fun at times, wasn't as exciting as previous. [Jack]

However, technical problems, the absence non-verbal cues and synchronicity afforded by the medium proved difficult for some respondents during discussions.

> ...technical issues like browsers, connection speed(delay in messages). [Alan]

> ... Sometimes demotivates us for not contributing because our senses cant feel our present [Tony]

> Communication is slower because you have to type. You also have to spend a fair amount of energy following threads. It doesn't stop you but it does slow you down. [Pete]

> At times I found that I had a lot of things to say, but by the time I had thought of how to word my comments appropriately and typed them, the discussion had moved on. As I didn't want to refer back to a previous part of the discussion, my comments were deleted before being posted. This is similar to what would happen in face-to-face communications, but seemed to either occur more often, or become more noticeable when it happened. [Jack]

While a respondent stated that participation was encouraged when "tutorial presenters throw questions" (Diane), others noted certain areas for improvement in *presenter* moderation or facilitation skills.

> When the presenter asks questions which are totally unrelevant to the topic, or the ones which I simply just do not understand. [Wendy]

> ... sometimes maybe too hard to read a long presentation at once ... [Alvin]

The *quality of online interaction* characterized by the sharing of multiple perspectives was regarded as a motivating factor for participation in discussions.

> … one of the main factors is when i disagree with a point made by anyone. [Barry]

> IT was a good tutorial because everyone had a say and had a laugh …[Ian]

> Well I guess what encouraged me... was that everyone in the tutorial group was open and accepting of other ideas and feelings. They were all willing to listen. [Robin]

However, some respondents emphasized the difficulties with turn-taking in an online environment, concerns over the 'visibility' of one's own messages, dominance of certain speakers, and even the high quality of others' contributions as inhibiting participation.

> Sometimes I feel that by contributing during a persons presentation of the tutorial, that it will either be overseen, or disrupt the flow of the presentation. [Colin]

> … you do get people who are more dominant speakers than others, it goes for online and face-to-face environments, so at times, you can be influenced by what they say. [Scott]

> Often topic being discussed was off subject. [Mike]

> The level of matureness of other students, their use of words and how they had smart answers in which i felt more comfy reading and taking in then expressing my views. I did that in my journal entries. [Bill]

The main factors identified by respondents to have both motivated and inhibited participation will be further discussed in relation to online tutorial factors regarded by respondents as affecting their understanding of course content[91].

Overall, the results indicate that the greater agreement in G4 on the presence and use of participation opportunities during tutorial discussions compared to G1 could be attributed to the following factors:
- *turn-taking patterns* since G4 respondents were more likely to make early and additional contributions to discussions.
- *presenter role* since G4 respondents as presenters reported less difficulty with all aspects of online communication and management of discussions.
- *tutor facilitation style* as there was unanimous agreement among G4 respondents on the positive impact of tutor facilitation style on encouraging participation.
- *assessment by the tutor* since a higher percentage of G4 respondents reported that participation was encouraged by tutor assessment.
- *other factors* i.e., the synchronous CMC medium, the presenter, and the quality of online interaction.

Although compared to G4, there was less agreement among G1 respondents over the presence and use of participation opportunities, within the group, most G1 respondents reported that participation opportunities were both present and taken up

---

[91] Refer to this chapter, section 5.8.

during discussions. The results suggest that within G1, the following factors may account for respondents' perception of the presence and use of participation opportunities:
- *turn-taking pattern* since a higher percentage of G1 respondents were likely to make additional contributions to discussions.
- *presenter facilitation style* as a higher percentage of G1 respondents reported that participation was encouraged by the facilitation style of the presenters rather than the tutor.
- *peer and tutor assessment* given that an equal percentage of G1 respondents reported that participation was encouraged by both peer and tutor assessment.
- *other factors* i.e., the synchronous CMC medium, the presenter, and the quality of online interaction.

The extent to which *roles* could account for G1 respondents' perception of the presence and use of participation opportunities was determined by a within group comparison of three aspects of online communication (Q.1a/2a, Q.1e/2c, Q.1f/2d) that were common to both roles (Table 5.43). The results indicate little difference in the levels of ease/difficulty reported by G1 respondents with all three aspects in both roles of presenter and participant. These results suggest that the factor of roles may not have affected, to any great extent, perception of the presence and use of participation opportunities in G1.

Table 5.43. Group 1: Responses for common aspects in presenter and participant roles (Q.1a/2a; Q.1e/2c; Q.1f/2d)

As a presenter/participant, I found it easy to		SA&A	SD&D
1a./2a. keep up with the speed of the discussion	G1-as presenter	10 (76.9%)	3 (23.1%)
	G1-as participant	10 (76.9%)	3 (23.1%)
1e./2c. explain and justify my views during the presentation	G1-as presenter	10 (76.9%)	3 (23.1%)
	G1-as participant	10 (76.9%)	3 (23.1%)
1f./2d. communicate my views without face-to-face contact with other students during the discussion	G1-as presenter	10 (76.9%)	3 (23.1%)
	G1-as participant	11 (84.6%)	2 (15.4%)

The survey results also reveal several noteworthy findings regarding turn-taking patterns and the ability to keep pace with the speed of chat discussions which are discussed below.
Survey results on turn-taking patterns indicate that compared to G4, G1 respondents were more likely to refrain from responding with additional contributions to discussions. The results substantiated RQ1 findings that G1 produced a lower percentage of (R) turns (40%) compared to G4 (57.3%) and tended to start new exchanges than follow up on what was said in previous turns.

While presenter/participant roles did not seem to affect G1 in terms of keeping up with the speed of discussions, G4 respondents as presenters experienced less difficulty with this aspect than as participants. Since the survey demographic data show that G4 comprised mainly experienced users of chat media (Table 5.44), the reported difficulty in keeping pace with discussions in the participant role could be explained by RQ1 findings that the G4 tutor maintained a high intensity of involvement during discussions. The tutor support provided by Fay could therefore have directly helped G4 respondents, in their role as presenter rather than participant, with the online communication and management of discussions.

Table 5.44. Groups 1 and 4: Previous experience with chat media (Q.15; Q.16)

	Daily	Weekly	Monthly	Hardly Ever	Never
G1	7 (53.8%)	2 (15.4%)	1 (7.7%)	2 (15.4%)	1 (7.7%)
G4	5 (62.5%)	1 (12.5%)	2 (25.0%)	0 (0.0%)	0 (0.0%)

5.6.3 Summary

The examination of participation opportunities in chat tutorials as the perception of availability and exercise of opportunities showed overall greater agreement in G4 on the presence and utilization of participation opportunities compared to G1. Further analyses revealed that compared to G1, participation in G4 was mainly affected by the following factors identified from the literature: turn-taking patterns, presenter role, tutor facilitation style, and tutor assessment of participation. Other factors reported by respondents that both motivated and inhibited participation included: the synchronous CMC medium, the presenter, and the quality of online interaction.

Of particular interest was the finding that G4 respondents as presenters experienced less difficulty in keeping up with the speed of discussions than as participants. Since G4 comprised mainly experienced users of chat media, it raised the possibility that tutor support in facilitating the online communication and management of discussions directly helped G4 respondents, in their role as presenter rather than participant, with the online communication and management of discussions. The next section presents the results on respondent perceptions of the availability of learning support from tutors and peers during the collaborative learning process.

5.7 Results for Research Question 2: Learning Support

Earlier findings raised the possibility that tutor support helped G4 presenters with the online communication and management of discussions. This section presents the results from examining student experiences of the adequacy of *learning support* defined as the extent of help perceived to be available from the *tutor* and *peers* on clarifying content issues during tutorial discussions.

5.7.1 Tutor learning support

The extent of *learning support* perceived to be available from the tutor on clarifying content issues during online discussion was measured by the following question where respondents indicated their extent of agreement on a 4-point scale from *Strongly Agree* (SA) to *Strongly Disagree* (SD).

- Q.3a: *The tutor clarified issues on content that were raised during the discussion.*

Results from a between group comparison (Figure 5.12) show
- 100% (8) G4 respondents agreed (*SA&A*) that the *tutor* clarified issues on content during tutorial discussions compared to 92.3% (12) G1 respondents.
- more intense agreement (*SA*) in G4 that the *tutor* clarified issues on content during tutorial discussions.

Group 1: Extent of tutor learning support (Q.3a)   Group 4: Extent of tutor learning support (Q.3a)

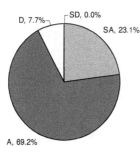 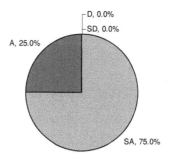

Figure 5.12. Groups 1 and 4: Extent of tutor learning support (Q.3a)

5.7.2 Peer learning support

The extent of *learning support* perceived to be available from *peers* was measured by three sets of questions (listed in Table 5.45). When taken together, the responses could indicate availability of clarification and different ideas from other students in the group, and the extent of mutuality in both information exchange and attainment of learning.

- *Set 1*: Q.3b and Q.5g for availability of clarification and different ideas
- *Set 2*: Q.5e and Q.5f for quantity of contributions provided and received.
- *Set 3*: Q.5h and Q.5i for mutual attainment of learning.

Table 5.45. Question sets 1-3: Measures of peer learning support

Set 1	
Q. 3b	How much help was available from other students during online tutorials?
	The other *students* clarified issues on content that were raised during the discussion
Q. 5g	To what extent do the following statements accurately reflect your overall experience of online tutorials in this unit?
	The other students contributed different ideas to the discussion
Set 2	To what extent do the following statements accurately reflect your overall experience of online tutorials in this unit?
Q.5e	I usually contribute more to the discussion than the others
Q.5f	Everyone in the tutorial group contributed about the same amount to the discussion
Set 3	To what extent do the following statements accurately reflect your overall experience of online tutorials in this unit?
Q.5h	I learned from other students' contributions during the discussion
Q.5i	I helped other students learn through my contributions during the discussion

In *Set 1*, a between group comparison (Table 5.46) found:
- more intense agreement (*SA*) in G4 that peers clarified issues and contributed different ideas during discussions.
- overall greater agreement (*SA&A*) among G4 respondents (100%) on the availability of clarification and different ideas from peers compared to G1 (84.6%)

Table 5.46. Groups 1 and 4: Extent of learning support from other students (Q.3b, Q.5g)

		SA	A	D	SD	UJ
3b. The other *students* clarified issues on content that were raised during the discussion	G1	2 (15.4%)	9 (69.2%)	2 (15.4%)	0 (0.0%)	-
	G4	4 (50.0%)	4 (50.0%)	0 (0.0%)	0 (0.0%)	-
5g. The other students contributed different ideas to the discussion	G1	2 (15.4%)	9 (69.2%)	2 (15.4%)	0 (0.0%)	0 (0.0%)
	G4	3 (37.5%)	5 (62.5%)	0 (0.0%)	0 (0.0%)	0 (0.0%)

Note: The UJ option was not available for Q.3b.

In *Set 2*, a between group comparison (Table 5.47) showed higher percentages of G1 respondents reported lower levels of own contributions to discussions *and* relatively unequal levels of contributions from others compared to G4.

Table 5.47. Groups 1 and 4: Quantity of contributions provided and received (Q.5e; Q.5f)

		SA	A	D	SD	UJ
5e. I usually contribute more to the discussion than the others	G1	0 (0.0%)	1 (8.3%)	6 (50.0%)	1 (8.3%)	4 (33.3%)
	G4	0 (0.0%)	3 (37.5%)	4 (50.0%)	0 (0.0%)	1 (12.5%)
5f. Everyone in the tutorial group contributed about the same amount to the discussion	G1	0 (0.0%)	2 (15.4%)	5 (38.5%)	4 (30.8%)	2 (15.4%)
	G4	0 (0.0%)	3 (37.5%)	1 (12.5%)	3 (37.5%)	1 (12.5%)

*Note: James (G1) submitted a blank response to Q.5e.

In *Set 3*, a between group comparison (Table 5.48) found:
- 100% G4 respondents reported that *they learnt* from other students' contributions compared to 92.3% in G1.
- a small difference in the percentage of respondents from both groups who reported that *other students learnt* from their contributions to the discussion.
- approximately half the respondents in both groups disagreed and were unable to judge that peers learnt from their contributions.

Table 5.48. Groups 1 and 4: Mutuality in attainment of learning (Q.5h; Q.5i)

		SA	A	D	SD	UJ
5h. I learned from other students' contributions during the discussion	G1	4 (30.8%)	8 (61.5%)	1 (7.7%)	0 (0.0%)	0 (0.0%)
	G4	3 (37.5%)	5 (62.5%)	0 (0.0%)	0 (0.0%)	0 (0.0%)
5i. I helped other students learn through my contributions during the discussion	G1	1 (7.7%)	6 (46.2%)	3 (23.1%)	0 (0.0%)	3 (23.1%)
	G4	1 (12.5%)	3 (37.5%)	2 (25.0%)	0 (0.0%)	2 (25.0%)

Results from comparative group analyses of *Question Sets 1 and 2* were consistent. The finding of greater agreement in G4 on the availability of clarification and different ideas from peers corroborated G4 reports of greater mutuality in the exchange of ideas during discussions. Additionally, the results substantiated earlier RQ1 findings that compared to G1, G4 exchanges displayed higher levels of reciprocity.

There were respondents from both groups who selected the *Unable to Judge* (UJ) option for *Set 2* indicating difficulties in judging the quantity of own and peer contribution which they explained below.

> …hard to keep track what everyone says … [Sam]

> Sometimes it was hard to tell and remember who said what, as I work better with face to face communication, rather then reading text that various people type. [Colin]

> I was unable to judge that everyone in the tutorial group contributed about the same amount to the discussion, because everyone would have their input, usually the same people. It was not a constant trend. [Scott]

> i wasn't really monitoring everyone else against myself too much so its hard to judge ... [Ian]

The explanations also highlighted a methodological issue[92] with this measure of the quantity of own and peer contributions to discussions. For some respondents, the text-based environment and rapid pace of discussions characteristic of the synchronous CMC mode had apparently posed difficulties for accurate recall of online interactions and monitoring of the level of own contributions against others. Results from comparative group analysis of *Set 3* indicate that most respondents from both groups reported own achievement of learning that was supported by peer contributions to discussions. However, results on perception of peer achievement of learning from own contributions were equivocal. Almost half the respondents in both groups disagreed and were unable to judge that peers learnt from their contributions. The difficulty experienced in judging attainment of learning by others was explained by some respondents.

> I have not heard any comments from other students about them having learnt from my contributions. [Diane]

> Sometimes I contributed more, sometimes didn't. Am not sure whether other students can learn through my contributions. [Wendy]

---

[92] Refer to Chapter 4, section 4.4.3 for discussion on the provision of an *Unable to Judge* (UJ) option.

Overall, compared to G1, there was stronger perception by G4 regarding the availability of peer learning support in terms of efforts in clarification, provision of different ideas, and mutual exchange of ideas during discussions. However, there were smaller differences between groups regarding own attainment of learning from peer contributions to discussions. There were equivocal findings on mutuality in attainment of learning as perception of own *and* others' achievement of learning which were attributed by some respondents to the lack of peer feedback.

5.7.3 Summary
Comparative group analyses of student experiences of the adequacy of tutor and peer learning support during tutorial discussions found:
- greater agreement in G4 on the availability of tutor and peer learning support as efforts in clarification and provision of different ideas.
- greater agreement in G4 regarding mutuality in the quantity of contributions or ideas exchanged.
- small differences between groups on perception on own attainment of learning.
- equivocal results in both groups regarding perception of own *and* peers' or mutual attainment of learning.

The results on *tutor* learning support substantiated RQ1 findings that compared to Rachel; Fay was more involved in G4 discussions with turns that convey information of some depth, thereby enhancing clarity of meanings during interaction. Results on *peer* learning support corroborated RQ1 findings of higher reciprocity levels in G4 exchanges and that G4 actors displayed greater mutuality in sharing information as *Carriers*; who sent and received ties, compared to G1 actors who being mainly *Receivers*, primarily received rather than sent ties.

The equivocal findings on mutuality in attainment of learning present certain implications for the design of collaborative learning activities which will be further discussed in Chapter 6. The next section presents the results on respondent perceptions of the overall quality of the online learning experience and collaborative work process.

5.8 Results for Research Question 2: Quality of Learning Experience and Collaborative Work Process
This section presents the results from a broader examination of the *quality of learning experience and collaborative work process* which was defined along two dimensions: the extent to which the chat tutorial activity is perceived to be integrated in the course design, and student satisfaction with experiences of chat tutorial factors.

5.8.1 Integration of chat tutorial activity in the course design
The *integration of chat tutorial activity in the course design* refers to the degree of fit between online tutorial experiences to the OI unit purpose of enhancing understanding of content. In other words, the concept concerns aspects of the chat tutorial experience regarded by respondents as affecting their understanding of the course content; and it was operationalized as Q.11: *What were the 1 or 2 specific things in the online tutorials that affected your understanding of the course topics?*

The results are presented according to the main factors that emerged from the analysis of responses to the open-ended question. The response rate for Q.11 is shown in Table 5.49. Quotes from survey responses and extracts from the transcript dataset are used to provide 'rich' descriptions of the findings.

Table 5.49. Groups 1 and 4: Response rate for Q.11

		Q.11	
Group	Survey Returns	Completed	Blank
G1	13	9 (69.2%)	4 (30.8%)
G4	8	7 (87.5%)	1(12.5%)

Note: *Completed returns* refer to instances where answers were given.
Blank returns refer to instances where no answers were given.

An analysis of the responses revealed the following main factors in chat tutorial experiences regarded by respondents as affecting their understanding of the course content:
(a) The synchronous CMC medium
(b) The presenter
(c) The quality of online interaction

(a) The synchronous CMC medium
Some respondents stated that the synchronous CMC medium had a positive impact on their understanding of course content by reducing inhibitions leading to greater willingness to discuss issues and exchange ideas.

> Everyone could discuss issues without being shy.Hence a lot of ideas could be exchanged. [Diane]

> Just recently there was a tutorial where many of the participants didn't understand the topic very well. after several explanations from both the presenter and the supervisor, I think everyone, including myself, understood the topic better. In a classroom, this may not have been as easy, as the presenter may not have been so forward in their 'teachings'. [Jack]

> … its easier to find get help in explaining cause not only the tutor speaks … [Ian]

However, other respondents maintained that the chat medium led to superficial discussions and added to difficulties in comprehension.

> ... lack of elaborate discussion and ability to express physical and facial communication. [James]

> ... harder to understand how someone expresses words in text ...[Ian]

The impact of English language proficiency on communicating via a text-based medium was highlighted by a G1 respondent. Cliff said, "... [o]ther group members lack of English skills" affected his understanding of the course content and the respondent had previously answered that he was motivated to participate by the "lack of English skills by other members of the group. If I didn't say anything, I had difficulty understanding what others were talking about." [93] These responses could be explained by the demographic survey data reported earlier (Table 5.34) which showed that there were 5 (38.5%) ESL/EFL speakers in G1. The composition of ESL/EFL speakers in the group could account for the different levels of English language proficiency perceived by Cliff.

(b) The presenter
While a respondent noted that understanding of course content was enhanced given "[t]he way the topics were explained by the people presenting" (Eric), Wendy maintained that when "the presenter is focusing on a topic too specific within the readings", her understanding of the topics was affected. To an extent, Wendy's observation on the presenter's moderation skill corresponded with RQ1 findings that G1 participants tended to focus on information-sharing rather than development of discussion threads during the collaborative learning process.

(c) The quality of online interaction
The quality of online discussions was held to have enhanced learning by enabling
- sharing of real-life examples and work experiences;
- exchange of different perspectives or interpretations of the set-readings; and
- active engagement reflected by the presence of questions and responses that clarified meanings of concepts or issues.

> ... The real examples ... [Max]

> Differing interpretations of the weekly readings, and also the work experiences and perspectives tutorial members brough to the discussion. [Pete]

> People's opinions on the related readings. As we did critiques we gave our point of view on the readinds, then in the tutorials, you got to see what other people thought and at times it went against what the readings were about. [Scott]

> Educated opinions are a valuable resource for learning topic material. [Mike]

> The questions that where asked during the presentations in the tutorials reinforced my knowledge of the topics. [Colin]

---

[93] Cliff's response was for Q.6. *Were there other factors that encouraged or motivated you to contribute to tutorial discussions in this unit?* Refer to discussion in this chapter, section 5.6.2.

That we as a group discussed the readings themes, points etc... I sometimes found I didn't understand some things... but was able to after the chat tutorial ... [Robin]

These observations on the quality of online interaction experienced during chat tutorials were supported by the following abridged exchanges from the transcript dataset.

Example of sharing work experiences in abridged exchange:

No.	Participant	Turn	EXG-7-g4S10-E2				
89	Evan>>	you would surprise the number of big projects I have had to fix up after people have just thought they would give it a go	I				INF
93	Fay>>	can you give us an example evan?	RI				CLA
97	Evan>>	Cant mention names but a large confectionary company recently upgraded their infrastructure		R+			INF
98	Evan>>	with no project plan and		R+			INF
99	Evan>>	the result was have to restore the Windows Infrastructure and start from scratch, end up costing them about $20K		R+			INF
100	Evan>>	more than it should have, cost is the determining factor I think, they weight the risk		R+			INF
102	Evan>>	vs doing it properly			R		INF
103	Robin>>	wow... just shows you how much having a project plan can be on a big project				R	INF

Example of active engagement with questions and responses that clarified meanings in abridged exchange:

No.	Participant	Turn	EXG-5-g4S9-E1												Code
64	Pete>>	Question from Jack: Is there any Practical DGSS, either real or conceptual, which would actually do what it would be required to do: support the group decision making process?	I+												INQ
66	Pete>>	This ties back to Hwee's question - has anyone used a GDSS?	I												INQ
68	Evan>>	Not in a formal way		R											INF
71	Fay>>	i've used a system that had a model similar to a nominal group technique		R											INF
76	Robin>>	could you give an example of when you used it fay			RI+										CLA
82	Robin>>	i think to better understand it... i don't about anyone else.. but i think with examples i could better understand it			RI										CLA
80	Fay>>	we separated into groups				R+									INF
81	Fay>>	and we were mostly co-located				R+									INF
83	Fay>>	and each group entered brainstorming ideas				R+									INF
84	Fay>>	and then we all looked at the ideas and evaluated them				R+									INF
85	Fay>>	the advantage being that everything was then recorded				R+									INF
87	Fay>>	the aim was a feasibility study of the division of arts				R									INF
99	Lim>>	so is GDSS a decision making methodology or is it a software system? I'm confused					RI								CHK
100	Robin>>	yes so am i						RC							FBK-E
102	Eric>>	From the example it looks like it can be both						R							INF
101	Fay>>	both lim						R							INF
104	Pete>>	So its a methodology which can have varying levels of software support?							RI						CHK
105	Fay>>	here's what i said before - basically a gdss comprises groupware + dss capabilities + telecommunications							R						INF
106	Lim>>	but that definition emphasizes the technical features								R					JUS
109	Fay>>	but it is also a decision methodology									R+				JUS
111	Fay>>	usually of brainstorming, analysis and evaluation									R				JUS
110	Pete>>	I think the Bannon article emphasises the CMC but not the DSS										R			INF
117	Lim>>	ok, now its clearer											RC		FBK-A
119	Robin>>	yes i can understand it easier now												RC	FBK-E

Example of different interpretations of set-readings in abridged exchange:

No.	Participant	Turn	EXG-8-g1S4-E2				
94	Diane>>	internet culture itself differs in different orgs	I				INF
95	Wendy>>	actually i wud c internet as having a very general culture :S	RI				CHA
98	Jason>>	difference is a part of live..whether it be in culture or character so an organisation has to embrace that learn on working with it....	R				REA
99	Alvin>>	yeah, i agree			RC		FBK-E
101	Derek>>	But to flip that, societies that refuse to adapt their culture to that of the multinational organisations can often find themselves passed over by the organisations			R		JUS
103	Sam>>	ya but normaly the company will adapt to the culture of the country.....or else the have no business				R	REA
104	Rachel>>	good point sam					RC FBK-E

Responses on the quality of online interaction indicate appreciation of the different perspectives shared as part of the learning process. Additionally, there was respondent awareness of the significance of active engagement as presence of questions and responses, which led to self-reflection or reconsideration of individual understandings during the construction of learning conversations.

Yet, the sheer quantity of information shared could prove daunting for cognitive processing during the rapid chat discussions. Tony said, "misinterpretation and understanding the interpretation differently from the topic" could occur during discussions. Hence, the presence of diverse and/or contradictory messages may not necessarily lead to better understanding when they are not clarified or followed up during the discussion as shown below.

No.	Participant	Turn	EXG-8-g1S2-E2			
95	Diane>>	With CMC can you escape F2F issues such as **gender prototyping?**	I			
101	Barry>>	wat do u mean by gender prototyping ?	RI			
105	Diane>>	gender prototyping as in		R+		
110	Diane>>	you know how some people expect men to be a certain way		R+		
111	Diane>>	or women to behave a certain way		R+		
113	Diane>>	gender discrimination		R+		
115	Diane>>	problems always occur cos of that		R		
114	Barry>>	icic			RC	

No.	Participant	Turn	EXG-8-g1S4-E2			
41	Alan>>	So how do these differ from soft systems methodology?	I			
42	Rachel>>	anyone?	I			
43	Diane>>	in soft systems....our PW affects our ideas....and our ideas affect our PW?		R+		
44	Diane>>	2 way?		R		
45	Tony>>	whay is PW			RI	
46	Diane>>	percieved world			R	
47	Tony>>	ok				RC
49	Tony>>	what differs from what alan	RI			

Overall, the examination of the degree of fit between online tutorial experiences to the OI unit purpose of enhancing understanding of content found three main factors identified by respondents as having both positively and negatively their understanding of the course content.

- *The synchronous CMC medium* that reduced inhibitions to share and discuss ideas leading to better understanding, but also presented difficulties in comprehending messages, and superficial discussions attributed to the speed and reduced non-verbal cues characteristic of the text-based medium.
- *Moderation or facilitation skill of presenters* who displayed different efforts in explaining difficult concepts and developing discussion threads beyond the immediate issues in the set-readings.

- *Quality of online interaction* which reflected both exchange of information and active engagement; with questions and answers that clarified meanings, but the diverse and/or contradictory messages that were not followed up during discussions did not further understanding of course content.

These factors were also found to correspond with those stated by respondents to have encouraged and inhibited participation during chat tutorial discussions[94] (Table 5.50). The findings present certain implications for the design of collaborative group learning activities which will be further discussed in Chapter 6.

Table 5.50. Impact of factors: Synchronous CMC medium, presenter, quality of online interaction

| | Impact on participation and understanding of course content | |
	Positive Impact	Negative Impact
Synchronous CMC medium	Text-based chat medium reduces inhibitions hence - supports participation by shy students. - improves understanding with greater willingness to share different ideas and development of CMC skills in context.	Text-based chat medium lacks non-verbal cues hence - inhibits participation given difficulty in sensing online presence. - reduces understanding when text contributions are unclear. Synchronicity of CMC medium increases pace of discussion hence - inhibits participation given difficulty in forming complete expressions of thought. - reduces understanding when rapid speed of discussions leads to superficial contributions.
Presenter skills	The presenter - encourages participation when there is eliciting of information with questions. - enhances understanding when there are efforts made to stimulate discussion and explain difficult concepts.	The presenter - inhibits participation when irrelevant questions are posed and lengthy postings are provided. - reduces understanding when discussions are not developed beyond immediate issues in set-readings.
Quality of online interaction	Quality of online interaction - encourages participation when different perspectives are shared. - improves understanding when engagement with questions and answers clarify meaning and add to individual knowledge.	Quality of online interaction - inhibits participation when discussions are not relevant to the course content. - reduces understanding when different or contradictory perspectives are not clarified or followed up during discussions.

Although respondents from both groups expressed mixed views on the degree of fit between chat tutorial experience to the OI unit purpose of enhancing understanding of content, further analysis of respondent satisfaction with chat tutorial factors in the next section will reveal clearer results on students' perceptions of the quality of learning experience and collaborative work process.

5.8.2 Satisfaction with experiences of chat tutorial factors
The extent of *student satisfaction with experiences of chat tutorial factors* was measured by two sets of questions below[95] (listed in Table 5.51).

- *Set 1*: Q.8 and Q.9 for levels of importance and satisfaction with online tutorial factors.
- *Set 2*: Q.17 for other factors or aspects of the overall online learning experience.

---

[94] Refer to results in this chapter, section 5.6.2.
[95] Responses from Q.10 were inconclusive and hence not included in the reporting of the results.

Table 5.51. Question sets 1-2: Measures of quality of learning experience and collaborative work process (Q.8; Q.9; Q.17)

Set 1	
Q.8	To what extent are the following factors important to you for online tutorials in this unit? Rate each factor from *Very Important* to *Not Important*.
Q.9	From your experience of online tutorials in this unit, how satisfied are you with each of the given factors? Rate each factor from *Very Satisfied* to *Not Satisfied*.
Set 2	
Q.17	Please share any other comments about your online learning experience in this unit *ICT329*.

In this section, the results are presented according to five online tutorial factors identified from the literature as potential influences on student satisfaction with the quality of learning experience (Table 5.52). The quantitative findings from comparative group analyses for each factor are accompanied by qualitative responses, where provided by respondents from the open-ended question (Q.17). The response rate for Q.17 is shown in Table 5.53. The results are also examined in relation to findings from RQ1.

Table 5.52. Online tutorial factors with potential impact on student satisfaction of learning experience

Online Tutorial Factors	References*
a. Opportunity to participate in discussions	Opportunities for participation (Carr et al., 2002; Cox et al., 2004; Dykes & Schwier, 2003; Gunawardena & Duphorne, 2000; McLoughlin & Luca, 1999; Spencer & Hiltz, 2003).
b. Discussions are relevant to the unit readings	Facilitation or management of interaction (Carr et al., 2002; Cox et al., 2004; Hara & Kling, 1999).
c. Communication skills in CMC environments are developed	Enhancement of understanding and learning experience (Dykes & Schwier, 2003; McLoughlin & Luca, 1999; Newman et al., 1997; Sudweeks, 2003a; 2003c; Sudweeks & Simoff, 2000).
d. Understanding of course content is increased	Convenience afforded by the CMC medium (Goh & Tobin, 1999; Pilkington et al., 2000).
e. Online learning experience is enhanced with chat tutorials	Availability of learning support (Hong, et al., 2003; Pilkington et al., 2000; Thomas et al., 2004).

*Note: References include studies on online synchronous and/or asynchronous learning experiences

Table 5.53. Groups 1 and 4: Response rate for Q.17

		Q.17	
Group	Survey Returns	Completed	Blank
G1	13	11 (84.6%)	2 (15.4%)
G4	8	7 (87.5%)	1(12.5%)

Note: *Completed returns* refer to instances where answers were given.
Blank returns refer to instances where no answers were given.

In the analysis of *Set 1*, the relationship between importance and satisfaction with chat tutorial factors was measured by the difference between the percentage of respondents who reported levels of importance (Q.8) and satisfaction (Q.9) with five chat tutorial factors (Factors a-e). This measure shows the extent of difference or gap between the proportion of respondents within a group who rated a factor as important and were satisfied with their experiences of the factor. In other words, responses to Q.8 established the level of importance for each factor reflecting certain expectations; the fulfillment of which were then determined by responses to Q.9 on the degree of satisfaction experienced with the factor.

The gap value is computed with the following formula: (VI&I% - VS&S%) where VI&I% and VS&S% denote respectively the percentage of respondents who rated a factor *Very Important* (VI) *and Important* (I), and *Very Satisfied* (VS) *and Satisfied* (S).

The gap value obtained reflects one of four possible states below (Table 5.54):
- *State 1*: where a factor was rated important and respondents were satisfied with their experiences of the factor i.e., gap value =0%.
- *State 2*: where a factor was rated not important and respondents were not satisfied with their experiences of the factor i.e., gap value =0%.
- *State 3*: where a factor was rated important and respondents were not satisfied with their experiences of the factor i.e., gap value >0%.
- *State 4*: where a factor was rated not important and respondents were satisfied with their experiences of the factor i.e., gap value <0% (negative value).

Table 5.54. States and parameters of gap value for online tutorial factors

State	Rating of Factor		Gap value	Parameters of value
	Importance	Satisfaction		
1	✓	✓	=0%	If VI&I% = VS&S%, and if VI&I% and VS&S% > SI&NI% and SS&NS%. • If there was no difference between the percentage of respondents who rated a factor as important and were satisfied with their experiences of the factor, and • if the percentage of respondents who rated the factor as VI&I and VS&S exceeded the percentage of respondents who rated the factor SI&NI and SS&NS.
2	✗	✗	=0%	If VI&I% = VS&S%, and if SI&NI% and SS&NS% > VI&I% and VS&S%. • If there was no difference between the percentage of respondents who rated a factor as important and were satisfied with their experiences of the factor, and • if the percentage of respondents who rated the factor as SI&NI and SS&NS exceeded the percentage of respondents who rated the factor VI&I and VS&S.
3	✓	✗	>0%	If VI&I% > VS&S% • if the percentage of respondents who rated a factor as important exceeded the percentage of respondents who were satisfied with their experiences of the factor.
4	✗	✓	<0%	If VS&S% > VI&I% • if the percentage of respondents who were satisfied with their experiences of the factor exceeded the percentage of respondents who rated the factor as important.

Note:
VI&I%: percentage of respondents who rated a factor *Very Important and Important*.
VS&S%: percentage of respondents who rated a factor *Very Satisfied and Satisfied*.
SI&NI%: percentage of respondents who rated a factor *Somewhat Important and Not Important*.
SS&NS%: percentage of respondents who rated a factor *Somewhat Satisfied and Not Satisfied*.
VI&I: ratings *Very Important and Important*.
VS&S: ratings *Very Satisfied and Satisfied*.
SI&NI: ratings *Somewhat Important and Not Important*.
SS&NS: ratings *Somewhat Satisfied and Not Satisfied*.

Correlation procedures were also performed on the two ratings (Importance, Satisfaction) for each factor. However, given the interpretation of *State 4* from negative gap values and small respondent numbers, scores obtained were more meaningful for strength of relationship than direction or statistical significance.

In *Set 1*, respondents indicated the levels of importance and satisfaction for five chat tutorial factors (Factors a-e) on a 4-point scale from *Very Important/Very Satisfied* (VI, VS) to *Not Important/Not Satisfied* (NI, NS). Table 5.55 shows the frequency/percentage of respondents from both groups who reported importance (Q.8) and satisfaction levels (Q.9) for each factor, and the gap values. Table 5.56 ranks the factors according to the gap value and corresponding state.

Table 5.55. Groups 1 and 4: Distribution of respondents who reported levels of importance and satisfaction with online tutorial factors (Q.8; Q.9)

Question		Rating	VI&I	SI&NI	Gap Value	State
Q.8a/9a.	G1	Importance (Q.8a)	92.3% (12)	7.7% (1)	0	1
Opportunity to			VS&S	SS&NS		
participate in		Satisfaction (Q.9a)	92.3% (12)	7.7% (1)		
discussions			VI&I	SI&NI		
	G4	Importance (Q.8a)	87.5% (7)	12.5% (1)	0	1
			VS&S	SS&NS		
		Satisfaction (Q.9a)	87.5% (7)	12.5% (1)		
Q.8b/9b.			VI&I	SI&NI		
Discussions are	G1	Importance (Q.8b)	92.3% (12)	7.7% (1)	0	1
relevant to the unit			VS&S	SS&NS		
readings		Satisfaction (Q.9b)	92.3% (12)	7.7% (1)		
			VI&I	SI&NI		
	G4	Importance (Q.8b)	100.0% (8)	0.0% (0)	12.5	3
			VS&S	SS&NS		
		Satisfaction (Q.9b)	87.5% (7)	12.5% (1)		
Q.8c/9c.			VI&I	SI&NI		
Communication skills in	G1	Importance (Q.8c)	100.0% (13)	0.0% (0)	25.0	3
CMC environments are			VS&S	SS&NS		
developed		Satisfaction (Q.9c)	75.0% (9)	25.0% (3)		
			VI&I	SI&NI		
	G4	Importance (Q.8c)	87.5% (7)	12.5% (1)	0	1
			VS&S	SS&NS		
		Satisfaction (Q.9c)	87.5% (7)	12.5% (1)		
Q.8d/9d.			VI&I	SI&NI		
Understanding of	G1	Importance (Q.8d)	100.0% (13)	0.0% (0)	30.8	3
course content is			VS&S	SS&NS		
increased		Satisfaction (Q.9d)	69.2% (9)	30.8% (4)		
			VI&I	SI&NI		
	G4	Importance (Q.8d)	75.0% (6)	25.0% (2)	-25.0	4
			VS&S	SS&NS		
		Satisfaction (Q.9d)	100.0% (8)	0.0% (0)		
Q.8e/9e.			VI&I	SI&NI		
Online learning	G1	Importance (Q.8e)	84.6% (11)	15.4% (2)	7.7	3
experience is enhanced			VS&S	SS&NS		
with chat tutorials		Satisfaction (Q.9e)	76.9% (10)	23.1% (3)		
			VI&I	SI&NI		
	G4	Importance (Q.8e)	37.5% (3)	62.5% (5)	-33.9	4
			VS&S	SS&NS		
		Satisfaction (Q.9e)	71.4%(5)	28.6% (2)		

*Note: James (G1) submitted a blank response to Q.9c. Mike (G4) submitted a blank response to Q.9e.

Table 5.56. Groups 1 and 4: Online tutorial factors ranked by gap value and state

G1 – Ranked online tutorial factors		Gap value	State
Q.8a/9a.	Opportunity to participate in discussions	0.0	1
Q.8b/9b.	Discussions are relevant to the unit readings	0.0	1
Q.8e/9e.	My online learning experience is enhanced with chat tutorials	7.7	3
Q.8c/9c.	Communication skills in CMC environments are developed	25.0	3
Q.8d/9d.	Understanding of course content is increased	30.8	3
G4 – Ranked online tutorial factors		**Gap value**	**State**
Q.8a/9a.	Opportunity to participate in discussions	0.0	1
Q.8c/9c.	Communication skills in CMC environments are developed	0.0	1
Q.8b/9b.	Discussions are relevant to the unit readings	12.5	3
Q.8d/9d.	Understanding of course content is increased	-25.0	4
Q.8e/9e.	My online learning experience is enhanced with chat tutorials	-33.9	4

A between group comparison for *Factor a* found:
- no difference between the percentage of respondents in both groups who rated *the opportunity to participate in discussions* as important and were satisfied with their experiences of the factor i.e., gap value =0%.
- most respondents in both groups regarded the factor as important and were satisfied with their experiences (State 1), with correlation scores of G1 r =0.63; G4 r =0.80.

Responses in Q.17 from both groups provided more insight into respondents' experiences with participation in chat tutorials that may account for their ratings of the factor. The opportunity to participate in chat tutorial discussions was held to be a positive experience by some respondents.

> I have learnt how to identify my ideas online by using chat room because while during face-to-face I usually don't share that much as I shared in this unit using chat room ... [Max]

> ... I think another online learning experiences i felt was that i was made to think on the spot in away... with chat you have to think quick to write responses. [Robin]

However, other respondents highlighted difficulties experienced when participating in chat tutorials.

> ... It made it hard to participate and share views because the speed of the discussion was too fast for me. [Bill]

> I hope there is something which can further encourage all our participation during discussions. [Wendy]

With regard to *Factor b*, the results show
- no difference between the percentage of G1 respondents who rated *relevance of discussions* as important and were satisfied with their experiences of the factor i.e., gap value =0%.
- most G1 respondents regarded the factor as important and were satisfied with their experiences (State 1), with a correlation of r =0.19.

- a gap value of 12.5% in G4, indicating State 3 whereby the factor was regarded as important but respondents were not satisfied with their experiences, and a correlation of r =0.18.

The results suggest a higher degree of satisfaction in G1 with the relevance of tutorial discussions compared to G4. While there were no responses in Q.17 that related to this factor, RQ1 findings corroborated the results since compared to G4, G1 produced a lower frequency of *Off-Topic* (OT) turns that were not directly related to the set-readings for all episodes (G1=322, G4=1077). Moreover, G1 tended to focus on information-sharing than the development of divergent discussion threads compared to G4.

Concerning *Factor c*, the results show
- no difference between the percentage of G4 respondents who rated *the development of CMC skills* as important and were satisfied with their experiences of the factor i.e., gap value =0%.
- most G4 respondents regarded the factor as important and were satisfied with their experiences (State 1), with a correlation of r =0.55.
- a gap value of 25% in G1, indicating State 3 whereby the factor was regarded as important but respondents were not satisfied with their experiences, and a correlation of r = -0.07.

Although there were respondents in both groups who were not very satisfied regarding the development of CMC skills through chat tutorials, comments in Q.17 were mainly positive; emphasizing the advantages of developing CMC skills that were transferable to real-life contexts.

I thought that having a tutorial online was an excellent idea. It opened up my way of thinking and i was not limited to face-to-face communication. There are still barriers surrounding this form of communication, but i think that the more people are willing to adopt to these environments, we can enhnace our skills using CMC. [Scott]

… very interesting and is definitly an eye opener to what will be a highly adopted form of communcation in all aspects of life. [James]

I loved the online learning experiences in this unit. I think its great, being able to communicate this way via online because i chat everyday online on yahoo, msn, icq, paltalk the list goes on. Its amazing just how many ways there are to communicate in various forms online. [Robin]

For *Factor d*, the results show
- a gap value of 30.4% in G1, indicating State 3 whereby *the increase in understanding of course content* was regarded as important but respondents were not satisfied with their experiences, and a correlation of r =0.25.
- a gap value of -25% in G4, indicating State 4 whereby satisfaction experienced with the factor exceeded its importance, and a correlation of r =0.39.

Comments in Q.17 regarding this factor were mainly positive with some respondents highlighting that understanding of course content was enhanced by the sharing of different views afforded by the online discussions, and the fit between the chat tutorial experience and the content topics.

> I think given the topics that are covered in this unit, using online tutorials to talk about them is the best way to learn, as it provides a more practical or hands-on experience which the students can identify with. [Jack]

> CMC tutorials turned out to be a great way to learn about the subject and learn opinions of others. [Mike]

> ... it was a very interesting experience and i think was very relevant to what they were teaching us. The world that we live in is changing toward the technology age very quickly and these activitys are vey important ... [Sam]

Regarding *Factor e*, the results show
- a gap value of 7.7% in G1, indicating State 3 whereby *the enhancement of their learning experience* through chat tutorials was regarded as important but respondents were not satisfied with their experiences, and a correlation of r =0.52.
- a gap value of -33.9% in G4, indicating State 4 whereby satisfaction experienced with the factor exceeded its importance, and a correlation of r = -0.14.

Responses in Q.17 that pertained to the enhancement of learning experience through chat tutorials reflected the respondents' mixed experiences with this factor. Some G4 respondents explained how their learning experience in the OI unit was enhanced through chat tutorials.

> ... an online chat doesn't quite have the same dynamic as a live tutorial, but in terms of convenience and learning is a very good option for a group fo externals. [Pete]

> It was good fun communicating over a communication chat medium overall, a new experience doing for the tutorials. [Eric]

Other respondents suggested that the learning experience in the OI unit could be improved by a combination of face-to-face and CMC communication modes in the design of the tutorials.

> It was a very interesting experience.However I still feel that there has to be a combination of face to face and CMC styles. [Diane]

> I would have preffered meeting face to face as tutorial group in the first week before doing online tutorials. [Alan]

Overall, the results reflect distinctly different quality of learning experience and collaborative work process perceived by student participants in the two groups (Table 5.56).
- Both groups reported two factors that reflected *State 1*; whereby the factors were regarded as important and respondents were satisfied with their experiences of the factors (G1=Factors a and b, G4=Factors a and c).
- G1 reported three factors (c, d and e) that reflected *State 3*; whereby the factors were regarded as important but respondents were not satisfied with their

experiences of the factors, compared to one factor (Factor b) reported by G4 respondents.
- G4 reported two factors (d and e) that reflected *State 4*; whereby satisfaction experienced with the factors exceeded their importance.

When the quality of learning experience and collaborative work process was defined as the extent of student satisfaction with experiences of chat tutorial factors, it would appear that compared to G1, G4 reported an overall higher quality of learning experience which was afforded by the online synchronous tutorials in the OI unit.

5.8.3 Summary
The examination of the broad construct *quality of learning experience and collaborative work process* was conducted along two dimensions: the extent to which the chat tutorial activity is perceived to be integrated in the course design; and the extent of student satisfaction with experiences of five chat tutorial factors.

Respondents from both groups expressed mixed views on the degree of fit between chat tutorial experiences to the OI unit purpose of enhancing understanding of content. Three main factors were identified by respondents as having both positively and negatively their understanding of the course content: the synchronous CMC medium, moderation or facilitation skill of presenters, and quality of online interaction.

Further analysis of student satisfaction with five chat tutorial factors revealed that:
- for both groups, expectations of *participation opportunities* afforded by the synchronous CMC medium were satisfied.
- while G1 respondents reported satisfaction with the *relevance of tutorial discussions*, G4 respondents were not satisfied with the factor.
- while G1 respondents reported that the expected *development of CMC skills*, *enhanced understanding of content* and *learning experience* were not met by their experiences of chat tutorials, G4 respondents not only reported satisfaction with development of CMC skills, but also indicated that satisfaction with enhanced understanding of content and learning experience actually exceeded their expectations for these factors.

Essentially, there were distinct differences in the overall quality of online learning experience between the two groups; with G4 reporting a more positive, higher quality of learning experience and collaborative work processes afforded by the chat tutorials in the OI unit than G1. The findings of student satisfaction and dissatisfaction with aspects of the chat tutorial present implications for the online learning process which will be discussed in Chapter 6.

5.9 Summary of Results for Research Question 2

In this chapter, sections 5.6 to 5.8 presented the results for RQ2 that examined student experiences of chat tutorial interaction in terms of participation opportunities, adequacy of learning support, and quality of learning experience and collaborative work process. Survey data was subjected to descriptive statistical analysis and interpretive content analysis. The results were presented as tables and illustrated with quotes from the survey responses and/or examples from the transcript dataset where relevant.

Results from comparative group analyses of *participation opportunities* in chat tutorials showed overall greater agreement in G4 on the presence and use of perceived opportunities which were attributed mainly to the following factors: turn-taking patterns, presenter role, tutor facilitation style, and tutor assessment of participation. Other factors reported by respondents that both motivated and inhibited participation included: the synchronous CMC medium, the presenter, and the quality of online interaction.

Further analyses on the adequacy of *tutor and peer learning support* during tutorial discussions found greater agreement in G4, compared to G1, on the availability of tutor and peer learning support as efforts in clarification and provision of different ideas. G4 also reported greater mutuality in the quantity of ideas exchanged. However, small differences between groups were found on perception on *own* attainment of learning. Additionally, equivocal results were found in both groups regarding perception of own *and* peers' (mutual) attainment of learning which were attributed to difficulties encountered with accurate recall of the rapid chat interactions, and the lack of peer feedback on the impact of own contributions on supporting peer learning processes.

The results on tutor learning support substantiated RQ1 findings that compared to Rachel; Fay was more involved in G4 discussions with turns that convey information of some depth, thereby enhancing clarity of meanings during interaction. Results on *peer* learning support corroborated RQ1 findings of higher reciprocity levels in G4 exchanges and that G4 actors displayed greater mutuality in sharing of information compared to G1.

Results on the *quality of learning experience and collaborative work process* revealed mixed views on the degree of fit between chat tutorial experiences to the OI unit purpose of enhancing understanding of content. Respondents identified three main factors as having both positively and negatively their understanding of the course content: the synchronous CMC medium, moderation or facilitation skill of presenters, and quality of online interaction. Further analysis of student satisfaction with five chat tutorial factors showed distinct differences in the overall quality of online learning experience between the two groups; with G4 reporting a more positive, higher quality of learning experience and collaborative work processes afforded by the chat tutorials in the OI unit than G1.

The results from RQ2 presented were based primarily on student perceptions of learning experiences during chat tutorials which were interpreted in conjunction with RQ1 findings that were based on educational interactions from the transcript dataset. The synthesis of results from the transcript and self-reported data provided a more holistic understanding of the construction of learning conversations. The next chapter discusses the substantive findings from Chapter 5, and highlights implications of the findings for the theory and practice of online synchronous activity design from a collaborative-sociocultural constructivist perspective.

CHAPTER 6

DISCUSSION AND CONCLUSIONS

6.1 Introduction

The aim of this study was to gain insight into the impact of online synchronous interaction on the learning process from a sociocultural constructivist perspective, in the context of an online undergraduate unit. Three main concepts pertaining to the role of chat interaction in facilitating collaborative-constructivist learning and group work processes were addressed by the research questions in this study: *participation, knowledge construction*, and *quality of online learning experience*. These concepts were examined in a single case comprising student and staff participants from two tutorial groups (G1 and G4), and the researcher as participant observer in G4.

The next section in this last chapter of the book discusses the substantive findings from Chapter 5, and the implications of the findings for the theory and practice of online synchronous activity design from a collaborative-sociocultural constructivist perspective. Section 6.3 highlights the limitations of this study and recommends possible directions for future research.

6.2 Discussion and Implications of Results

This study views interaction as vital to the sociocultural constructivist learning process (Vygotsky, 1962/1986; Wertsch, 1985) and assumes that *participation* in the instructional context of chat tutorials supports individual and group *knowledge construction* processes. Within the zone of proximal development (ZPD) established between the students, tutor and the virtual learning environment, scaffolding as support from the tutor and peers are held to affect the *quality of online learning experience* perceived by student participants. The mediation means of the synchronous CMC technology and the language of chat discourse enable, respectively, immediacy of interaction that reduces transactional distance (Moore & Kearsley, 1996) and the formation of learning conversations from which participants appropriate (Rogoff, 1990) for their own use the resulting shared understandings. This knowledge construction process is assumed to be empirically observable through an examination of the educational chat exchanges as well as student participants' self-reflection on their learning experiences.

The conceptualization of educational chat discourse as a hierarchical model comprising of exchanges, turns, and moves enabled the examination of participation patterns and the knowledge construction process, during chat tutorial discussions of G1 and G4, through discourse and social network analyses which were further informed by self-reports of student participants on their online learning experiences. Findings on the impact of chat interaction on the learning process pertaining to participation, knowledge construction, and quality of online learning experience are discussed below.

6.2.1 Participation

- *Were there opportunities for participation?*

The issue of opportunities for participation afforded by the synchronous CMC medium has attracted debate in the literature. The largely text-based chat medium is assumed to filter out visual and social cues (Kiesler, 1992; Kiesler et al., 1984) enabling participants to have (or perceive to have) equal opportunities for contributing to discussions. However, its synchronicity and conversational characteristics (Kortti, 1999; Murphy & Collins, 1997) led to unfavourable comparisons with the asynchronous CMC mode which was held to offer an ever-present window for 'speaking' (Meyer, 2003) that is not constrained by time or competition for turn allocation.

Results from comparative group analyses established that participation opportunities in chat tutorial discussions were not only perceived to be *present*, but also *exercised* by most respondents. With regard to the use of participation opportunities, most participants were present rather than lurking for most episodes i.e., logged in the tutorial chat room and made at least one contribution to the discussion rather than logged in and made no contributions. There was also a low prevalence of exchanges with inclusiveness of <1; suggesting that actors were largely connected to one another by relational ties that indicate the exercise of participation opportunities through activities of sending and/or receiving information during discussions.

The integration of discourse and social network analytical concepts enabled a further interpretation of the participation patterns found and their implications for the collaborative-constructivist learning process. Connections between actors in a network represent the existence of communication channels that facilitate the flow of information. The high prevalence of exchanges with inclusiveness of =1 found indicates the presence of these conduits that enable information to be shared among tutorial group members. Additionally, exchanges with inclusiveness of <1 signal the presence of Isolate actors who have no contact with other actors being neither senders (sources) nor receivers (sinks) of information (Scott, 2000). Being positioned apart from the discourse, these actors or participants could be considered less reachable compared to other connected actors in terms of the exchange of information within the network. The finding that participants in this study were largely connected to one another at the exchange level implies both ready accessibility to network resources, in the form of shared knowledge, and the availability of learning support within the network.

- *Were participation opportunities valued, avoided or withheld?*
Even as participation opportunities in chat tutorial discussions were mainly found to be present and exercised, there were contrary experiences reported in both groups. Although conversational turn-taking rules theoretically govern 'orderly talk' so as to minimize "gap and overlap" (Sacks et al., 1974, p.704), the rules are held to establish conditions for turn-taking, but do not guarantee their occurrences. Variations in the symmetry of turn-taking patterns could signal instances when participation opportunities were "valued, sought, or avoided" (Sacks et al., 1974, p.701), hence reflecting the degree of cooperation or control in the dialogue.

Results for both groups showed that opportunities to participate in chat tutorial discussions was a factor *valued* by most respondents who rated it as an *important* aspect of their online learning experience. However, there was a minority who reported an inability to utilize the opportunities perceived to be available which could explain the presence of lurkers in some episodes and variations in individual total frequency of ALL turns. These exceptions were in line with findings from a number of studies which indicated varying levels of participation in terms of frequency of chat contributions within online learning groups in spite of the democratizing effect of the text-based chat medium (Carr et al., 2002; Cox et al., 2004; Kneser et al., 2001; Pilkington et al., 2000).

A between group comparison found a greater tendency by G1 respondents to *avoid* making additional contributions when others had posted similar ideas to discussions, compared to G4. G1 participants were also more likely to refrain from making early contributions; preferring to let the discussion develop before joining in. Although such turn-taking behaviours by G1 conform to the rules of 'orderly talk' (Sacks et al., 1974) and cooperative maxims (Grice, 1967; 1978) that add to chat discourse coherence, they could undermine the assumption in this study that active participation in the dialogic sharing of individual understandings supports knowledge building. When opportunities to participate are deliberately avoided, a possible consequence is a reduced involvement in the construction of learning conversations from which shared understandings could be appropriated.

As participation opportunities are valued, it is reasonable to expect efforts by participants to *withhold* such opportunities from others by maintaining control of discussions. Application of the social network analytical concept of *degree* provided a dynamic representation of engagement by participants in each other's contributions in terms of their overall tendency to send or receive ties. The finding of wider variability in the tendency of certain actors to send ties than to receive ties within both groups suggested the presence of a hierarchical engagement pattern which is typical of 'teacher-oriented' interaction. Further analysis between groups showed that in G1, ties were mainly sent by the presenter for the episode and directed to all rather than specific students in the group. In contrast, G4 out-ties tended to originate from more actors other than the presenter and tutor; and ties received by G4 actors were more likely to be specifically directed to them i.e., G4 participants were more likely to receive individual attention in exchanges compared to G1.

Even though compared to G1, G4 displayed a less hierarchical engagement pattern whereby the flow of information tended to originate from more actors, the asymmetrical relational ties between actors in each group signal that control of discussion was exerted, albeit in varying extent. However, it is possible that the asymmetry resulted from the design of the learning activity where control of discussion was formally vested in the presenter and tutor. Since the learning activity required students in the presenter role to manage and stimulate discussions, with support from the tutor, patterns of control found do not necessarily mean that there was a less effective communication process for information exchange and meaning negotiation.

The synthesis of results from social network and discourse analyses offered a clearer understanding of this phenomenon. In discourse analysis, control of discussion was operationalized in various studies as the number of postings (Carr et al., 2002), turn sequences (Kneser et al., 2001), and exchanges initiated (Cox et al., 2004). This study utilized finer measures of I-SEQ, RI-SEQ and R-SEQ types of extended turn sequences[96], with which participants could avoid being interrupted and ensure the

---

[96] An extended turn sequence is a sequence of two or more turns of the same ES turn type (by the same speaker) that may/may not immediately follow each other in the transcript due to system lag and/or use of multiple short postings by the

'speaking' time necessary to communicate the message given that others in the group would refrain from posting until the perceived completion of the turn sequences. A between group comparison found the use of extended turn sequences in varying proportions and for different pragmatic purposes which raised the possibility that even as certain participants were excluded from the chat interaction, the effect may not necessarily be detrimental to learning.

Compared to G1, G4 produced higher percentages of R-SEQ and RI-SEQ that signal, respectively, control of discussion for extended sharing of new/additional information among members of the learning community, and for development of main conversational threads or re-direction of discussions to further understanding of the issues raised. Hence, such patterns of control could be interpreted as supporting exchange of learning resources at some depth that enhances the meaning negotiation process. Compared to G4, G1 produced a higher percentage of I-SEQ that point to control of discussion, primarily employed by presenters, for providing known information in metastatements (as summaries of set-readings) and eliciting information from others in order to start new exchanges. Such patterns of control in G1 could be construed as displaying a more limited sharing of individual knowledge and a stronger concentration on the gathering rather than sharing of information.

Essentially, the findings established that chat interaction enabled participation opportunities in tutorial discussions which were valued as important but variations in chat interaction patterns indicated instances when opportunities were avoided or withheld. While withholding of participation opportunities through control of discussion may not necessarily be detrimental to learning, avoidance of opportunities to participate implies the absence of certain participants from dialogic interaction that supports formation of shared knowledge. This study further examined factors that could have motivated or inhibited participation, hence affecting the extent to which participation opportunities were taken up.

Main factors located in the literature that accounted for whether participation opportunities in conversations are taken up included structural constraints in exchanges set by adjacency pairs (Sacks et al., 1974) and participants' degree of understanding regarding pragmatic intentions of turns (Levinson, 1983). In synchronous CMC discussions, participation opportunities available could be missed due to the characteristics of the largely text-based CMC medium which displays rapid speed of discussion (Dykes & Schwier, 2003; Mercer, 2003), and multiple concurrent discussion threads (Werry, 1996) that appear to lack interactional coherence (Herring, 1999) and discussion focus (Pilkington & Walker, 2004).

In the context of public chat discussion, Weger, Jr. and Aakhus (2003) found that the apparent lack of discourse coherence enables participation opportunities to be intentionally ignored when participants wish to evade questions, or deliberately avoided when there is concern over the visibility of one's own contributions. Additionally, Stromer-Galley and Martinson (2004) identified the topic as a motivating factor in participation in public chat discussions.

---

participant in order to convey a message. I-SEQ, RI-SEQ and R-SEQ refer respectively to Initiate, Reinitiate and Respond types of extended turn sequences.

In educational chat discussions, besides factors of the CMC medium, characteristics of chat discourse and topic of discussion, additional factors that accounted for whether participation opportunities are utilized included:

- mandated participation in assessed instructional activities (Sudweeks & Simoff, 2000),
- tutor facilitation style (Cox et al., 2004; Kneser et al., 2001; Pilkington et al., 2000),
- student moderation style (Chou, 2002),
- English language proficiency (Cox et al., 2004; Dykes & Schwier, 2003; Pilkington et al., 2000; Warschauer, 1996),
- prior experience with the chat medium and its linguistic conventions (Murphy & Collins, 1997; Pfister & Miihlpfordt, 2002), and
- gender (Chou, 2002).

Informed by the literature, the following factors were explicitly addressed by this study enabling a comparison of their impact on participation in the two groups: turn-taking behaviour, tutor/presenter facilitation styles, tutor/peer assessment of participation, and presenter/participant roles. Additional factors provided by respondents that both motivated and inhibited participation included: the synchronous CMC medium, facilitation skill of presenters, discussion topic, and gender which were consistent with the literature. However, the quality of online interaction noted by respondents appeared to be a factor that is specific to the context of this case. Since the results indicated that these factors do not exclusively motivate or inhibit participation, it implies that the combinatory effect of these factors should be considered when designing collaborative-constructivist group learning activities.

A between group comparison revealed the following main factors *common to both groups* that motivated and inhibited participation during tutorial discussions:

- *Turn-taking behaviour* as different tendencies towards making early contributions and responding with additional information or views.
- The *synchronous CMC medium* that encouraged expression of views and provided a novel learning experience generating greater collaborative efforts, but also presented technical problems and difficulties for complete expression of thought attributed to the speed and reduced non-verbal cues characteristic of the text-based medium.
- The *presenters* who displayed different abilities in facilitating, stimulating participation and ensuring relevance of discussion.
- The *quality of online interaction* which motivated contributions by reflecting the presence, acceptance, and acknowledgement of different perspectives, but also posed problems with dominance of discussion by certain participants that compounded difficulties of turn-allocation and ensuring the visibility of own contributions in an online environment.

Even though both groups underwent the same learning activity involving weekly critical discussion of the same set of readings in WebCT™ chat tutorial rooms, facilitated by student presenters and a tutor, there were factors highlighted by the survey responses that appeared to *motivate* participation within *one group more than another.*

In G4, participation was largely encouraged by
- the *presenter role* in which there was less difficulty reported with all aspects of online communication and management of discussion;
- the *tutor facilitation style* which supports the presenter in the management and stimulation of discussion; and
- *tutor assessment* or evaluation of participation.

However, participation in G1 was mainly motivated by
- the *presenter facilitation style* which stimulates participation and ensures relevance of discussion; and
- *tutor* and *peer assessment* or evaluation of participation.

Of particular interest was the different impact of the tutors on participation suggested by the findings. G1 participation was found to be largely motivated by peer-related factors (facilitation and assessment) while G4 participation was mainly encouraged by tutor-related factors (facilitation and assessment) with the greater ease reported in the presenter role attributed to tutor support received by G4 presenters in the online communication and management of discussions. It is possible that the overall minimal involvement in the learning process by Rachel (G1 tutor) and the greater efforts by Fay (G4 tutor) to scaffold interactions contributed to the different motivational sources for participation reported by the two groups. The more intense involvement by the G4 tutor could be explained by Fay's roles as both the tutor and the OI unit coordinator with the accompanying implication that Fay has a higher stake in ensuring the success of the learning process. The aspects of tutor and peer learning support are further discussed in section 6.2.2.

- *Should/could there be equality of participation?*
While this study assumes that participation supports the collaborative-constructivist learning process, it does not prescribe a normative state of *equal* participation. When the pedagogical aims of the learning activity, characteristics of the chat medium, and the totality of the learning environment in this case study are considered, a possible implication for the theory and design of online synchronous learning activities is that not every opportunity for participation could or needed to be taken up.

As stated in Chapter 3, a broad aim of the OI unit is to "facilitate reflective construction of knowledge [and] encourage the acquisition of cooperative and lifelong learning skills" (Sudweeks, 2004, p.90). The online tutorial learning activity was designed to develop "reflective construction of knowledge and active participation" (Sudweeks, 2004, p.85), as well as sustain "students' continuous engagement in discovering and applying knowledge and skills in the context of authentic problem solving" (p.92). In congruence with these pedagogical aims, both tutor and peer assessment of active participation emphasized the "level and quality of participation, effort, and sense of responsibility" (Peer Assessment of Participation, 2005, p.1 in Appendix A.2) displayed by students throughout the online learning process rather than mere equivalence of contributions made to discussions.

The sharing and negotiation of individual interpretations of concepts that integrate new and existing information are social-cognitive processes that require time. With the speed of interaction afforded by the chat medium, participants expressed the need for time to reflect on what was said in earlier turns.

No.	Participant	Turn
109	Tony>>	AQre you all still with me
116	Cliff>>	i'm still here, i'm just......thinking.....
117	Alvin>>	yeah, we need time 2 think.......................hehe....................

To acquire time for reflection, participants were observed to let pass immediate opportunities to participate only to take them up at a later stage of the discussion.

No.	Participant	Turn
65	Evan>>	This is a Question from Jack - Should computer scientists who have little social experience with interacting with an organisation, have to take a course on understanding how to interact with the organisation before designing or implementing a new technology?, and when studying computer science at university, how much of that time should be spent learning how to be interact with an organisations before introducing a new system?
69	Fay>>	what are your thoughts on your own question, jack?
70	Jack>>	haven't a clue at the moment....give me a second to gather my thoughts and I'll let you know
91	Jack>>	I actually thought my experience at uni so far has taught that quite well....maybe I just picked up on the idea by myself?

It could be further argued that attempts to be involved in all discussion threads at all times could result in information overload while selective involvement in exchanges enables a thoughtful filtering of information received during which incongruities in meanings were noted that enhances quality of learning conversations, as shown below.

No.	Participant	Turn
104	Robin>>	this one is Ian's: Can we have confidence in our communities HRO, or does more need to be done?
105	Robin>>	Ian do you have any comments you would like to add to this??....and comments from everyone
111	Ian>>	typin
106	Mike>>	HRO ?
107	Lim>>	high risk organizations - mike
108	Ian>>	high reliability organizations
113	Ian>>	like fire dep,
114	Ian>>	high reliability organizations
116	Ian>>	i think hwee
112	Eric>>	so that what it stands for
115	Bill>>	ahh it makes sense now
117	Lim>>	yes, Ian, essential services that cannot afford to fail

Moreover, as participants engage directly in selective exchanges, it is possible that surrounding threads are being monitored in a manner similar to eavesdropping during face-to-face settings. As noted in McDaniel et al. (1996), "overhearing conversations" (p.47) in the interweaving threads could result in greater awareness by various work groups of the totality of their collaborative environments.

Since no one could be expected to be active in all things at all times, it is possible that chat interaction impacts on the learning process by enabling a mix of active and peripheral participation by individuals as described by a participant: "Sometimes I contributed more, sometimes didn't ..." (Wendy). The construct *legitimate peripheral participation* (Lave & Wenger, 1991) refers broadly to a process by which "newcomers [learn to] become a part of a community of practice" (p.29) through gradual participation in the sociocultural practices of the community. Although the construct is not directly relevant to this study, given that students enrolled in the OI unit are usually 'newcomers', with tutorial groups formed from different student cohorts each academic year, the varying levels of educational chat interaction within and between groups reported in this study raise the wider issue of the impact of peripheral participants as *lurkers* on the collaborative learning process.

This study argues that lurkers in chat tutorials are not necessarily 'free-riders' (Albanese & van Fleet, 1984; Jones, 1984) but are "potentially productive participant[s]" (Shumar & Renninger, 2002, p.6) who could have contributed to the learning process through other means. The OI unit adopted a hybrid course delivery design that offers face-to-face lectures and online tutorials, supported by the WebCT™ virtual learning environment which provides both synchronous and asynchronous communication tools such as chat, bulletin boards, and e-mail. Learning could therefore be experienced in a range of physical and virtual instructional contexts. Hence, this study views participation in chat tutorial discussion as one learning activity which is integrated with other learning activities that participants may be engaged in within other contexts. While students move along gradients of participation in chat tutorials, they also occupy other fields of participation defined by the learning environment of the OI unit which are beyond the scope of this study.

In other words, although a participant may produce fewer turns during chat tutorials, s/he may seek to share individual understanding of concepts and ideas through other communication channels available, as described by a G4 participant: "The level of matureness of other students, their use of words and how they had smart answers in which i felt more comfy reading and taking in then expressing my views. I did that in my journal entries." (Bill).

6.2.2 Knowledge construction
The sociocultural constructivist learning perspective broadly assumes that knowledge building occurs during interaction which involves the sharing of multiple perspectives on experiences or concepts, and negotiation of individual interpretations (Vygotsky, 1962/1986; Wertsch, 1985) that may or may not eventually lead to shared meanings. As members of the learning community share individual understandings of concepts, a zone of proximal development (ZPD) is established where intellectual growth is supported by the availability of scaffolding as guidance from peers and tutors, mediated by technology and language. The tutor establishes a facilitator relationship with learners for the provision of guidance *when necessary* that supports gradual attainment of learner control over own beliefs in face of multiple perspectives (Duffy & Cunningham, 1996).

Additionally, this knowledge construction process is contextualized within the *Community of Inquiry* (Garrison et al., 2000) that comprised three mutually interacting and reinforcing elements of cognitive, social, and teaching presences in a virtual learning environment. Guided by the literature, this study examined the impact of chat interaction on supporting the knowledge building process which was held to be characterized by the presence of tutor/peer learning support, phases of information-sharing and topic development, and indications of gradual withdrawal of learning support from the tutor as students gain greater control of the dialogue.

• *Was there peer learning support?*
Results from this study established that chat interaction enabled peer support in varying extent which was consistent with findings from the literature (Heift & Caws, 2000; Mercer, 2003). A between group comparison showed agreement by most G1 respondents that other students clarified issues on content and contributed different ideas during discussions, but there was unanimous agreement among G4 respondents on the availability of such support which help to establish *cognitive presence* in the learning community. These different perceptions were consistent with findings of greater mutuality in the exchange of information during G4 discussions, and greater tendency towards reciprocation of ties by G4 compared to G1. Additionally, more G4 participants adopted a broader range of Moves for all episodes, indicating greater efforts to contribute ideas, prompt, probe for additional information, or shape the direction of discussions than G1 participants. Therefore, even as peer support was available in both groups, there was also greater collaborative peer learning present in G4 compared to G1. However, further analysis on the aspect of tutor learning support was necessary to establish whether G4 participants gained greater control of the learning process as well.

• *Tutor learning support: too little, too much, when needed?*
Several studies that examined the extent of tutor support during knowledge building, using earlier versions of the ESA framework, had largely reported patterns of tutor domination during chat sessions in terms of frequency of words and turns produced (Pilkington et al., 2000); number of words and dialogue roles held (Pilkington & Walker, 2004); number of turns, turn types and argument roles adopted (Cox et al., 2004; Kneser et al., 2001). The results were generally based on the observation of one tutor (Kneser et al., 2001; Pilkington et al., 2000; Pilkington & Walker, 2004) although when tutors of different learning groups were compared (Cox et al., 2004), they were involved in dissimilar learning activities i.e., general discussion and decision-making. From the analyses of selective chat sessions, the studies generally found no conclusive evidence of gradual withdrawal of tutor control over time in the dialogue.

In this study, the extent of tutor involvement the online learning process was examined from multiple perspectives including student perceptions of experiences and interpretations of interactions in chat transcripts with ESA and SNA measures. This study observed two tutors of different groups (G1 tutor-Rachel, G4 tutor-Fay) who facilitated the same learning activity involving critical discussion of the same set-readings. The findings were based on the analysis of a full transcript dataset, obtained over the entire 11 weeks of the OI unit, triangulated with self-reports which reflected overall learning experiences of the unit, and information from secondary data sources.

In general, both tutors were found to provide support which encompassed all three elements in the COI model, but a comparison of their involvement in establishing *cognitive* and *teaching presences* over time revealed very different extent of learning support provided. Contrary to findings of tutor domination from studies in the literature, this study found minimal involvement by Rachel in the learning process while Fay maintained a more visible presence with evidence of gradual withdrawal of control over time.

The results from discourse and social network analyses showed strong efforts by Fay to scaffold the learning process within G4 based on the following findings:

- *provision of information* indicated by highest frequency of TASK turns that convey content directly related to the discussion topics; highest frequency R-SEQ that provide information at some depth; and main preference for (R) turn types.
- involvement in *mutual information exchange* as *Carrier* for all episodes and *Isolate* in few exchanges.
- *shared control of discussion* with presenters at the start of new exchanges through I-SEQ.
- *shared responsibility of discussion* with other students through efforts to convey meaning, prompt, probe for additional information, or shape the direction of discussions with adoption of a broad range of Moves.

Compared to Fay, Rachel maintained a less distinct tutor presence reflecting little effort to guide learning within G1 based on the following findings:

- *provision of minimal information* indicated by lowest frequency of TASK turns, lowest turn density, and main preference for (RC) turn types.
- involvement in *information gathering* as *Receiver* for the most episodes in G1 and *Isolate* in more exchanges than Fay.
- *negligible control of discussion* with use of one extended turn sequence (I-SEQ) for all episodes.
- *adoption of minimal responsibility of discussion* with other students through the use of a narrower Move range than Fay.

These findings from the transcripts were confirmed by survey results that showed unanimous agreement among G4 respondents that the tutor clarified issues on content during discussions which helped to establish cognitive and teaching presences. In contrast, G1 respondents were more equivocal about the support available from Rachel with disagreement expressed by one respondent. Moreover, while most G4 respondents indicated intense agreement, the majority of G1 respondents expressed less emphatic agreement over the availability of tutor support during discussions.

Essentially, the results established that chat interaction enabled tutor support as well but such patterns of scaffolding found hold certain implications for the collaborative-constructivist learning process. When students are expected to gradually assume greater responsibility for the learning conversation, a consistently strong tutor presence may undermine this process. With these findings, it would seem that, compared to G1, G4 participants had less control over tutorial discussions with corresponding less responsibility for the learning process. However, a comparison of extended turn sequences used by Fay, in the first and last half of the 22 episodes in the transcript dataset, showed a declining prevalence of I-SEQ and R-SEQ while the frequency of RI-SEQ remained unchanged, indicating gradual withdrawal of tutor control over time. Since Rachel was found to use only one extended turn sequence for all episodes, it was not possible to observe meaningful changes over time in her case. With these findings, it is possible to conclude that in the case of G4, chat interaction enabled the provision of strong tutor support when necessary at the initial learning stages with gradual withdrawal of scaffolding when students gained greater mastery of the process.

Even as G1 participants appeared to have consistently assumed responsibility of their learning process given Rachel's negligible control over tutorial discussions, it could be argued that they experienced an accompanying loss of scaffolding from a more knowledgeable source. Although there was initial strong tutor control of G4 discussions, it also implies a corresponding presence of scaffolding with direction and information of some depth available during the learning process. Additionally, the less collaborative peer learning found during G1 discussions as noted earlier suggests a need for more educator support in conjunction with facilitation by peers. This study's comparison of tutor learning support over time highlighted these areas of tension between the cognitive, social and teaching elements of the theoretical COI in actual practice. While it is beyond the scope of this study to suggest the ideal proportions of each element that would constitute the most effective educational experience, it is reasonable to conclude that largely reduced teaching and cognitive presences throughout the learning process in the form of low tutor activity (as in the case of G1) implies an overall diminished online educational experience.

- *Were there information-sharing and topic development phases?*
Several studies that used earlier versions of ESA framework to examine educational chat discourse had mainly focused on the extent to which the coding scheme captured the structural organization, dialogue strategies, and roles in chat exchanges rather than explicitly tracked the depth of learning achieved (Carr et al., 2002; Cox et al., 2004; Kneser et al., 2001). Other studies linked the level of participation measured by ESA coding scheme to learning outcomes in the form of grades obtained for collaborative group work (Pilkington et al., 2000; Pilkington & Walker, 2004).

Extending on previous research, this study applied a refined ESA scheme for examining two crucial facets in learning conversations: information-sharing and topic development phases in chat exchanges indicative of the construction of new knowledge. During the *information-sharing* phase, participants concentrate mainly on their own contributions as they put forward ideas for consideration. This phase was measured by the combined presence of R-SEQ and {INF, EXD} Moves[97] (*Move Set 1*)[98] that indicate extended information giving, and {JUS, REA} Moves (*Move Set 2*) that indicate a more advanced stage of information-sharing that involves working through of implications or hypotheses. At the *topic development* phase, rather than merely accepting the information shared, participants give critical consideration to the meanings or implications of what others have said by questioning, checking, clarifying, and challenging previous turns in the exchanges. This phase was measured by the combined presence of {INQ, CHK, CLA, CHA} Moves (*Move Set 4*) that elicit more information to make meaning clearer/understanding easier, and propose another direction for thought or discussion. Hence at this phase, discussions are taken further in depth and direction which essentially reflect the meaning negotiation process that builds new knowledge.

---

[97] For definitions and examples of Move categories, see Chapter 4, section 4.4.1 and the codebook (Appendix B.1).
[98] For descriptors of Move Sets, see Tables 5.29 and 5.32 in Chapter 5, section 5.4.2.

This study found information-sharing phases in both groups and a between group comparison showed similar percentages of R-SEQ, Move Sets 1 and 2 produced. However, within each group, R-SEQ and Move Set 1 formed a greater proportion of the information-sharing phase. Such a pattern suggests that at this phase, participants were more occupied with exchanging information at some depth than with justifying beliefs, presenting implications or extended reasoning as represented by Move Set 2. This impression was substantiated by the overall lower prevalence of {JUS, REA} Moves compared to {INF} found in both groups.

These findings appear to reinforce perceptions in the literature that compared to chat interaction, online asynchronous interaction more effectively supports extended reflection (Harasim et al., 1995; Lapadat, 2002) necessary for developing higher order skills such as reasoning. However, this study argues that the greater involvement of participants in extended information giving compared to justifying/reasoning activities was not an unexpected result given the nature of the learning activity. In Cox et al (2004), higher instances of {REA} were found in exchanges of a learning group involved in decision-making compared to another which was set a general discussion task. Similarly, Kneser et al. (2001) found that {REA} was not the predominant Move adopted by participants involved in general discussion learning activities.

In this study, the chat tutorial activity involved critical discussion of issues in the set-readings rather than engagement in decision-making or problem-solving deliberations. The explicit priorities of the student presenter included moderating the tutorial sessions, stimulating comments from all members, and ensuring coherence of discussions. Consequently, instances of {JUS, REA} were anticipated and found, but the Move types were not expected to be predominantly adopted by the participants given the learning activity.

In the course of critical discussion, other than information-sharing, participants were expected to evaluate the meaning of what others have said by questioning, checking, clarifying, and challenging previous turns in exchanges. This study also found topic development phases in both groups, as represented by Move Set 4, which reflected presence of meaning negotiation during the learning process. Additionally, a between group comparison showed that compared to G1, G4 tended to develop main conversational threads further in terms of direction and depth.

A particularly interesting result emerged from an analysis of the proportion of Move types that constitute Move Set 4 which holds certain implications for the collaborative learning process. While {INQ, CHK, CLA} formed the larger part of *Set 4* within both groups, G1 produced a higher percentage of {CHA} than G4 in the form of questions/statements to assert or propose other views for consideration. When coupled with the less collaborative peer learning process during G1 discussions in the form of a narrower range of Moves, there appeared to be more *disputational talk* (Wegerif & Mercer, 1997) in G1 which is characterized by conflict and disagreement. However, in view of the corresponding presence of {INF} as the predominant Move type adopted by G1, it is argued that G1 discussions reflect more closely the characteristics of *exploratory talk* (Wegerif & Mercer, 1997) as participants cooperate to share information, yet contribute critical responses that prompt efforts from others to justify or explain their views. This study further argues that within the social constructivist framework where shared understandings are formed from meaning negotiation, {CHA} Moves in educational chat interaction are essential for their function as sources of 'perturbations' that lead to changes in individual interpretations of experiences or concepts (von Glasersfeld, 1989).

Essentially, the results from discourse and social network analyses established that chat interaction facilitated both information-sharing and topic development phases in both groups, which this study considered as indicating collaborative sharing of individual understandings and meaning negotiation of shared information that are characteristic of the sociocultural constructivist learning process. Additionally, scaffolding as peer and tutor learning support were largely found to be available during the knowledge building process. Although it is beyond the scope of this study to determine the exact form or extent of knowledge constructed, attainment of learning perceived by respondents was examined to ascertain if there was *appropriation of shared knowledge* during the online learning process.

Overall, results from this study also established that chat interaction during online tutorials was largely perceived to enable both individual and mutual appropriations of the shared knowledge. Most G1 respondents reported *individual* attainment of learning while there was unanimous agreement in G4 that they learnt from other students' contributions during discussions. However, the results were more equivocal regarding *mutual* attainment of learning. Although approximately half the respondents in both groups agreed that other students learnt from their contributions, the rest were equally divided between disagreement and being unable to judge whether peers had learnt from their contributions.

Even as the inability to provide an accurate answer on the behaviour of other participants was anticipated, it presented certain possibilities for modifying existing self-assessment practices in the OI unit. Following on the explanation by a G1 respondent that the lack of peer feedback on whether others learnt from her contributions led to the selection of the UJ option, the end of semester *peer assessment of participation* could therefore be modified to include this aspect and made accessible to other group members so as to raise awareness of the impact of one's own contributions on scaffolding the learning process.

6.2.3 Quality of online learning experience
Quality of online learning experience in higher education is a contentious issue stemming from the use of different institutional guidelines on quality practices or quality assurance frameworks for evaluating online programs and learner experiences (McLoughlin, 2003). In this study, a successful online learning experience is held to be largely determined by the presence and interactions between social, cognitive, and teaching presences within the COI model (Garrison et al., 2000). Although results from both groups established the presence of the three elements, focusing particularly on the interactions between cognitive and teaching presences, more could be learnt about the quality of learning experience from examining student expectations and perceptions of the value of chat interaction in supporting collaborative learning and group work processes.

This study defined the construct *quality of learning experience and collaborative work process* along two dimensions: the extent to which the chat tutorial activity is perceived to be integrated in the course design; and the extent of student satisfaction with experiences of five chat tutorial factors.

• *Was experience of chat tutorials perceived to enhance understanding of content?*
Several studies have identified the extent to which chat learning activities are integrated into the course design, with formal instructional objectives, schedules and assessment, as affecting student perceptions of learning experiences (Carr et al., 2002; Cox et al., 2004; Pilkington et al., 2000; Spencer & Hiltz, 2003). Since the chat tutorials in the OI unit are already based on a formal pedagogical framework; with clear learning objectives, scheduled sessions and assessment criteria (described in Chapter 3), this study extended previous research by examining the integration of the chat tutorial activity in the course design in terms of the degree of fit between chat tutorial experience to the OI unit purpose of enhancing understanding of content.

Essentially, student perceptions of the extent to which the chat tutorial experience enhanced their understanding of content were mixed, with the following main factors cited in responses to an open-ended question (Q.11) as having both positively and negatively affected understanding of course content:

- *the synchronous CMC medium* that reduced inhibitions to share and discuss ideas leading to better understanding, but also presented difficulties in comprehending messages, and superficial discussions which were attributed to the speed and reduced non-verbal cues characteristic of the text-based medium.
- *facilitation skill of presenters* who displayed different efforts in explaining difficult concepts and developing discussion threads beyond the immediate issues in the set-readings.
- *quality of online interaction* which reflected both exchange of information and active engagement; with questions and answers that clarified meanings, but the diverse and/or contradictory messages that were not followed up during discussions did not further understanding of course content.

It was interesting to note that these factors were similar to those identified by respondents to have both motivated and inhibited participation. When participation in chat tutorials is held to involve sharing of multiple perspectives and negotiation of individual interpretations that leads to greater understanding, these results suggest that the impact of the chat medium, facilitation style, and quality of online interaction should be considered in tandem in designing collaborative-constructivist group learning activities that enhance participation and understanding of content.

• *What was the overall quality of online learning experience for both groups?*
Several studies that surveyed student perceptions of online synchronous and/or asynchronous learning experiences have identified the following main factors as potential influences on learner satisfaction with the quality of experience:

- opportunities for participation (Carr et al., 2002; Cox et al., 2004; Dykes & Schwier, 2003; Gunawardena & Duphorne, 2000; McLoughlin & Luca, 1999; Spencer & Hiltz, 2003),
- facilitation or management of interaction (Carr et al., 2002; Cox et al., 2004; Hara & Kling, 1999),

- enhancement of understanding and learning experience (Dykes & Schwier, 2003; McLoughlin & Luca, 1999; Newman et al., 1997; Sudweeks, 2003a; 2003c; Sudweeks & Simoff, 2000),
- convenience afforded by the CMC medium (Goh & Tobin, 1999; Pilkington et al., 2000), and
- availability of learning support (Hong, et al., 2003; Pilkington et al., 2000; Thomas et al., 2004).

Informed by the literature, the following five chat tutorial factors (Factors a-e) were explicitly addressed by the online survey questions in this study, enabling a between group comparison of the extent to which respondents' expectations of the factors were satisfied by their experiences of chat tutorials:

- *Factor a:* opportunity to participate in discussions
- *Factor b:* discussions are relevant to the unit readings
- *Factor c:* communication skills in CMC environments are developed
- *Factor d:* understanding of course content is increased
- *Factor e:* online learning experience is enhanced with chat tutorials

Generally, the results showed that for both groups, expectations of *participation opportunities* afforded by the synchronous CMC medium were satisfied which were consistent with findings that participation opportunities in chat tutorial discussions were perceived to be present and exercised by most respondents. However, there were marked differences in experiences found between the two groups for the remaining factors. While G1 respondents reported satisfaction with the *relevance of tutorial discussions*, G4 respondents were not satisfied with the factor, which were consistent with findings that G4 produced a higher percentage of Off-Topic (OT) turns compared to G1.

Although respondents from both groups expressed mixed views on the degree of fit between chat tutorial experience to the OI unit purpose of enhancing understanding of content, further analysis of student satisfaction with this factor revealed clearer results. For G1 respondents, the expected *development of CMC skills, enhanced understanding of content and learning experience* were not met by their experiences of chat tutorials. In contrast, G4 respondents not only reported satisfaction with development of CMC skills but also indicated that satisfaction with enhanced understanding of content and learning experience actually exceeded their expectations for these factors.

Essentially, where quality of learning experience and collaborative work process is defined as the extent to which respondents' expectations of each factor were fulfilled through their experiences of chat tutorials, this study found distinct differences in the overall quality of online learning experience between the two groups; with G4 reporting a more positive, higher quality of learning experience and collaborative work processes afforded by the chat tutorials in the OI unit than G1.

The findings of greater dissatisfaction among G1 respondents with these factors are of concern when chat tutorials were designed to introduce students, in an active and experiential way, to the theory and practice of CMC processes which are directly relevant to the OI unit content. In particular, the development of CMC skills and understanding of course content are factors that situate the chat tutorial experience (Brown et al., 1989), enabling the tutorial activity to reflect real-world practices and settings hence making learning more relevant and transferable to other contexts. Taken further, the findings that expectations were not fulfilled for these factors signal potential sources of student frustrations over the nature of chat interaction that could impede learning and overwhelm students to the point of abandoning "the formal content of the course" (Hara & Kling, 1999, p.23). Conversely, the reported satisfaction experienced with these factors by other respondents could translate to greater receptivity to their value and use in other educational and communication contexts (Spencer & Hiltz, 2003).

6.2.4 Summary of findings

The aim of this in-depth qualitative case study was to gain insight into the impact of chat interaction on the learning process from a sociocultural constructivist perspective in the context of an online undergraduate unit. The impact of chat interaction in facilitating participation, knowledge construction, and quality of online learning experience of two online tutorial groups were examined and compared using discourse and social network analytical methods as well as self-reports of online learning experiences. The overall findings from this study are summarized below.

Regarding the issue of participation, the results established that chat interaction enabled participation opportunities in tutorial discussions which were valued as important, but variations in chat interaction patterns within and between groups indicated instances where opportunities were avoided or withheld. Compared to G4, G1 showed a greater tendency towards avoidance of opportunities to participate based on reported turn-taking behaviours and displayed a more hierarchical engagement pattern whereby asymmetrical relational ties in G1 indicated that the flow of information tended to originate from fewer actors. The avoidance of participation opportunities, which implies the absence of certain participants from dialogic interaction that supports learning, was attributed to the combinatory effect of factors of turn-taking behaviour, facilitation style, assessment of participation, and roles that did not exclusively motivated or inhibited participation.

While G4 was found to control discussion largely for extended sharing of information and further development of main conversational threads, G1 displayed a stronger concentration on the gathering rather than sharing of information. Although the withholding of participation opportunities implies the exclusion of certain participants from the learning conversation, it was not necessarily detrimental to learning since control of discussion was found to be exerted mainly for the gathering and exchange of learning resources at some depth that enhance meaning negotiation. Overall, these findings raised the possibility that chat interaction impacts on the learning process by enabling a mix of active and peripheral participation during which participants contribute to the knowledge building process through involvement in other learning contexts offered by the learning environment of the OI unit besides the chat tutorials.

Since participation in mere generation of dialogue does not necessarily indicate that learning had taken place, results from discourse and social network analyses established that chat interaction facilitated both information-sharing and topic development phases in both groups which this study considered as indicating collaborative sharing of individual understandings and meaning negotiation of shared information that are characteristic of the sociocultural constructivist learning process. Although it is beyond the scope of this study to determine the exact form or extent of knowledge constructed, the results showed that chat interaction was largely perceived to enable both individual and mutual appropriations of the shared knowledge.

Additionally, scaffolding as peer and tutor learning support were largely found to be available during the knowledge building process, albeit in varying extent, with greater collaborative peer learning support present in G4 compared to G1. Distinct variations in patterns of tutor scaffolding were found with minimal involvement by Rachel in the learning process while Fay maintained a more visible presence with evidence of gradual withdrawal of control over time. Such patterns of tutor scaffolding indicated that, in the case of G4, chat interaction enabled the provision of strong tutor support when necessary at the initial learning stages, with gradual withdrawal of scaffolding when students gained greater mastery of the process. However, low tutor activity in the case of G1 implies an overall diminished online educational experience which was confirmed by findings on the quality of learning experiences for the group.

In terms of the quality of learning experience as the extent of student satisfaction with experiences of five chat tutorial factors, distinct differences were found in the overall quality of online learning experience between the two groups. In contrast to G1, G4 reported greater satisfaction with more factors; indicating an overall more positive, higher quality of learning experience and collaborative work processes afforded by the chat tutorial discussions in the OI unit. Such findings on the extent to which student expectations of their online learning experiences were fulfilled presented pedagogical implications for the design of situated learning activities that enhance relevance and transferability of knowledge gained as well as minimize potential sources of frustrations over the nature of chat interaction that could impede learning.

Specific recommendations for the pedagogical design of online collaborative-constructivist learning activities arising from this research are presented below.
- A consideration of the combinatory effect of factors that could both motivate and inhibit participation such as student/tutor facilitation skill, assessment of participation, presenter/participant roles, discussion topic, and turn-taking behaviour manifested through the chat medium.
- The provision of physical and virtual contexts integrated within the learning environment for contributing to the learning process which could enable students to utilize participation opportunities in a range of learning activities and at different levels of intensity.
- The cyclical activity of reflection on educator practice regarding the effects of social, cognitive and teaching elements on the online educational experience.
- The modification of the end of semester *peer assessment of participation* activity to raise student awareness of the impact of own contributions on scaffolding the learning process.

In conclusion, the similarities and variations found in G1 and G4 regarding participation patterns, the knowledge construction process, and overall quality of learning experiences enabled a deeper understanding of this single-embedded case (Yin, 1994) whereby within a single case of the OI unit, the sub-units of analysis, namely, the two tutorial groups were bounded by the highly personalized experiences of teaching and learning (Stake, 1988). When extrapolated to comparable cases, findings from this study could guide the pedagogical design of online collaborative-constructivist learning that takes into account the impact of synchronous CMC interaction in the construction of learning conversations.

6.3 Limitations of Study and Future Directions
6.3.1 Limitations of study
In order to further understand the impact of online synchronous interaction on the learning process from a sociocultural constructivist perspective in the context of an online undergraduate unit, this qualitative study specifically examined the discourse of task-oriented chat interactions for indications of active participation and knowledge construction, and explored the perceptions of student participants on the impact/value of chat interactions in supporting collaborative learning and group work processes. Certain characteristics inherent in the design of the study resulted in three main limitations.

The first limitation concerns the *methodological frameworks of this study*. As described in Chapter 4, the constructionist and sociocultural constructivist assumptions of this study located it at the paradigmatic level within the qualitative research framework. Hence, the research process reflected "an interpretive, naturalistic approach" involving the study of phenomena in their natural settings (Denzin & Lincoln, 2000, p.3). Given such an interpretive approach, this qualitative study sought to illuminate and gain greater understanding of the knowledge construction process in the context of a unique case. The in-depth knowledge from the interpretive analysis of transcript data gathered over time and participant self-reports are not claimed to be generalizable to wider populations. However, the implications for the theory and practice of online synchronous activity design that were derived from the findings may be extrapolated to similar contexts "in the sense of pointing out lessons learned and potential applications to future efforts" (Patton, 2002, p.584).

The second limitation concerns the *transcript data*. Given the available features of the synchronous CMC tool in WebCT™, information captured in the chat transcripts were limited to the textual content of messages, server messages providing time/date stamps of tutorial sessions, participant names and their login/logout activities. This study acknowledges that the transcript data did not reflect all the details surrounding the events in the tutorial chat rooms and that findings from transcript analysis alone present a restricted and subjective account of the analyst's perspective on participants' interpretations of what occurred during the discussions (Wooffitt, 2001). Moreover, such data by definition reflects the presence of only those who contribute to the discussion (Harris & Muirhead, 2004). However, this study took into account these limitations with the use of a multi-method research design and multiple data sources which included insights from a key informant, unit document artifacts, and participant self-reports. The triangulation of different perspectives on the chat interaction afforded by the integration of discourse and social network analytical methods with participant perceptions and various data sources enhanced validity of this study based on the constructionist criteria of *authenticity* (Patton, 2002) which is in keeping with the qualitative research framework adopted.

The third limitation concerns the *self-reported data*. The validity of self-reports of perceptions or experiences assumes that respondents are able to provide accurate information on the phenomena examined (Kuh, 2001). As discussed in Chapter 4, the inclusion of an *Unable to Judge* (UJ) option in several closed survey questions took into consideration instances when respondents may not have sufficient knowledge to provide accurate answers on the behaviour of *other* participants during tutorial discussions. Interestingly, the UJ option was also selected to indicate an inability to provide an accurate report of *own* behaviour which some respondents attributed to the rapid pace of discussion and text-based CMC environment (Chapter 5). However, it is likely that the mandated *peer assessment of participation* activity and the availability of tutorial logs for review enhanced both recall and reflection on own and others' behaviour during online interactions.

These main limitations in this study are acknowledged but do not detract from the value of the findings. Instead, the limitations indicate several avenues for future research stemming from the contributions made by this study which are discussed below.

6.3.2 Future research directions

In its areas of inquiry, this study is essentially cross-disciplinary since it involves education, linguistics, information and communication technology (ICT), and educational technology which presents a number of potential areas for future research in these fields.

The single-embedded case methodological design (Yin, 1994) adopted by this study enabled an in-depth investigation of one particularly informative case and a comparison of the impact of chat interaction on the online learning process of two tutorial groups within the case. Although unique cases are, by definition, not easily available, there is scope for further research with a methodological design that encompasses all the tutorial groups in the OI unit and other units offering similar learning experiences. Alternatively, one tutorial group could be examined in greater depth in terms of the relationship between learning processes that are supported by the range of face-to-face, online asynchronous and synchronous instructional environments afforded by the OI unit. Such research efforts could yield valuable insights on the appropriate incorporation of the various CMC technologies in supporting online educational processes.

Given this study's focus on the examination of task-related turns which establish cognitive and teaching presences in the *Community of Inquiry* (Garrison et al., 2000), coding categories in the ESA instrument developed for this study were naturally more comprehensive for TASK turns while non task-oriented turns were simply categorized as *Off-Topic* (with sub-categories of OT-Administration, OT-Social, OT-Technical) or *Repair* (with sub-categories of RPR-Self, RPR-Other). Further analysis of the transcript data could be conducted on the OT turn type that could provide more insight for online facilitators on practical strategies for managing educational chat discussions. Additionally, the analysis of the RPR turn type could offer greater theoretical understanding on the linguistic features of repair by self and others in turn-taking sequences of chat discourse.

The integration of discourse and social network analytical methods enabled the examination and visualization of both pedagogical exchange structure and the dynamic engagement patterns of chat exchanges over time during the collaborative knowledge construction process. Since the primary focus of the transcript analysis was the chat exchanges, future work could investigate the actors in terms of shifts in actor positions within networks over time that could be highly informative regarding the effect of cliques or subgroups, centrality, power and influence of participants on the online learning process.

6.4 Summary of Study

Interaction has a vital role in the success of online learning as it supports collaborative-constructivist learning strategies and fosters relational ties that bind virtual learning communities, leading to higher levels of student satisfaction and quality learning outcomes. Although the literature largely regarded online synchronous interaction as fragmented and characterized by interactional incoherence (Lapadat, 2002; Herring, 1999) that disrupt the dialogic knowledge construction process, findings from this case study on the online learning processes of two tutorial groups over time showed that chat interaction is more structured and complex than the literature suggests.

Through the application of a new methodological design that integrated discourse and social network analytical concepts as well as self-reports of online learning experiences, educational chat discourse was found to be coherent at the level of exchange structure, and reflective of information-sharing and topic development phases that indicate the collaborative sharing of individual understandings and critical negotiation of meaning. Together with findings of scaffolding as peer and tutor learning support suggested by the chat exchange patterns, there were ultimately individual and mutual appropriations of shared knowledge reported by the participants.

With its methodological design, instruments and findings, this research effort has contributed to existing knowledge on online interaction, extended previous studies regarding the pedagogical impact of synchronous CMC technology, and increased understanding of the impact of online synchronous interaction on the learning process from a sociocultural constructivist perspective.

REFERENCES

Aaker, D., Kumar, V., & Day, G. (2004). *Marketing research* (8th ed.). New York: John Wiley & Sons, Inc.

Albanese, R., & van Fleet, D. (1985). Rational behavior in groups: The free-riding tendency. *Academy of Management Review, 10*(2), 244-255.

Anderson, T. (2002). *An updated and theoretical rationale for interaction - paper presented at ITFORUM.* Retrieved 13 July, 2004, from http://it.coe.uga.edu/itforum/paper63/paper63.htm

Anderson, T. (2003). Getting the mix right again: An updated and theoretical rationale for interaction. *International Review of Research in Open and Distance Learning, 4*(2), Online.

Anderson, T. (2004). Toward a theory of online learning. In T. Anderson & F. Elloumi (Eds.), *Theory and practice of online learning* (pp. 33-60). Canada: Athabasca University.

Anderson, T., & Garrison, D. (1998). Learning in a networked world: New roles and responsibilities. In C. Gibson (Ed.), *Distance learning in higher education.* (pp. 97-112). Madison WI: Atwood Publishing.

Anderson, T., Rourke, L., Garrison, D., & Archer, W. (2001). Assessing teaching presence in a computer conferencing context. *Journal of Asynchronous Learning Networks, 5*(2), 1-17.

Armitt, G., Slack, F., Green, S., & Beer, M. (2002, January 2002). *The development of deep learning during a synchronous collaborative on-line course.* Paper presented at the CSCL 2002, Boulder, Colorado.

Ary, D., Jacobs, L., & Razavieh, A. (2002). *Introduction to research in education* (6th ed.). Belmont, CA: Wardsworth/Thomson Learning.

Austin, J. (1962). *How to do things with words.* Oxford: Clarendon Press.

Aviv, R., Erlich, Z., Ravid, G., & Geva, A. (2003). Network analysis of knowledge construction in asynchronous learning networks. *Journal of Asynchronous Learning Networks, 7*(3).

Babbie, E. (1990). *Survey research methods* (2nd ed.). Belmont, California: Wadsworth, Inc.

Barnes, J. (1954). Class and committee in a Norwegian island parish. *Human Relations, 7*, 39-58.

Baym, N. (1998). The emergence of on-line community. In S. Jones (Ed.), *Cybersociety 2.0: Revisiting computer-mediated communication and community* (pp. 35-68). Thousand Oaks, California: Sage.

Benbasat, I., Goldstein, D., & Mead, M. (1987). The case research strategy in studies of information systems. *MIS Quarterly, 11*(3), 369-386.

Berge, Z. (2002). Active, interactive and reflective learning. *The Quarterly Review of Distance Education, 3*(2), 181-190.

Berzenyi, C. (1999). Teaching interlocutor relationships in electronic classrooms. *Computers and Composition, 16*, 229-246.

Boer, P., De Negro, R., Huisman, M., Snijders, T., Steglich, C., & Zeggelink, E. (2004). *StOCNET: An open software system for the advanced statistical analysis of social networks. Version 1.5.* Groningen: ICS/Science Plus Group, University of Groningen.

Bonk, C., & Reynolds, T. (1997). Learner-centered web instruction for higher-order thinking, teamwork and apprenticeship. In B. Khan (Ed.), *Web-based instruction* (pp. 167-178). Englewood Cliffs, New Jersey: Educational Technology Publications.

Bonk, C. J., & Cunningham, D. J. (1998). Searching for learner-centered, constructivist, and sociocultural components of collaborative educational learning tools. In C. J. Bonk & K. S. King (Eds.), *Electronic collaborators: Learner-centered technologies for literacy, apprenticeship, and discourse* (pp. 25-50). New Jersey: Lawrence Erlbaum Associates.

Bonk, C. J., Daytner, K., Daytner, G., Dennen, V., & Malikowski, S. (2001). Using web-based cases to enhance, extend, and transform pre-service teacher training: Two years in review. In C. D. Maddux & D. LaMont Johnson (Eds.), *The Web in higher education: Assessing the impact and fulfilling the potential* (pp. 189-211). New York: The Haworth Press, Inc.

Bonk, C. J., Hansen, E. J., Grabner-Hagen, M. M., Lazar, S. A., & Mirabelli, C. (1998). Time to "connect": synchronous and asynchronous case-based dialogue among preservice teachers. In C. J. Bonk & K. S. King (Eds.), *Electronic collaborators: Learner-centered technologies for literacy, apprenticeship, and discourse* (pp. 289-314). New Jersey: Lawrence Erlbaum Associates.

Bonk, C. J., & Kim, K. A. (1998). Extending sociocultural theory to adult learning. In M. C. Smith & T. Pourchot (Eds.), *Adult learning and development* (pp. 67-88). Mahwah, NJ: Erlbaum.

Booth, S., & Hulten, M. (2004). Opening dimensions of variation: An empirical study of learning in a web-based discussion. In P. Goodyear, S. Banks, V. Hodgson & D. McConnell (Eds.), *Advances in research on networked learning* (Vol. 4, pp. 153-174). Massachusetts, USA: Kluwer Academic Publishers.

Borgatti, S., Everett, M., & Freeman, L. (2002). UCINET 6 for Windows: Software for social network analysis. Harvard: Analytic Technologies.

Bott, E. (1955). Urban families: Conjugal roles and social networks. *Human Relations, 8*, 345-383.

Bott, E. (1956). Urban families: The norms of conjugal roles. *Human Relations, 9*, 325-341.

Brabazon, T. (2002). *Digital hemlock: Internet education and the poisoning of teaching.* Sydney, Australia: University of New South Wales Press.

Breiger, R. (1974). The duality of persons and groups. *Social Forces, 53*(2), 181-190.

Breiger, R. (2004). The analysis of social networks. In M. Hardy & A. Bryman (Eds.), *Handbook of data analysis* (pp. 505-526). London: Sage.

Bromseth, J. (2002). Public places-public activities? Methodological approaches and ethical dilemmas in research on computer-mediated communication contexts. In A. Morrison (Ed.), *Researching ICTs in context* (Vol. Report 3, pp. 44-72). Oslo: Intermedia, Unipub forlag.

Brown, G., & Yule, G. (1983). *Discourse analysis.* Cambridge: Cambridge University Press.

Brown, J., Collins, A., & Duguid, P. (1989). Situated cognition and the culture of learning. *Educational Researcher, 18*(1), 32-42.

Bruner, J. (1961). The act of discovery. *Harvard Educational Review, 31*(1), 21-32.

Bruner, J. (1966). *Toward a theory of instruction.* Cambridge, MA: Harvard University Press.

Buckingham, S. (2003). Perspectives on the experience of the learning community through online discussions. *Journal of Distance Education, 18*(2), 74-91.

Burt, R. (1988). The stability of American markets. *American Journal of Sociology, 94*(2), 356-395.

Burt, R. (1991). STRUCTURE. Version 4.2. New York: Columbia University.

Carr, S. (2000). As distance education comes of age, the challenge is keeping the students. *The Chronicle of Higher Education, 46*(23), 39-41.

Carr, T., Cox, G., Eden, A., & Loopuyt, M. (2002). *An analysis of face to face and online learning conversations in three mixed mode courses.* Paper presented at the Multimedia Educational Group (MEG) Colloquium October 2002, Sport Science Institute of South Africa.

Cartwright, D., & Harary, F. (1956). Structural balance: A generalization of Heider's theory. *Psychological Review, 63*, 277-292.

Cashion, J., & Palmieri, P. (2002). *'The secret is the teacher': The learner's view of online learning.* SA: Australia: NCVER.

Chan, H., Tan, B., & Tan, W.-P. (2000). A case study of one-to-one video-conferencing education over the Internet. In A. Aggarwal (Ed.), *Web-based learning and teaching technologies: Opportunities and challenges* (pp. 275-299): Idea Group Publishing.

Chesebro, J., & McCroskey, J. (2000). The relationship between students' reports of learning and their actual recall of lecture material: A validity test. *Communication Education, 49*, 297-301.

Chi, M. (1997). Quantifying qualitative analyses of verbal data: A practical guide. *The Journal of the Learning Sciences, 6*(3), 271-315.

Chickering, A., & Gamson, A. (1987). Seven principles for good practice in undergraduate education. *AAHE Bulletin, 39*(7), 3-7.

Chou, C. (2002). *A comparative content analysis of student interaction in synchronous and asynchronous learning networks.* Paper presented at the 35th Annual Hawaii International Conference on System Sciences, Hawaii.

Chun, M. (2002). Looking where the light is better: A review of the literature on assessing higher education quality. *peerReview, Winter/Spring*, 16-25.

Clayman, S., & Gill, V. (2004). Conversation analysis. In M. Hardy & A. Bryman (Eds.), *Handbook of data analysis* (pp. 589-606). London: Sage.

Cobb, P. (1994). Where is the mind? Constructivist and sociocultural perspectives on mathematical development. *Educational Researcher, 23*(7), 13-20.

Collet, M., & Belmore, N. (1996). Electronic language: A new variety of English. In S. Herring (Ed.), *Computer-mediated communication* (pp. 13-28). Philadelphia, USA: John Benjamins Publishing Company.

Conrad, D. (2002). Deep in the hearts of learners: Insight into the nature of online community. *Journal of Distance Education, 17*(1).

Cooney, D. (1998). Sharing aspects within ASPECTS: Real-time collaboration in the high school English classroom. In C. J. Bonk & K. S. King (Eds.), *Electronic collaborators: Learner-centered technologies for literacy, apprenticeship, and discourse* (pp. 263-287). New Jersey: Lawrence Erlbaum Associates.

Coulthard, M., & Brazil, D. (1992). Exchange structure. In M. Coulthard (Ed.), *Advances in spoken discourse analysis* (pp. 50-78). London: Routledge.

Couper, M., Traugott, M., & Lamias, M. (2001). Web survey design and administration. *Public Opinion Quarterly, 65*(2 (Summer)), 230-253.

Cox, G., Carr, T., & Hall, M. (2004). Evaluating the use of synchronous communication in two blended courses. *Journal of Computer Assisted Learning, 20*, 183-193.

Crook, C., & Light, P. (2002). Virtual society and the cultural practice of study. In S. Woolgar (Ed.), *Virtual society? Technology, cyberbole, reality.* Oxford: Oxford University Press.

Crotty, M. (1998). *The foundations of social research: Meaning and perspective in the research process.* Sydney, Australia: Allen & Unwin.

Culnan, M., & Markus, M. (1987). Information technologies. In F. Jablin, L. Putnam, K. Roberts & L. Porter (Eds.), *Handbook of organizational communication: An introductory perspective* (pp. 420-443). Newbury Park, California: Sage.

Cunningham, D. (1991). Assessing constructions and constructing assessments: A dialogue. *Educational Technology, 31*(5), 13-17.

Cutler, R. (1995). Distributed presence and community in cyberspace. *Interpersonal Computing and Technology (IPCT): An Electronic Journal for the 21st Century, 3*(2), 12-32.

Cyram. (2004). Cyram NetMiner II. Version 2.5.0: Cyram Co., Ltd.

Daft, R., & Lengel, R. (1986). Organizational information requirements: Media richness and structural design. *Management Science, 32*(5), 554-571.

Davis, A., Gardner, B., & Gardner, M. (1941). *Deep South: A social anthropological study of caste and class.* Chicago: University of Chicago Press.

De Laat, M., & Lally, V. (2004). Complexity, theory and praxis: Researching collaborative learning and tutoring processes in networked learning community. In P. Goodyear, S. Banks, V. Hodgson & D. McConnell (Eds.), *Advances in research on networked learning* (Vol. 4, pp. 11-42). Massachusetts, USA: Kluwer Academic Publishers.

de Vicente, A., Bouwer, A., & Pain, H. (1999). *Initial impressions on using the DISCOUNT scheme.* Paper presented at the Workshop on Analysing Educational Dialogue Interaction: Towards Models that Support Learning (AI-ED'99).

December, J. (1993, July 8 1993). *Characteristics of oral culture in discourse on the Net.* Paper presented at the 12th Annual Penn State Conference on Rhetoric and Composition, University Park, Pennsylvania.

Delamont, S. (2004). Ethnography and participant observation. In C. Seale, G. Gobo, J. Gubrium & D. Silverman (Eds.), *Qualitative research practice* (pp. 217-229). London: Sage.

Denzin, N., & Lincoln, Y. (2000). Introduction: The discipline and practice of qualitative research. In N. Denzin & Y. Lincoln (Eds.), *Handbook of qualitative research* (2nd ed., pp. 1-28). London: Sage Publications.

Dewey, J. (1938). *Experience and education.* New York: Macmillan.

Dillman, D., Tortora, R., & Bowker, D. (1998). *Principles for constructing web surveys.* Washington.: Pullman.

Duemer, L., Fontenot, D., Gumfory, K., & Kallus, M. (2002). The use of online synchronous discussion groups to enhance community formation and professional identity development. *The Journal of Interactive Online Learning, 1*(2).

Duffy, T., & Cunningham, D. J. (1996). Constructivism: Implications for the design and delivery of instruction. In D. Jonassen (Ed.), *Handbook of research for educational communications and technology* (pp. 170-198). New York: Simon & Schuster Macmillan.

Duffy, T., & Jonassen, D. (1991). Constructivism: New implications for instructional technology? *Educational Technology, 31*(5), 7-12.

Dykes, M., & Schwier, R. (2003). Content and community redux: Instructor and student Interpretations of online communication in a graduate seminar. *Canadian Journal of Learning and Technology, 29*(2 Spring).

Edwards, C. (2002, 26-28 March). *Discourse on collaborative networked learning.* Paper presented at the Networked Learning Conference 2002, University of Sheffield.

Eggins, S., & Slade, D. (1997). *Analyzing casual conversation.* London: Cassell.

Ertmer, P., & Newby, T. (1993). Behaviourism, cognitivism, constructivism. Comparing critical features. *Performance Improvement Quarterly, 6*(4), 50-70.

Eysenbach, G., & Till, J. (2001). Ethical issues in qualitative research on internet communities. *BMJ, 323,* 1103-1105.

Fernback, J. (1997). The individual within the collective: Virtual ideology and the realization of collective principles. In S. Jones (Ed.), *Virtual culture: Identity and communication in cybersociety* (pp. 36-54). Thousand Oaks, California: Sage Publications.

Ferris, P. (1991). *What is CMC? An overview of scholarly definitions.* Retrieved 23 June, 2005, from http://www.december.com/cmc/mag/1997/jan/ferris.html

Forsyth, E., & Katz, L. (1946). A matrix approach to the analysis of sociometric data: Preliminary report. *Sociometry, 9*(2), 340-347.

Francis, G., & Hunston, S. (1992). Analysing everyday conversation. In M. Coulthard (Ed.), *Advances in spoken discourse analysis* (pp. 123-161). London: Routledge.

Freeman, L. (2000a). *Visualizing social networks.* Retrieved 2 November, 2004, from http://www.cmu.edu/joss/content/articles/volume1/Freeman.html

Freeman, L. (2000b). Social network analysis: Definition and history. In A. Kazdan (Ed.), *Encyclopedia of Psychology* (Vol. 6, pp. 350-351). New York: Oxford University Press.

Fricker Jr., R., & Rand, M. (2002). Advantages and disadvantages of internet research surveys: Evidence from the literature. *Field Methods, 14*(4), 347-367.

Fulk, J., Schmitz, J., & Steinfeld, C. (1990). A social influence model of technology use. In J. Fulk & C. Steinfield (Eds.), *Organizations and communication technology* (pp. 117-140). Newbury Park, CA: Sage.

Fulk, J., Steinfield, C., Schmitz, J., & Power, J. (1987). A social information processing model of media use in organizations. *Communication Research, 14,* 529-552.

Galaskiewicz, J., & Wasserman, S. (1989). Mimetic and normative processes within an interorganizational field: An empirical test. *Administrative Science Quarterly, 34*(3), 454-480.

Garfinkel, H. (1967). *Studies in ethnomethodology.* Englewood Cliffs, N.J.: Prentice-Hall.

Garrison, D. (2003). Cognitive presence for effective asynchronous online learning: The role of reflective inquiry, self-direction and metacognition. In J. Bourne & J. Moore (Eds.), *Elements of quality online education: Practice and direction* (Vol. 4). Needham, MA: The Sloan Consortium.

Garrison, D., & Anderson, T. (2003). *E-learning in the 21th century.* London: RoutledgeFalmer.

Garrison, D., Anderson, T., & Archer, W. (2000). Critical inquiry in a text-based environment: Computer conferencing in higher education. *Internet and Higher Education, 11*(2), 1-14.

Garrison, D., Anderson, T., & Archer, W. (2001). Critical thinking, cognitive presence, and computer conferencing in distance education. *American Journal of Distance Education, 15*(1), 7-23.

Garton, L., Haythornthwaite, C., & Wellman, B. (1997). Studying online social networks. *Journal of Computer Mediated Communication, 3*(1).

Geetz, C. (1973). *The interpretation of cultures: Selected essays by Clifford Geertz.* New York: Basic Books, Inc. Publishers.

Goetz, J., & LeCompte, M. (1984). *Ethnography and qualitative design in educational research.* London: Academic Press.

Goffman, E. (1955). On face work: An analysis of ritual elements in social interaction. *Psychiatry, 18,* 213-231.

Goffman, E. (1983). The interaction order. *American Sociological Review, 48,* 1-17.

Goh, S.-C., & Tobin, K. (1999). Student and teacher perspectives in computer-mediated learning environments in teacher education. *Learning Environments Research, 2,* 169-190.

Good, T., & Brophy, J. (1990). *Educational psychology- A realistic approach* (4th ed.). New York: Longman.

Granovetter, M. (1974). *Getting a job.* Cambridge, MA: Harvard University Press.

Grice, H. (1967). *Logic and conversation.* Unpublished manuscript, Harvard University.

Grice, H. (1978). Further notes on logic and conversation. In P. Cole (Ed.), *Syntax and Semantics 9: Pragmatics* (pp. 113-128). New York: Academic Press.

Gunawardena, C., & Duphorne, P. (2000). Predictors of learner satisfaction in an academic computer conference. *Distance Education, 21*(1), 101-117.

Gunn, H. (2002). Web-based surveys: Changing the survey process. *First Monday, 7*(12).

Hammersley, M. (1998). *Reading ethnographic research: A critical guide* (2nd ed.). London: Longman.

Hammersley, M. (2003). Conversation analysis and discourse analysis: Methods or paradigms? *Discourse and Society, 14*(6), 751-781.

Hancock, J., & Dunham, P. (2001). Language use in computer-mediated communication: The role of coordination devices. *Discourse Processes, 31*(1), 91–110.

Hanneman, R., & Riddle, M. (2005). *Introduction to social network methods.* Retrieved 19 July, 2005, from http://faculty.ucr.edu/~hanneman/

Hara, N., Bonk, C. J., & Angeli, C. (2000). Content analysis of online discussions in an applied educational psychology course. *Instructional Science, 28,* 115-152.

Hara, N., & Kling, R. (1999). Students' frustrations with a web-based distance education course. *First Monday, 4*(12).

Harary, F., & Norman, R. (1953). *Graph theory as a mathematical model in social science.* Ann Arbor: University of Michigan Press.

Harary, F., Norman, R., & Cartwright, D. (1965). *Structural models: An introduction to the theory of directed graphs.* New York: John Wiley and Sons.

Harasim, L., Calvert, T., & Groeneboer, C. (1997). Virtual-U: A web-based system to support collaborative learning. In B. Khan (Ed.), *Web-based instruction* (pp. 149-158). Englewood Cliffs, New Jersey: Educational Technology Publications.

Harasim, L., Hiltz, S. R., Teles, L., & Turoff, M. (1995). Network learning: A paradigm for the twenty-first century. In *Learning networks: A field guide to teaching and learning Online* (pp. 271-278). Cambridge. MA: MIT Press.

Harris, R., & Muirhead, A. (2004). *Online learning community research- Some influences of theory on methods.* Paper presented at the Networked Learning Conference 2004.

Haythornthwaite, C. (2000). Online personal networks: Size, composition and media use among distance learners. *New Media and Society, 2*(2), 195-226.

Haythornthwaite, C. (2001). Exploring multiplexity: Social network structures in a computer-supported distance learning class. *The Information Society, 17*(3), 211-226.

Haythornthwaite, C., Kazmer, M., Robins, J., & Shoemaker, S. (2000). Community development among distance learners: Temporal and technological dimensions. *Journal of Computer Mediated Communication, 6*(1).

Heift, T., & Caws, C. (2000). Peer feedback in synchronous writing environments: A case study in French. *Educational Technology and Society, 3*(3).

Hendriks, V. (2002). *Implications of social constructivist theory for students' construction of knowledge through computer-mediated communications.* Unpublished Degree of Doctor of Science Education, Curtin University of Technology, Perth.

Hepburn, A., & Potter, J. (2004). Discourse analytic practice. In C. Seale, G. Gobo, J. Gubrium & D. Silverman (Eds.), *Qualitative research practice* (pp. 180-196). London: Sage.

Heritage, J. (2001). Goffman, Garfinkel and conversation analysis. In M. Wetherell, S. Taylor & S. Yates (Eds.), *Discourse theory and practice: A reader* (pp. 47-56). London: Sage.

Herring, S. (1999). Interactional coherence in CMC. *Journal of Computer Mediated Communication, 4*(4).

Herring, S. (2000). *Gender differences in CMC: Findings and implications.* Retrieved 19 April, 2005, from http://www.cpsr.org/issues/womenintech/herring

Herring, S. (2003). Computer-mediated discourse. In D. Schiffrin, D. Tannen & H. Hamilton (Eds.), *The handbook of discourse analysis* (pp. 612-634). Oxford: Blackwell.

Herzog, A., & Bachman, J. (1981). Effects of questionnaire length on response quality. *The Public Opinion Quarterly, 45*(4), 549-559.

Hillman, D., Willis, D., & Gunawardena, C. (1994). Learner-interface interaction in distance education: An extension of contemporary models and strategies for practitioners. *The American Journal of Distance Education, 8*(2), 30-42.

Hirumi, A. (2002). A framework for analyzing, designing, and sequencing planned e-learning interactions. *The Quarterly Review of Distance Education, 3*(2), 141-160.

Homans, G. (1951). *The human group.* London: Routledge and Kegan Paul.

Hong, K.-S., Lai, K.-W., & Holton, D. (2003). Students' satisfaction and perceived learning with a web-based course. *Educational Technology and Society, 6*(1), 116-124.

Huisman, M., & van Duijn, M. (2004). *Software for statistical analysis of social networks.* Paper presented at the 6th International Conference on Logic and Methodology (RC33), August 16-20, Amsterdam.

Hymes, D. (1974). *Foundations in sociolinguistics: An ethnographic approach.* Philadelphia: University of Pennsylvania Press.

Institute for Higher Education Policy. (2000). *Quality on the line: Benchmarks for success in internet based distance education*. Washington, D.C.: Blackboard, National Education Association.

Jacobson, D. (1999). Doing research in cyberspace. *Field Methods, 11*(2), 127-145.

Jennings, H. (1937). Structure of leadership-development and sphere of influence. *Sociometry, 1*(1/2), 99-143.

Johnson, D., & Johnson, R. (1996). Cooperation and the use of technology. In D. Jonassen (Ed.), *Handbook of research for educational communications and technology* (pp. 1017-1044). New York: Simon & Schuster Macmillan.

Jonassen, D. (1991a). Objectivism versus Constructivism: Do we need a new philosophical paradigm? *Educational Technology Research and Development, 39*(3), 5-14.

Jonassen, D. (1991b). Evaluating constructivistic learning. *Educational Technology, 31*(6), 28-33.

Jonassen, D., Davidson, M., Collins, M., Campbell, J., & Haag, B. (1995). Constructivism and computer-mediated communication in distance education. *The American Journal of Distance Education, 9*(2), 7-26.

Jones, G. (1984). Task visibility, free riding, and shirking: Explaining the effect of structure and technology on employee behavior. *Academy of Management Review, 9*(4), 684-695.

Jones, R., Lou, J., Yeung, L., Leung, V., Lai, I., Man, C., et al. (2001, 28 November-2 December). *Beyond the screen: A participatory study of computer mediated communication among Hong Kong youth*. Paper presented at the Annual Meeting of the American Anthropological Association.

Jones, S. (1998). Information, internet, and community: Notes toward an understanding of community in the information age. In S. Jones (Ed.), *Cybersociety 2.0: Revisiting computer-mediated communication and community* (pp. 1-34). Thousand Oaks, California: Sage.

Jurczyk, J., Kushner Benson, S., & Savery, J. (2004). Measuring student perceptions in web-based courses: A standards-based approach. *Distance Learning Administration, 7*(4).

Kahn, R., & Cannell, C. (2004). The formulation of questions. In M. Bulmer (Ed.), *Questionnaires* (Vol. 1, pp. 55-78). London: Sage Publications.

Kanuka, H., & Anderson, T. (1998). Online social interchange, discord and knowledge construction. *Journal of Distance Education, 13*(1), 57-74.

Kanuka, H., & Garrison, D. (2004). Cognitive presence in online learning. *Journal of Computing in Higher Education, 15*(2), 1-18.

Kiesler, S. (1992). Talking, teaching, and learning in network groups: Lessons from research. In A. Kaye (Ed.), *Collaborative learning through computer conferencing: The Najaden papers* (pp. 147-165). Berlin: Springer-Verlag.

Kiesler, S., Siegel, J., & McGuire, T. (1984). Social psychological aspects of computer-mediated communication. *American Psychologist, 39*(10), 1123-1134.

King, S. (1996). Researching Internet communities: Proposed ethical guidelines for the reporting of results. *The Information Society, 12*(12), 119-127.

Kneser, C., Pilkington, R., & Treasure-Jones, T. (2001). The tutor's role: An investigation of the power of Exchange Structure Analysis to identify different roles in CMC seminars. *International Journal of Artificial Intelligence in Education, 12*, 63-84.

Kolko, B., & Reid, E. (1998). Dissolution and fragmentation: Problems in on-line communities. In S. Jones (Ed.), *Cybersociety 2.0: Revisiting computer-mediated communication and community* (pp. 212-229). Thousand Oaks, California: Sage.

Kortti, H. (1999). *On some similarities between discourse in the IRC and the conventions of spoken English.* Retrieved 9 November, 2004, from http://www.student.oulu.fi/~hkortti/proseminar-final.html

Krebs, V. (2002). Mapping networks of terrorist cells. *Connections, 24*(3), 43-52.

Krosnick, J., & Alwin, D. (1987). An evaluation of a cognitive theory of response-order effects in survey measurement. *The Public Opinion Quarterly, 51*(2), 201-219.

Kuh, G. (2001). Assessing what really matters to student learning. *Change, 33*(3).

Kuhn, T. (1961). The functions of measurement in modern physical science. In T. Kuhn (Ed.), *The essential tension* (1977 ed., pp. 178-224). Chicago: University of Chicago Press.

Kuhn, T. (1970). *The structure of scientific revolution.* Chicago, IL: University of Chicago Press.

Kumar, A., Kumar, P., & Basu, S. C. (2002). Student perceptions of virtual education: An exploratory study. In M. Khosrow-Pour (Ed.), *Web-based instructional learning* (pp. 132-141). London: IRM Press.

Labov, W. (1972). *Language in the inner city: Studies in the Black English vernacular.* Philadelphia: University of Pennsylvania Press.

Lapadat, J. (2002). Written interaction: A key component in online learning. *Journal of Computer-Mediated Communication, 7*(4).

Laurillard, D. (2002). *Rethinking university teaching: A conversational framework for the effective use of learning technologies* (2nd ed.). London: RoutledgeFalmer.

Lave, J., & Wenger, E. (1991). *Situated learning: Legitimate peripheral participation.* Cambridge: Cambridge University Press.

Lee, N. (1969). *The search for an abortionist.* Chicago: University of Chicago Press.

Levine, J. (1972). The sphere of influence. *American Sociological Review, 37*(1), 14-27.

Levinson, S. (1983). *Pragmatics.* Cambridge: Cambridge University Press.

Lipman, M. (1991). *Thinking in education.* New York: Cambridge University Press.

Lipponen, L., Rahikainen, M., Lallimo, J., & Hakkarainen, K. (2001). *Analyzing patterns of participation and discourse in elementary students' online science discussion.* Paper presented at the European Perspectives on Computer-Supported Collaborative Learning. Proceedings of the First European Conference on CSCL, Maastricht, The Netherlands.

Mann, W., & Thompson, S. (1988). Rhetorical structure theory: Toward a functional theory of text organization. *Text, 8*(3), 243-281.

Mason, L. (2001). Introducing talk and writing for conceptual change: A classroom study. *Learning and Instruction, 11*, 305-329.

Mason, R. (1992). Evaluation methodologies for computer conferencing applications. In A. Kaye (Ed.), *Collaborative learning through computer conferencing: The Najaden papers* (pp. 105-116). Berlin: Springer-Verlag.

Mason, R., & Weller, M. (2000). Factors affecting students' satisfaction on a web course. *Australian Journal of Educational Technology, 16*(2), 173-200.

McDaniel, S., Olson, G., & Magee, J. (1996). *Identifying and analyzing multiple threads in computer-mediated and face-to-face conversations.* Paper presented at the 1996 ACM Conference on Computer Supported Cooperative Work, Boston, Massachusetts, US.

McIsaac, M., & Gunawardena, C. (1996). Distance education. In D. Jonassen (Ed.), *Handbook of research for educational communications and technology* (pp. 403-437). New York: Simon & Schuster Macmillan.

McKlin, T., Harmon, S., Evans, W., & Jones, M. (2002). *Cognitive presence in web-based learning: a content analysis of students' online discussion.* Paper presented at the ITFORUM 2002.

McLeod, P. (1997). *A comprehensive model of anonymity in computer-supported group decision making.* Paper presented at the Proceedings of the 18th International Conference on Information Systems, Atlanta, Georgia, United States.

McLoughlin, C. (2003, 11-12 February). *How does the quality debate relate to the nature of the student experience online?* Paper presented at the Partners in Learning. Proceedings of the 12th Annual Teaching Learning Forum, Perth.

McLoughlin, C., & Luca, J. (1999). *Lonely outpourings or reasoned dialogue? An analysis of text-based conferencing as a tool to support learning.* Paper presented at the ASCILITE 99, Brisbane, Australia.

Mehan, H. (1985). The structure of classroom discourse. In T. van Dijk (Ed.), *Handbook of discourse analysis: Discourse and dialogue* (Vol. 3, pp. 119-129). London: Academic Press.

Mercer, D. (2003). *Using synchronous communication for online social constructivist learning.* Paper presented at the 2003 CADE-ACED Conference, St Johns, Newfoundland.

Meyer, D., & Turner, J. (2002). Using instructional discourse analysis to study the scaffolding of student self-regulation. *Educational Psychologist, 37*(1), 17-25.

Meyer, K. (2003). Face-to-face versus threaded discussions: the role of time and higher-order thinking. *Journal of Asynchronous Learning Networks, 7*(3), 55-65.

Meyer, K. (2004). Evaluating online discussions: Four different frames of analysis. *Journal of Asynchronous Learning Networks, 8*(2), 101-114.

Microsoft Press. (2002). *Microsoft computer dictionary* (5th ed.). Redmond, Washington: Microsoft Press.

Milroy, L. (1987). *Language and social networks* (2nd ed.). Oxford, UK: Blackwell.

Milroy, L. (2000). Social network analysis and language change: Introduction. *European Journal of English Studies. Special Issue: Social Networks and the History of English, 4*(3), 217-223.

Mitchell, J. (1969). The concept and use of social networks. In J. Mitchell (Ed.), *Social networks in urban situations* (pp. 1-50). Manchester: Manchester University Press.

Molm, L., & Cook, K. (1995). Social exchange and exchange networks. In K. Cook, G. Fine & J. House (Eds.), *Sociological perspectives on social psychology* (pp. 209-235). Boston: Allyn and Bacon.

Moore, M. (1989). Three types of interaction. *The American Journal of Distance Education, 3*(2).

Moore, M., & Kearsley, G. (1996). *Distance education: A systems view.* California: Wadsworth Publishing Company.

Moreno, J. (1932). *Application of the group method to classification.* New York: National Committee on Prisons and Prison Labor.

Moreno, J. (1934). *Who shall survive?* Washington, DC: Nervous and Mental Disease Publishing Company.

Moreno, J., & Jennings, H. (1944). Sociometric methods of grouping and regrouping with reference to authoritative and democratic methods of grouping. *Sociometry, 7*(4), 397-414.

Moreno, J., Jennings, H., & Stockton, R. (1943). Sociometry in the classroom. *Sociometry, 6*(4), 425-428.

Muirhead, B., & Juwah, C. (2004). Interactivity in computer-mediated college and university education: A recent review of the literature. *Educational Technology and Society, 7*(1), 12-20.

Murphy, K., & Collins, M. (1997). Communication conventions in instructional electronic chats. *First Monday, 2*(11).

Newman, D., Johnson, C., Webb, B., & Cochrane, C. (1997). Evaluating the quality of learning in computer supported co-operative learning. *Journal of the American Society for Information Science, 48*(6), 484-495.

Ngwenya, J., Annand, D., & Wang, E. (2004). Supporting asynchronous discussions among online learners. In T. Anderson & F. Elloumi (Eds.), *Theory and practice of online learning* (pp. 319-347). Canada: Athabasca University.

Nolan, J., & Weiss, J. (2002). Learning in cyberspace: An educational view of virtual community. In K. Renninger & W. Shumar (Eds.), *Building virtual communities: Learning and change in cyberspace* (pp. 293-320). New York: Cambridge University Press.

Ong, W. (1982). *Orality and literacy: The technologizing of the word.* New York: Methuen.

Palloff, R., & Pratt, K. (2003). *The virtual student: a profile and guide to working with online learners.* San Francisco, CA: Jossey-Bass.

Paolillo, J. (1999). The virtual speech community: Social network and language variation on IRC. *Journal of Computer-Mediated Communication, 4*(4).

Parker, N. (2004). The quality dilemma in online education. In T. Anderson & F. Elloumi (Eds.), *Theory and practice of online learning.* (pp. 385-421). Canada: Athabasca University.

Patton, M. Q. (2002). *Qualitative research and evaluation methods* (3rd ed.). Thousand Oaks, CA: Sage.

Pawan, P., Paulus, T., Yalcin, S., & Chang, C. (2003). Online learning: patterns of engagement and interaction among in-service teachers. *Language Learning and Technology, 7*(3), 119-140.

Payne, S. (2004). Who left it open? A description of the free-answer question and its demerits. In M. Bulmer (Ed.), *Questionnaires* (Vol. 1, pp. 131-147). London: Sage.

Pfister, H.-R., & Miihlpfordt, M. (2002, January 7-11). *Supporting discourse in a synchronous learning environment: The learning protocol approach.* Paper presented at the CSCL 2002, Boulder, Colorado, USA.

Pike, G. (1999). The constant error of the halo in educational outcomes research. *Research in Higher Education, 40*(1), 61-86.

Pilkington, R. (1997). *Analyzing educational discourse: The DISCOUNT scheme. Technical report no. 019703.* UK: Computer Based Learning Unit, The University of Leeds.

Pilkington, R. (1999). *Analysing educational discourse: The DISCOUNT Scheme.* Leeds: Computer Based Learning Unit, The University of Leeds.

Pilkington, R., Bennett, C., & Vaughan, S. (2000). An evaluation of computer mediated communication to support group discussion in continuing education. *Educational Technology and Society, 3*(3), 349-359.

Pilkington, R., & Walker, S. (2004). Facilitating debate in networked learning: Reflecting on online synchronous discussion in higher education. In P. Goodyear, S. Banks, V. Hodgson & D. McConnell (Eds.), *Advances in research on networked learning* (Vol. 4, pp. 67-90). Massachusetts, USA: Kluwer Academic Publishers.

Polin, L. (2000, 28 April). *Affordances of a VR world as a place for learning: Discourse patterns and contextualization cues framing learning experiences for adults in a real-time, text-based, virtual reality setting.* Paper presented at the AERA 2000 Symposium, New Orleans, LA.

Postmes, T., Spears, R., & Lea, M. (1998). Breaching or building social boundaries? SIDE-effects of computer-mediated communication. *Communication Research, 25,* 689-715.

Postmes, T., Spears, R., & Lea, M. (1999). Social identity, group norms, and "deindividuation": Lessons from computer-mediated communication for social influence in the group. In R. Ellemers, R. Spears & B. Doosje (Eds.), *Social identity: Context, commitment, content* (pp. 164-183). Oxford: Blackwell.

Potter, J. (2003). Practical scepticism. *Discourse and Society, 14*(6), 799-801.

Potter, J. (2004). Discourse analysis. In M. Hardy & A. Bryman (Eds.), *Handbook of data analysis* (pp. 607-624). London: Sage.

Potter, J., & Wetherell, M. (1987/2001). Unfolding discourse analysis. In M. Wetherell, S. Taylor & S. Yates (Eds.), *Discourse theory and practice: A reader* (pp. 198-209). London: Sage.

Principia Products. (2005). Remark Web Survey® (Version 2).

Rafaeli, S., & Sudweeks, F. (1997). Networked interactivity. *Journal of Computer-Mediated Communication, 4*(2).

Rafaeli, S., & Sudweeks, F. (1998). Interactivity on the Nets. In F. Sudweeks, M. McLaughlin & S. Rafaeli (Eds.), *Network and netplay: Virtual groups on the Internet* (pp. 173-190). Cambridge, MA: MIT Press.

Ramsden, R. (1992). *Learning to teach in higher education.* London: Routledge.

Rehberg, S., Ferguson, D., & McQuillian, J. (2001). *The ultimate WebCT handbook: A pedagogical and practical guide.* Georgia: Pullen Library, Georgia State University.

Reid, E. (1991). *Electropolis: Communication and community on Internet Relay Chat.* Unpublished Honours Dissertation, University of Melbourne.

Riffe, D., Lacy, S., & Fico, F. (1998). *Analyzing media messages: Using quantitative content analysis in research.* Mahwah, New Jersey: Lawrence Erlbaum Associates, Inc.

Roethlisberger, F., & Dickson, W. (1939). *Management and the worker.* Cambridge, MA: Harvard University Press.

Rogers, E. (1979). Network analysis of the diffusion of innovations. In P. Holland & S. Leinhardt (Eds.), *Perspectives on social network research* (pp. 137-164). New York: Academic Press.

Rogoff, B. (1990). *Apprenticeship in thinking.* New York: Oxford University Press.

Romiszowski, A., & Mason, R. (1996). Computer-mediated communication. In D. Jonassen (Ed.), *Handbook of research for educational communications and technology* (pp. 438-456). New York: Simon & Schuster Macmillan.

Rose, M. (2002). *Cognitive dialogue, interaction patterns, and perceptions of graduate students in an online conferencing environment under collaborative and cooperative structures.* Unpublished Doctorate in Education, Indiana University.

Rourke, L., Anderson, T., Garrison, D., & Archer, W. (2001). Assessing social presence in asynchronous text-based computer conferencing. *Journal of Distance Education, 14*(2).

Rovai, A., & Barnum, K. (2003). On-line course effectiveness: An analysis of student interactions and perceptions of learning. *Journal of Distance Education, 18*(1), 57-73.

Ruhleder, K. (2000). The virtual ethnographer: Fieldwork in distributed electronic environments. *Field Methods, 12*(1), 3-17.

Ryen, A. (2004). Ethical issues. In C. Seale, G. Gobo, J. Gubrium & D. Silverman (Eds.), *Qualitative research practice* (pp. 230-247). London: Sage.

Sacks, H., Schegloff, E., & Jefferson, G. (1974). A simplest systematics for the organization of turn-taking for conversation. *Language, 50*(4), 696-735.

Schegloff, E., Jefferson, G., & Sacks, H. (1977). The preference for self-correction in the organization of repair in conversation. *Language, 53*(2), 361-382.

Schleyer, T., & Forrest, J. (2000). Methods for the design and administration of web-based surveys. *Journal of the American Medical Informatics Association, 7*(4 (July/August)), 416-425.

Schwandt, T. (2001). *Dictionary of qualitative inquiry* (2nd ed.). Thousand Oaks, California: Sage.

Schwier, R., & Balbar, S. (2002). The interplay of content and community in synchronous and asynchronous communication: Virtual communication in a graduate seminar. *Canadian Journal of Learning and Technology, 28*(2 Spring).

Scott, J. (1991). Networks of corporate power. *Annual Review of Sociology, 17*, 181-203.

Scott, J. (2000). *Social network analysis* (2nd ed.). Thousand Oaks, CA: Sage Publications.

Searle, J. (1969). *Speech acts: An essay in the philosophy of language.* Cambridge: Cambridge University Press.

Shale, D., & Garrison, D. (1990). Education and communication. In D. Garrison & D. Shale (Eds.), *Education at a distance: From issues to practice.* (pp. 23-39). Malabar, Florida: R.E.Krieger Publishing Company Inc.

Sherman, R. (2001). The mind's eye in cyberspace: Online perceptions of self and others. In G. Riva & C. Galimberti (Eds.), *Towards cyberpsychology: Mind, cognitions and society in the Internet age* (pp. 53-72). Amsterdam: IOS Press.

Sherron, G., & Boettcher, J. (1997). Distance learning: The shift to interactivity. *CAUSE Professional Paper Series, 7*, 1-39.

Shoemaker, P. (1996). *Levels and units- Studying increments of content.* Retrieved 27 July, 2005, from http://web.syr.edu/~snowshoe/frames/content_analysis/levels_units_hando ut.doc

Short, J., Williams, E., & Christie, B. (1976). *The social psychology of telecommunications.* London: John Wiley & Sons.

Shumar, W., & Renninger, K. (2002). Introduction: On conceptualizing community. In K. Renninger & W. Shumar (Eds.), *Building virtual communities: Learning and change in cyberspace* (pp. 1-17). New York: Cambridge University Press.

Siegel, J., Dubrovsky, V., Kiesler, S., & McGuire, T. (1986). Group processes in computer-mediated communication. *Organizational Behavior and Human Decision Processes, 37*, 157-187.

Sims, R. (1995). Interactivity: A forgotten art? *Instructional Technology Research Online.*

Sims, R., Dobbs, G., & Hand, T. (2002). Enhancing quality in online learning: Scaffolding planning and design through proactive evaluation. *Distance education, 23*(2), 135-148.

Sinclair, J., & Coulthard, M. (1975). Towards an analysis of discourse. In M. Coulthard (Ed.), *Advances in spoken discourse analysis* (pp. 1-35). London: Routledge.

Sinclair, J., & Coulthard, M. (1992). Towards an analysis of discourse. In M. Coulthard (Ed.), *Advances in spoken discourse analysis* (pp. 1-34). London: Routledge.

Spencer, D., & Hiltz, S. (2003). *A field study of use of synchronous chat in online courses.* Paper presented at the 36th Annual Hawaii International Conference in System Sciences (HICSS 03), Big Island, Hawaii.

Sproull, L., & Kiesler, S. (1986). Reducing social context cues: Electronic mail in organizational communication. *Management Science, 32*(11), 1492-1512.

Stacey, E. (2000). Quality online participation: Establishing social presence. In T. Evans (Ed.), *Research in Distance Education 5* (pp. 138-253). Geelong: Deakin University.

Stake, R. (1988). Case study methods in educational research: Seeking Sweet Water. In R. Jaeger (Ed.), *Contemporary methods for research in education* (pp. 253-265). Washington, D.C.: American Educational Research Association.

Stake, R. (1995). *The art of case study research.* Thousand Oaks: Sage Publications.

Stake, R. (2000). Case studies. In N. Denzin & Y. Lincoln (Eds.), *Handbook of qualitative research* (2nd ed., pp. 435-454). London: Sage Publications.

Stein, D., & Wanstreet, C. (2004, 6-8 October). *Presence and interaction in an inquiry-based learning environment.* Paper presented at the Midwest Research-to-Practice Conference in Adult, Continuing, and Community Education, Indiana University, Indianapolis, IN.

Stromer-Galley, J., & Martinson, A. (2004, September, 2004). *Coherence or fragmentation?: Comparing serious and social chat online.* Paper presented at the Association for Internet Researchers Annual Conference, Sussex, England.

Stubbs, M. (1981). Motivating analyses of exchange structure. In M. Coulthard & M. Montgomery (Eds.), *Studies in discourse analysis* (pp. 107-119). London: Rutledge.

Stubbs, M. (1983). *Discourse analysis: The sociolinguistic analysis of natural language.* Oxford: Blackwell.

Sudweeks, F. (2003a). *Promoting cooperation and collaboration in a web-based learning environment.* Paper presented at the 2003 Informing Science and Information Technology Education Conference, Informing Science Institute, Santa Rosa, CA.

Sudweeks, F. (2003b). *The reflective learner: A framework for reflective e-learning.* Paper presented at the ICIER03, Seattle, WA.

Sudweeks, F. (2003c). Connecting students with group work. In C. Constantinou & Z. Zacharia (Eds.), *Computer-based learning in science* (Vol. 1, pp. 173-183). Nicosia, Cyprus: University of Cyprus.

Sudweeks, F. (2004). *Development and leadership in computer-mediated collaborative groups.* Unpublished PhD Thesis, Murdoch University, Perth, Australia.

Sudweeks, F. (2005). *Unit outline.* School of Information Technology: Murdoch University.

Sudweeks, F., & Allbritton, M. (1996). *Working together apart: Communication and collaboration in a networked group.* Paper presented at the 7th Australasian Conference of Information Systems (ACIS96), Department of Computer Science, University of Tasmania.

Sudweeks, F., & Simoff, S. (1998). Complementary explorative data analysis: The reconciliation of quantitative and qualitative principles. In S. Jones (Ed.), *Doing internet research* (pp. 29-56). Thousand Oaks: Sage Publications.

Sudweeks, F., & Simoff, S. (2000). *Participation and reflection in virtual workshops.* Paper presented at the 3rd Western Australian Workshop on Information Systems Research, Perth, Australia.

Sudweeks, F., & Simoff, S. (2005). *Leading conversations: Communication behaviour of emergent leaders in virtual teams.* Paper presented at the 38th Hawaii International Conference on System Sciences (HICSS05), Hawaii, USA.

Taylor, S. (2001). Locating and conducting discourse analytic research. In M. Wetherell, S. Taylor & S. Yates (Eds.), *Discourse as data: A guide for analysis* (pp. 5-48). London: Sage Publications Ltd.

Teles, L., Gillies, M., & Ashton, S. (2001). A case study in online classroom interaction to enhance graduate instruction in English literature. In C. D. Maddux & D. LaMont Johnson (Eds.), *The web in higher education: Assessing the impact and fulfilling the potential* (pp. 231-248). New York: The Haworth Press, Inc.

ten Have, P. (2001). Applied conversation analysis. In A. McHoul & M. Rapley (Eds.), *How to analyse talk in institutional settings: A casebook of methods* (pp. 3-11). London: Continuum.

Thomas, B., Jones, P., Packham, G., & Miller, C. (2004, 5-7 April). *Student perceptions of effective e-moderation: A qualitative investigation of E-college Wales.* Paper presented at the Networked Learning Conference 2004, Lancaster University, England, UK.

Thomsen, S., Straubhaar, J., & Bolyard, D. (1998). *Ethnomethodology and the study of online communities: Exploring the cyber streets.* Paper presented at the IRISS 98, Bristol, UK.

Tse, A. (1998). Comparing the response rate, response speed and response quality of two methods of sending questionnaires: E-mail vs. mail. *Journal of the Market Research Society, 40*(4), 353-359.

Tsvetovat, M., & Carley, K. (2005). Structural knowledge and success of anti-terrorist activity: The downside of structural equivalence. *Journal of Social Structure, 6*(2).

Ubon, N., & Kimble, C. (July 2004). *Exploring social presence in asynchronous text-based online learning communities (OLCs)*. Paper presented at the 5th International Conference on Information Communication Technologies in Education, Greece.

van Dijk, T. (1997). The study of.discourse. In T. van Dijk (Ed.), *Discourse studies: A multidisciplinary introduction* (Vol. 1, pp. 1-34). London: Sage.

Veerman, A., Andriessen, J., & Kanselaar, G. (2000). Learning through synchronous electronic discussion. *Computers and Education, 34*(Third Quarter), 269-290.

von Glasersfeld, E. (1981). An introduction to radical constructivism. In W. P. (Ed.), *The invented reality* (pp. 17-40). New York: Norton.

von Glasersfeld, E. (1989). Cognition, construction of knowledge, and teaching. *SYNTHESE, 80*(1), 121-140.

von Glasersfeld, E. (1992, August). *Aspects of radical constructivism and its educational implications*. Paper presented at the ICMe-7, Working Group #4, Quebec.

von Glasersfeld, E. (1995). A constructivist approach to teaching. In L. Steffe & J. Gale (Eds.), *Constructivism in education* (pp. 3-15). Hillsdale, New Jersey: Lawrence Erlbaum Associates, Inc., Publishers.

von Glasersfeld, E. (1997a, May 1997). *Piaget's legacy: Cognition as adaptive activity*. Paper presented at the Presented at International Congress "Does Representation need Reality?" Vienna.

von Glasersfeld, E. (1997b). Homage to Jean Piaget (1896-1982). *Irish Journal of Psychology, 18*(2), 293-306.

Vygotsky, L. (1962). *Thought and language*. Cambridge, MA: MIT Press. Revised and edited by A. Kozulin, 1986.

Vygotsky, L. (1978). *Mind in society: The development of higher processes* (V. John-Steiner, E. Souberman, M. Cole & S. Scribner, Trans.). Cambridge, MA: Harvard University Press.

Wall, A. (2001). Evaluating an undergraduate unit using a focus group. *Quality Assurance in Education, 9*(1), 23.

Walther, J. (1996). Computer-mediated communication: Impersonal, interpersonal, and hyperpersonal interaction. *Communication Research, 23*(1), 3-43.

Warner, W., & Lunt, P. (1941). *The social life of a modern community*. New Haven, CT: Yale University Press.

Warschauer, M. (1996). Comparing face-to-face and electronic discussion in the second language classroom. *CALICO Journal, 13*(2-3), 7-26.

Waskul, D., & Douglass, M. (1996). Considering the electronic participant: Some polemical observations on the ethics of on-line research. *The Information Society, 12*(2), 129-141.

Wasserman, S., & Faust, K. (1994). *Social network analysis: Methods and applications*. Cambridge: Cambridge University Press.

Webster, C., Freeman, L., & Aufdemberg, C. (2001). The impact of social context on interaction patterns. *Journal of Social Structure, 2*(1), 1-13.

Wedemeyer, C. (1981). *Learning at the back door: Reflections on non-traditional learning in the lifespan*. Madison, Wisconsin: University of Wisconsin Press.

Weger Jr, H., & Aakhus, M. (2003). Arguing in Internet chat rooms: Argumentative adaptations to chat room design and some consequences for public deliberation at a distance. *Argumentation and advocacy, 40*(1), 23-38.

Wegerif, R., & Mercer, N. (1997). A dialogical framework for investigating talk. In R. Wegerif & P. Scrimshaw (Eds.), *Computers and talk in the primary classroom* (pp. 49-65.). Clevedon: Multilingual Matters.

Werry, C. (1996). Linguistic and interactional features of Internet Relay Chat. In S. Herring (Ed.), *Computer-mediated communication* (pp. 47-64). Philadelphia, USA: John Benjamins Publishing Company.

Wertsch, J. (1985). *Vygotsky and the social formation of mind*. Cambridge, MA: Harvard University Press.

Wetherell, M. (2001a). Part three: Editor's introduction. In M. Wetherell, S. Taylor & S. Yates (Eds.), *Discourse theory and practice: A reader* (pp. 186-197). London: Sage.

Wetherell, M. (2001b). Debates in discourse research. In M. Wetherell, S. Taylor & S. Yates (Eds.), *Discourse theory and practice: A reader* (pp. 380-399). London: Sage.

Winn, W. (1991). The assumptions of constructivism and instructional design. *Educational Technology, 31*(6), 38-40.

Wooffitt, R. (2001). Researching psychic practitioners: Conversation analysis. In M. Wetherell, S. Taylor & S. Yates (Eds.), *Discourse as data: A guide for analysis* (pp. 49-92). London: Sage Publications Ltd.

Yates, S. (2001). Researching internet interaction: Sociolinguistics and corpus analysis. In M. Wetherell, S. Taylor & S. Yates (Eds.), *Discourse as data: A guide for analysis* (pp. 93-146). London: Sage Publications Ltd.

Yeung, D. (2001). Toward an effective quality assurance model of web-based learning: The perspective of academic staff. *Online Journal of Distance Learning Administration, 4*(4).

Yin, R. (1993). *Applications of case study research* (Vol. 34). Newbury Park, California: Sage Publications.

Yin, R. (1994). *Case study research: Design and methods* (Vol. 5). Thousand Oaks, CA: Sage Publications.

APPENDIX A

CASE STUDY DOCUMENTS

A.1 Unit Outline Semester 2, 2005

---

1. Contact

1.1. Unit Coordinator

Fay Sudweeks

--- --- ---

Please do not hesitate to contact the Unit Coordinator if (and as soon as) you have any difficulties with the unit, or just to talk over the work, or to receive some encouragement to carry on! Generally you will deal with your tutor on a week-by-week basis. The unit coordinator, however, can deal with urgent problems. Other than the consultation time listed above, it is best to arrange an appointment by email.

1.2. Tutor

You will be advised of your tutor's name by the end of Week 1. Both internal and external students are expected to attend tutorials, which are in the chat room of WebCT (see section 4.3 Tutorials). Your tutor will mark your assignments and assist you with your study. If you have any questions, do not hesitate to ask your tutor during tutorials. Your tutor is also the first person you should contact if you have concerns about the marking of the assessment work.

Tutors are usually not on campus. Tutors are not expected (not paid) to be available outside tutorial times. In order to ensure that you can contact your tutor, you should attend your tutorial session. You can also contact your tutor by email (when advised).

1.3. Administrative Contact

If you have any queries about your enrolment, please contact Division of Arts Student Administration Office, tel: ---, fax: ---, email: ---

---

2. Unit Aims and Objectives

The aim of this unit is to provide you with a range of skills associated with the organisational aspects of the design and development of information systems, including development methodologies, CMC, CSCW, group dynamics, globalisation and organisational culture. You will be able to critically assess and manage numerous issues that impact both on knowledge and knowledge workers in the context of today's organisation. Part of the lecture time will be devoted to discussions in which all students are expected to participate actively. In addition to required reading, students are encouraged to extend their knowledge with additional suggested reading. Assessments are intended to encourage the development of written and oral communication skills, group skills, and research skills.

---

3. WebCT and iLecture

ICT329 is organised within a virtual learning environment called WebCT (Web Course Tools). WebCT is the university's online course server. The ICT329 WebCT site includes this unit outline, unit materials and readings, lecture notes, assignments, resources, and all information you need for the unit. All lectures are also digitally recorded (iLecture) and available from a link in WebCT a few hours after the lectures. To access WebCT you will need reliable Internet access and a web browser.

To access ICT329 on WebCT, you will need a login name (also called "User ID") and password. Your login name is your student number. Your password is your University Password or MAIS (Murdoch Authorisation and Identification System) PIN. For more information about login and passwords, see http:// ---
To access all your online units, go to http:// --- and click on **myWebCT**. You will then get a list of all your units which have a WebCT site. Click on **ICT329 Organisational Informatics (S2, 2005).** (See http:// --- for more information about **myWebCT**).

If you are unable to log on to ICT329 using your login name and password by the end of Week 1 of the semester, you must contact the unit coordinator immediately. The usual reason for not being able to log on is that your enrolment in ICT329 is still being processed. If this is the case, you may use the guest account temporarily, which is   --- as a login name and --- as password.

On WebCT, you will find a variety of communication tools:

- The **Bulletin Board** allows communication among all course participants, the unit coordinator, and the tutors. It is used for general discussions. WebCT keeps track of which articles are read by each student. Messages can have embedded links to web sites (URLs) which are active in WebCT.

- The **Chat Rooms** provide real-time, text-based communication among course participants, unit coordinator and tutors. ICT329 tutorials take place in the chat rooms. There is one general chat room to which all course participants have access, and there are private chat rooms to which only tutorial group participants have access.

- The **Calendar** is like a daily planner, telling you about course events. Important announcements will be posted to the Calendar.

- The **Private Mail** tool can be used to send private mail to any course participant, tutor or coordinator.

Be aware that WebCT provides real-time monitoring of your participation in this unit and automatically logs all discussions in the private chat rooms.

4. Unit Organisation

4.1. Prerequisite

B107/ICT107 Principles of Information Systems **or** B208/ICT208 Commercial Computing **or** C247/BUS247 Concepts in Electronic Commerce

4.2. Lectures

There is one 2-hour lecture each week at 14:30-16:30, Mondays, in SS1.36.

4.3. Tutorials

There is one 1-hour tutorial each week, beginning in Week 2 and finishing in Week 13 (i.e. there are no tutorials in Week 1). The tutorial is "supervised" and is conducted online in the WebCT tutorial (chat) rooms using a seminar format. The computer labs are booked for two hours to give you the opportunity of using the computer for the second hour for preparing your journal for the following week, or for doing web searches. You may also use this time to visit the library as resources for information about your project and research essay (see the Unit Assessment section for more information about the journal and assignments).
However, although there are labs allocated for internal students to log on to the WebCT chat room, you are encouraged to log on from work or home. Note, however, that many organisations do not allow access to synchronous environments (such as the WebCT chat room) from their network. So if you intend to log on from your workplace, please check well before the first tutorial that you are able to do so.

Both internal and external students are required to sign up for a tutorial time. To do this, you will use the online tutorial signup system (OTSS) at http:// ---. There is a link to this URL on the ICT329 WebCT site. You will be prompted for a login and password when accessing the OTSS. The login is your student number and the password is ---. This system will be operational in Week 1. Allocation is computerised and does not operate on a first-come first-served basis.
After hours (19:00-07:00) access to labs is available. Ensure that you have your student ID card and security card on you (at all times) in the event that a security guard requests to verify it. If the labs are closed, contact a security guard. The security office is located at the east end of the Chancellery building.

If you are unable to access WebCT, you can contact the helpdesk at (08) 9360 2000, or email --- (also see http:// ---. If the problem is not resolved by the helpdesk, you must contact the unit coordinator. Contacting the unit coordinator or other tutorial staff in the first instance would result in a delay as the unit coordinator and tutorial staff do not have administrative access to WebCT and will have to forward your request to helpdesk.

5. Lecture Schedule

Week	Date	Lecture Topic
1	25 July	Introduction to the Unit and Organisational Informatics
2	1 August	Computer-mediated communication in organisations
3	8 August	Organisational design and group processes
4	15 August	Organisational culture
NTW	22 August	
5	29 August	Virtual organisations and communities
6	5 September	Work in the Information Age
7	12 September	Globalisation
8	19 September	Computer-mediated collaborative work
9	26 September	Organisational decision-support systems
NTW	3 October	
10	10 October	Systems theory
11	17 October	Systems theory (cont'd)
12	24 October	Managing information and information technology
13	31 October	Unit review and exam hints

6. Unit Assessment

This unit will be assessed by a group project, a research essay, a tutorial presentation, reflective journals, participation in discussions, and a final examination. The assessments have the following weights:

Research essay	15%
Group project	15%
Reflective journals (11)	20%
Tutorial presentation	10%
Discussion participation	5%
Examination	35%

In order to pass this unit you must achieve at least 50% for the aggregate of all assessment (see Section 11 of the assessment code regarding grades at http:// ---. Final unit grades will be awarded using the approximate scale:

Notation	Grade	Notional Percentage Scores
HD	High Distinction	80-100%
D	Distinction	70-79%
C	Credit	60-69%
P	Pass	50-59%
S*	Supplementary assessment	45-49%
DNS	Fail	did not submit any assignments after HECS census date
N	Fail	Below 50

*The award of S shall be at the discretion of the unit coordinator

6.1. Assessments

6.1.1. Group Project
The group project is a PowerPoint presentation. It is a group activity among both on-campus and off-campus students and collaboration is entirely online. It is marked out of 100. The Group Project is to be submitted on disk or CD with a cover sheet. If possible, arrange for an on-campus student in your group to submit the assignment in the assignment box. If this cannot be done for some reason, then an off-campus student may submit the files (including a cover sheet) of their group's assignment to their tutor by email.

Group Project	**Due:** 10:00, Monday 19 September (beginning of Week 8)

6.1.2. Research Essay

The research essay is to be 2,000-2,500 words. It is individual work and it is marked out of 100. You will be given a list of topics from which to choose. The essay topics and requirements will be available on WebCT. See the "Submission" section for the procedure for submitting this work.

The research essay is to be submitted as follows:

Submission for Internal students. The essay is to be placed in the ICT329 assignment box (ECL building, opposite the School of Information Technology office, ECL3.037) by the due date. It must be attached to an assignment cover sheet, which is available from WebCT.

Submission for external students. The essay must be submitted through the External Studies Office. See http:// --- for detailed instructions on submitting assignments. The assignment can be submitted by post, personal delivery, fax --- or email ---.

Research Essay	**Due:** 10:00, Monday 17 October (beginning of Week 11)

6.1.3. Reflective Journals

You are required to submit *reflective journals* throughout the semester. The purpose of writing these journals is to give you experience in critically reviewing and recording your thoughts about the readings for the unit, as well as from a variety of other sources if you want to read further on particular topics.

Your journals should **not** be just summaries of the readings, although you may include this as well. What is really required is your reactions to the articles for each topic, and how they relate to the lectures, other topics and other material; that is, comparisons, themes, disagreements and relevant experiences of your own.

Source material for your thoughts, and hence comments, can include the required readings, recommended and other readings, web sites, lectures and readings in other units, TV programs and anything else which you can meaningfully relate to the topics of this unit.

You are required to submit 11 journals (from Week 2 to Week 12 inclusive). Each journal is to be at least 500 words. *You must also include at the beginning of your journal (with a clearly identified heading) at least one question about an issue or issues from one of the articles that you want clarified and/or discussed during your tutorial.*

Submission for internal and external students. Journals are to be posted as a message to your *tutorial group's bulletin board*. Do **not** submit the journal as an attachment. The reason for posting your journals to the bulletin board is that other group members can read your comments and thus facilitate collaborative learning.

Reflective Journals (11)	**Due:** 20:00 each Sunday beginning 31 July

6.1.4. Tutorial Presentation

Each student will be required to present two readings. This involves a brief presentation in a chat room in WebCT. The presenter will identify key issues in each reading, relate the issues to lecture material and/or other readings, and lead the group in discussions. Assessment will be based on a clear (and very brief) summary, identification of key issues, knowledge of the topic, expressions of opinions on the topic(s), efforts to stimulate discussion, and management of the group discussion.

6.1.5. Discussion Participation

Assessment for participation will be based on both quantity and quality of interactions. The evaluation of each student's participation is a combination of peer and tutor assessment, based on active and thoughtful participation in discussion sessions. Students who attend regularly but make little or no contribution to the discussion should not expect a pass mark in this component of the assessment. The peer assessment form is available on WebCT. As part of the assessment of the discussion you are to assess the participation level of each tutorial group member at the end of semester and email it to your tutor.

6.1.6. Examination

The examination is a closed-book examination covering all aspects of the unit.

6.2. Late submission

If an extension is needed, contact the Unit Coordinator **prior** to the due date. Assessment submissions that are not received by the due time and date will be regarded as late unless an extension has been granted.

Please note:

- Applications for extensions must be made to the Unit Coordinator by email ---. You will receive an email response.
- Applications for extensions will not be granted unless there is a good reason. Not being able to organise your time is **not** a good reason.
- Applications for extensions on the grounds of sickness must be backed up with a medical certificate, a copy of which should be attached to the submitted assignment.
- Applications for extensions should be made as soon as a problem is experienced. Under normal circumstances, extensions will not be granted if application is made after the due date and time.

If an assignment is handed in late without an approved extension, a penalty will apply. Late work will attract a penalty in the form of a reduction in the mark given for your assignment. The penalty is 5 marks deducted each day (including each weekend day). For further details about assessment, see the current *University Handbook and Calendar*.

7. Unit Materials

7.1. Textbook

There is no textbook for this course.

7.2. Lecture Notes and Other Unit Materials

Lecture notes (PowerPoint, RTF, PDF) will be added to WebCT each week shortly after the lecture. Lecture notes from 2004 are available at the beginning of the semester.

7.3. Resource Materials

ICT329 Resource Materials is a booklet available from the campus bookstore which includes the required readings. The readings are also available on WebCT. If you are giving the tutorial presentation, you should read the required and recommended readings. Another category of readings – additional readings – has been added for students interested in exploring the topic further and/or as a resource for assignments.

7.4. Information Distribution

Information will be distributed via the Calendar, the Bulletin Board, and Private Email in WebCT. Occasionally, information will also be sent to your email address. You should check WebCTand your email every day. The email address used by the unit coordinator and tutors is the one you have provided to the university.

8. University policy on assessment

Assessment for this unit is in accordance with the provisions of Degree regulations 40–48. Check these in the current *Murdoch University Handbook and Calendar* or
http:// ---

Please refer to the University Policy Regarding Assessment Roles and Responsibilities at
http:// ---

For guidelines on honesty in assessment including avoiding plagiarism, see also: http:// ---

A.2. Peer Assessment of Participation

ABOUT YOU

Your name: _____

Your student number: _____

Please put an X against the appropriate category.

Your age (optional):
[ ] <25   [ ] 25-35   [ ] 35-45   [ ] >45

Your native language (optional):
[ ] English
[ ] Other than English (please specify) _____

YOUR ASSESSMENT OF GROUP MEMBERS

Please rate the degree to which each member of your tutorial group fulfilled his/her responsibilities in participating in the discussions throughout the semester. The possible ratings are:

5   **Excellent**: Went beyond the material, very well prepared, contributed significantly, cooperative
4   **Very good**: Did what he/she was supposed to do, very well prepared and cooperative
3   **Satisfactory**: Did what he/she was supposed to do, acceptably prepared and cooperative
2.5 **Ordinary**: Did what he/she was supposed to do, minimally prepared and cooperative
2   **Unsatisfactory**: Showed up, unprepared, little participation
1   **Superficial**: Showed up, practically no participation
0   **No show**: Did not show up, no participation at all

These rating should reflect each individual's level and quality of participation, effort, and sense of responsibility, not his or her academic or language ability.

GROUP MEMBER	RATING

A.3. Reflective Journal

Due Date	8:00pm each Sunday, beginning 31 July.
Format	Individual work
Length	500 words
Unit contribution	20% (11 journals)
Submission	Prepare in text format and post to your tutorial group's bulletin board by 8:00pm each Sunday.
Aims	To enable you to identify and critically assess the main points/issues of each week's topic. To encourage you to have a deeper understanding of the lecture material. To provide a mechanism for encouraging more knowledgeable participation. To provide a forum for you to think of broader issues beyond the lecture material.
Your task:	**A critique of the week's required readings from the unit reader.** Each week you are to submit a journal of at least 500 words. The journal is a critique - **not** a summary - of the readings. It should be a critical review of the articles including, e.g., your opinion of the articles, did you understand it, did the authors provide a persuasive argument, is it well-written, do you agree/disagree with the author's statements, did it help you to understand more about the topic. In other words, comparisons, supporting themes, agreements/disagreements, relevant experiences of your own. You can compare and relate the articles to other material, e.g. lecture notes, other readings in the Reader or from other units or from the Web or the library, TV programs, newspapers, magazines, etc. **Your journal must include at least one question about an issue(s) from one of the articles that you want clarified and/or discussed during your tutorial. The question must be at the beginning of the journal, clearly labelled, so that the presenter can compile the questions before the tutorial.** Your journal is to be posted as a message to your group's bulletin board (which will be set up by the end of Week 1) no later than 8:00pm each Sunday. Do **not** post your journal as an attachment. By completing your journal before the tutorial, you will be able to participate more knowledgeably in the discussions and therefore learn more.
Assessment	Each journal will be marked out of 10.
Late Submission	Late submission will attract a penalty of 10% per day.
Marking criteria	Identification of main issues of reviewed readings. Relevancy and strength of arguments in support of your opinions about the reviewed readings. Relating the readings to other material (lecture notes, other readings, web sites, TV programs, your own experiences). Citing other material accurately and using a consistent reference style.

A.4. Guidelines for Tutorial Presenters

1. Tutorials are online and conducted in the WebCT Chat Rooms - log on to WebCT and go to your designated tutorial "room" about 5 minutes before the tutorial is due to start. **All** students (both external and internal) are expected to attend tutorials each week and give a tutorial presentation one week during the semester.

2. When you do your presentation, you will present **two** readings from the list of required readings for that particular week. Note that the topic list starts from Topic 1 and tutorials start in Week 2. So if your tutorial presentation is in Week 6, for example, you will present two readings from Topic 5. The Tutorial Readings web page in WebCT (go to "Tutorials" then click on "Readings") indicates both the topic number and the week number. I have announced the topic number for each week on the calendar, so you can check that also if you are confused.

3. For some weeks, there are more than two required readings given so you will have a choice. For most weeks, however, there are only two required readings so you will **not** have a choice. If there are more than two required readings, advise your tutorial group members which readings you will be presenting **at least a week** before your presentation. You can advise your group members via your tutorial group's forum (bulletin board). Private forums for each tutorial group will be created once tutorial groups are finalised.

4. As there are only 11 weeks of tutorials (Week 13 is for group presentations) and an average of 15 people per tutorial, there will be two people presenting in some weeks.

5. If there are two people presenting, each presenter is required to prepare two presentations but actually present only one. The second prepared presentation should be posted to your group's forum. The two presenters should also liaise before the tutorial and ensure that each one presents a different article.

6. If there is only one person presenting, aim to have about 10-20 minutes of prepared comments and questions on the articles; that is, about 5-10 minutes per article. The remaining time should be used for discussions among the group.

7. If there are two people presenting, aim to have about 5-10 minutes presentation and 20-25 minutes discussion each.

8. You can assume that everyone in your tutorial group has read the required readings so it's not necessary to summarise the readings. Rather, you should review or critique each reading. Highlight the main issues addressed in each reading and give your opinions on the issues. Your opinions may agree or disagree with the author's research. Support your opinions, where possible, by referring to other literature or documented examples. I advise you to read at least one other reading from the "recommended" or "additional" reading list for the week in which you are presenting to give you a broader knowledge of the topic.

9. Include in your presentation the questions posed by other group members in their journals posted to the tutorial group bulletin board. There will probably not be sufficient time to discuss all the questions but try to prioritise the questions and focus the discussions on these questions. You can also use these questions as a strategy to involve group members who are not participating in the discussions. For example, you could ask a particular person to comment on his/her question. It is most important to stimulate comments from all tutorial group members.

10. Although you will have prepared about 5-10 minutes of comments on each article, do not present all comments in one block as a monologue. Intersperse your comments with questions for the group to discuss so that the tutorial becomes more interactive and the group maintains interest in the topic.

11. Prepare your presentation in a text file (e.g. in Notepad). Have the prepared file opened in one window of your computer and the chat room in another window. Copy a paragraph at a time from your prepared file and paste into the message field of the chat room window (where it says "Type your message below and press [enter]").

12. In addition to presenting your critique of the readings, you primary role is to moderate the group discussions. This means that you will need to keep the discussions flowing and coherent. If there is a lag in the discussions, you may need to ask another question - either one from a group member or one of your own. If too many people want to "talk", you may need to interrupt and stipulate an order. It is best to ask a question of the whole group, however if you find that some group members are not participating, you may need to address them individually in order to draw them into the discussions.

13. In the first tutorial in Week 2, your tutor will be asking everyone to post to the tutorial group bulletin board their preferred week to present. The tutor will post the schedule to the bulletin board in Week 3.

A.5. Ecoms Guidelines

If you want to say more than a line, enter the first line followed by three dots (…) to indicate there is more to come.

Keep comments as short as possible to allow every the opportunity to "talk".

Be polite and don't interrupt.

It helps to indicate who you are responding to, e.g. "Lauren, why do you think that?"

You can communicate privately to any one person by click on their name in the right window. Be sure to unclick the name when you want to "go public".

Abbreviations are used to save typing, such as:
imho – in my humble (honest) opinion
btw – by the way
lol – laughing out loud
rofl – rolling on the floor laughing
np – no problems
brb – be right back
wb – welcome back
u – you
r – are

It is quite acceptable to use lower case at all times as it saves time (and is also more friendly and casual)

Shouting is usually indicated by upper case letters, so avoid upper case unless you mean to shout

Emoticons are very popular to convey expression:
:-) to indicate a smile
:-(to indicate displeasure or being unhappy about something
;-) to indicate a wink

A.6. Research Sites for Possible Study

The following research sites were located in September 2004 and the course details provided below are correct at that time.

NET24 – Virtual Communities
Open Learning Australia/Curtin University of Technology
This hybrid online unit is hosted on WebCT™. Its instructional design emphasizes online asynchronous interaction between students and the tutor. On-campus students attend weekly face-to-face instructional sessions (lecture and tutorial). The unit covers issues and implications of social and professional interactions mediated by networked technologies with additional focus on the characteristics of successful online communities.

Students are required to
- read works
- carry out research for other resources
- complete set tasks
- contribute to discussions to create new resources for assignments

Areas of assessment include a written report, essay, case study and participation in online discussions.

REA11 – Applied Reasoning
Open Learning Australia/Curtin University of Technology
This purely online unit is hosted on WebCT™. Its instructional design emphasizes online asynchronous interactions with no face-to-face instruction. The unit aims to develop critical thinking skills and use of reasoning for effective communication and analysis in the academic context.

Students are required to
- read works
- carry out necessary research for additional materials
- complete set exercises and self-tests
- contribute to online discussions

Areas of assessment include three essays and participation in online discussions.

Although both units would be next available in March 2005, formal permission for site access could not be confirmed in 2004.

LAW150 – Australian Legal System and LEG171 – Legal Writing
Murdoch Law School, Murdoch University
Both hybrid online units are hosted on WebCT™. The units offer online asynchronous activities and materials with face-to-face lectures and tutorials. The units introduce students to the workings of the Australian justice system as well as the role and influence of the main players in that system.

The common aims of the two units are the development of the legal research and writing skills that include
- active reading of legal texts
- use of legal resources
- clarity and precision in legal writing
- critical thinking about legal issues

The quality of online discussions in the asynchronous forum is mainly *social*; characterized by queries on location of resources, social events and technical problems. Solutions to problems or mutual confirmation that give comfort are often offered in discussions. Content-related queries from students are usually e-mailed to the tutor rather than posted on the forum for general discussion.

Areas of assessment include online research quizzes, a research essay and a mid-semester examination.

LAW150 and LEG171 are offered every year in Semester 1 and 2 respectively.

LEG180 – Justices of the Peace and the Justice System
Murdoch Law School, Murdoch University
This law unit is a commercially contracted distance learning course on the various duties and rights of practicing Justices of the Peace. This unit incorporates the theoretical aspects of the position of Justice of the Peace with practical exercises and activities. The Murdoch Law School awards students who successfully complete this unit a credit (Pass/Fail grade) towards a degree in the Bachelor of Legal Studies or a Graduate Certificate in Law.

This unit does not utilize WebCT™ or equivalent learning management systems. Interaction is mainly between the tutor and students which occurs via e-mail. The tutor sends course materials as e-mail attachments and answers e-mail queries from students. There are no opportunities for face-to-face or online common between the distant students themselves.

Assignments include a Reading Log (journal) and five case studies with which students are expected to
- explain and discuss legal issues
- list steps to be taken
- justify their actions/legal decisions
- provide practical examples from working experience
- reflect on possible impact of their own biases on decisions

The unit would be offered by Murdoch in 2005 if the university is successful in tendering for it.

VET620 – Diagnostic Imaging Unit for Masters of VET Studies Program
School of Veterinary Clinical Science, Murdoch University
The postgraduate unit is offered as a distance course to veterinary practitioners for developing diagnostic interpretation skills. The unit uses WebCT™ to provide students with additional learning materials such as answers to submitted assignments. The WebCT™ chat facility is available but not used by students. The online asynchronous discussion forum is available but there are usually few postings that are mainly announcements by the tutor. The online asynchronous discussions are usually between the tutor and the students with few instances of peer interaction.

Unit materials include printed texts (with CD), a Unit Reader and x-ray sheets on case studies with which students are expected to
- examine sample case studies and answers
- complete practice case studies by describing the medical condition in the x-ray, making a diagnosis, and suggesting interventions

Areas of assessments include a written assignment and a final written examination.

The unit is offered once every two years in Semester 1 and it would be next available in January 2006.

ICT329 – Organizational Informatics
School of Information Technology, Murdoch University
This online unit is hosted on WebCT™ and uses both online synchronous and asynchronous communication tools in learning activities. It covers issues in organizational aspects of information system design and development, and aims to develop skills related to online communication, group work and research. The unit offers weekly instructional sessions (face-to-face lecture, online synchronous tutorial). The online synchronous tutorial involves critical discussion on issues arising from the set-readings. Roles and duties of students during discussions (i.e. student-presenter and participant) are clearly defined.

Students are required to
- read works
- post critiques of readings to online asynchronous forum
- contribute actively to chat tutorial discussions
- carry out necessary research for additional materials
- complete set assignments

Assessments include
- a group project
- an essay assignment
- a chat tutorial presentation
- critiques of set-readings
- participation in chat tutorial discussions
- final written examination

The unit is offered every year in Semester 2 and it would be next available in July 2005.

A.7. Information Letter and Consent Form

Research Project - Constructing Learning Conversations: A Study of the Discourse and Learner Experiences of Online Synchronous Discussions

I am a PhD student at Murdoch University investigating the impact of online synchronous discussions on the learning experiences of students in the unit, Organisational Informatics (ICT329) offered by Murdoch University, under the supervision of Dr Fay Sudweeks.

The purposes of this research project are to examine the discourse structure and student experiences of synchronous interaction or 'chat' to gain better understanding of the impact of chat in supporting the learning process in this online course. Findings from the study can contribute to enhancing the course design and your online learning experiences in this unit.

You can help in this project by consenting to complete a survey, and permitting the use of the tutorial logs and information from your reflective journals (critiques of course readings).

The online survey questionnaire, which will be open from Week 11, contains background questions on gender, English language ability as well as other questions on your frequency of chat usage and your experiences of participating in chat tutorial discussions. You will probably need about twenty (20) minutes to complete the questionnaire.

All information given in the survey will be treated as confidential. Your name or other information that might identify you, will not be disclosed to the course tutor or the coordinator, nor used in any publication arising from the project. You can decide to withdraw your consent at any time, without penalty. All participants will receive information on the outcomes of this project.

If you have any questions about this research project, you can contact me (Hwee Ling, Lim) at ----@murdoch.edu.au, 0423--- or Dr Sudweeks at ---@murdoch.edu.au, 9360---. We will be happy to discuss any concerns you may have on how this project is conducted. You can also contact Murdoch University's Human Research Ethics Committee at 9360---.

If you are willing to participate in this study, please read the following statement.

I have read the information above. Any questions I have asked have been answered to my satisfaction and I know that I may change my mind and stop at any time. I consent to take part in the following activities as part of this research project:

1. complete a survey at the end of the semester
2. permit the use of the tutorial group logs, information from my critiques of course readings (journals).

I agree that the data gathered in this research project may be published provided my name or other information that may identify me is not used. I understand that all information provided is treated as confidential and will not be released by the investigator unless required to do so by law.

APPENDIX B

INSTRUMENTATION DOCUMENTS

B.1 Codebook: Introduction to Exchange Structure Analysis[99]

CONTENTS

---

[99] **NOTE**: Examples in the codebook include both hypothetical turn/exchanges and those taken from the transcript dataset. The turn labels are hypothetical and do not refer to the transcript dataset in this study.

1 DEFINITIONS AND SEGMENTATION

1.1 Session
A Session, like a lesson, is "the highest unit of classroom discourse" (Sinclair & Coulthard, 1992, p.33). A Session refers to the entire (1 hour) online synchronous tutorial period comprising *episodes* and *social spaces*. 11 Sessions were obtained from each tutorial group.
- The start of a session is signalled by the presence of the first utterance in the transcript.
- The end of a session is signalled by the presence of the last utterance in the transcript.

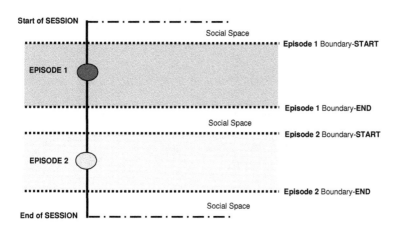

Week	Date	Session	Episode	
1	25 July 2005	---	---	---
2	1 August 2005	1	1	2
3	8 August 2005	2	1	2
4	15 August 2005	3	1	2
5	29 August 2005	4	1	2
6	5 September 2005	5	1	2
7	12 September 2005	6	1	2
8	19 September 2005	7	1	2
9	26 September 2005	8	1	2
10	10 October 2005	9	1	2
11	17 October 2005	10	1	2
12	24 October 2005	11	1	2
13	31 October 2005	---	---	---

Chat Log: Group x Mon 19:30 xx August - Week x

```
*_A*****************************************************************************
```
New session has begun in ICT329s2_Roomx.
Monday, August xx, 200x 7:06pm
```
*_A*****************************************************************************
```

*+**** Participant J entered ICT329s2_Roomx. Monday, August xx, 2005 7:06pm

*+**** Participant E entered ICT329s2_Roomx. Monday, August xx, 2005 7:21pm

START OF SESSION

```
================================================================
```
Participant E>>hi

Participant J>>howdy

*+**** Participant B entered ICT329s2_Roomx. Monday, August xx, 2005 7:23pm

Participant B>>hi, hows it going..

Participant E>>good, busy with work, yourself

//
//

Participant F>>bye and thanks everyone

Participant J>>ciao

Participant R>>see you later
```
================================================================
```
END OF SESSION

*-**** Participant L left ICT329s2_Roomx. Monday, August xx, 2005 8:40pm

*-**** Participant Fleft ICT329s2_Roomx. Monday, August xx, 2005 8:41pm

```
***************************************************************
```
Session in ICT329s2_Roomx ended. (all participants have left).
Monday, August xx, 2005 9:32pm
```
***************************************************************
```

1.2 Episode

An Episode refers to a discussion slot (usually 20-30 mins), within a Session, during which a student presents a critique on one set-reading and moderates the discussion (refer to 1.6 *discussion*) based on the issue(s) in the reading. Only turns that fall within the Episode boundaries, in the transcript, are included in the analysis.

There are usually 2 Episodes (i.e. two student presentations) in each Session. The 2 Episodes are delimited by boundaries marking the transition from one student presentation to another, within the Session.
- The start of an Episode is usually signalled by the first turn from the presenter that directly relates to the task of critiquing the set-reading (refer to 1.6 *metastatement*).
- The end of an Episode is usually signalled by the last turn from any participant that relates to the issue(s) in the set-reading and closes the current presentation (refer to 1.6 *conclusion*).

Episode Boundary-START
==

Participant A>>Howdy people my name is Participant A, I guess it is assumed that since my name is shown on the post oh well oops, I guess it is time to get to started, I would like to thank everyone for joining this session based on Topic 3: Organisational Design and Group Processes.

Participant A>>What this is basically about is team work, the fascination behind having teamwork within the organisations and the benefits that it may bring to the organisation such as boosting production. As well as critical issues involved with teamwork and how it is not the only thing that will increase production of a particular product, it also takes a closer look into teamwork with the GroupThink symptom and the causes of GroupThink as well as what can be a possible solution for it.

Participant A>>Is there a fundamental difference between a group of people and a team

Participant A>>of people?

Participant P>>Is it because team members have roles which are accountable to the entire team, but a group is just
a collective?

Participant L>>agree w Participant P, a team is purposive, group can be just a random gathering of ple

//
//

Participant M>>its the same as the dictator question before, if you put a bunch of people to decide what video to rent
they dont get anywhere

Participant M>>in the end someone has to come along and take the recommendations and get the job done.

Participant J>>agreed
==
Episode Boundary-END
Participant F>>reminds me of travelling with a bus load of ppl

Participant A>>I eblieve I should go onto next topic now if everyone finished

1.3 Social Space

A Social Space refers to a period, within a Session, during which participants discuss topic(s) not directly related to the issue(s) in the set-reading(s). Utterances that fall within the social spaces, in the transcript, are excluded from the analysis.

There are usually 3 Social Spaces in each Session.
- The 1st Social Space is located between the start of the Session and before the start of Episode 1.
- The 2nd Social Space is located between the Episode boundaries that mark the transition from one presentation to another, within the Session.
- The 3rd Social Space is located between the end of Episode 2 and the end of the Session.

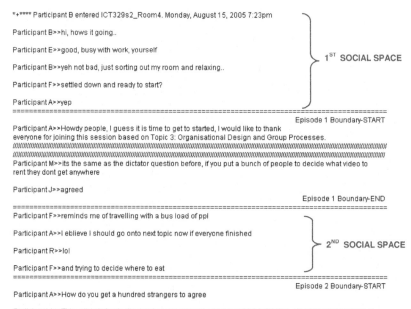

*+**** Participant B entered ICT329s2_Room4. Monday, August 15, 2005 7:23pm

Participant B>>hi, hows it going..

Participant E>>good, busy with work, yourself

Participant B>>yeh not bad, just sorting out my room and relaxing..

Participant F>>settled down and ready to start?

Participant A>>yep

1ST SOCIAL SPACE

===
Episode 1 Boundary-START

Participant A>>Howdy people, I guess it is time to get to started, I would like to thank everyone for joining this session based on Topic 3: Organisational Design and Group Processes.

Participant M>>its the same as the dictator question before, if you put a bunch of people to decide what video to rent they dont get anywhere

Participant J>>agreed

Episode 1 Boundary-END
===

Participant F>>reminds me of travelling with a bus load of ppl

Participant A>>I eblieve I should go onto next topic now if everyone finished

Participant R>>lol

Participant F>>and trying to decide where to eat

2ND SOCIAL SPACE

===
Episode 2 Boundary-START

Participant A>>How do you get a hundred strangers to agree

Participant A>>This article is basically about a research project dubbed ?PROJECTH?. What it basically looks at is how we behave using an online text computer mediated communication.

Participant A>>Conclusion

Participant A>>From both readings you can see that group work is essential for communication in both environments. However one must use group work to discuss all possible outcomes of a task before going into the, because if everyone just agrees with how to do the task the way someone has set it, and they have an objection as to how it is conducted, and they do not voice there opinion. It would be said that the group will show symptoms of Groupthink.

Episode2 Boundary-END
===

Participant F>>thanks for facilitating tonight

Participant A>>thanks

Participant R>>good presentation

*-**** Participant J left ICT329s2_Room4. Monday, August 15, 2005 8:40pm

*-**** Participant F left ICT329s2_Room4. Monday, August 15, 2005 8:41pm

3RD SOCIAL SPACE

1.4 Utterance and Turn

An Utterance is defined as "everything said by one speaker before another began to speak" (Sinclair & Coulthard, 1992, p.2). Refer to 1.6 *speaker*. The term *utterance* refers to all contributions made by participants within a Session. System generated messages in the transcript are excluded from this category and from analysis (refer to 1.6 *system generated messages*).

In conventional spoken discourse, a Turn is defined as "a contribution by a particular participant and is delimited by them starting and stopping speaking" (Kneser, Pilkington, & Treasure-Jones, 2001, p.67).
In Chat discourse, "a carriage return effectively sends a message and automatically delimits a turn" (Kneser et al., 2001, p.67). The term *turn* is reserved for contributions that fall within Episode boundaries in the transcript. Turns are considered structural units of exchanges and are hence included in the analysis. Turns are identified by Session, Episode and Number; e.g.: the label ($_{tu}$03.1.214) refers to Session 3, Episode 1, Turn 214.

TURNS

$_{tu}$03.1.214 Participant M>>its the same as the dictator question before, if you put a bunch of people to decide what video to rent they dont get anywhere

$_{tu}$03.1.215 Participant M>>

$_{tu}$03.1.216 Participant M>>in the end someone has to come along and take the recommendations and get the job done.

$_{tu}$03.1.217 Participant J>>agreed

Episode 1 Boundary-END
===

Participant F>>reminds me of travelling with a bus load of ppl

Participant A>>I eblieve I should go onto next topic now if everyone finished

Participant R>>lol

Participant F>>and trying to decide where to eat

1.5 Exchange

An *exchange* is defined as "the smallest unit of dialogue that can stand alone and still make sense" (Kneser et al., 2001, p.67). A well-formed exchange consists of "at least one initiating and one responding turn and a minimum of two participants" (Pilkington, 1999, p.12). An exchange may contain sub-exchanges that reinitiate the current exchange (Pilkington, 1999, p.14) with "an intermediary question or statement" (Pilkington, 1999, p.14).

In chat discourse, an exchange may comprise of turns that may/may not be immediately adjacent due to system lag, posting patterns of participants, and gaps or overlaps (referring respectively to when no one is speaking and when more than one participant is speaking) in the discussion. Private chats or exchanges, when reflected in the transcript, are excluded from analysis.

No.	Participant Turn	Exchange EXG-4-g4S3-E1					
69	Participant F>> what is the best way to resolve conflicts in a team?	I+					
72	Participant F>> as an example, if you had conflict in your team project, how would you deal with it?	I					
73	Participant R>> i think open communication....and perhaps also having time during the project just to discuss if any problems come with other team members	R					
74	Participant J>> if it was over the internet there would be a lot of flaming! =)	R					
76	Participant A>> in a civilised manner group consensus	R+					
84	Participant A>> considering all the alternatives of course	R					
80	Participant F>> all good suggestions Participant A		RC				
81	Participant J>> in an ideal world you would want to discuss the problem among all members of the team and come to a unanimous consensus	R					
82	Participant L>> in not so ideal world Participant J?			RI			
87	Participant J>> there would be a last-minute decision made by someone in a dictatorship-like role				R		
92	Participant E>> but a good dictator might be able to get things done faster					R	
93	Participant J>> it's good to be the king, but only if you're seen to be a "good" king (which obviously differs depending on who you ask)						R
85	Participant P>> Democracy if there are an odd number of people in the team? The will of the majority?				R		
88	Participant A>> what if the will has made a bad choice					RI	
91	Participant P>> Democracy is the freedom to make choices...even if they're bad. Its the price for social cohesion						R
83	Participant F>> what do you think, Participant M?			RI			
89	Participant M>> about how to resolve a team conflict? if it's tolerable, you take it, if it crosses your line, you argue with the party you believe to be at fault.			R			

Sub-exchanges ─────────┘

1.6 Other Terms

- *Speaker*: the participant who originates the utterance or turn in the discourse.
- *Hearer/addressee*: the participant(s) who receive(s) the utterance or turn in the discourse.
- *Discussion/dialog*: the discourses produced by more than one speaker.
- *System generated messages*: Information generated by the WebCT™ chat application on aspects such as the chat room number, session date/time, participant login and logout times.
- *Metastatement*: According to Sinclair and Coulthard (1992), a metastatement functions to "state what the discourse is going to be about" and refers to "some future time when what is described will occur" (p.17). In classroom discourse, metastatements "help pupils to see the structure of the lesson ... understand the purpose of the subsequent exchange, and see where they are going" (Sinclair & Coulthard, 1992, p.21). Sinclair and Coulthard (1992) consider the metastatement to be "technically not part of the discourse but a commentary on the discourse" (p.17) because "the teacher is not telling the children something, he is telling them what he is going to tell them (p.18). However, this study regards metastatements as turns made by participants, within an Episode and metastatements are included in the analysis for what they can reveal regarding how the student views his or her own role in the dialogue and their progress on learning tasks" (Pilkington, 1999, p.20).
- *Conclusion*: According to Sinclair and Coulthard (1992), the conclusion is "the converse of the metastatement", that functions to "summarize what the preceding chunk of discourse was about" (p.21).Turns that function as conclusions are included in the analysis for what they can reveal about participant dialog roles and classroom discourse structure.

1.7 Methodological Units of Analysis

- *Sampling unit*: refers to the document that is selected for study i.e. the transcript of the session (adapted from Shoemaker, 1996).
- *Context unit*: forms the portion of the text to be analyzed i.e. to the *episode* which forms the context in which the recording unit is interpreted.
- *Recording unit(s)*: Forms what is actually measured within the context unit i.e. the *turns* and *exchanges*.

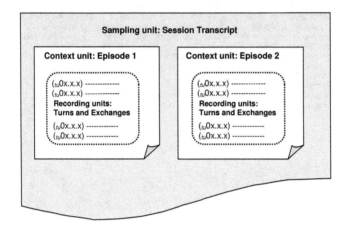

2 CODING CONVENTIONS

2.1 Coding Conventions

General coding symbol	Description
[ ]	Exchange boundaries
( )	EXCHANGE STRUCTURE (ES) and OTHER categories
{ }	MOVE category
< >	Optional item
($_{tu}$04.1.200)	Turn label
/	Double/multiple assignment of categories
+	Extended turn sequence

ES Level Category	
(I)	Initiate
(RI)	Reinitiate
(R)	Respond
(RC)	Response-Complement

MOVE Level Category	
{INF}	Inform
{INQ}	Inquire
{JUS}	Justify
{REA}	Reason
{CLA}	Clarify
{CHK}	Check
{EXD}	Extend
{CHA}	Challenge
{FBK}	Feedback

OTHER Category	
OT	Off-Topic
RPR	Repair

2.2 General Coding Notes

2.2.1 Overlapping episodes
Due to system lag, turns from Episode 1 may be found within the boundaries of Episode 2 in a session transcript. In this case, the turns were extracted from their original location and inserted within the boundaries of Episode 1.

Participant E>>how many people here would say they are received adequate training on the systems they use

Participant J>>it's taken me 10 years and I'm still an amateur

Participant A>>What if the end user has no technical expertise to fix the problem

Turns inserted into boundaries of Episode 1

Participant R>>hmm....i'd say i've taught myself more then anything

Episode 1 Boundary-END

==

Episode 2 Boundary-START

Participant E>>The second article is about simplifying the interaction between human

Participant R>>but i feel like every day there is something else new to learn

Participant J>>that's where the IT Pro should spend a little extra time educating the person, rather than just fixing the problem

Participant I>>id agree with that

Participant E>>and machine and taking into account the diversities of different users

Participant A>>but it takes time to learn new things which the organisation may not want to waste

2.2.2 Postings from students who are not part of the study
Since the tutorial chat rooms were open to all students in the OI unit, occasionally students who were not part of the groups selected for this study contributed brief messages. In such cases, the messages were removed from the transcript and excluded from analysis.

2.2.3 Private chat messages
The WebCT™ chat application supports *private chat* whereby a participant could send messages to designated receiver(s) in the chat room. These messages are hidden from the view of non-designated receivers and usually do not appear in the transcripts. However, messages from private chats were reflected in some transcripts. In such cases, these messages were removed.

2.2.4 Treatment of turn content
The correctness and accuracy of the content in the turns were not considered.

2.2.5 Punctuation in chat discourse
Punctuation in chat discourse is not always a definitive indication of the turn intention. Given the paucity of punctuation in chat discourse, requests are not always indicated by question marks and conversely, the presence of a question mark does not necessarily indicate a request due to different behaviors in font/character conversion. Therefore, turns that function as requests and statements were largely interpreted as such from the discussion context.

2.2.6 Turn count for extended turn sequences

Due to system lag and/or use of multiple short postings by participants, extended turn sequences may be present that consist of 2 or more turns (by the same speaker) that may/may not immediately follow each other in the transcript. In such cases, each turn in the sequence was coded as a single instance of the coding category.

No.	Participant	Turn	Exchange
			EXG-4-g4S3-E1
69	Participant F>>	what is the best way to resolve conflicts in a team?	I+
72	Participant F>>	as an example, if you had conflict in your team project, how would you deal with it?	I
73	Participant R>>	i think open communication....and perhaps also having time during the project just to discuss if any problems come with other team members	R
74	Participant J>>	if it was over the internet there would be a lot of flaming! =)	R
76	Participant A>>	in a civilised manner group consensus	R+
84	Participant A>>	considering all the alternatives of course	R
80	Participant F>>	all good suggestions Participant A	RC
81	Participant J>>	In an ideal world you would want to discuss the problem among all members of the team and come to a unanimous consensus	R

ES Categories	Turn Count
(I)	2
(RI)	0
(R)	5
(RC)	1
Total	**8**

2.2.7 Double-coding for MOVE Level categories

At the ES Level, there is no double-coding and each turn was coded based on its predominant structural function. However, there is double-coding at the MOVE Level and a turn could be interpreted as simultaneously performing different pragmatic functions associated with the ES category determined for the turn. For instance, an (I) could function to {INF} and {INQ} but not to {FBK} since the Feedback MOVE category is associated only with (RC) turns.

In cases of double coding at the MOVE level, more than one MOVE category was assigned to the turn for the functions it was interpreted to perform. Each turn was counted as a single instance of the Move categories assigned.

No.	Participant	Turn	Exchange ES categories			MOVE categories
140	Participant J>>	I use Trillian, which allows connections to MSN, Yahoo, ICQ and AIM...but is a totally different program...does that make it a "bad" program for cmc?	I			INF / INQ
142	Participant R>>	well i don't think its bad...it just doesn't have the features if you have individual chat programs	R+			JUS
148	Participant R>>	see i tried using trillian....but after awhile, got rid of it, went back to the old way of having half a dozen messengers up...you get much more features	R			JUS
141	Participant I>>	you can communication to more ppl	R			INF
143	Participant J>>	that's why I use it...but it doesn't have all the same functionalities		R		INF
144	Participant M>>	yeah but it complicates and de-standardises.		R		JUS
145	Participant I>>	tue			RC	FBK-E

Double coded turn at Move Level _____

ES Categories	Turn Count	Move Categories	Turn Count
(I)	1	(I)-{INFORM}	1
		(I)-{INQUIRE}	1
(RI)	0		
(R)	5	(R) -{INFORM}	2
		(R) -{JUSTIFY}	3
(RC)	1	(RC)-{FBK-E}	1
Total	7	**Total**	8

2.3 Summary of ESA Coding Procedure

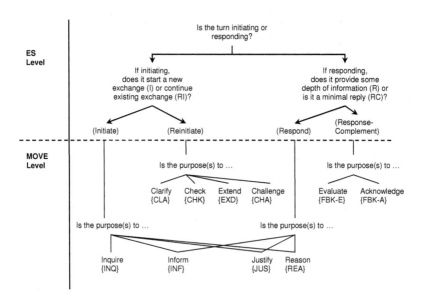

3 EXCHANGE STRUCTURE (ES) LEVEL: CODING CATEGORIES

3.1 Initiate (I)

CODING CATEGORY	DESCRIPTORS		
Initiate (I)	A turn that is "initial in the exchange, it predicts a subsequent turn by another participant and it is not predicted by the preceding turn" (Kneser et al., 2001, p.67). Initiates include statements and requests, in an exchange, with the following characteristics: ■ initial in the exchange ■ not predicted from a previous turn ■ anticipate a following turn by another participant		
Examples		ES LEVEL	
(ᵣ06.1.17)	Participant A>> Can anyone suggest the – 've ways IFC can impact socially?	[I	
(ᵣ06.1.18)	Participant B>> decrease in physical exercise		R
(ᵣ06.1.20)	Participant C>> less f2f		R
(ᵣ06.1.38)	Participant A>> Good response, Thanks all (no reponse needed)		RC]
(ᵣ04.1.90)	Participant A>> macdonals is able to better provide a service for differing countries by using the nations cultural norms…Vegie burgers in India	[I	
(ᵣ04.1.91)	Participant B>> agree		RC
(ᵣ04.1.94)	Participant C>> thats true…understanding different culture..help organisation to be more productive		R]
(ᵣ05.1.78)	Participant A>> telephone is better communication than e-mail	[I	
(ᵣ05.1.84)	Participant B>> I would say they are different but to judge a technology without a context and say its better is a hard thing to do		R]

CODING NOTES: Initiate

- Differentiate between *Initiate* and *Reinitiate* turns on the basis of "whether a new exchange is being started" (Kneser et al., 2001, p.68).
- Code a turn as an Initiate when it is unclear whether it is a response (R, RC) or a continuation of the current exchange (RI).
- In chat discourse, an Initiate may consist of a sequence of 2 or more turns (by the same speaker) that may/may not immediately follow each other in the transcript. The sequence of turns function to set the background for the final Initiate turn in the exchange. In such cases, code each turn in the *Initiate sequence* as a single instance of Initiate.

Examples		ES LEVEL	
(ᵣ04.2.64)	Participant A>> the biggest flaw is the fact the culture is unstructured, understanding is a matter of belonging and sometimes not even knowing it … in his defence he drove points that made people think about it	I+	
(ᵣ04.2.67)	Participant A>> this proves some understanding … and that is an art under the circumstances	I	

3.2 Reinitiate (RI)

CODING CATEGORY	DESCRIPTORS
Reinitiate (RI)	A turn that signals "a continuation of the current exchange. RI predicts a response but is non-predicted and non-initial" (Kneser et al., 2001, p.67). Reinitiates include turns, in an exchange, with the following characteristics: • not initial (similar to a *Response*) • not predicted from earlier turn • anticipates a following turn by another participant (similar to an *Initiate*) • a continuation of the current exchange (signals intention to start a sub-exchange that is related in content/topic)

Examples

			ES LEVEL
(a04.1.47)	Participant A>>	The paper is mainly focused on the access issue, as this is the only quantifiable means to determine networked activity within cultures	[I
(a04.1.57)	Participant B>>	so they are really talking about qualitative aspects for now until they find more quantitative measures??	RI
(a04.1.60)	Participant C>>	yup…as they said need more research…	R]
(a05.1.24)	Participant A>>	Do you think that Virtual Organisations should be based on High Reliability Organisations (HROs)?	[I
(a05.1.28)	Participant B>>	not really, they are a special case	R
(a05.1.29)	Participant A>>	special in what way?	RI
(a05.1.33)	Participant B>>	seem to form for vary short timeframes and only a single objective. A bit different frm normal VOs	R]

CODING NOTES: Reinitiate

- An interruption or need to re-focus the discussion may result in a turn that re-states or repeats a previous Initiate. In such cases, code the turn as a Reinitiate.
- In chat discourse, a Reinitiate may consist of a sequence of 2 or more turns (by the same speaker) that may/may not immediately follow each other in the transcript. In such cases, code each turn in the *Reinitiate sequence* as a single instance of Reinitiate.

Examples

			ES LEVEL
(a06.1.307)	Participant A>>	what community do you feel a part of?	RI+
(a06.1.309)	Participant A>>	the virtual one here, the one physically around you doorstep	RI+
(a06.1.311)	Participant A>>	or the mental university student one etc	RI

3.3 Respond (R)

CODING CATEGORY	DESCRIPTORS
Respond (R)	A turn that is "not initial, it does not predict a following turn by another participant and usually completes the exchange, indeed an exchange without a Responding turn is not considered a well-formed exchange. However Respond is not always the terminal category in an exchange" (Kneser et al., 2001, p.67). Responds include turns, in an exchange, with the following characteristics: ■ not initial (a reply/response) ■ predicted from a previous turn that can be (I) or (RI) e.g.s: [I-*R*], [RI-*R*] ■ does not anticipate a following turn by another participant ■ usually completes/closes an exchange but not always due to possibility of a Response-Complement

Examples

			ES LEVEL
(ₐ₀5.1.78)	Participant A>>	telephone is better communication than e-mail	[I
(ₐ₀5.1.84)	Participant B>>	I would say they are different but to judge a technology without a context and say	R]
		its better is a hard thing to do	
(ₐ₀6.1.17)	Participant A>>	Can anyone suggest the—'ve ways IFC can impact socially?	[I
(ₐ₀6.1.18)	Participant B>>	decrease in physical exercise	R
(ₐ₀6.1.38)	Participant A>>	Good response, Thanks all (no reponse needed)	RC]

CODING NOTES: Respond

- A turn is coded as a Respond based on its position/function in the exchange, and interpretation of its relevance as a reply to previous turn(s) guided by the context and co-text.
- In chat discourse, a Respond may consist of a sequence of 2 or more turns (by the same speaker) that may/may not immediately follow each other in the transcript. In such cases, code each turn in the *Respond sequence* as a single instance of Respond.

Examples

			ES LEVEL
(ₐ₀6.1.77)	Participant A>>	yes…because…there are still peple that feel isolated…even though they may be	R+
		talking to others on the internet	
(ₐ₀6.1.79)	Participant A>>	it creates the impression of knowing someone , but we don't actually know them …	R
		that's the paradox	

- A Respond turn is distinguished from a Response-Complement by the presence an extended reply that provides more/new information (with explanation or elaboration) rather than a minimal response.

Examples

			ES LEVEL
(ₐ₀6.1.128)	Participant A>>	People who use e-mail regard it as less valuble than other modes of	[I
		comm.. We all use e-mail regularly do we agree/disagree why?	
(ₐ₀6.1.130)	Participant B>>	agree	RC
(ₐ₀6.1.137)	Participant C>>	Disagree. Depends on context	R+
(ₐ₀6.1.147)	Participant C>>	Email is great 4 work stuff	R]

3.4 Response-Complement (RC)

CODING CATEGORY	DESCRIPTORS
Response-Complement (RC)	A turn, in an exchange, with the following characteristics: ■ not initial (a reply/response) ■ predicted from a previous turn that can be (I) or (RI) e.g.s: [I-*RC*], [RI-*RC*] ■ not predicted from an earlier turn, an optional turn that may follow a (R) e.g.: [I-R-RC] ■ does not anticipate a following turn by another participant ■ usually signals intention to close the exchange: [I-RC] or [I-R-RC] ■ marks point for possible new exchange

Although (RC) shares some characteristics of a Respond, a (RC) can be both predicted and not predicted from an earlier turn. In a well-formed exchange, a (RC) can occupy the position after an Initiate/Reinitiate and can also occupy the position after a Respond. Unlike a Respond that provides more/new information, (RC) is a minimal reply to an earlier turn without additional explanation or elaboration. (R) and (RC) are more clearly distinguished at the Move level.

Examples

			ES LEVEL		
(ᵤ04.1.6)	Participant A>>	does everyone understand what i have said	[I		
(ᵤ04.1.7)	Participant B>>	yes, understood		RC]	
(ᵤ05.2.64)	Participant A>>	But comp access is definitely cheaper than flying all the way to the other side of the world for business purpose rite	[...RI		
(ᵤ05.2.65)	Participant B>>	yes		RC]	
(ᵤ06.2.8)	Participant A>>	Antecedents are the contributing factors of Self-efficacy and are incorporated in the investigation of one?s degree of self-efficacy. What are some antecedents you can think of?	[I		
(ᵤ06.2.9)	Participant B>>	er... previous experience		R	
(ᵤ06.2.19)	Participant A>>	yes - Remote working experience & training			RC]
(ᵤ04.1.90)	Participant A>>	macdonals is able to better provide a service for differing countries by using the nations cultural norms... Vegie burgers in India	[I		
(ᵤ04.1.91)	Participant B>>	agree		RC	
(ᵤ04.1.94)	Participant C>>	thats true...understanding different culture..help organisation to be more productive		R]	

4 MOVE (MV) LEVEL: CODING CATEGORIES

4.1 Inform {INF}

CODING CATEGORY	DESCRIPTORS	
Inform {INF}	INFORM moves are used for making "*observations*, including stating facts or rules either retrieved from memory or from external sources. Inform moves represent commitments – more or less strongly held – about the state of the world" (Pilkington, 1999, p.19 – emphasis in original).	
	An INFORM move usually functions to • describe or make observations of facts or events • state retrieved beliefs, definitions/rules • summarize/repeat information from memory or external sources	
	Can be	**Examples**
	- to describe or make observations of facts or events	(₄04.1.64) (₄04.1.90) (₄06.1.237)	culture is just another way of stereo typing macdonals is able to better provide a service for differing countries by using the nations cultural norms… Vegie burgers in India My parents and in-laws do. Mum to look up recipes Dad to see the sport news neither ever happen.
	- to state retrieved beliefs, definitions/rules - to summarize/repeat information from memory or external sources	(₄04.1.24) (₄06.1.4)	as defined by management … its the collective of that members expect the bechaviour is, never defined by policies but understood by all Studies by Kraut and colleagues in 98 looked at 93 households for their 1st 12-18 months OL & found heavy users became less socially involved, more lonely & depressed even though they were using the Internet for communication.

4.2 Inquire {INQ}

CODING CATEGORY	DESCRIPTORS	
Inquire {INQ}	An INQUIRE move usually functions to • elicit or request for information • bid/solicit for favor that participants can permit or deny Since the INQUIRE move functions to seek or elicit information, it shares some of the characteristics of CLARIFY and CHALLENGE moves that take the form of requests. However, {INQ} is associated with *Initiate* at the ES level whereas {CLA} and {CHA} are associated with (RI)	
	Can be	**Examples**
	- to elicit or request for information	(₄04.1.76) (₄04.2.88) (₄05.1.24)	In the article Geert Hofstede's studies are spoken about. What are his practical applications for his research on cultural differences? What is McSweeney trying to gain out of this article for his readers? Do you think that Virtual Organisations should be based on High Reliability Organisations (HROs)?
	- bid/solicit for favor that participants can permit or deny	(₄04.2.11) (₄05.1.2) (₄05.2.183)	nope - maybe you have some for us? First the summary?? any conclusion

4.3 Justify {JUS}

CODING CATEGORY	DESCRIPTORS
Justify {JUS}	A move that is used to respond to a stated position/point of view with supporting or contrary evidence/information. The {JUS} moves usually take the form of "yes/no/point-of-view...because..."

A JUSTIFY move usually functions to
- defend a stated position (in previous or current turn) with information/evidence
- challenge/dispute a stated position (in previous turn) with information/evidence

The {JUS} move differs from {REA} and {FBK} in the following aspects:
- respond with information/beliefs retrieved from external sources in contrast to {REA} application of constructed beliefs/extended reasoning
- respond with more/new information in contrast to {FBK} minimal comment on/reply to an earlier turn

Can be	Examples	
to defend a stated position (in previous or current turn) with *supportive evaluative element and information*	(ₐ04.1.180) (ₐ04.1.199) (ₐ04.2.100) (ₐ05.1.31) (ₐ05.1.107)	yeah, same... I think it has the ability to expose you to different cultures exactly, look at the CAPS situation, thats a part of the internet culture. yes he has envested a lot in his theory and become a little to attached to it at the expense of loosing his perspective VO is more risky because of its status. Mind you no one would not like to venture into a tempory entity Trust is importnt as a lot of VO's include the saftely of ppl eg. health maintenence systems, fire and emergency etc.
to challenge/dispute a stated position (in previous turn) with *direct non-supportive evaluative element and information*	(ₐ04.1.49) (ₐ04.2.34) (ₐ06.2.31) (ₐ05.1.112)	i don't think so, too many sub-groups in each culture I don't think it was flawed, I believe it was a good start no i was more leaning towards phycological states u can't build trust that way, but trust can be developed through the right way of communicating n policies
to challenge/dispute a stated position (in previous turn) with *indirect non-supportive evaluative element and information*, "performed in positive syntax, with added mitigation and accounts" (Stubbs, 1983, p.117)	(ₐ04.1.72) (ₐ04.2.104) (ₐ05.2.94) (ₐ06.1.202)	yes, but a culture within an org. can be more readily grouped than say of a nation yes, but as stated b4, that brings about a lot of bias' in the results yes but not all send money back Well yes but numbers would be more appropriate, saying more than 10hours is heavy for example

4.4 Reason {REA}

CODING CATEGORY	DESCRIPTORS		
Reason {REA}	"Reasoning moves include constructed rather than retrieved beliefs and are used to present; *goals, problems and solutions, contraindications,* and *support for alternative hypotheses*" (Pilkington, 1999, p.19). "*Reasoning* involves the retrieval of relevant rules or operators and their application to the problem space e.g. the construction of working hypotheses or the implications of a claim" (Pilkington, 1999, p.18).		
	The REASON move is usually a declarative statement that functions to ■ present problem-solution or cause-consequence: 'if…then'; 'unless…then' ■ present support or contraindication for alternative hypotheses: 'because…'; 'hence/so….'; 'but/so…then' ■ state constructed (reasoned) beliefs/implications: 'this/which means…'; 'that is why…'; 'so/therefore…'		
	The {REA} move differs from {INF} and {JUS} in the following aspect: ■ respond with constructed beliefs/extended reasoning in contrast to information/beliefs retrieved from external sources		
	Can be		Examples
	- to present problem-solution or cause-consequence: 'if…then'; 'unless…then'	(₀06.1.105) (₀06.1.304) (₀06.2.71)	it can be used without a control group if the groups studied are more selective but if u build a repore with someone, then u r more comfortable meeting them f2f if the expert makes things seem easy, then the novice will try harder to begin with, but may become more easily discouraged in the long run.
	- to present support or contraindication for alternative hypotheses: 'because…'; 'hence/so….'; 'but/so…then'	(₀06.1.76) (₀04.1.105)	because people are keen support new technology…but they don't realize they are unrealistic agree, I think Hofstede's studies is important to consider but not solid enough to be a sole consideration
	- to state constructed (reasoned) beliefs/implications: 'this/which means…'; 'that is why…'; 'so/therefore…'	(₀04.1.152) (₀04.1.173) (₀04.2.37)	I think even though its impacts cannot be quantified, it still needs to be considered, just like org. informatics, you can't measure how impressed an employee is with a new product, but you still need to take their opinion into the equation of success yes, cultural difference affect me as a person…sometimes the differences may be extreme or surprising, so it requires me to keep my composure in a business situation This study was conducted on a group of employees of one of the largest computer organisations in the world. Therefore the study would not be representative of the entire nation of any of the countries, as these employees would be technologically focused for reason of the company that they are employed by.

4.5 Check {CHK}

CODING CATEGORY	DESCRIPTORS
Check {CHK}	A CHECK move is used to make certain/sure the meaning of previous turn(s) and associated with repair work.[100] It can take "any declarative move type and turn it into an inquiry of the form 'do you mean....?' or 'is it the case that....'" (Pilkington, 1999, p.19). Usually, the CHECK statement/request[100] gives or specifies the information to be confirmed (provided as options by the speaker) hence reflecting a situation when speakers "ask questions which they have reasons for asking, and have hopes and expectations about answers" (Stubbs, 1983, p.115).

A CHECK move usually functions to
- make certain the meaning of previous turn(s)
- check readiness of participants, ascertain if there are any problems[102]

Can be		Examples
- to make certain the meaning of previous turn(s)	(₍ᵤ₎05.1.160) (₍ᵤ₎05.2.165) (₍ᵤ₎06.1.54)	so manager is of critical importance in VO threat to culture or transnational integration? You mean extro or introvert
- to check readiness of participants, ascertain if there are any problems	(₍ᵤ₎05.2.11) (₍ᵤ₎06.1.68)	everyone ok? are you guys all taking about the same article?

4.6 Clarify {CLA}

CODING CATEGORY	DESCRIPTORS
Clarify {CLA}	A CLARIFY move is used to seek more information on previous turn(s) for making meaning clearer or understanding easier and associated with repair work.[103] The CLARIFY move is usually a request in the form of an open-ended question that seeks information from the hearer(s)/addressee(s). It differs from the CHECK move as the information sought is not provided as options by the speaker.

A CLARIFY move usually functions to
- seek more information on previous turn(s)
- make meaning clearer or understanding easier

Can be		Examples
- to seek more information on previous turn(s) to make meaning clearer	(₍ᵤ₎04.1.31) (₍ᵤ₎05.1.29) (₍ᵤ₎05.1.67) (₍ᵤ₎06.1.59) (₍ᵤ₎06.1.186)	– organisational culture? special in what way? why is it so how do u prove u worked whole weekend? Why are we heavy internet users?

---

[100] This does not refer to the *Repair (Self/Other)* category that is outside ES level analysis.
[101] Given the paucity of punctuation in chat discourse, requests are not always indicated by question marks and conversely, the presence of question mark does not necessarily indicate a request due to different behaviors in font/character conversion. Where a turn cannot be clearly interpreted as a request from the context, it is regarded as a statement.
[102] When it is unclear whether a turn functions as a (RI)–{CHK} or OT-A, its interpretation should be guided by the discussion context.
[103] This does not refer to the *Repair (Self/Other)* category that is outside ES level analysis.

APPENDIX B

301

4.7 Extend {EXD}

CODING CATEGORY	DESCRIPTORS
Extend {EXD}	An EXTEND move is used to provide more information and add to what is said in a previous Initiate. Although an EXTEND move shares some characteristics of an INFORM, {EXD} is associated with *Reinitiate* at the ES level. An EXTEND move usually functions to ▪ describe or make observations of facts or events ▪ state retrieved beliefs, definitions/rules ▪ summarize/repeat information from memory or external sources

	Can be	Examples
	- to provide more information or continue the topic raised in a previous Initiate	(₀₀05.1.146) also don't forget word of mouth and personal testimonies. they go far nowadays 2 (₀₀06.2.47) note tht there a need of self motivation upon past experience as well (₀₀06.1.236) it also shows who buys second hand computers (non internet users) and those who buy the newest and best

4.8 Challenge {CHA}

CODING CATEGORY	DESCRIPTORS
Challenge {CHA}	A CHALLENGE move usually functions to ▪ propose/suggest another direction for discussion or thought ▪ assert the need for another direction for discussion or thought The {CHA} statement/request usually contains a proposal/suggestion in the form of 'then/maybe, we should...' or 'why do/should we...?' Although the {CHA} request shares the characteristic of an {INQ} in asking for information, {CHA} is associated with *Reinitiate* at ES level.

	Can be	Examples
	- to propose/assert the need for another direction for discussion or thought	(₀₀04.1.142) So why bother with culture, and not stick to quantifiable methods like GDP, and uptake of IT? (₀₀04.1.176) or does internet have it's own culture? (₀₀04.1.183) maybe it drags u away frp, traditional cultures (₀₀04.2.102) brendan may seem to think that hof is very narrow-minded but on the other hand, hof might be tryin to localise his research on 'IBM organisational culture' (₀₀06.2.58) it can help to begin with, but if a person gets half way through a task and it falls down, what then? (₀₀05.1.74) i believe its advanced technology, how else can you communicate over distances, f2f doesn't go further than the sound of your voice

4.9 Feedback {FBK}

CODING CATEGORY	DESCRIPTORS
Feedback (FBK)	A FEEDBACK move is used to answer or comment on previous turn(s) and may contain evaluative content or a form of acknowledgement.
	A Feedback-Evaluation (FBK-E) move functions to ■ validate the truth/correctness of previous turn(s) or ■ comment on the quality of the previous turn(s)
	A Feedback-Acknowledgement (FBK-A) move functions to ■ report the state of the speaker ■ claim or acknowledge understanding/hearing of the previous turn(s)
	The {FBK-A} move does not imply agreement/disagreement or support/non-support of previous turn(s). In other words, the {FBK-A} move "does not commit the speaker to any opinion about the truth, correctness or validity of the response. Rather, it acknowledges having heard [or understood] the speaker and signals intention to close or 'finish' the exchange" (Kneser et al, 2001, p.67). Since the {FBK} move functions to provide information, it shares some of the characteristics of {INF}, {JUS}, {REA} moves that are used to respond to previous turns. However, {FBK} differs in the following aspects: ■ comments on/answers a previous turn with a minimal (can be single word) response in contrast to extended information-sharing in {INF} or the working through of implications/hypotheses in {JUS} and {REA} moves ■ comments on/answers a previous turn by close repetition/summary of the content in the previous turn ■ associated mainly with *Response-Complement* (RC) at the ES level whereas {INF}, {JUS}, {REA} are mainly associated with (I) and (R)

SUB-CATEGORIES

Feedback-Evaluation {FBK-E}	A {FBK-E} move functions to ■ validate the truth/correctness of previous turn(s) or ■ comment on the quality of the previous turn(s)		
	Can be		**Examples**
	- {FBK-E} Positive (to indicate Support; Agreement)	(ₙ06.2.147) (ₙ04.1.48) (ₙ04.1.181) (ₙ04.1.67) (ₙ06.2.40)	yes That's true good point wait agree yes – past experience
	- {FBK-E} Negative (to indicate Non-Support; Disagreement)	(ₙ05.1.18) (ₙ06.1.189) (ₙ06.1.179) (ₙ04.1.89) (ₙ04.1.128)	no No it's not true I don't agree Not as serious tho I don't belive adding culture does make it easier
	- {FBK-E} Neutral (to indicate No Commitment)	(ₙ04.2.55) (ₙ06.1.48) (ₙ06.1.75)	well… depends Well its hard to assess,

Feedback-Acknowledgment {FBK-A}	A {FBK-A} move functions to ■ report the state of the speaker ■ claim or acknowledge understanding/hearing of the previous turn(s)

	Can be	Examples	
-	{FBK-A} Confirm	(ₐ04.1.7) (ₐ04.1.13) (ₐ05.1.13) (ₐ05.1.10) (ₐ05.2.30)	yes, understood got it go on all good yup…no questions
-	{FBK-A} Deny	(ₐ04.2.12) (ₐ04.2.17) (ₐ04.2.14)	nope…go on nup no
-	{FBK-A} Accept (to indicate acceptance of information, without confirmation/refutation; serves mainly phatic function to establish or maintain contact)	(ₐ04.1.123) (ₐ05.2.3) (ₐ05.2.127) (ₐ05.2.199) (ₐ06.2.57)	ok cool i c take that ah

CODING NOTES: Feedback {FBK}

- FEEDBACK moves in the forms of *yes*, *no* should be interpreted in the context of the discussion to determine their sub-categories: {FBK-E} or {FBK-A}.

Examples			ES Level		MV Level
(ₐ04.1.6)	Participant A>>	does everyone understand what i have said	[I		{INQ}
(ₐ04.1.8)	Participant B>>	yes		RC]	{FBK-A}
(ₐ04.2.10)	Participant A>>	any questions	[I		{INQ}
(ₐ04.2.14)	Participant B>>	no		RC]	{FBK-A}
(ₐ06.1.291)	Participant A>>	extrovers use the net to extend themselves while introvert use the net to remove themselves	[…R		{REA}
(ₐ06.1.293)	Participant B>>	Yes		RC]	{FBK-E}
(ₐ05.2.161)	Participant A>>	so textbased cmc is a threat?	[RI		{CHK}
(ₐ05.2.164)	Participant B>>	no		RC]	{FBK-E}

APPENDIX B

304

5 ASSOCIATED ES AND MOVE CODING CATEGORIES

MOVE	Exchange Structure			
	(Initiate)	(Reinitiate)	(Respond)	(Response-Complement)
{Inform}	1		1	
{Inquire}	1			
{Justify}	1		1	
{Reason}	1		1	
{Check}		1		
{Clarify}		1		
{Extend}		1		
{Challenge}		1		
{Feedback}				1

Explanatory Note:
- (INITIATE) to {Inform}, {Inquire}, {Justify}, {Reason}
- (REINITIATE) to {Check}, {Clarify}, {Extend}, {Challenge}
- (RESPOND) to {Inform}, {Justify}, {Reason}
- (RESPONSE-COMPLEMENT) to {Feedback}

6 OTHER CODING CATEGORIES

6.1 Off Topic (OT)

CODING CATEGORY	DESCRIPTORS
Off Topic	A turn, within episode boundaries, that contains content not directly related to the issue(s) in the set-reading(s).
SUB-CATEGORIES	
Off Topic-Social (OT-S)	▪ A turn for "facilitating the development of group relationships" (Kneser et al., 2001, p.69). ▪ A turn that conveys a social act "aimed at distracting from the subject matter, intentionally or unintentionally" (Cox et al., 2004, p.187). Can be **Examples** - Social banter (ₙ06.1.260) Hes a married man! - Appreciation (ₙ04.1.204) Thank you - Invitation (ₙ04.1.03) let's chart after tutorial - Greeting (ₙ06.1.25) hello - Acknowledgement (ₙ05.2.186) yep - Reassurance (ₙ05.1.51) no worries … - Encouragement/praise (ₙ05.2.209) gj - Apology* (see RPR category) (ₙ04.1.161) sorry about the CAPS - Emoticons/emotags (ₙ05.2.27) :((ₙ06.1.250) grin

Off Topic-Administration (OT-A)	▪ A turn that deals with/discusses housekeeping issues for the OI unit and/or tutorial group.
	
	Can be **Examples**
	- Time-calls (ₙ04.2.140) 3 mins
	- Reminders (ₙ04.2.143) Thanks, do you want to wrap it up?
	- Comments on management of (ₙ05.2.182) This has really slowed down
	  presentation; schedules; assignments; (ₙ04.1.127) back on track
	  projects, etc.

Off Topic-Technical (OT-T)	▪ A turn that is created or results from technical problems/issues. ▪ A turn that could be the 'trouble source' for Repair (refer to 6.2 *Repair*). Can be turns resulting from **Examples** - Mistyping (ₙ04.2.80) i dowhy? - Problems with network connection; (ₙ05.2.02) [blank] equipment; software; etc.

CODING NOTES: Off Topic

- A turn coded OT, within Episode boundaries, is included in the total count of turns for the Episode.
- A turn coded OT is excluded from analysis at ES and MOVE levels.
- OT sub-categories are not mutually exclusive. A turn that performs more than one OT function is double coded.

Examples   OT Category

($_{io}$04.2.143)   Thanks, do you want to wrap it up?   OT-S/OT-A

6.2 Repair (RPR)

CODING CATEGORY	DESCRIPTORS
Repair (RPR)	A turn, within the episode boundaries, that repairs or corrects a previous turn. The general concept of *Repair* includes *correction* as a type of repair and also covers phenomena that are "neither contingent upon error, nor limited to replacement" (Schegloff, Jefferson, & Sacks, 1977, p.363). A *Repair* can occur even when there is no "hearable [or obvious] error, mistake, or fault", hence "it appears that nothing is, in principle, excludable from the class 'repairable'" (Schegloff et al., 1977, p.363). The term *Trouble-source* (or repairable) refers to "that which the repair addresses" (Schegloff et al., 1977, p.363). The terms *Self* and *Other* refer to "two classes of participants in interactive social organizations" (Schegloff et al., 1977, pp.361-362).

SUB-CATEGORIES

Repair-Self (RPR-S)	A turn that repairs/corrects a previous turn. The 'speaker' of the trouble-source or repairable item carries out the repair.		
	Can be - Word replacement that repairs the error with what is correct	**Examples**	
		Participant A>> (n04.2.5)	3discrete component (organisational culture, occupational, and national. The national as micro-local which is being identified as in uniformity and an average tendency). National culture creates questionnaire response differences. National culture can be identified by response different anaylysis	I
		Participant A>> (n04.2.6)	analysis	RPR-S
		Participant B>> (n04.2.96)	McSweeney states that H "has never acknowledged any significant errors or weaknesses in the research"	I+
		Participant B>> (n04.2.97)	which I find very narrow-minded!	I
		Participant B>> (n04.2.98)	*minded	RPR-S
		Participant A>> (n06.2.158)	and the results can be found in a long term...which most manager want it S.O.S	R
		Participant A>> (n06.2.159)	I mean sonn as possible	RPR-S

Repair-Other (RPR-O)	A turn that repairs/corrects a previous turn. Another participant (not the 'speaker' of the trouble-source) carries out the repair.		
	Can be - Word replacement that repairs the error with what is correct	**Examples**	
		Participant A>> (n06.2.115)	seeing more work brings on more stress thus ness gets done in the end	R
		Participant B>> (n06.2.116)	or less	RPR-O

CODING NOTES: Repair

- A turn coded RPR, within the Episode boundaries, is included in the total count of turns for the Episode.
- A turn coded RPR is excluded from analysis at ES and MOVE levels.
- Apologies may function to 'repair' utterances. If the corrected form/amendment is present, code the turn as RPR, otherwise code the turn as OT-S.

B.2 NetMiner II: Features, System Requirements and Limitations

Information adapted from User Manual Version 2.5.0 (2004), pp.1-3.

Last revised 16 August 2004

NetMiner Web site http://www.netminer.com

About Cyram NetMiner II

Cyram NetMiner II version 2.5.0 is an innovative software tool for Exploratory Network Data Analysis and Visualization. Its unique feature lies in the integration of standard social network analysis (SNA) methodology with modern network visualization (or graph drawing) techniques in the spirit of *Exploratory Data Analysis* (EDA).

NetMiner allows you to explore your network data visually and interactively, and helps you to detect underlying patterns and structures of the network. Cyram NetMiner can be used for general research, teaching and professional analysis in social networks. Also, it can be effectively applied to various business fields, where network-structural factors have great deal of influences on the performance: e.g. intra- and inter-organizational, financial, criminal/intelligence, Web, telecommunication, distribution, transportation networks.

Features

- Integration of network analysis and network visualization in one software package
- Dynamic linking of network-analytic substance with network map
- Incorporates standard and latest set of network analysis tools and data manipulation facilities
- Highly interactive user interface which supports quick exploratory data analysis
- Generalized data architecture makes it easy to model multi-layered network and inter-connections among relational, affiliation and attribute variables

System Requirements

System Requirement of NetMiner for Windows:

- Computer/Processor : IBM PC or compatible with Pentium III 600 MHz or higher processor required
- Operation System : Microsoft Windows 98, Windows ME, Windows NT, Window 2000, Windows XP, Windows 2003, Linux, Unix (Linux & Unix version requires other installation package. Contact us for information.)
- Memory: at least 64 MB of RAM required. (128MB recommended)
- Hard Disk: 60 MB (including 30 MB for JRE) of available hard-disk space is required
- Display: Super VGA (800x600) or higher-resolution monitor with 256or more colors
- Java Runtime Environment : NetMiner is Java application and requires JRE 1.3 or higher
- Network: NetMiner II Enterprise edition requires Internet-connected computer to support database facilities.
- For printed output, an Windows-supported printer that can print bitmaps

Limitations

- Performance: Network analysis and visualization is highly memory and processor intensive. So performance of NetMiner II depends heavily on the performance of processor and available size of memory on user's computer.
- Number of Variables: No predefined limit to the number of adjacency variables, affiliation variables, categories per affiliation variable, attribute variable.
- Number of Nodes: No predefined limit. But large network size affects functional performance in analyses and visualization, especially Flow Betweenenss, Clique, Community, Lambda Set or Equivalences finding. The number of nodes and edges that NetMiner II can handle is similar with some other network 'visualization-only' software. NetMiner II is not designed simply to visualize network dataset with an automatic layout algorithm – for example, Spring Embedding - and a fixed layout input data, normally geodesic distance matrix, which is the case with most of other network visualization software. Rather, NetMiner is so designed to enable various additional 'exploratory data analysis on the Map Frame, and much more values are computed and stored in memory for each nodes and edges.
- Built-in Matrix Editor: No limit but should be smaller than preset number in Editor of Options.

Survey on Student Experiences of Online Synchronous Tutorials

This survey is carried out as part of my doctoral project on the discourse and student experiences of online synchronous/chat tutorials. The following questions cover your views and experiences of participating in chat tutorials conducted in ICT329-Organisational Informatics offered by Murdoch University. Your comments will contribute greatly to both improving the unit design and research in educational technology.

As you have consented to be a participant in this project, all information given in this survey will be treated as confidential. Your name or other information that might identify you will not be disclosed to the unit tutor or coordinator, nor used in any publication arising from the research. You will receive information on the outcomes of this study at a later stage.

Please answer all questions and complete this survey by 7th November 2005. Thank you!

If you have technical problems submitting the survey, please contact xx (xx@murdoch.edu.au)

Please enter your name and student number below.

Name:

Student ID number:
Your survey will not be accepted without your student ID number.

PART A

1. As a presenter during a tutorial session in this unit, to what extent were the following aspects of the online discussion easy for you? Indicate your responses to the following statements from Strongly Agree to Strongly Disagree.

As a presenter, I found it easy to

	Strongly agree	Agree	Disagree	Strongly disagree
a. keep up with the speed of the discussion	☐	☐	☐	☐
b. manage the discussion to keep it relevant to the topic	☐	☐	☐	☐
c. answer questions from others during the presentation	☐	☐	☐	☐
d. initiate the discussion on the reading(s)	☐	☐	☐	☐
e. explain and justify my views during the presentation	☐	☐	☐	☐
f. communicate my views without face-to-face contact with other students during the discussion	☐	☐	☐	☐

2. When you were not a presenter, as a participant during tutorial sessions for this unit, to what extent were the following aspects of the online discussion easy for you? Indicate your responses to the following statements from Strongly Agree to Strongly Disagree

As a participant, I found it easy to

	Strongly agree	Agree	Disagree	Strongly disagree
a. keep up with the speed of the discussion	☐	☐	☐	☐
b. contribute actively to the discussion	☐	☐	☐	☐
c. explain and justify my views during the discussion	☐	☐	☐	☐
d. communicate my views without face-to-face contact with other students during the discussion	☐	☐	☐	☐

3. How much help was available from your tutor and other students during online tutorials? Indicate your responses to the following statements from Strongly Agree to Strongly Disagree

	Strongly agree	Agree	Disagree	Strongly disagree
a. The tutor clarified issues on content that were raised during the discussion	☐	☐	☐	☐
b. The other students clarified issues on content that were raised during the discussion	☐	☐	☐	☐

4. To what extent did the following factors encourage you to participate during tutorial discussions in this unit? Indicate your responses to the following statements from Strongly Agree to Strongly Disagree.

I was encouraged to participate in the discussion by

	Strongly agree	Agree	Disagree	Strongly disagree
a. the facilitation style of the tutor	☐	☐	☐	☐
b. the facilitation styles of student presenters	☐	☐	☐	☐
c. the assessment of my participation by the tutor	☐	☐	☐	☐
d. the assessment of my participation by other students	☐	☐	☐	☐

5. To what extent do the following statements accurately reflect your overall experience of online tutorials in this unit? Indicate your responses to the following statements from Strongly Agree to Strongly Disagree or Unable to Judge (UJ).

	Strongly agree	Agree	Disagree	Strongly disagree	Unable to judge
a. I had plenty of opportunities to participate in the discussion	☐	☐	☐	☐	☐
b. I was able to make best use of the opportunities available for participation	☐	☐	☐	☐	☐
c. I usually prefer to let the discussion develop before joining in	☐	☐	☐	☐	☐
d. During discussions, I contributed my views even when I saw that others had already posted similar ideas	☐	☐	☐	☐	☐
e. I usually contribute more to the discussion than the others	☐	☐	☐	☐	☐
f. Everyone in the tutorial group contributed about the same amount to the discussion	☐	☐	☐	☐	☐
g. The other students contributed different ideas to the discussion	☐	☐	☐	☐	☐
h. I learned from other students' contributions during the discussion	☐	☐	☐	☐	☐
i. I helped other students learn through my contributions during the discussion	☐	☐	☐	☐	☐

If you were unable to rate any of the above factors (i.e. selected Unable to Judge), why is this so? Please explain below.

6. Were there other factors that encouraged or motivated you to contribute during tutorial discussions in this unit? Please describe them below.

7. Were there other factors that discouraged or inhibited you from contributing during tutorial discussions in this unit? Please describe them below.

8. To what extent are the following factors important to you for online tutorials in this unit?

	Very important	Important	Somewhat important	Not important
a. Opportunity to participate in discussions	☐	☐	☐	☐
b. Discussions are relevant to the unit readings	☐	☐	☐	☐
c. Communication skills in CMC environments are developed	☐	☐	☐	☐
d. Understanding of course content is increased	☐	☐	☐	☐
e. My online learning experience is enhanced with chat tutorials	☐	☐	☐	☐

9. From your experience of online tutorials in this unit, how satisfied are you with each of the given factors?

	Very satisfied	Satisfied	Somewhat satisfied	Not satisfied
a. Opportunity to participate in discussions	☐	☐	☐	☐
b. Discussions are relevant to the unit readings	☐	☐	☐	☐
c. Communication skills in CMC environments are developed	☐	☐	☐	☐
d. Understanding of course content is increased	☐	☐	☐	☐
e. My online learning experience is enhanced with chat tutorials	☐	☐	☐	☐

10. Rank the following factors on online tutorials in order of importance. For each factor, enter your choice of ranking from -

Most Important 5---4---3---2---1 Least Important.

(No ties allowed)

a. Opportunity to participate in discussions ☐

b. Discussions are relevant to the unit readings ☐

c. Communication skills in CMC environments are developed ☐

d. Understanding of course content is increased ☐

e. My online learning experience is enhanced with chat tutorials ☐

11. What were the 1 or 2 specific things in the chat tutorials that affected your understanding of the course topics?

PART B

12. Gender

☐ Male

☐ Female

13. Do you use English as a Second or Foreign Language?

☐ Yes

☐ No

14. With which ethnic group(s) or culture(s) do you identify most?

15. Before attending online tutorials for this unit, how often did you normally use text-based synchronous CMC or chat media (such as Yahoo/Windows Messenger Chat, WebCT Chat, ICQ, etc.) to communicate with other people?

☐ Daily

☐ Weekly

☐ Monthly

☐ Hardly ever*

☐ Never*

*If you indicated in Q. 15 that you Hardly Ever or Never use the chat medium to communicate with others before attending online tutorials for this unit, please answer Q16.
Otherwise, click here to go to Q17.

16. You indicated in Q. 15 that you Hardly Ever or Never use the chat medium to communicate with others before attending online tutorials for this unit. Why is this so? Select all applicable options

- [ ] I didn't have adequate Internet/computer access at home
- [ ] I didn't know how to use Chat
- [ ] I didn't need to use Chat
- [ ] I wasn't comfortable with using Chat
- [ ] I wasn't interested in using Chat
- [ ] Other reasons: (please explain below)

17. Please share any other comments about your online learning experience in this unit ICT329.

Thank you for completing this survey.

Please hit the submit button once only.

Submit | Reset

B.4 Draft Questionnaire (Print Version)

Survey on Student Experiences of Online Synchronous Tutorials

This survey is carried out as part of a doctoral study on the discourse structure and student experiences of online synchronous or chat tutorials. The following questions cover your views and experiences of chat tutorials conducted in the unit *Organisational Informatics* offered by Murdoch University. Your comments will contribute greatly to improving the course and research in the area of educational technology. Please complete this survey and return it by xx June 2005 using the enclosed self-addressed envelop. Thank you!

NAME

PART A: Instructions: Please select **ONE** answer for each question unless otherwise stated.

1. As a **presenter** during a tutorial session in this unit, how did you feel about the following aspects of the online discussion? Rate each aspect from **4** to **1** *(4-Love It, 1-Hate It)* or **UJ** *(Unable to Judge)*.

	Love It 4	Like It 3	Dislike It 2	Hate It 1	UJ*
a. Initiating the discussion on the reading(s)	O	O	O	O	O
b. Explaining and justifying own views during the presentation	O	O	O	O	O
c. Facing questions from others during the presentation	O	O	O	O	O
d. Managing the discussion to keep it relevant to the topic	O	O	O	O	O
e. Keeping up with the speed of the discussion	O	O	O	O	O

*If you were unable to rate any of the given aspects, why is this so? Please explain below.

2. When you are not a presenter, as a **participant** during tutorial sessions for this unit, how did you feel about the following aspects of online discussion? Rate each aspect from **4** to **1** *(4-Love It, 1-Hate It)* or **UJ** *(Unable to Judge)*.

	Love It 4	Like It 3	Dislike It 2	Hate It 1	UJ*
a. Grading of participation in the discussion	O	O	O	O	O
b. Lacking face-to-face contact with other students during the discussion	O	O	O	O	O
c. Keeping up with the speed of the discussion	O	O	O	O	O
d. Contributing actively to the discussion	O	O	O	O	O
e. Explaining and justifying own views during the discussion	O	O	O	O	O

*If you were unable to rate any of the given aspects, why is this so? Please explain below.

3. How much help was available from your tutor and other students during online tutorials? Indicate your responses to the following statements from **4** to **1** (*4 – Strongly Agree, 1 – Strongly Disagree*).

		Strongly Agree 4	Agree 3	Disagree 2	Strongly Disagree 1
a.	The *tutor* clarified issues on content that were raised during the discussion	O	O	O	O
b.	The other *students* clarified issues on content that were raised during the discussion	O	O	O	O
c.	The other *students* contributed different ideas to the discussion	O	O	O	O

4. Do the following statements accurately reflect your overall experience of online tutorials in this unit? Indicate your responses to the following statements from **4** to **1** (*4 – Strongly Agree, 1 – Strongly Disagree*) or **UJ** (*Unable to Judge*).

		Strongly Agree 4	Agree 3	Disagree 2	Strongly Disagree 1	UJ*
a.	I had plenty of opportunities to participate in the discussion	O	O	O	O	O
b.	I was able to make best use of the opportunities available for participation	O	O	O	O	O
c.	I usually prefer to let the discussion develop before joining in	O	O	O	O	O
d.	During discussions, I contributed my views even when I saw that others had already posted similar ideas	O	O	O	O	O
e.	Negotiation and debate were acceptable ways of interacting with the *tutor*	O	O	O	O	O
f.	Negotiation and debate were acceptable ways of interacting with other *students*	O	O	O	O	O
g.	The facilitation style of the *tutor* encouraged me to participate in the discussion	O	O	O	O	O
h.	The facilitation styles of *student presenters* encouraged me to participate in the discussion	O	O	O	O	O

*If you were unable to rate any of the given aspects, why is this so? Please explain below.

5. Were there other factors that **encouraged** you to contribute during tutorial discussions in this unit? Please describe them below.

6. Were there other factors that **inhibited** you from contributing during tutorial discussions in this unit? Please describe them below.

7. To what extent are the following factors important to you for online tutorials in this unit? Rate each factor from **5** to **1** *(5-High Importance, 1-No Importance).*

	IMPORTANCE TO ME				
	High Importance	Important	Some Importance	Low Importance	No Importance
ONLINE TUTORIAL FACTORS	5	4	3	2	1
a. Opportunities for participating in discussions are available	O	O	O	O	O
b. Discussions are relevant to the unit readings	O	O	O	O	O
c. Communication skills in CMC environments are developed with participation in discussions	O	O	O	O	O
d. Understanding of course content is increased with participation in discussions	O	O	O	O	O
e. My online learning experience is enhanced with chat tutorials	O	O	O	O	O

8. From your experience of online tutorials in this unit, how satisfied are you with each of the given factors? Rate each factor from **5** to **1** *(5-Very High, 1-Very Low).*

	SATISFACTION LEVEL WITH EXPERIENCE				
	Very High	High	Medium	Low	Very Low
ONLINE TUTORIAL FACTORS	5	4	3	2	1
a. Opportunities for participating in discussions are available	O	O	O	O	O
b. Discussions are relevant to the unit readings	O	O	O	O	O
c. Communication skills in CMC environments are developed with participation in discussions	O	O	O	O	O
d. Understanding of course content is increased with participation in discussions	O	O	O	O	O
e. My online learning experience is enhanced with chat tutorials	O	O	O	O	O

9. What were the 1 or 2 specific things in the chat tutorials that affected your understanding of the course topics?

PART B: Instructions: Please select **ONE** answer for each question unless otherwise stated.

10. Gender
a.   Male   O
b.   Female   O

11. Do you use English as a Second or Foreign Language?
a.   Yes   O
b.   No   O

12. Before attending online tutorials for this unit, how often did you normally use Chat to communicate with other people?

a.   Daily   O
b.   Weekly   O
c.   Monthly   O
d.   Hardly Ever* O
e.   Never*   O

* If you have selected this option, **go to Q. 13**.

13. You indicated in Q. 12 that you usually *Hardly Ever* or *Never* use Chat to communicate with others before attending online tutorials for this unit. Why is this so? Select all applicable options.

a.   I didn't have adequate Internet/computer access at home   ☐
b.   I didn't know how to use Chat   ☐
c.   I didn't need to use Chat   ☐
d.   I wasn't comfortable with using Chat   ☐
e.   I wasn't interested in using Chat   ☐
f.   Other reasons: (please explain below)   ☐

Thank you for completing this survey.
Please return it by xx June 2005 using the enclosed self-addressed envelop.

B.5 Survey announcement message

Dear xx

We have now reached the final stage of my research project on the discourse and student experiences of online tutorials that involves completing an e-survey on your views and experiences of participating in ICT329 chat tutorials. The e-survey is open on 17 October 2005 (Monday) at https://www.tlc.murdoch.edu.au/survey--- . You will probably need about 20 minutes to complete the questionnaire. All information given in this survey will be treated as confidential. Your name or other information that might identify you will not be disclosed to the unit tutor or coordinator, nor used in any publication arising from the research.

As a token of appreciation for consenting to participate in this project, I will be giving a A$100 shopping voucher to one student randomly selected from your tutorial group at the end of the semester. If you have any questions, please contact me (Hwee Ling, Lim) at ---@murdoch.edu.au, 0423-- or Dr Sudweeks at ---@murdoch.edu.au, 9360--.

Thank you.
Hwee Ling, LIM

APPENDIX C

RESULTS FROM DATA ANALYSIS

TABLE OF CONTENTS

C.1.1. Frequency of Out-Ties by G1 Participants

G1		S1-E1	S1-E2	S2-E1	S2-E2	S3-E1	S3-E2	S4-E1	S4-E2	S5-E1	S5-E2	S6-E1	S6-E2	S7-E1	S7-E2	S8-E1	S8-E2	S9-E1	S9-E2	S10-E1	S10-E2	S11-E1	S11-E2	Total
r1	Derek	x	x	19	12	5	6	0	76	1	279	16	6	7	17	x	x	x	x	x	x	x	x	444
r2	Max	243	278	16	34	8	8	0	16	4	12	4	2	2	1	10	29	x	x	x	1	6	3	677
r3	Alvin	44	6	11	11	10	21	50	49	2	93	24	21	28	9	15	13	10	1	3	444	23	24	912
r4	Cliff	2	0	7	5	x	x	1	78	3	22	9	5	448	180	7	18	6	0	16	1	12	11	831
r5	Colin	2	0	2	1	2	0	2	1	659	6	x	x	0	0	x	x	3	0	1	0	x	x	679
r6	Ted	7	4	50	8	7	16	x	x	2	0	0	557	24	5	5	1	5	1	x	x	x	x	692
r7	Sam	5	3	10	9	8	2	2	6	3	4	10	2	4	0	5	1	4	0	1	0	3	183	265
r8	Diane	9	5	824	667	x	11	3	25	1	0	9	7	x	x	7	2	3	0	6	4	x	x	1583
r9	James	x	x	5	3	15	2	x	4	2	5	305	6	x	x	x	x	3	1	1	2	x	x	354
r10	Alan	2	0	3	0	6	3	0	1	2	3	2	0	0	0	3	1	2	4	163	0	2	3	200
r11	Jason	x	x	x	x	x	x	2	130	4	16	x	x	x	11	x	x	4	1	1	1	194	0	364
r12	Scott	2	0	5	7	4	5	217	213	1	0	4	0	x	x	x	x	1	0	x	x	x	x	459
r13	Barry	21	7	7	29	0	0	x	x	x	0	x	x	9	8	237	137	x	0	x	0	x	x	456
r14	Tony	5	4	5	60	21	30	1	8	3	2	19	23	1	3	x	x	679	541	7	5	x	x	1417
r15	Wendy	38	0	13	15	339	219	4	16	6	4	9	19	x	x	11	52	8	1	5	6	8	12	785
r16	Rachel	0	1	2	4	1	3	0	2	0	5	0	0	0	1	6	1	2	28	37	0	0	0	93
	Total	380	308	979	865	426	326	282	625	693	451	411	648	523	235	306	255	730	578	242	464	248	236	**10211**

Note: x denotes absent participant.

APPENDIX C

324

C.1.2. Frequency of In-Ties by G1 Participants

G1		S1-E1	S1-E2	S2-E1	S2-E2	S3-E1	S3-E2	S4-E1	S4-E2	S5-E1	S5-E2	S6-E1	S6-E2	S7-E1	S7-E2	S8-E1	S8-E2	S9-E1	S9-E2	S10-E1	S10-E2	S11-E1	S11-E2	Total
n1	Derek	x	x	67	62	30	28	22	68	46	74	39	55	54	26	x	x	x	x	x	x	x	x	571
n2	Max	23	23	63	66	32	25	22	40	50	29	27	48	46	17	35	27	x	x	17	36	33	28	687
n3	Alvin	34	23	67	57	33	34	24	50	46	34	32	57	50	20	31	34	60	47	17	20	32	31	833
n4	Cliff	28	23	62	64	x	x	22	47	47	27	29	51	52	28	28	26	61	47	22	37	39	39	779
n5	Colin	28	23	64	52	29	20	22	40	33	27	x	x	45	17	x	x	58	47	17	36	x	x	558
n6	Ted	34	24	65	56	38	29	x	x	47	25	26	41	50	19	25	23	56	47	x	x	x	x	605
n7	Sam	29	24	63	57	31	20	23	48	46	26	31	48	46	17	25	23	56	47	17	36	29	27	769
n8	Diane	30	24	74	62	x	21	22	41	46	25	26	50	x	x	27	23	56	47	21	38	x	x	633
n9	James	x	x	65	52	31	20	x	47	46	25	62	54	x	x	x	x	56	47	17	37	x	x	559
n10	Alan	29	23	62	52	30	22	22	39	47	26	26	48	45	17	25	23	57	52	25	36	29	27	762
n11	Jason	x	x	x	x	x	x	24	45	49	31	x	x	x	19	x	x	59	47	17	37	27	26	381
n12	Scott	27	23	66	53	30	20	8	41	46	25	27	48	x	x	x	x	56	47	x	x	x	x	517
n13	Barry	30	25	64	65	29	20	x	x	x	x	x	x	45	18	56	30	x	x	17	36	x	x	435
n14	Tony	27	26	67	60	35	19	23	40	48	25	31	52	45	20	x	x	42	6	20	38	x	x	624
n15	Wendy	34	23	67	55	49	28	26	40	50	26	29	48	x	x	29	23	57	48	20	41	30	32	755
n16	Rachel	27	24	63	52	29	20	22	39	46	26	26	48	45	17	25	23	56	49	15	36	29	26	743
	Total	380	308	979	865	426	326	282	625	693	451	411	648	523	235	306	255	730	578	242	464	248	236	10211

Note: x denotes absent participant.

C.1.3. Frequency of Out-Ties by G4 Participants

	G4	S1-E1	S1-E2	S2-E1	S2-E2	S3-E1	S3-E2	S4-E1	S4-E2	S5-E1	S5-E2	S6-E1	S6-E2	S7-E1	S7-E2	S8-E1	S8-E2	S9-E1	S9-E2	S10-E1	S10-E2	S11-E1	S11-E2	Total
n1	Evan	144	101	6	85	24	6	x	x	x	x	x	x	89	8	x	x	54	7	1	20	22	73	640
n2	Bill	2	4	87	191	7	2	4	2	1	23	x	x	17	0	x	x	x	x	x	0	11	0	351
n3	Mike	x	x	x	x	16	27	27	11	34	33	42	17	81	4	3	3	3	5	73	112	7	28	526
n4	Eric	26	13	10	31	258	137	14	27	18	25	33	14	25	5	21	21	17	12	15	0	50	23	795
n5	Karl	x	x	x	x	x	x	13	12	14	8	24	7	210	28	x	x	x	x	x	x	6	12	334
n6	Jack	21	35	9	48	47	11	111	166	14	42	56	8	36	0	72	39	33	13	0	22	68	41	892
n7	Ian	22	6	10	43	x	x	13	29	33	47	40	71	27	3	29	21	13	6	22	1	36	44	732
n8	Pete	15	20	x	x	20	6	19	53	x	x	266	1	x	x	28	15	115	75	x	0	78	104	641
n9	Robin	17	16	9	21	11	7	6	8	124	62	x	53	x	x	31	13	17	8	10	0	25	23	409
n10	Lim	x	x	7	20	8	5	17	18	30	26	60	15	23	2	31	15	17	11	8	0	23	35	365
n11	Fay	34	62	32	224	67	48	168	145	59	166	45	70	118	14	133	152	51	123	43	1	78	72	1905
	Total	281	257	170	663	458	249	392	471	327	432	566	256	626	64	322	279	320	260	115	217	410	455	7590

Note: x denotes absent participant.

C.1.4. Frequency of In-Ties by G4 Participants

	G4	S1-E1	S1-E2	S2-E1	S2-E2	S3-E1	S3-E2	S4-E1	S4-E2	S5-E1	S5-E2	S6-E1	S6-E2	S7-E1	S7-E2	S8-E1	S8-E2	S9-E1	S9-E2	S10-E1	S10-E2	S11-E1	S11-E2	Total
n1	Evan	58	28	19	85	57	23	x	x	x	x	x	x	73	8	x	x	32	24	16	21	26	31	501
n2	Bill	21	27	39	84	43	31	34	35	29	44	x	x	63	5	x	x	x	x	x	14	23	33	525
n3	Mike	x	x	x	x	56	37	40	41	37	47	61	24	66	8	29	27	23	28	3	41	33	34	635
n4	Eric	27	30	15	76	42	16	41	32	32	47	64	23	68	5	40	26	29	26	16	18	28	37	745
n5	Karl	x	x	x	x	x	x	40	34	34	40	61	23	76	12	x	x	x	x	x	x	27	39	387
n6	Jack	37	30	18	94	50	33	58	87	32	55	71	22	75	5	52	38	39	26	16	19	55	42	954
n7	Ian	27	30	17	75	x	x	40	40	39	48	79	32	65	6	33	43	23	24	16	16	32	39	718
n8	Pete	36	29	x	x	61	29	56	x	x	x	61	38	x	x	37	36	44	x	x	15	51	56	621
n9	Robin	31	38	15	75	45	26	37	37	35	40	38	22	69	5	33	27	36	26	16	15	27	36	614
n10	Lim	x	x	14	75	49	27	39	48	48	43	84	30	69	5	36	42	41	35	16	26	44	50	807
n11	Fay	44	45	33	99	55	27	55	41	41	68	85	42	71	10	62	40	44	27	16	47	64	58	1083
	Total	281	257	170	663	458	249	392	471	327	432	566	256	626	64	322	279	320	260	115	217	410	455	7590

Note: x denotes absent participant.

APPENDIX C

C.2.1. Frequency of (l) by G1 Participants

G1	S1-E1	S1-E2	S2-E1	S2-E2	S3-E1	S3-E2	S4-E1	S4-E2	S5-E1	S5-E2	S6-E1	S6-E2	S7-E1	S7-E2	S8-E1	S8-E2	S9-E1	S9-E2	S10-E1	S10-E2	S11-E1	S11-E2	Total
1 Derek	0	0	1	0	0	0	0	3	0	10	1	0	0	1	0	0	0	0	0	0	0	0	16
2 Max	18	22	1	2	0	1	0	1	0	0	0	0	0	0	0	3	0	0	0	0	0	0	48
3 Alvin	4	0	0	0	0	1	4	2	0	5	0	1	0	0	0	0	0	0	35	0	2	2	56
4 Cliff	0	0	0	0	0	0	0	5	0	1	0	0	42	16	0	1	0	0	0	1	1	0	67
5 Colin	0	0	0	0	0	0	0	0	46	0	0	0	0	0	0	0	0	0	0	0	0	0	46
6 Ted	0	0	1	0	1	0	0	0	0	0	0	45	0	0	0	0	0	0	0	0	0	0	47
7 Sam	0	0	0	0	0	0	0	0	0	0	0	0	0	0	0	0	0	0	0	0	22	0	22
8 Diane	0	0	55	44	0	0	0	1	0	0	0	0	0	0	0	0	0	0	0	0	0	0	100
9 James	0	0	0	0	0	0	0	0	0	0	24	0	0	0	0	0	0	0	0	0	0	0	24
10 Alan	0	0	0	0	0	0	0	0	0	0	0	0	0	0	0	0	0	0	0	13	0	0	13
11 Jason	0	0	0	0	0	19	0	9	0	0	0	2	0	0	0	5	0	0	0	0	0	0	35
12 Scott	0	0	0	0	0	0	17	15	0	0	0	0	0	0	0	0	0	0	0	0	0	0	32
13 Barry	1	0	0	0	0	0	0	0	0	0	0	0	0	0	25	13	0	0	0	0	0	0	39
14 Tony	0	0	2	4	1	0	0	0	0	0	0	0	0	0	0	0	54	44	0	0	4	0	109
15 Wendy	2	0	0	0	24	0	0	0	0	0	0	0	0	0	0	0	0	0	0	0	0	22	48
16 Rachel	0	0	0	0	0	0	0	0	0	1	0	0	0	0	0	0	0	2	0	2	0	0	5
Total	25	22	60	50	26	21	21	36	46	17	25	48	42	17	25	22	54	46	35	16	29	24	707

APPENDIX C

C.2.2. Frequency of (RI) by G1 Participants

G1	S1-E1	S1-E2	S2-E1	S2-E2	S3-E1	S3-E2	S4-E1	S4-E2	S5-E1	S5-E2	S6-E1	S6-E2	S7-E1	S7-E2	S8-E1	S8-E2	S9-E1	S9-E2	S10-E1	S10-E2	S11-E1	S11-E2	Total
1 Derek	0	0	0	2	0	1	0	3	0	14	1	0	2	1	0	0	0	0	0	0	0	0	24
2 Max	2	1	0	1	1	1	0	0	0	1	0	0	0	0	2	0	0	0	0	0	0	0	9
3 Alvin	1	2	1	2	0	2	0	0	0	0	1	0	3	2	0	1	0	0	2	0	1	0	18
4 Cliff	0	0	0	0	0	0	1	0	1	0	1	0	2	0	0	2	0	0	0	0	0	4	11
5 Colin	0	0	0	0	0	0	0	0	2	0	0	0	0	0	0	0	0	0	0	0	0	0	2
6 Ted	1	0	2	3	1	0	0	0	0	0	0	0	1	1	0	0	0	0	0	0	0	0	9
7 Sam	0	0	1	0	1	0	0	0	0	0	0	0	0	0	0	0	0	0	0	0	0	0	2
8 Diane	0	0	3	1	0	1	0	2	0	0	0	0	0	0	1	0	1	1	0	0	0	0	10
9 James	0	0	1	0	0	0	0	1	0	0	4	0	0	0	0	0	1	0	0	0	0	0	7
10 Alan	0	0	0	0	1	0	0	0	0	0	0	0	0	0	0	0	0	0	0	1	0	0	2
11 Jason	0	0	0	0	0	0	0	2	1	0	0	0	0	0	0	0	2	0	0	0	2	0	7
12 Scott	0	0	0	0	0	0	0	0	0	0	0	0	0	0	0	0	0	0	0	0	0	0	0
13 Barry	1	2	0	2	0	0	0	0	0	0	0	0	0	0	5	1	0	0	0	0	0	0	11
14 Tony	0	1	2	0	0	0	0	0	0	0	1	0	0	0	0	0	4	0	2	0	0	0	10
15 Wendy	2	0	2	3	2	0	2	3	0	1	0	0	0	0	1	0	0	1	2	0	0	0	19
16 Rachel	0	0	1	0	0	0	0	0	0	0	0	0	0	0	0	0	0	0	2	1	0	0	4
Total	7	6	13	14	6	5	3	11	4	16	8	0	8	4	9	4	8	2	8	2	3	4	145

C.2.3. Frequency of (R) by G1 Participants

G1	S1-E1	S1-E2	S2-E1	S2-E2	S3-E1	S3-E2	S4-E1	S4-E2	S5-E1	S5-E2	S6-E1	S6-E2	S7-E1	S7-E2	S8-E1	S8-E2	S9-E1	S9-E2	S10-E1	S10-E2	S11-E1	S11-E2	Total
1 Derek	0	0	4	9	4	5	0	10	0	3	3	6	5	5	0	0	0	0	0	0	0	0	54
2 Max	0	1	1	3	5	4	0	2	3	8	2	2	1	1	6	2	0	0	1	0	5	2	49
3 Alvin	5	2	4	5	8	4	2	19	1	19	19	8	11	6	9	7	6	1	1	5	6	8	156
4 Cliff	2	0	4	5	0	0	0	9	0	7	8	5	3	3	2	4	4	0	3	1	5	7	72
5 Colin	2	0	1	1	1	0	1	0	8	5	0	0	0	0	0	0	2	0	0	0	0	0	21
6 Ted	6	4	5	3	5	2	0	0	1	0	0	7	18	2	0	0	1	1	0	0	0	0	55
7 Sam	5	1	4	6	5	1	1	5	1	2	8	0	3	0	0	1	0	0	1	0	2	14	60
8 Diane	5	4	11	21	0	4	1	3	1	0	5	5	0	0	0	0	1	0	3	4	0	0	68
9 James	0	0	3	3	2	1	0	2	0	3	11	6	0	0	0	0	0	1	0	1	0	0	33
10 Alan	2	0	2	0	4	2	0	0	1	1	2	0	0	0	0	0	1	4	3	0	2	3	27
11 Jason	0	0	0	0	0	0	2	10	1	14	0	0	0	11	0	0	2	0	0	1	11	0	52
12 Scott	2	0	2	6	2	3	1	2	0	0	4	0	0	0	0	0	0	0	0	0	0	0	22
13 Barry	2	3	1	6	0	0	0	0	0	0	0	0	7	6	2	5	0	0	0	0	0	0	32
14 Tony	4	3	3	4	7	4	1	6	2	1	4	7	1	2	8	0	5	2	3	2	0	0	61
15 Wendy	0	0	8	7	11	10	2	7	6	0	7	3	0	0	0	7	6	1	0	5	3	9	100
16 Rachel	0	1	0	0	0	0	0	0	0	0	0	0	0	0	0	0	1	1	1	0	0	0	4
Total	35	19	53	79	54	40	11	75	25	63	73	49	49	36	27	26	29	11	15	20	34	43	866

C.2.4. Frequency of (RC) by G1 Participants

G1	S1-E1	S1-E2	S2-E1	S2-E2	S3-E1	S3-E2	S4-E1	S4-E2	S5-E1	S5-E2	S6-E1	S6-E2	S7-E1	S7-E2	S8-E1	S8-E2	S9-E1	S9-E2	S10-E1	S10-E2	S11-E1	S11-E2	Total
1 Derek	0	0	1	1	1	0	0	0	1	5	0	0	0	0	0	0	0	0	0	0	0	0	9
2 Max	3	1	1	2	2	2	0	1	1	3	2	0	1	0	2	0	0	0	0	0	1	1	23
3 Alvin	1	2	6	4	2	2	0	4	1	4	4	1	5	1	6	5	4	0	2	3	2	2	61
4 Cliff	0	0	3	0	0	0	0	4	2	1	0	0	3	1	5	3	2	0	1	0	0	0	25
5 Colin	0	0	1	0	1	0	1	1	5	1	0	0	0	0	0	0	1	1	0	0	0	0	12
6 Ted	0	0	1	2	1	1	0	0	1	0	0	10	0	0	5	1	4	0	0	0	0	0	33
7 Sam	0	2	5	3	2	1	1	1	2	2	2	2	5	2	5	0	4	0	0	0	0	3	37
8 Diane	4	1	13	16	0	6	2	7	0	0	4	2	1	0	6	2	1	0	2	0	1	3	66
9 James	0	0	1	0	1	1	0	1	2	2	3	0	0	0	0	0	2	0	1	1	0	0	15
10 Alan	0	0	1	0	1	0	0	1	1	2	0	0	0	0	3	1	1	0	3	0	0	0	15
11 Jason	0	0	0	0	0	0	0	1	2	2	0	0	0	0	0	0	0	1	0	0	0	0	6
12 Scott	0	0	3	1	2	0	1	4	1	0	0	0	0	0	0	0	1	0	0	0	0	0	15
13 Barry	6	2	6	8	0	2	0	0	0	0	0	0	2	2	5	6	0	0	0	0	0	0	38
14 Tony	1	0	0	0	2	0	0	2	1	1	2	4	0	1	0	0	1	0	2	3	0	0	20
15 Wendy	1	0	3	5	6	1	0	6	0	3	2	4	0	0	4	0	2	0	3	1	4	3	48
16 Rachel	0	0	1	4	1	3	0	2	0	4	0	0	0	1	4	1	1	1	0	0	0	0	23
Total	16	8	46	46	22	20	5	35	20	30	19	23	17	8	45	19	24	2	16	8	8	9	446

APPENDIX C

C.2.5. Frequency of (I) by G4 Participants

G4	S1-E1	S1-E2	S2-E1	S2-E2	S3-E1	S3-E2	S4-E1	S4-E2	S5-E1	S5-E2	S6-E1	S6-E2	S7-E1	S7-E2	S8-E1	S8-E2	S9-E1	S9-E2	S10-E1	S10-E2	S11-E1	S11-E2	Total
1 Evan	16	12	0	3	0	0	0	0	0	0	0	0	7	1	0	0	4	0	0	2	1	6	53
2 Bill	0	0	10	24	0	0	0	0	0	2	0	0	1	0	0	0	0	0	0	0	1	0	38
3 Mike	0	0	0	0	1	0	2	0	3	2	4	1	9	0	0	0	0	0	15	8	0	2	47
4 Eric	0	0	0	0	30	12	0	0	0	1	0	0	0	0	0	0	0	0	0	0	3	1	47
5 Karl	0	0	0	0	0	0	0	0	0	0	0	0	15	4	0	0	0	0	0	0	0	0	19
6 Jack	0	4	0	2	1	0	7	13	1	4	3	0	2	0	7	3	2	0	0	1	4	3	57
7 Ian	0	0	0	1	0	0	0	1	2	3	28	6	0	0	1	0	0	0	0	0	1	3	46
8 Pete	0	2	0	0	0	0	1	1	0	0	2	5	0	0	1	0	12	9	0	0	5	9	47
9 Robin	0	1	0	0	0	0	0	0	13	6	0	0	0	0	0	0	0	0	0	0	1	0	23
10 Lim	0	0	0	1	0	0	1	1	3	2	5	1	1	0	2	1	1	1	0	1	1	3	24
11 Fay	5	6	1	24	7	4	15	12	5	16	3	8	13	1	15	18	1	15	0	4	5	6	184
Total	21	25	11	55	40	16	26	28	27	36	45	21	48	6	27	22	20	24	15	16	22	34	585

C.2.6. Frequency of (RI) by G4 Participants

G4	S1-E1	S1-E2	S2-E1	S2-E2	S3-E1	S3-E2	S4-E1	S4-E2	S5-E1	S5-E2	S6-E1	S6-E2	S7-E1	S7-E2	S8-E1	S8-E2	S9-E1	S9-E2	S10-E1	S10-E2	S11-E1	S11-E2	Total
1 Evan	5	3	0	10	0	0	0	0	0	0	0	0	3	0	0	0	0	1	2	0	0	1	25
2 Bill	0	0	3	6	1	0	0	0	0	0	0	0	0	0	0	0	0	0	0	0	0	0	10
3 Mike	0	0	0	0	0	1	1	1	1	0	2	0	2	0	0	0	1	1	0	1	1	0	10
4 Eric	2	0	0	3	4	6	0	0	0	2	4	1	3	0	1	2	2	2	3	0	0	0	35
5 Karl	0	0	0	0	0	0	0	0	0	1	2	0	8	1	0	0	0	0	0	0	0	0	12
6 Jack	5	2	0	1	3	0	3	7	2	2	3	0	3	0	4	5	6	3	2	0	13	5	69
7 Ian	2	0	0	0	0	0	1	1	1	2	9	0	2	0	0	3	1	0	0	2	4	3	31
8 Pete	0	1	0	0	2	1	1	5	0	0	2	1	0	0	1	2	10	0	0	0	4	3	33
9 Robin	1	1	0	0	2	0	0	0	1	0	0	0	0	0	1	0	3	1	0	1	3	1	14
10 Lim	0	0	0	4	3	1	1	0	2	2	5	1	2	1	1	2	3	0	0	3	4	2	37
11 Fay	3	1	3	8	6	2	2	6	3	5	2	1	1	1	5	2	4	8	0	1	4	3	64
Total	18	8	6	33	21	11	8	20	10	14	29	4	24	3	13	16	29	8	0	14	33	18	340

APPENDIX C

C.2.7. Frequency of (R) by G4 Participants

G4	S1-E1	S1-E2	S2-E1	S2-E2	S3-E1	S3-E2	S4-E1	S4-E2	S5-E1	S5-E2	S6-E1	S6-E2	S7-E1	S7-E2	S8-E1	S8-E2	S9-E1	S9-E2	S10-E1	S10-E2	S11-E1	S11-E2	Total
1 Evan	14	5	6	16	15	6	0	0	0	0	0	0	21	0	0	0	8	6	1	9	9	12	128
2 Bill	1	2	5	14	6	2	4	1	0	3	0	0	6	0	0	0	0	0	0	0	1	0	45
3 Mike	0	0	0	0	8	10	8	10	6	16	5	8	7	4	3	3	3	4	1	8	6	8	118
4 Eric	23	11	8	23	9	5	12	17	10	13	19	8	13	5	14	7	13	11	0	11	18	11	261
5 Karl	0	0	0	0	0	0	10	7	11	4	13	5	14	1	0	0	0	0	0	0	5	10	80
6 Jack	16	4	9	24	19	10	12	13	1	8	22	7	14	0	15	10	7	8	0	11	12	6	228
7 Ian	18	6	9	27	0	0	11	15	13	17	22	13	20	3	14	11	6	4	1	7	19	11	247
8 Pete	15	4	0	0	18	4	8	12	0	0	19	11	0	0	17	12	7	3	0	0	5	11	146
9 Robin	15	4	8	17	6	5	5	4	9	6	0	1	0	0	17	9	9	6	0	5	9	11	146
10 Lim	0	0	7	8	4	3	6	6	2	7	13	6	14	1	1	6	5	10	0	10	13	11	133
11 Fay	6	11	9	22	6	6	14	20	7	12	15	3	17	5	16	10	28	2	0	15	22	6	252
Total	108	47	61	151	91	51	90	105	59	86	128	62	126	19	97	68	86	54	3	76	119	97	1784

C.2.8. Frequency of (RC) by G4 Participants

G4	S1-E1	S1-E2	S2-E1	S2-E2	S3-E1	S3-E2	S4-E1	S4-E2	S5-E1	S5-E2	S6-E1	S6-E2	S7-E1	S7-E2	S8-E1	S8-E2	S9-E1	S9-E2	S10-E1	S10-E2	S11-E1	S11-E2	Total
1 Evan	0	3	0	2	1	0	0	0	0	0	0	0	2	0	0	0	0	0	0	0	3	0	11
2 Bill	1	2	3	3	0	0	0	1	1	4	0	0	3	0	0	0	0	0	0	0	0	0	18
3 Mike	0	0	0	0	0	0	0	0	1	0	1	1	0	0	0	0	0	0	1	0	0	0	4
4 Eric	2	2	2	5	5	4	2	10	8	2	4	5	9	0	7	6	2	1	0	1	2	2	81
5 Karl	0	0	0	0	0	0	3	5	3	3	9	2	6	1	0	0	0	0	0	0	1	2	35
6 Jack	0	1	0	3	3	1	1	4	3	0	4	1	3	0	4	3	4	2	0	1	3	0	41
7 Ian	2	0	1	8	0	0	2	4	3	4	9	3	5	0	7	7	6	2	0	3	3	0	69
8 Pete	0	1	0	0	0	1	1	3	0	0	5	1	0	0	3	1	2	0	0	0	1	0	19
9 Robin	1	4	1	4	3	2	1	4	3	8	0	0	0	0	7	4	4	2	0	4	3	1	56
10 Lim	0	0	0	1	1	1	1	3	2	1	1	0	0	0	1	0	2	1	0	1	2	1	19
11 Fay	2	2	1	6	5	1	1	3	2	5	1	2	3	0	4	2	4	0	1	2	2	3	52
Total	8	15	8	32	18	10	12	37	26	27	34	15	31	1	33	23	24	8	1	13	20	9	405

APPENDIX C

C.3.1. Frequency of I-[INF] by G1 Participants

G1	S1-E1	S1-E2	S2-E1	S2-E2	S3-E1	S3-E2	S4-E1	S4-E2	S5-E1	S5-E2	S6-E1	S6-E2	S7-E1	S7-E2	S8-E1	S8-E2	S9-E1	S9-E2	S10-E1	S10-E2	S11-E1	S11-E2	Total
1 Derek	0	0	1	0	0	0	0	3	0	5	1	0	0	0	0	0	0	0	0	0	0	0	10
2 Max	16	18	1	1	0	0	0	1	0	0	0	0	0	0	0	3	0	0	0	0	0	0	40
3 Alvin	1	0	0	0	0	0	4	2	0	5	0	1	0	0	0	0	0	0	0	29	1	0	43
4 Cliff	0	0	0	0	0	0	0	4	0	1	0	0	30	11	0	1	0	0	1	0	1	0	49
5 Colin	0	0	0	0	0	0	0	0	39	0	0	0	0	0	0	0	0	0	0	0	0	0	39
6 Ted	0	0	1	0	0	0	0	0	0	0	0	39	0	0	0	0	0	0	0	0	0	0	40
7 Sam	0	0	0	0	0	0	0	0	0	0	0	0	0	0	0	0	0	0	0	0	0	16	16
8 Diane	0	0	42	33	0	0	0	1	0	0	0	0	0	0	0	0	0	0	0	0	0	0	76
9 James	0	0	0	0	1	0	0	0	0	0	16	0	0	0	0	0	0	0	0	0	0	0	17
10 Alan	0	0	0	0	0	0	0	0	0	0	0	0	0	0	0	0	0	0	7	0	0	0	7
11 Jason	0	0	0	0	0	0	0	8	0	0	0	0	0	0	0	0	0	0	0	0	22	0	30
12 Scott	0	0	0	0	0	0	15	13	0	0	0	0	0	0	0	0	0	0	0	0	0	0	28
13 Barry	0	0	0	0	0	0	0	0	0	0	0	0	0	0	18	11	0	0	0	0	0	0	29
14 Tony	0	0	2	2	1	2	0	0	0	0	0	1	0	0	0	0	42	42	0	0	0	0	92
15 Wendy	1	0	0	0	15	12	0	0	0	0	0	1	0	0	0	5	0	0	0	0	0	0	34
16 Rachel	0	0	0	0	0	0	0	0	0	0	0	0	0	0	0	0	0	0	0	0	0	0	0
Total	18	18	47	36	17	14	19	32	39	11	17	42	30	11	18	20	42	42	8	29	24	16	550

C.3.2. Frequency of I-[INQ] by G1 Participants

G1	S1-E1	S1-E2	S2-E1	S2-E2	S3-E1	S3-E2	S4-E1	S4-E2	S5-E1	S5-E2	S6-E1	S6-E2	S7-E1	S7-E2	S8-E1	S8-E2	S9-E1	S9-E2	S10-E1	S10-E2	S11-E1	S11-E2	Total
1 Derek	0	0	0	0	0	0	0	0	0	8	0	0	0	0	0	0	0	0	0	0	0	0	8
2 Max	2	4	0	0	0	1	0	0	0	0	0	0	0	0	0	0	0	0	0	0	0	0	7
3 Alvin	3	0	0	0	0	1	0	1	0	0	0	0	0	0	0	0	0	0	6	0	1	2	14
4 Cliff	0	0	0	0	0	0	0	0	0	0	0	0	12	5	0	0	0	0	0	0	0	0	17
5 Colin	0	0	0	0	0	0	0	0	6	0	0	0	0	0	0	0	0	0	0	0	0	0	6
6 Ted	0	0	0	0	0	1	0	0	0	0	0	6	0	0	0	0	0	0	0	0	0	0	7
7 Sam	0	0	0	0	0	0	0	0	0	0	0	0	0	0	0	0	0	0	0	0	0	6	6
8 Diane	0	0	5	5	0	0	0	0	0	0	0	0	0	0	0	0	0	0	0	0	0	0	10
9 James	0	0	0	0	0	0	0	0	0	0	10	0	0	0	0	0	0	0	0	0	0	0	10
10 Alan	0	0	0	0	0	0	0	0	0	0	0	0	0	0	0	0	0	0	0	6	0	0	6
11 Jason	0	0	0	0	0	0	0	1	0	0	0	0	0	0	0	0	0	0	0	0	4	0	5
12 Scott	0	0	0	0	0	0	2	3	0	0	0	0	0	0	0	0	0	0	0	0	0	0	5
13 Barry	1	0	0	0	0	0	0	0	0	0	0	0	0	0	7	2	0	0	0	0	0	0	10
14 Tony	0	0	0	1	0	0	0	0	0	0	1	0	0	0	0	0	12	2	0	0	0	0	16
15 Wendy	1	0	0	0	9	4	0	0	0	0	0	0	0	0	0	0	0	0	0	0	0	0	14
16 Rachel	0	0	0	0	0	0	0	0	0	1	0	0	0	0	0	0	0	2	2	0	0	0	5
Total	7	4	5	6	9	7	2	5	6	9	11	6	12	5	7	2	12	4	8	6	5	8	146

C.3.3. Frequency of (I-JUS) by G1 Participants

G1	S1-E1	S1-E2	S2-E1	S2-E2	S3-E1	S3-E2	S4-E1	S4-E2	S5-E1	S5-E2	S6-E1	S6-E2	S7-E1	S7-E2	S8-E1	S8-E2	S9-E1	S9-E2	S10-E1	S10-E2	S11-E1	S11-E2	Total
1 Derek	0	0	0	0	0	0	0	0	0	0	0	0	0	0	0	0	0	0	0	0	0	0	0
2 Max	0	0	0	0	0	0	0	0	0	0	0	0	0	0	0	0	0	0	0	0	0	0	0
3 Alvin	0	0	0	0	0	0	0	0	0	0	0	0	0	0	0	0	0	0	0	0	0	0	0
4 Cliff	0	0	0	0	0	0	0	2	0	0	0	0	0	0	0	0	0	0	0	0	0	0	2
5 Colin	0	0	0	0	0	0	0	0	0	0	0	0	0	0	0	0	0	0	0	0	0	0	0
6 Ted	0	0	0	0	0	0	0	0	0	0	0	0	0	0	0	0	0	0	0	0	0	0	0
7 Sam	0	0	0	0	0	0	0	0	0	0	0	0	0	0	0	0	0	0	0	0	0	0	0
8 Diane	0	0	0	4	0	0	0	0	0	0	0	0	0	0	0	0	0	0	0	0	0	0	4
9 James	0	0	0	0	0	0	0	0	0	0	0	0	0	0	0	0	0	0	0	0	0	0	0
10 Alan	0	0	0	0	0	0	0	0	0	0	0	0	0	0	0	0	0	0	0	0	0	0	0
11 Jason	0	0	0	0	0	0	0	0	0	0	0	0	0	0	0	0	0	0	0	0	0	0	0
12 Scott	0	0	0	0	0	0	0	0	0	0	0	0	0	0	0	0	0	0	0	0	0	0	0
13 Barry	0	0	0	0	0	0	0	0	0	0	0	0	0	0	0	0	0	0	0	0	0	0	0
14 Tony	0	0	0	0	0	0	0	0	0	0	0	0	0	0	0	0	0	0	0	0	0	0	0
15 Wendy	0	0	0	0	0	0	0	0	0	0	0	0	0	0	0	0	0	0	0	0	0	0	0
16 Rachel	0	0	0	0	0	0	0	0	0	0	0	0	0	0	0	0	0	0	0	0	0	0	0
Total	0	0	0	4	0	0	0	2	0	0	0	0	0	0	0	0	0	0	0	0	0	0	6

C.3.4. Frequency of I-(REA) by G1 Participants

G1	S1-E1	S1-E2	S2-E1	S2-E2	S3-E1	S3-E2	S4-E1	S4-E2	S5-E1	S5-E2	S6-E1	S6-E2	S7-E1	S7-E2	S8-E1	S8-E2	S9-E1	S9-E2	S10-E1	S10-E2	S11-E1	S11-E2	Total
1 Derek	0	0	0	0	0	0	0	0	0	0	0	0	0	0	0	0	0	0	0	0	0	0	1
2 Max	0	0	0	0	0	0	0	0	0	0	0	0	0	1	0	0	0	0	0	0	0	0	1
3 Alvin	0	0	0	0	0	0	0	0	0	0	0	0	0	0	0	0	0	0	0	0	0	0	0
4 Cliff	0	0	0	0	0	0	0	0	0	0	0	0	0	0	0	0	0	0	0	0	0	0	0
5 Colin	0	0	0	0	0	0	0	0	1	0	0	0	0	0	0	0	0	0	0	0	0	0	1
6 Ted	0	0	0	0	0	0	0	0	0	0	0	0	0	0	0	0	0	0	0	0	0	0	0
7 Sam	0	0	0	0	0	0	0	0	0	0	0	0	0	0	0	0	0	0	0	0	0	0	0
8 Diane	0	0	4	6	0	0	0	0	0	0	0	0	0	0	0	0	0	0	0	0	0	0	10
9 James	0	0	0	0	0	0	0	0	0	0	0	0	0	0	0	0	0	0	0	0	0	0	0
10 Alan	0	0	0	0	0	0	0	0	0	0	0	0	0	0	0	0	0	0	0	0	0	0	0
11 Jason	0	0	0	0	0	0	0	0	0	0	0	0	0	0	0	0	0	0	0	0	0	0	0
12 Scott	0	0	0	0	0	0	0	0	0	0	0	0	0	0	0	0	0	0	0	0	0	0	0
13 Barry	0	0	0	0	0	0	0	0	0	0	0	0	0	0	0	0	0	0	0	0	0	0	0
14 Tony	0	0	0	1	0	0	0	0	0	0	0	0	0	0	0	0	0	0	0	0	0	0	1
15 Wendy	0	0	0	0	0	0	0	0	0	0	0	0	0	0	0	0	0	0	0	0	0	0	0
16 Rachel	0	0	0	0	0	0	0	0	0	0	0	0	0	0	0	0	0	0	0	0	0	0	0
Total	0	0	4	8	0	0	0	0	1	0	0	0	0	1	0	0	0	0	0	0	0	0	14

G1	S1-E1	S1-E2	S2-E1	S2-E2	S3-E1	S3-E2	S4-E1	S4-E2	S5-E1	S5-E2	S6-E1	S6-E2	S7-E1	S7-E2	S8-E1	S8-E2	S9-E1	S9-E2	S10-E1	S10-E2	S11-E1	S11-E2	Total
1 Derek	0	0	0	1	0	0	0	2	0	14	0	0	1	1	0	0	0	0	0	0	0	0	19
2 Max	2	1	0	0	0	0	0	0	0	0	0	0	0	0	0	0	0	0	0	0	0	0	3
3 Alvin	1	2	1	0	0	2	0	0	0	0	0	0	3	2	0	0	0	0	0	0	1	0	12
4 Cliff	0	0	0	0	0	0	0	0	0	0	0	0	1	0	0	0	0	0	0	0	0	4	5
5 Colin	0	0	0	0	0	0	0	0	0	0	0	0	0	0	0	0	0	0	0	0	0	0	0
6 Ted	0	0	2	1	0	0	0	0	0	0	0	0	0	0	0	0	0	0	0	0	0	0	3
7 Sam	0	0	1	0	1	0	0	0	0	0	0	0	0	0	0	0	0	0	0	0	0	0	2
8 Diane	0	0	3	1	0	0	0	1	0	0	0	0	0	0	0	0	1	0	1	0	0	0	7
9 James	0	0	0	0	0	0	0	0	0	0	2	0	0	0	0	0	0	0	0	0	0	0	2
10 Alan	0	0	0	0	0	0	0	0	0	0	0	0	0	0	0	0	0	0	1	0	0	0	1
11 Jason	0	0	0	0	0	0	0	2	1	0	0	0	0	0	0	0	2	0	0	0	0	0	5
12 Scott	0	0	0	0	0	0	0	0	0	0	0	0	0	0	0	0	0	0	0	0	0	0	0
13 Barry	1	1	0	0	0	0	0	0	0	0	0	0	0	0	0	0	0	0	0	0	0	0	2
14 Tony	0	0	2	0	0	0	0	0	0	0	0	0	0	0	0	0	4	0	0	0	0	0	6
15 Wendy	2	0	1	2	2	0	0	2	0	0	0	0	0	0	0	0	0	0	1	0	1	0	11
16 Rachel	0	0	0	0	0	0	0	0	0	0	0	0	0	0	0	0	0	0	1	0	0	0	1
Total	6	4	10	5	3	2	0	7	1	14	2	0	5	3	0	0	7	0	4	0	2	4	79

C.3.6. Frequency of RI-(CLA) by G1 Participants

G1	S1-E1	S1-E2	S2-E1	S2-E2	S3-E1	S3-E2	S4-E1	S4-E2	S5-E1	S5-E2	S6-E1	S6-E2	S7-E1	S7-E2	S8-E1	S8-E2	S9-E1	S9-E2	S10-E1	S10-E2	S11-E1	S11-E2	Total
1 Derek	0	0	0	1	0	0	0	0	0	0	0	0	0	0	0	0	0	0	0	0	0	0	1
2 Max	0	0	0	0	1	0	0	0	0	1	0	0	0	0	2	0	0	0	0	0	0	0	4
3 Alvin	0	0	0	0	0	0	0	0	0	0	1	0	0	0	0	0	0	0	2	0	0	0	3
4 Cliff	0	0	0	0	0	0	1	0	0	0	0	0	0	0	0	1	0	0	0	0	0	0	2
5 Colin	0	0	0	0	0	0	0	0	2	0	0	0	0	0	0	0	0	0	0	0	0	0	2
6 Ted	0	0	2	0	1	0	0	0	0	1	0	0	0	1	0	0	0	0	0	0	0	0	5
7 Sam	0	0	0	0	0	0	0	0	0	0	0	0	0	0	0	0	0	0	0	0	0	0	0
8 Diane	0	0	0	0	0	0	0	0	0	0	0	0	0	0	0	0	0	0	0	0	0	0	0
9 James	0	0	0	0	0	0	0	0	0	0	2	0	0	0	0	0	0	0	0	0	0	0	2
10 Alan	0	0	0	0	0	1	0	1	0	0	0	0	0	0	0	0	0	0	2	0	0	0	4
11 Jason	0	0	0	0	0	0	0	0	0	0	0	0	0	0	0	0	0	0	0	0	1	0	1
12 Scott	0	0	0	2	0	0	0	0	0	0	0	0	0	0	0	0	0	0	0	0	0	0	2
13 Barry	0	1	0	2	0	0	0	0	0	0	0	0	0	0	5	0	0	0	0	0	0	0	8
14 Tony	0	1	0	0	0	0	0	0	0	0	0	0	0	0	1	0	1	0	0	0	0	0	3
15 Wendy	0	0	0	0	0	0	0	0	0	0	0	0	0	0	1	0	0	0	0	2	0	0	3
16 Rachel	0	0	0	0	0	0	0	0	0	0	0	0	1	0	0	0	0	2	0	0	0	0	3
Total	0	2	2	5	2	1	1	1	2	2	3	0	1	1	9	1	1	2	4	2	1	0	43

C.3.7. Frequency of RI-[EXD] by G1 Participants

G1	S1-E1	S1-E2	S2-E1	S2-E2	S3-E1	S3-E2	S4-E1	S4-E2	S5-E1	S5-E2	S6-E1	S6-E2	S7-E1	S7-E2	S8-E1	S8-E2	S9-E1	S9-E2	S10-E1	S10-E2	S11-E1	S11-E2	Total
1 Derek	0	0	0	0	0	1	0	2	0	0	0	0	0	0	0	0	0	0	0	0	0	0	3
2 Max	0	0	0	0	0	0	0	0	0	0	0	0	0	0	0	0	0	0	0	0	0	0	0
3 Alvin	0	0	0	0	0	0	0	0	0	0	0	0	0	0	0	1	0	0	0	0	0	0	1
4 Cliff	0	0	0	0	0	0	0	0	0	0	0	0	1	0	0	0	0	0	0	0	0	0	1
5 Colin	0	0	0	0	0	0	0	0	0	0	0	0	0	0	0	0	0	0	0	0	0	0	0
6 Ted	0	0	0	0	0	0	0	0	0	0	0	0	0	0	0	0	0	0	0	0	0	0	0
7 Sam	0	0	0	0	0	0	0	0	0	0	0	0	0	0	0	0	0	0	0	0	0	0	0
8 Diane	0	0	0	0	0	1	0	0	0	0	0	0	0	0	0	0	0	0	0	0	0	0	1
9 James	0	0	0	0	0	0	0	1	0	0	0	0	0	0	0	0	0	0	0	0	0	0	1
10 Alan	0	0	0	0	0	0	0	0	0	0	0	0	0	0	0	0	0	0	0	0	0	0	0
11 Jason	0	0	0	0	0	0	0	0	0	0	0	0	0	0	0	0	0	0	0	0	0	0	0
12 Scott	0	0	0	0	0	0	0	0	0	0	0	0	0	0	0	0	0	0	0	0	0	0	0
13 Barry	0	0	0	0	0	0	0	0	0	0	0	0	0	0	0	1	0	0	0	0	0	0	1
14 Tony	0	0	0	0	0	0	0	0	0	0	0	0	0	0	0	0	0	0	0	0	0	0	0
15 Wendy	0	0	0	0	0	0	0	0	0	0	0	0	0	0	0	0	0	0	0	0	0	0	0
16 Rachel	0	0	0	0	0	0	0	0	0	0	0	0	0	0	0	0	0	0	0	0	0	0	0
Total	0	0	0	0	0	2	0	3	0	0	0	0	1	0	0	2	0	0	0	0	0	0	8

C.3.8. Frequency of RI-(CHA) by G1 Participants

G1	S1-E1	S1-E2	S2-E1	S2-E2	S3-E1	S3-E2	S4-E1	S4-E2	S5-E1	S5-E2	S6-E1	S6-E2	S7-E1	S7-E2	S8-E1	S8-E2	S9-E1	S9-E2	S10-E1	S10-E2	S11-E1	S11-E2	Total
1 Derek	0	0	0	0	0	0	0	0	0	0	1	0	1	0	0	0	0	0	0	0	0	0	2
2 Max	0	0	0	1	1	0	0	0	0	0	0	0	0	0	0	0	0	0	0	0	0	0	2
3 Alvin	0	0	0	2	0	0	0	0	0	0	0	0	0	0	0	0	0	0	0	0	0	0	2
4 Cliff	0	0	0	0	0	0	0	0	1	0	1	0	0	0	0	2	0	0	0	0	0	0	4
5 Colin	0	0	0	0	0	0	0	0	0	0	0	0	0	0	0	0	0	0	0	0	0	0	0
6 Ted	1	0	0	0	0	0	0	0	0	0	0	0	0	0	0	0	0	0	0	0	0	0	1
7 Sam	0	0	0	0	0	0	0	0	0	0	0	0	0	0	0	0	0	0	0	0	0	0	0
8 Diane	0	0	0	0	0	0	0	0	0	0	0	0	0	0	0	0	0	0	0	0	0	0	0
9 James	0	0	0	0	0	0	0	0	0	0	0	0	0	0	0	0	0	0	0	0	0	0	0
10 Alan	0	0	0	0	0	0	0	0	0	0	0	0	0	0	0	0	0	0	0	0	0	0	0
11 Jason	0	0	0	0	0	0	0	0	0	0	0	0	0	0	0	0	0	0	0	0	0	0	0
12 Scott	0	0	0	0	0	0	0	0	0	0	0	0	0	0	0	0	0	0	0	0	0	0	0
13 Barry	0	0	0	0	0	0	0	0	0	0	0	0	0	0	0	0	0	0	0	0	0	0	0
14 Tony	0	0	0	0	0	0	0	0	0	0	1	0	0	0	0	0	0	0	0	0	0	0	1
15 Wendy	0	0	1	1	0	0	2	1	0	0	0	0	0	0	0	0	0	0	0	0	0	0	5
16 Rachel	0	0	0	0	0	0	0	0	0	0	0	0	0	0	0	0	0	0	0	0	0	0	0
Total	1	0	1	4	1	0	2	1	1	0	3	0	1	0	0	2	0	0	0	0	0	0	17

C.3.9. Frequency of R-(INF) by G1 Participants

G1	S1-E1	S1-E2	S2-E1	S2-E2	S3-E1	S3-E2	S4-E1	S4-E2	S5-E1	S5-E2	S6-E1	S6-E2	S7-E1	S7-E2	S8-E1	S8-E2	S9-E1	S9-E2	S10-E1	S10-E2	S11-E1	S11-E2	Total
1 Derek	0	0	3	1	2	2	0	3	0	0	2	4	2	1	0	0	0	0	0	0	0	0	20
2 Max	0	1	1	2	2	0	0	0	3	8	2	1	1	1	3	0	0	0	1	0	2	0	28
3 Alvin	2	2	1	2	2	1	0	2	1	7	10	2	6	0	1	1	3	0	4	1	2	3	53
4 Cliff	1	0	3	0	0	0	0	3	0	2	6	2	3	1	1	2	2	0	1	3	3	2	35
5 Colin	2	0	2	1	0	0	1	0	0	3	0	0	0	0	0	0	0	0	0	0	0	0	9
6 Ted	2	3	1	1	2	0	0	0	2	0	0	2	10	0	0	0	1	0	0	0	0	0	23
7 Sam	3	0	2	1	3	0	1	2	1	2	5	0	1	0	0	1	0	0	1	0	2	2	30
8 Diane	5	4	9	15	0	2	1	3	1	0	5	5	0	0	0	0	1	0	3	4	0	0	58
9 James	0	0	2	3	2	1	0	0	0	3	3	6	0	0	0	0	0	1	0	1	0	0	22
10 Alan	2	0	2	0	3	2	0	0	1	0	2	0	0	0	0	0	1	1	3	0	2	2	21
11 Jason	0	0	0	0	0	0	2	4	1	6	0	0	0	5	0	0	2	0	0	1	5	0	26
12 Scott	1	0	1	1	2	1	1	2	0	0	4	0	0	0	0	0	0	0	0	0	0	0	12
13 Barry	0	3	0	1	0	0	0	0	0	0	0	0	3	0	2	0	0	0	0	0	0	0	9
14 Tony	4	3	1	4	6	3	1	5	2	1	4	7	1	2	0	4	5	1	1	0	0	0	55
15 Wendy	0	0	0	7	3	0	2	3	6	0	2	3	0	0	1	0	1	0	0	9	3	3	43
16 Rachel	0	1	0	0	0	0	0	0	0	0	0	0	0	0	0	0	1	1	1	0	0	0	4
Total	22	17	28	40	27	12	9	27	19	32	45	32	27	10	8	8	17	3	15	19	19	12	448

C.3.10. Frequency of R-(JUS) by G1 Participants

G1	S1-E1	S1-E2	S2-E1	S2-E2	S3-E1	S3-E2	S4-E1	S4-E2	S5-E1	S5-E2	S6-E1	S6-E2	S7-E1	S7-E2	S8-E1	S8-E2	S9-E1	S9-E2	S10-E1	S10-E2	S11-E1	S11-E2	Total
1 Derek	0	0	1	5	1	2	0	5	0	2	1	1	2	1	0	0	0	0	0	0	0	0	21
2 Max	0	0	0	1	3	4	0	2	0	0	0	1	0	0	3	2	0	0	0	0	3	1	20
3 Alvin	3	0	3	3	2	1	2	14	0	9	9	6	2	6	6	4	3	1	0	0	4	5	83
4 Cliff	1	0	1	4	0	0	0	5	0	0	2	3	0	2	1	2	2	0	0	0	1	4	28
5 Colin	0	0	0	0	1	0	0	0	3	2	0	0	0	0	0	0	0	0	0	0	0	0	6
6 Ted	1	1	3	2	2	1	0	0	0	0	0	5	8	0	0	0	0	1	0	0	0	0	26
7 Sam	2	1	2	2	2	1	0	2	0	0	3	0	2	0	0	0	0	0	0	0	0	9	26
8 Diane	0	0	2	6	0	2	0	0	0	0	0	0	0	0	0	0	0	0	0	0	0	0	10
9 James	0	0	0	0	0	0	0	1	0	0	2	0	0	0	0	0	0	1	0	0	0	0	4
10 Alan	0	0	0	0	1	0	0	0	0	1	0	0	0	0	0	0	0	3	0	0	0	1	6
11 Jason	0	0	0	0	0	0	0	3	0	3	0	0	0	5	0	0	0	0	0	0	6	0	17
12 Scott	1	0	1	4	0	2	0	0	0	0	0	0	0	0	0	0	0	0	0	0	0	0	8
13 Barry	2	0	1	5	0	0	0	0	0	0	0	0	4	6	0	5	0	0	0	0	0	0	23
14 Tony	0	0	2	0	1	1	0	1	0	0	0	0	0	0	0	0	0	1	0	0	0	0	6
15 Wendy	0	0	5	0	3	6	0	3	0	0	3	0	0	0	6	3	2	1	0	0	0	5	37
16 Rachel	0	0	0	0	0	0	0	0	0	0	0	0	0	0	0	0	0	0	0	0	0	0	0
Total	10	2	21	32	16	20	2	36	3	17	20	16	18	22	16	16	7	8	0	0	14	25	321

C.3.11. Frequency of R-(REA) by G1 Participants

G1	S1-E1	S1-E2	S2-E1	S2-E2	S3-E1	S3-E2	S4-E1	S4-E2	S5-E1	S5-E2	S6-E1	S6-E2	S7-E1	S7-E2	S8-E1	S8-E2	S9-E1	S9-E2	S10-E1	S10-E2	S11-E1	S11-E2	Total
1 Derek	0	0	0	3	1	1	0	2	0	1	0	1	1	3	0	0	0	0	0	0	0	0	13
2 Max	0	0	0	0	0	0	0	0	0	0	0	0	0	0	0	0	0	0	0	0	0	1	1
3 Alvin	0	0	0	0	4	2	0	3	0	3	0	0	3	0	2	2	0	0	0	1	0	0	20
4 Cliff	0	0	0	1	0	0	0	2	0	5	0	0	0	0	0	0	0	0	0	0	1	1	10
5 Colin	0	0	0	1	0	0	0	0	3	0	0	0	0	0	0	0	2	0	0	0	0	0	6
6 Ted	3	0	1	0	1	1	0	0	0	0	0	0	0	0	0	0	0	0	0	0	0	0	6
7 Sam	0	0	0	0	0	0	0	1	0	0	0	0	0	0	0	0	0	0	0	0	0	3	4
8 Diane	0	0	0	0	0	0	0	0	0	0	0	0	0	0	0	0	0	0	0	0	0	0	0
9 James	0	0	0	0	0	0	0	1	0	0	6	0	0	0	0	0	0	0	0	0	0	0	7
10 Alan	0	0	0	0	0	0	0	0	0	0	0	0	0	0	0	0	0	0	0	0	0	0	0
11 Jason	0	0	0	0	0	0	0	3	0	5	0	0	0	1	0	0	0	0	0	0	0	0	9
12 Scott	0	0	2	2	0	0	0	0	0	0	0	0	0	0	0	0	0	0	0	0	0	0	2
13 Barry	0	0	0	0	0	0	0	0	0	0	0	0	0	0	0	0	0	0	0	0	0	0	0
14 Tony	0	0	0	0	0	0	0	0	0	0	0	0	0	0	0	0	0	0	0	0	0	0	0
15 Wendy	0	0	3	0	5	4	0	1	0	0	2	0	0	0	1	0	3	0	0	0	0	1	20
16 Rachel	0	0	0	0	0	0	0	0	0	0	0	0	0	0	0	0	0	0	0	0	0	0	0
Total	3	0	4	7	11	8	0	13	3	14	8	1	4	4	3	2	5	0	0	1	1	6	98

C.3.12. Frequency of RC-[FBK-E] by G1 Participants

G1	S1-E1	S1-E2	S2-E1	S2-E2	S3-E1	S3-E2	S4-E1	S4-E2	S5-E1	S5-E2	S6-E1	S6-E2	S7-E1	S7-E2	S8-E1	S8-E2	S9-E1	S9-E2	S10-E1	S10-E2	S11-E1	S11-E2	Total
1 Derek	0	0	1	1	0	0	0	0	1	4	0	0	0	0	0	0	0	0	0	0	0	0	7
2 Max	2	1	1	2	2	1	0	1	1	3	2	0	1	0	2	0	0	0	0	0	0	1	20
3 Alvin	1	0	6	4	1	2	0	5	1	4	4	1	4	1	6	5	3	0	1	1	0	2	52
4 Cliff	0	0	3	0	0	0	0	4	2	1	0	0	2	0	5	3	1	0	1	0	1	0	22
5 Colin	0	0	1	0	0	0	0	1	5	1	0	0	0	0	0	0	1	0	1	0	0	0	10
6 Ted	0	0	1	2	0	1	0	0	1	0	0	10	5	2	5	1	4	0	0	0	0	0	32
7 Sam	0	1	5	3	1	1	1	1	2	2	2	2	1	0	5	0	4	0	0	1	3	0	35
8 Diane	4	0	12	16	0	6	2	6	0	0	4	2	0	0	5	2	1	0	1	0	0	0	61
9 James	0	0	1	0	1	1	0	1	2	2	3	0	0	0	0	0	2	0	1	0	0	1	15
10 Alan	0	0	1	0	0	1	0	1	1	2	0	0	0	0	3	1	1	0	0	1	0	0	12
11 Jason	0	0	0	0	0	2	1	0	1	0	0	0	0	0	0	0	0	1	0	0	0	0	5
12 Scott	0	0	3	1	1	0	0	0	1	2	0	0	0	0	0	0	1	0	0	2	1	0	12
13 Barry	3	0	5	7	0	0	0	0	0	0	0	0	2	2	4	6	0	0	1	0	0	0	30
14 Tony	1	0	0	0	1	0	0	2	1	1	2	4	0	1	0	0	1	0	3	0	0	0	17
15 Wendy	1	0	3	5	5	1	0	6	0	3	2	4	0	0	3	0	2	0	3	0	3	3	44
16 Rachel	0	0	1	4	1	3	0	2	0	3	0	0	0	1	3	1	1	1	0	0	0	0	21
Total	12	2	44	45	13	19	4	32	19	28	19	23	15	7	41	19	22	2	10	5	5	9	395

APPENDIX C

344

C.3.13. Frequency of RC-[FBK-A] by G1 Participants

G1	S1-E1	S1-E2	S2-E1	S2-E2	S3-E1	S3-E2	S4-E1	S4-E2	S5-E1	S5-E2	S6-E1	S6-E2	S7-E1	S7-E2	S8-E1	S8-E2	S9-E1	S9-E2	S10-E1	S10-E2	S11-E1	S11-E2	Total
1 Derek	0	0	0	0	1	0	0	0	0	1	0	0	0	0	0	0	0	0	0	0	0	0	2
2 Max	1	0	0	0	0	1	0	0	0	0	0	0	0	0	0	0	0	0	0	0	1	0	3
3 Alvin	0	2	0	0	1	0	0	0	1	0	0	0	1	0	0	0	1	0	2	0	1	0	9
4 Cliff	0	0	0	0	0	0	0	0	0	0	0	0	1	1	0	0	1	0	0	0	0	0	3
5 Colin	0	0	0	0	1	0	1	0	0	0	0	0	0	0	0	0	0	0	0	0	0	0	2
6 Ted	0	0	0	0	1	0	0	0	0	0	0	0	0	0	0	0	0	0	0	0	0	0	1
7 Sam	0	1	0	0	1	0	0	0	0	0	0	0	0	0	0	0	0	0	0	0	0	0	2
8 Diane	0	1	1	1	0	0	0	1	0	0	0	0	0	0	1	0	0	0	0	0	0	0	5
9 James	0	0	0	0	0	0	0	0	0	0	0	0	0	0	0	0	0	0	0	0	0	0	0
10 Alan	0	0	0	0	1	0	0	0	0	0	0	0	0	0	0	0	0	0	2	0	0	0	3
11 Jason	0	0	0	0	1	0	0	0	0	0	0	0	0	0	0	0	0	0	0	0	0	0	1
12 Scott	0	0	0	0	1	0	0	2	0	0	0	0	0	0	0	0	0	0	0	0	0	0	3
13 Barry	3	2	1	0	0	0	0	0	0	0	0	0	0	0	1	0	0	0	1	0	0	0	8
14 Tony	0	0	0	0	0	0	0	0	0	0	0	0	0	0	1	0	0	0	0	2	0	0	3
15 Wendy	0	0	0	0	1	0	0	0	0	0	0	0	0	0	0	0	0	0	1	1	1	0	4
16 Rachel	0	0	0	0	0	0	0	0	0	1	0	0	0	0	1	0	0	0	0	0	0	0	2
Total	4	6	2	1	9	1	1	3	1	2	0	0	2	1	4	0	2	0	6	3	3	0	51

C.3.14. Frequency of I-[INF] by G4 Participants

G4	S1-E1	S1-E2	S2-E1	S2-E2	S3-E1	S3-E2	S4-E1	S4-E2	S5-E1	S5-E2	S6-E1	S6-E2	S7-E1	S7-E2	S8-E1	S8-E2	S9-E1	S9-E2	S10-E1	S10-E2	S11-E1	S11-E2	Total
1 Evan	10	10	0	3	0	0	0	0	0	0	0	0	5	0	0	0	2	0	0	1	0	3	34
2 Bill	0	0	6	14	0	0	0	0	0	1	0	0	0	0	0	0	0	0	0	0	0	0	21
3 Mike	0	0	0	0	0	0	2	0	1	1	1	1	7	0	0	0	0	4	15	0	0	2	34
4 Eric	0	0	0	0	12	6	0	0	0	0	0	0	0	0	0	0	0	0	0	0	3	0	21
5 Karl	0	0	0	0	0	0	0	0	0	0	0	0	10	2	0	0	0	0	0	0	0	0	12
6 Jack	0	2	0	1	0	0	4	6	4	3	3	0	1	0	0	0	0	0	0	1	0	0	25
7 Ian	0	0	0	0	0	0	0	0	0	5	19	5	2	0	0	0	0	0	0	0	0	0	31
8 Pete	0	0	0	0	0	0	0	0	1	0	4	0	0	0	3	0	4	0	0	0	0	6	18
9 Robin	0	0	0	0	0	0	0	0	7	3	0	1	0	0	0	0	0	0	0	0	0	1	12
10 Lim	0	0	0	0	0	0	0	0	0	0	0	1	0	0	3	2	1	0	0	3	3	0	13
11 Fay	1	6	0	17	1	4	8	7	3	9	2	4	6	1	6	13	0	13	0	2	0	2	105
Total	11	18	6	35	13	10	14	13	16	22	29	12	31	3	12	15	7	17	15	7	6	14	326

C.3.15. Frequency of I-[INQ] by G4 Participants

G4	S1-E1	S1-E2	S2-E1	S2-E2	S3-E1	S3-E2	S4-E1	S4-E2	S5-E1	S5-E2	S6-E1	S6-E2	S7-E1	S7-E2	S8-E1	S8-E2	S9-E1	S9-E2	S10-E1	S10-E2	S11-E1	S11-E2	Total
1 Evan	6	2	0	0	1	0	0	0	0	0	0	0	2	1	0	0	2	0	0	1	1	3	19
2 Bill	0	0	5	10	1	0	0	0	1	1	0	0	0	0	0	0	0	0	0	0	0	0	18
3 Mike	0	0	0	0	0	0	0	0	0	0	1	0	0	0	2	0	0	5	0	0	0	3	11
4 Eric	0	0	0	0	18	6	0	0	1	0	0	0	0	0	0	0	0	0	0	0	0	1	26
5 Karl	0	0	0	1	0	0	0	0	0	0	0	0	5	1	0	0	0	0	0	0	0	0	7
6 Jack	0	2	0	1	1	0	5	7	0	0	9	0	0	0	0	0	3	0	0	0	0	3	31
7 Ian	0	0	0	0	0	0	0	0	0	3	0	0	1	0	3	0	0	0	0	5	3	0	15
8 Pete	0	2	0	0	0	0	0	1	6	3	0	0	2	0	8	0	0	0	0	0	0	3	25
9 Robin	0	1	0	0	0	0	0	0	0	0	0	3	0	1	0	0	0	0	0	0	3	3	11
10 Lim	0	0	0	1	0	0	0	1	1	0	0	0	0	0	0	1	3	0	0	1	3	0	11
11 Fay	4	0	1	7	6	0	6	5	1	7	5	4	7	0	2	5	5	2	0	2	4	4	77
Total	10	7	6	20	27	6	11	14	10	14	15	7	17	3	15	6	13	7	0	9	14	20	251

APPENDIX C

C.3.16. Frequency of I-I(JUS) by G4 Participants

G4	S1-E1	S1-E2	S2-E1	S2-E2	S3-E1	S3-E2	S4-E1	S4-E2	S5-E1	S5-E2	S6-E1	S6-E2	S7-E1	S7-E2	S8-E1	S8-E2	S9-E1	S9-E2	S10-E1	S10-E2	S11-E1	S11-E2	Total
1 Evan	0	0	0	0	0	0	0	0	0	0	0	0	0	0	0	0	0	0	0	0	0	0	0
2 Bill	0	0	0	0	0	0	0	0	0	0	0	0	0	0	0	0	0	0	0	0	0	0	0
3 Mike	0	0	0	0	0	0	0	0	0	0	0	0	0	0	0	0	0	0	0	0	0	0	0
4 Eric	0	0	0	0	0	0	0	0	0	0	0	0	0	0	0	0	0	0	0	0	0	0	0
5 Karl	0	0	0	0	0	0	0	0	0	0	0	0	0	0	0	0	0	0	0	0	0	0	0
6 Jack	0	0	0	0	0	0	0	0	0	0	0	0	0	0	1	0	0	0	0	0	0	0	1
7 Ian	0	0	0	0	0	0	0	0	0	0	0	0	0	0	0	0	0	0	0	0	0	0	0
8 Pete	0	0	0	0	0	0	0	0	0	0	0	0	0	0	0	0	0	0	0	0	0	0	0
9 Robin	0	0	0	0	0	0	0	0	0	0	0	0	0	0	0	0	0	0	0	0	0	0	0
10 Lim	0	0	0	0	0	0	0	1	0	0	0	0	0	0	0	0	0	0	0	0	0	0	0
11 Fay	0	0	0	0	0	0	0	0	0	0	0	0	0	0	0	0	0	0	0	0	0	0	1
Total	0	0	0	0	0	0	0	1	0	0	0	0	0	0	1	0	0	0	0	0	0	0	2

C.3.17. Frequency of I-(REA) by G4 Participants

G4	S1-E1	S1-E2	S2-E1	S2-E2	S3-E1	S3-E2	S4-E1	S4-E2	S5-E1	S5-E2	S6-E1	S6-E2	S7-E1	S7-E2	S8-E1	S8-E2	S9-E1	S9-E2	S10-E1	S10-E2	S11-E1	S11-E2	Total
1 Evan	0	0	0	0	0	0	0	0	0	0	0	0	0	0	0	0	0	0	0	0	0	0	0
2 Bill	0	0	0	0	0	0	0	0	0	0	0	0	0	0	0	0	0	0	0	0	0	0	0
3 Mike	0	0	0	0	0	0	0	0	1	0	2	0	0	0	0	0	0	0	0	0	0	0	3
4 Eric	0	0	0	0	0	0	0	0	0	0	0	0	0	0	0	0	0	0	0	0	0	0	0
5 Karl	0	0	0	0	0	0	0	0	0	0	0	0	0	0	0	0	0	0	0	0	0	0	0
6 Jack	0	0	0	0	0	0	0	0	0	0	0	0	0	0	1	0	0	0	0	0	0	0	1
7 Ian	0	0	0	0	0	0	0	1	0	0	0	0	0	0	0	0	0	0	0	0	0	0	1
8 Pete	0	0	0	0	0	0	0	0	0	0	0	3	0	0	0	0	0	0	0	0	1	0	4
9 Robin	0	0	0	0	0	0	0	0	0	0	0	0	0	0	0	0	0	0	0	0	0	0	0
10 Lim	0	0	0	0	0	0	0	0	0	0	0	0	0	0	0	0	0	0	0	0	0	0	0
11 Fay	0	0	0	0	0	0	0	0	0	0	0	0	0	0	0	0	0	0	0	0	1	0	1
Total	0	0	0	0	0	0	0	1	1	0	2	3	0	0	1	0	0	0	0	0	2	0	10

C.3.18. Frequency of RI-(CHK) by G4 Participants

G4	S1-E1	S1-E2	S2-E1	S2-E2	S3-E1	S3-E2	S4-E1	S4-E2	S5-E1	S5-E2	S6-E1	S6-E2	S7-E1	S7-E2	S8-E1	S8-E2	S9-E1	S9-E2	S10-E1	S10-E2	S11-E1	S11-E2	Total
1 Evan	2	2	0	4	0	0	0	0	0	0	0	0	1	0	0	0	0	0	0	0	0	1	10
2 Bill	0	0	3	5	0	0	0	0	0	0	0	0	0	0	0	0	0	0	0	0	0	0	8
3 Mike	0	0	0	0	0	1	1	1	0	0	2	0	2	0	0	0	0	0	0	0	1	0	7
4 Eric	0	0	0	0	1	1	0	0	0	0	1	0	0	0	1	1	0	1	0	0	0	0	6
5 Karl	0	0	0	0	0	0	0	0	0	1	0	0	8	0	0	0	0	0	0	0	0	0	9
6 Jack	4	1	0	0	0	0	3	4	1	2	2	0	2	0	2	4	3	0	0	0	11	3	44
7 Ian	2	0	0	1	0	0	0	1	0	2	8	0	1	0	0	2	0	0	2	0	4	1	24
8 Pete	0	0	0	0	2	1	0	1	0	0	2	1	0	0	0	2	7	0	0	0	2	1	19
9 Robin	1	0	0	0	1	0	0	0	1	0	0	0	0	0	1	0	1	0	0	0	3	1	9
10 Lim	0	0	0	2	2	0	0	0	1	1	3	1	2	0	1	0	2	0	1	0	2	0	18
11 Fay	2	0	2	3	5	1	1	5	1	2	1	0	0	0	4	2	3	1	0	1	0	2	35
Total	11	3	5	15	11	4	4	12	4	8	19	2	16	0	9	10	17	1	6	23	9	189

C.3.19. Frequency of RI-(CLA) by G4 Participants

G4	S1-E1	S1-E2	S2-E1	S2-E2	S3-E1	S3-E2	S4-E1	S4-E2	S5-E1	S5-E2	S6-E1	S6-E2	S7-E1	S7-E2	S8-E1	S8-E2	S9-E1	S9-E2	S10-E1	S10-E2	S11-E1	S11-E2	Total
1 Evan	3	1	0	0	0	0	0	0	0	0	0	0	1	0	0	0	0	0	2	0	0	0	7
2 Bill	0	0	0	1	1	0	0	0	0	0	0	0	0	0	0	0	0	0	0	0	0	0	2
3 Mike	0	0	0	0	0	0	1	0	1	0	0	0	0	0	0	0	0	1	0	0	0	0	3
4 Eric	2	0	0	2	3	3	0	0	0	0	3	1	2	0	1	1	1	1	2	2	0	0	20
5 Karl	0	0	0	0	0	0	0	0	0	0	2	0	0	0	0	0	0	0	0	0	0	0	3
6 Jack	1	0	0	1	1	0	0	3	0	0	0	0	1	0	4	0	3	3	0	0	2	2	21
7 Ian	0	0	0	0	0	0	0	0	1	0	1	0	0	0	0	1	1	0	0	0	1	0	5
8 Pete	0	1	0	0	0	0	1	1	0	0	0	0	0	0	1	0	3	0	0	0	0	2	8
9 Robin	0	1	0	0	1	0	0	0	0	0	0	0	0	0	0	0	2	1	1	0	2	0	5
10 Lim	0	0	0	2	1	1	1	0	1	1	0	0	1	1	2	2	1	0	2	2	1	1	18
11 Fay	1	1	1	3	1	0	1	1	2	3	1	1	1	1	0	1	0	4	1	4	1	1	25
Total	7	4	1	9	8	4	4	5	5	4	9	2	5	3	5	4	11	4	8	8	7	117

C.3.20. Frequency of RI-(EXD) by G4 Participants

G4	S1-E1	S1-E2	S2-E1	S2-E2	S3-E1	S3-E2	S4-E1	S4-E2	S5-E1	S5-E2	S6-E1	S6-E2	S7-E1	S7-E2	S8-E1	S8-E2	S9-E1	S9-E2	S10-E1	S10-E2	S11-E1	S11-E2	Total
1 Evan	0	0	0	6	0	0	0	0	0	0	0	0	1	0	0	0	0	0	0	0	0	0	7
2 Bill	0	0	0	0	0	0	0	0	0	0	0	0	0	0	0	0	0	0	0	0	0	0	0
3 Mike	0	0	0	0	0	0	0	0	0	0	0	0	0	0	0	0	0	0	0	0	0	0	0
4 Eric	0	0	0	0	0	2	0	0	0	2	0	0	1	0	0	0	0	0	0	0	0	0	5
5 Karl	0	0	0	0	0	0	0	0	0	0	0	0	0	0	0	0	0	0	0	0	0	0	0
6 Jack	0	0	0	0	2	0	0	0	0	0	0	0	0	0	0	1	0	0	0	0	0	0	3
7 Ian	0	0	0	0	0	0	0	0	0	0	0	0	0	0	0	0	0	0	0	0	0	1	1
8 Pete	0	0	0	0	0	0	0	3	0	0	0	0	0	1	0	0	0	0	0	0	2	0	6
9 Robin	0	0	0	0	0	0	0	0	0	0	0	0	0	0	0	0	0	0	0	0	0	0	0
10 Lim	0	0	0	0	0	1	0	0	0	0	0	0	0	0	0	0	0	0	0	0	0	0	1
11 Fay	0	0	0	2	0	0	0	0	0	0	0	0	0	0	0	0	1	0	0	0	0	1	4
Total	0	0	0	8	2	3	0	3	0	2	0	0	2	1	1	1	1	0	0	0	2	2	27

C.3.21. Frequency of RI-(CHA) by G4 Participants

G4	S1-E1	S1-E2	S2-E1	S2-E2	S3-E1	S3-E2	S4-E1	S4-E2	S5-E1	S5-E2	S6-E1	S6-E2	S7-E1	S7-E2	S8-E1	S8-E2	S9-E1	S9-E2	S10-E1	S10-E2	S11-E1	S11-E2	Total
1 Evan	0	0	0	0	0	0	0	0	0	0	0	0	0	0	0	0	0	1	0	0	0	0	1
2 Bill	0	0	0	0	0	0	0	0	0	0	0	0	0	0	0	0	0	0	0	0	0	0	0
3 Mike	0	0	0	0	0	0	0	0	0	0	0	0	0	0	0	0	0	0	0	0	0	0	0
4 Eric	0	0	1	0	0	0	0	0	0	0	0	0	0	0	0	1	0	2	0	0	0	0	4
5 Karl	0	0	0	0	0	0	0	0	0	0	0	0	0	0	0	0	0	0	0	0	0	0	0
6 Jack	0	1	0	0	0	0	0	0	1	0	1	0	0	0	0	0	0	0	0	0	0	0	3
7 Ian	0	0	0	0	0	0	0	0	0	0	0	0	1	0	0	0	0	0	0	0	0	0	1
8 Pete	0	0	0	0	0	0	0	0	0	0	0	0	0	0	0	0	0	0	0	0	0	0	0
9 Robin	0	0	0	0	0	0	0	0	0	0	0	0	0	0	0	0	0	0	0	0	0	0	0
10 Lim	0	0	0	0	0	0	0	0	0	0	0	0	0	0	0	0	0	0	0	0	0	0	0
11 Fay	0	0	0	0	0	0	0	0	0	0	0	0	0	0	0	0	0	0	0	0	0	0	0
Total	0	1	1	0	0	0	0	0	1	0	1	0	1	0	0	1	0	3	0	0	0	0	9

C.3.22. Frequency of R-[INF] by G4 Participants

G4	S1-E1	S1-E2	S2-E1	S2-E2	S3-E1	S3-E2	S4-E1	S4-E2	S5-E1	S5-E2	S6-E1	S6-E2	S7-E1	S7-E2	S8-E1	S8-E2	S9-E1	S9-E2	S10-E1	S10-E2	S11-E1	S11-E2	Total
1 Evan	13	5	5	13	7	4	0	0	0	0	0	0	5	0	0	0	5	3	1	7	5	10	83
2 Bill	1	1	4	10	5	2	4	1	0	3	0	0	3	0	0	0	0	0	0	0	1	0	35
3 Mike	0	0	0	0	2	4	7	3	4	8	2	4	1	3	2	0	1	0	1	5	4	3	54
4 Eric	9	5	4	15	7	1	12	13	5	7	12	2	10	2	10	6	10	7	0	9	11	9	166
5 Karl	0	0	0	0	0	0	7	5	5	3	10	5	13	0	0	0	0	0	0	0	3	6	57
6 Jack	11	3	3	14	8	5	5	8	0	4	12	2	10	0	12	8	7	7	0	5	8	4	136
7 Ian	12	4	5	12	0	0	9	14	10	8	12	6	10	3	12	8	5	2	1	5	10	10	158
8 Pete	8	0	0	0	11	2	6	10	0	0	15	4	0	0	6	6	4	0	0	0	4	8	90
9 Robin	14	1	5	12	4	5	2	3	6	3	0	1	0	0	6	6	5	4	0	4	5	9	101
10 Lim	0	0	6	7	1	3	3	4	2	4	7	2	10	1	1	4	3	6	0	8	7	8	87
11 Fay	4	6	7	13	6	5	8	10	1	8	9	1	16	3	10	1	21	2	0	5	22	6	164
Total	72	25	39	96	51	31	63	71	33	48	79	27	78	12	71	39	61	31	3	48	80	73	1131

C.3.23. Frequency of R-(JUS) by G4 Participants

G4	S1-E1	S1-E2	S2-E1	S2-E2	S3-E1	S3-E2	S4-E1	S4-E2	S5-E1	S5-E2	S6-E1	S6-E2	S7-E1	S7-E2	S8-E1	S8-E2	S9-E1	S9-E2	S10-E1	S10-E2	S11-E1	S11-E2	Total
1 Evan	1	0	1	2	5	0	0	0	0	0	0	0	12	0	0	0	0	3	0	2	3	1	33
2 Bill	0	1	1	4	1	0	0	0	0	0	0	0	3	0	0	0	0	0	0	0	0	0	10
3 Mike	0	0	0	0	1	3	1	4	0	7	0	0	3	1	1	0	0	1	0	1	1	1	25
4 Eric	12	6	3	6	1	4	1	4	5	5	7	4	2	3	3	1	3	3	0	1	5	2	81
5 Karl	0	0	0	0	0	0	3	0	4	1	3	0	1	1	0	0	0	0	0	0	2	4	19
6 Jack	0	0	5	6	7	4	4	2	1	4	6	4	3	0	1	1	0	1	0	4	3	1	57
7 Ian	5	1	4	12	0	0	2	0	2	3	10	7	10	0	2	3	0	1	0	2	6	1	72
8 Pete	1	4	0	0	4	2	2	2	0	0	4	5	0	0	3	1	2	2	0	0	0	3	35
9 Robin	1	3	3	6	1	0	3	1	3	3	0	0	0	0	5	2	4	1	0	0	4	1	41
10 Lim	0	0	1	1	3	0	2	1	0	2	4	4	0	0	0	0	1	4	0	2	5	3	36
11 Fay	2	5	2	8	0	0	4	8	6	4	2	2	1	2	6	2	6	0	0	10	0	0	70
Total	22	20	20	45	23	13	22	22	21	29	36	26	36	7	21	12	19	17	0	22	29	17	479

C.3.24. Frequency of R-(REA) by G4 Participants

G4	S1-E1	S1-E2	S2-E1	S2-E2	S3-E1	S3-E2	S4-E1	S4-E2	S5-E1	S5-E2	S6-E1	S6-E2	S7-E1	S7-E2	S8-E1	S8-E2	S9-E1	S9-E2	S10-E1	S10-E2	S11-E1	S11-E2	Total
1 Evan	0	0	1	0	3	2	0	0	0	0	0	0	4	0	0	0	0	0	0	0	1	1	12
2 Bill	0	0	0	0	0	0	0	0	0	0	0	0	0	0	0	0	0	0	0	0	0	0	0
3 Mike	0	0	0	3	5	3	0	3	2	1	4	3	3	0	0	3	2	3	2	0	1	4	39
4 Eric	2	0	2	0	1	0	0	0	0	1	0	2	1	1	1	0	0	1	1	0	2	0	15
5 Karl	0	0	0	0	0	0	0	2	2	0	0	0	0	0	0	1	0	0	0	0	0	1	4
6 Jack	5	1	4	4	4	1	3	3	0	6	4	1	1	0	2	1	0	0	2	0	3	1	36
7 Ian	1	1	3	0	0	0	0	1	1	0	0	0	0	0	0	0	1	1	0	0	1	0	17
8 Pete	6	0	0	3	3	0	0	0	0	0	2	2	0	0	2	5	1	1	0	1	0	0	23
9 Robin	0	0	0	0	1	0	0	0	0	0	0	0	3	0	0	1	0	1	1	0	1	0	5
10 Lim	0	0	0	0	0	0	1	1	0	1	2	0	0	0	0	0	1	0	0	1	0	0	10
11 Fay	0	0	1	0	0	1	3	2	0	0	4	0	0	0	0	7	1	0	0	0	0	0	19
Total	14	2	3	11	17	7	7	12	5	9	15	9	12	0	5	17	6	6	6	10	10	7	180

C.3.25. Frequency of RC-[FBK-E] by G4 Participants

G4	S1-E1	S1-E2	S2-E1	S2-E2	S3-E1	S3-E2	S4-E1	S4-E2	S5-E1	S5-E2	S6-E1	S6-E2	S7-E1	S7-E2	S8-E1	S8-E2	S9-E1	S9-E2	S10-E1	S10-E2	S11-E1	S11-E2	Total
1 Evan	0	2	0	2	1	0	0	0	0	0	0	0	2	0	0	0	0	0	0	0	3	0	10
2 Bill	1	2	3	2	0	0	0	1	1	1	0	0	3	0	0	0	0	0	0	0	0	0	13
3 Mike	0	0	0	0	0	0	0	0	0	0	1	1	0	0	0	0	0	0	0	0	0	0	2
4 Eric	2	1	2	5	3	3	1	10	7	2	3	5	9	0	6	6	1	1	1	0	1	2	71
5 Karl	0	0	0	0	0	0	3	5	3	2	9	2	6	1	0	0	0	0	0	0	1	2	34
6 Jack	0	1	0	2	3	1	1	4	3	0	4	1	3	0	3	2	4	2	0	1	3	2	38
7 Ian	2	0	1	8	0	0	2	3	2	4	8	3	5	0	7	6	5	2	0	3	1	0	62
8 Pete	0	1	0	0	0	1	1	3	0	0	5	1	0	0	3	1	1	0	0	0	0	0	18
9 Robin	1	4	1	4	3	2	1	4	3	7	0	0	0	0	6	3	4	2	0	3	3	1	52
10 Lim	0	0	0	1	1	1	1	3	2	0	1	0	0	0	1	0	1	1	0	1	2	2	17
11 Fay	2	1	1	3	3	0	1	3	2	2	1	2	3	0	2	2	4	0	0	2	2	3	39
Total	8	12	8	27	14	8	11	36	22	18	32	15	31	1	28	20	20	8	0	11	17	9	356

C.3.26. Frequency of RC-(FBK-A) by G4 Participants

G4	S1-E1	S1-E2	S2-E1	S2-E2	S3-E1	S3-E2	S4-E1	S4-E2	S5-E1	S5-E2	S6-E1	S6-E2	S7-E1	S7-E2	S8-E1	S8-E2	S9-E1	S9-E2	S10-E1	S10-E2	S11-E1	S11-E2	Total
1 Evan	0	1	0	0	0	0	0	0	0	0	0	0	0	0	0	0	0	0	0	0	0	0	1
2 Bill	0	0	0	1	0	0	0	0	1	3	0	0	0	0	0	0	0	0	0	0	0	0	5
3 Mike	0	0	0	0	0	0	0	0	1	0	0	0	0	0	0	0	0	0	1	0	0	0	2
4 Eric	0	1	0	0	2	1	1	0	1	0	1	0	0	0	1	0	1	0	0	0	1	0	10
5 Karl	0	0	0	0	0	0	0	0	0	1	0	0	0	0	0	0	0	0	0	0	0	0	1
6 Jack	0	0	0	0	0	0	0	0	0	0	0	0	0	0	1	1	1	0	0	0	0	0	3
7 Ian	0	0	0	1	0	0	0	0	1	1	1	0	0	0	0	1	1	0	0	0	1	0	7
8 Pete	0	0	0	0	0	0	0	0	0	0	0	0	0	0	0	0	0	0	0	0	1	0	1
9 Robin	0	0	0	0	0	0	0	0	0	1	0	0	0	0	1	0	1	0	1	0	0	0	4
10 Lim	0	0	0	0	0	0	0	1	0	0	0	0	0	0	0	1	0	0	0	0	0	0	2
11 Fay	0	1	0	3	2	1	0	0	0	3	0	0	0	0	2	0	0	0	0	1	0	0	13
Total	0	3	0	5	4	2	1	1	4	9	2	0	0	0	5	3	4	0	2	1	3	0	49

APPENDIX C

www.ingramcontent.com/pod-product-compliance
Lightning Source LLC
LaVergne TN
LVHW022300060326
832902LV00020B/3189